W9-AHM-297

SOUTHERN LITERARY STUDIES
Fred Hobson, Editor

SELECTED

LETTERS OF

ROBERT PENN

WARREN

Volume Two

THE "SOUTHERN REVIEW" YEARS

1935–1942

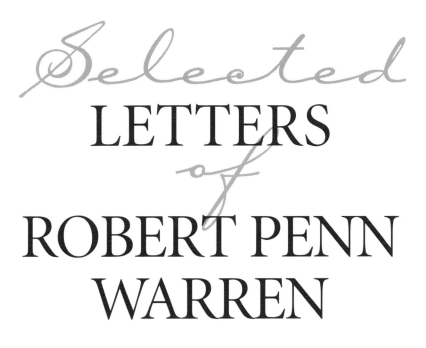

Selected LETTERS *of* ROBERT PENN WARREN

Volume Two

THE "SOUTHERN REVIEW" YEARS

1935–1942

EDITED,

WITH AN INTRODUCTION, BY

WILLIAM BEDFORD CLARK

LOUISIANA STATE UNIVERSITY PRESS

Baton Rouge

Copyright © 2001 by Gabriel Warren and Rosanna Warren Scully

All rights reserved

Manufactured in the United States of America

First printing

10   09   08   07   06   05   04   03   02   01

5   4   3   2   1

Designer: Rebecca Lloyd Lemna

Typeface: Minion

Typesetter: Coghill Composition Co., Inc.

Printer and binder: Thomson-Shore, Inc.

LIBRARY OF CONGRESS CATALOGING-IN-PUBLICATION DATA:

Warren, Robert Penn, 1905–

 [Correspondence. Selections]

 Selected letters of Robert Penn Warren / edited, with an introduction, by William
Bedford Clark.

  p.   cm.—(Southern literary studies)

 Includes bibliographical references (p.) and index.

 Contents: v. 1. The apprentice years, 1924–1934

 ISBN 0-8071-2536-9 (cloth : alk. paper)

 ISBN 0-8071-2657-8 (v. 2)

  1. Warren, Robert Penn, 1905—Correspondence.   2. Authors, American—Southern
States—Correspondence   3. Authors, American—20th century—Correspondence.   4.
Southern States—Intellectual life—20th century.   5. English teachers—United
States—Correspondence.   6. Critics—United States—Correspondence.   I. Clark,
William Bedford.   II. Title.   III. Series.

 PS3545.A748   Z48   2000

 813'.52—dc21

 [B]   99-056099

The paper in this book meets the guidelines for permanence and durability of the
Committee on Production Guidelines for Book Longevity of the Council on Library
Resources. ⊗

To
Michael Masopust,
best and brightest

I was living in Louisiana where there was a world that was very

dramatic and about which I had very ambivalent feelings. . . .

It feels strange talking about it now—it was so long ago; it's like

talking in your sleep.

> —ROBERT PENN WARREN, in conversation with
> Frank Gado (1966)

I think you deserved better;

Therefore I am writing you this letter.

> —ROBERT PENN WARREN, "Letter of a Coward
> to a Hero" (1935)

Contents

Illustrations

Acknowledgments

The present volume, like its predecessor, owes its existence to the confidence John Burt, Warren's literary executor, placed in me at the beginning, and to the encouraging support of Rosanna and Gabriel Warren. Shortly prior to her death, Eleanor Clark Warren gave this project her warm blessing, and during the planning stage Cleanth Brooks (of most happy memory) honored me with his wisdom and guidance. Joseph Blotner gave me the confidence to proceed, and the degree to which his brilliant and thorough *Robert Penn Warren: A Biography* (1997) informs these pages is unmistakable. In the process of putting together the annotations to this second volume in the series, I came to depend time and again upon the unfailing generosity and expertise of Charles East, author, journalist, and former director of Louisiana State University Press, whose knowledge of the Baton Rouge community and LSU proved nothing less than phenomenal. Not only was he personally acquainted with many of the principals mentioned in these pages, he managed to unearth information I had assumed was irretrievable. It would be impossible to thank him adequately. Lewis P. Simpson, that most astute and articulate student of the southern mind, likewise reviewed the manuscript and made useful suggestions. Closer to home, my department head, J. Lawrence Mitchell, found ways to support my research and writing throughout, and I owe an important debt to the Interdisciplinary Group for the Historical Study of Literature (now the Center for Humanities Research) at Texas A&M University and to my colleagues Jerome Loving, Janet McCann, Raymond Petrillo, Stanley L. Archer, Craig Kallendorf, James L. Harner, Claude Gibson,

David G. Myers, John McDermott, and Douglas A. Brooks. A sequence of dedicated students, undergraduate and graduate, assisted me along the way: Dean Wang, Martha Bradbury, Claire Carly, Tatyana and Mariam Khoubarian, Mi Su Kim, Christopher Stidvent, Dawn Weiner, and Pauline Wong. The technical and research skills of Christopher L. Morrow and Bridget Black proved indispensable when it came to putting the manuscript into final shape. The debt I owe my wife, Charlene Kerne Clark, and my daughters, Mary and Eleanor, defies articulation.

The catalog of individuals—writers, scholars, librarians, archivists, and interested laypersons—who made key contributions of various kinds to this project is a lengthy one, but my sense of obligation demands that each be mentioned individually: Jodi Allison-Bunnell, Ruth M. Alvarez, Joan Ashton, Jami Awalt, Amy Baptist, Frederick Bauman, Dennis Beach, Charlotte H. Beck, Peggy Beckett-Rinker, Candace Benefiel, Robert J. Bertholf, Catherine L. Bill, Alice Birney, Loyd M. Bishop, Andrea Blair, Paul Blanchard, Anthony S. Bliss, Judy Bolton, Georgianna Arnett Bonds, George and Joy Bale Boone, Elizabeth Brunett, Robert Buffington, Gil Campbell, Thomas Carlson, Robert Chapel, Saville T. Clark Jr., Christopher Colman, Ann Collins, George Core, Frederick Crews, Gwyneth Crowley, Bernard R. Crystal, Polly Lytle Darwin, Christopher Densmore, Donald L. DeWitt, Kathleen Donahue, Stephen Donato, Sarah East, William B. Eigelsbach, Stephen Ennis, Yvonne Evans, John Irwin Fischer, John and Jerre Fitts, Ed Folsom, Granville Frey, Robert D. and Tommie Lou Warren Frey, Kristine Frost, Wayne Fruman, Forrest W. Galey, Agnes Gentry, Howard B. Gotlieb, James A. Grimshaw Jr., Lee Gruver, Riley D. Handy, John Edward and Willene Hardy, Nancy D. Hargrove, Sarah Harwell, Diana Haskell, Robert B. Heilman, Cathy Henderson, Jo Jackson, John and Elinor Jacobs, Mary Jarrell, James H. Justus, Hilaire Kallendorf, Robert Karrow, J. Gerald Kennedy, Ethel W. Kerne, Elizabeth Kesler, Robert Koppelman, Alan K. Lathrop, Pamela Lytle Law, Paula Y. Lee, Bill Longhurst, William J. Maher, Frederick Manfred, Kathleen Manwaring, Amy Marks, Gregory and Kathleen Marks, Linda M. Matthews, Robert A. McCown, Cassandra McCraw, Kathleen McDonough, L. Rebecca Johnson Melvin, Susan Mabry Menees, William E. Meneray, Daniel Meyer, Sue Michel, David and Francine Middleton, Mark Miller, Mary Ellen Miller, Constance Mills, Chaddra Moore, Jeane and Dean Moore, Leslie A. Morris, Timothy D. Murray, James Olney, James A. Perkins, Patrick Phelps, Rodney Phillips, Anne

Posega, John Henry Raleigh, Carla Rickerson, Emily Robison, Dan and Dorothy Ross, Robert Rudnicki, Mattie K. Sanders, Nancy M. Shawcross, Alice G. Shepherd, Allen Shepherd, Margaret M. Sherry, William M. Short, Richard A. Shrader, Ethel C. Simpson, Melba Smith, Elaine B. Smyth, Sandra Stelts, Kristina Southwell, Donald E. Stanford, William Stoneman, Victor Strandberg, Suellen Stringer-Hye, Walter and Jane Sullivan, Ruth Tapia, Helen Tate, Saundra Taylor, Bess Barnett Turpin, Leonard and Sherley Unger, Philip Uzee, Barbara van der Lyke, Alphonse Vinh, Floyd C. Watkins, Robert C. Weller, Eudora Welty, Tara Wenger, Earl J. Wilcox, Susan Williams, Patricia Willis, Marice Wolfe, and Nancy Tate Wood. My special thanks to John Easterly, George Roupe, and Margaret Hart of LSU Press.

The letters in this volume are published with permission of the Warren estate, and I am likewise grateful to John Michael Walsh, Cleanth Brooks's literary executor, for enabling me to print correspondence signed by both Brooks and Warren. I am especially grateful to two of Robert Penn Warren's most valued friends, John Ellis Palmer and Pier Maria Pasinetti, for making their files of Warren correspondence available to me and for providing me with information that found its way into my notes. The other letters in this volume may be found in the following libraries and repositories and are published with the requisite permission.

Letters to Domenico Brescia and Emma "Cinina" Brescia Warren: Special Collections, Robert W. Woodruff Library, Emory University

——— to John Berryman: Manuscript Division, University of Minnesota Libraries

——— to Kenneth Burke: Rare Books and Manuscripts, Pennsylvania State University Libraries

——— to W. S. Campbell: William Stanley Campbell Collection, Western History Collections, University of Oklahoma

——— to James T. Farrell: Rare Book and Manuscript Library, University of Pennsylvania

——— to Eudora Welty: Eudora Welty Collection, Mississippi Department of Archives and History

——— to Lyle Saxon: Lyle Saxon Papers, Special Collections, Tulane University Library

——— to Paul Green: Paul Green Papers, Southern Historical Collection, Wilson Library, University of North Carolina at Chapel Hill

——— to Paul Engle: University of Iowa Libraries, Iowa City

——— to Muriel Ruykeyser, Randall Jarrell, and Harper & Brothers: Berg Collection of English and American Literature, New York Public Library (Astor, Lenox, and Tilden foundations)

——— to Louis Untermeyer and John Malcolm Brinnin: respective authors' papers, University of Delaware Library, Newark

——— to Lionel Trilling, Allen Nevins, and John Berryman (February 7, 1939): respective authors' papers, Rare Books and Manuscripts Library, Columbia University

——— to J. Kerker Quinn: University Archives, University of Illinois at Champaign-Urbana

——— to Editors of *Contempo* and Willard Maas: Harry Ransom Humanities Research Center, University of Texas at Austin

——— to Robert B. Heilman: Manuscripts and Special Collections, University of Washington Libraries

——— to George Marion O'Donnell: George Marion O'Donnell Papers, Special Collections, Washington University Libraries, St. Louis

——— to Hubert Creekmore and Jo Sinclair: Special Collections, Boston University Library

——— to William Carlos Williams and C. D. Abbott: Poetry/Rare Books Collection, University Libraries, State University of New York at Buffalo

——— to Paul M. Hebert and Thomas A. Kirby: Special Collections, Louisiana State University Libraries

——— to Katherine Anne Porter and Albert Erskine: Papers of Katherine Anne Porter, Special Collections, University of Maryland Libraries

——— to Thomas Wolfe (bMS Am 1883.1 [663]), Ferris Greenslet (bMS Am 1925 [1867]), Paul Brooks (bMS Am 1925 [1867]), and Oliver St. John Gogarty (bMS Am 1787 [554]): Houghton Library, Harvard University

——— to Alan Swallow: Alan Swallow Papers, Department of Special Collections, Syracuse University Library

——— to Merrill Moore: Merrill Moore Papers, Manuscripts Division, Library of Congress

——— to John Gould Fletcher: John Gould Fletcher Papers, Special Collections, University of Arkansas Libraries

——— to Seward Collins, Edward Davison, Edmund Wilson, Cleanth Brooks, Cleanth Brooks and John Palmer, David M. Clay, and F. O. Matthiessen: Beinecke Rare Book and Manuscript Library, Yale University

——— to Frank Lawrence Owsley, Andrew Lytle, Donald Davidson, Peter Taylor, Brainard Cheney, Arthur Mizener, Catherine Wilds, and Kate Zerfoss: Special Collections, Jean and Alexander Heard Library, Vanderbilt University

———— to Allen Tate, Caroline Gordon, R. P. Blackmur, T. J. Wilson, John Peale Bishop, C. A. Madison, William Sloane, and the Henry Holt Company: respective authors' papers and publisher's archives, Manuscripts Division, Department of Rare Books and Special Collections, Princeton University Library

———— to Herbert J. Muller: Manuscripts Division, Lilly Library, Indiana University, Bloomington, Indiana

———— to Josephine Miles: Rare Books and Literary Manuscripts, Bancroft Library, University of California, Berkeley

———— to Sherwood Anderson, Malcolm Cowley, and Morton Dauwen Zabel (November 10, 1936; March 23, October 11 and 13, and November 15, 1937; n.d. [Fall 1938]; March 2, 1939; October 19 and 29 and December 15 and 25, 1942): respective authors' papers, The Newberry Library, Chicago, Illinois

———— to Morton Dauwen Zabel (October 15, 1935; January 15 and November 4, 1936; April 26, 1937; n.d. [Spring 1937]), Ronald Lane Latimer, Alcestis Press, and H. T. Stuart: Special Collections, University of Chicago Library

Note on Editorial Procedures and List of Abbreviations

his volume, like its predecessor, employs a format derived from consulting, comparing, and combining the practices that inform a number of related editions: Joseph Blotner's *Selected Letters of William Faulkner* (1977), John Tyree Fain and Thomas Daniel Young's *The Literary Correspondence of Donald Davidson and Allen Tate* (1974), Thomas Daniel Young and George Core's *Selected Letters of John Crowe Ransom* (1985), Thomas Daniel Young and Elizabeth Sarcone's *The Lytle-Tate Letters* (1987), James A. Grimshaw Jr.'s *Cleanth Brooks and Robert Penn Warren: A Literary Correspondence* (1998), and Alphonse Vinh's *Cleanth Brooks and Allen Tate: Collected Letters, 1933–1976* (1998). My practice here represents a broad synthesis of the procedures followed by these distinguished scholars.

First and foremost, my goal has been the accurate transcription and reproduction of Warren's words as they appear in the original correspondence, though I have remained mindful of the legitimate requirements of the general reader, who is more interested in the contents of a given letter and what it might reveal than in the kinds of questions addressed by textual editing in the strictest sense. Thus, with minimal exceptions, I have followed Warren's own punctuation and spelling, while retaining the right to silently correct obvious typographical errors, unintended repetitions, and similar mistakes. Accordingly, I have tried to avoid excessive recourse to bracketed interpolations but have used them whenever clarity, editorial scruples, or other considerations demanded. On occasion, I have found it necessary to address a significant textual issue in my notes. There are, for instance, times when the date of a particular item is problematic. I have adopted a standardized format in laying out individual items of correspondence, regularizing otherwise anomalous spacing and the arrangement of lines and paragraphs on the page. Warren occasionally placed an internal address at the end of a letter. I have adjusted such variations in format with an eye toward uniformity, when this could be done without doing violence to the integrity of the original.

I have endeavored to annotate Warren's letters as thoroughly as possible, guided in part by George Core's sensible observation that what is obvious today may prove perplexing in the not too distant future. Even so, the identity of some persons and the significance of certain allusions and references have escaped me. In compiling my annotations, I had recourse to any number of standard reference works, but I also made use of several more specialized sources. These are listed in the Selected Bibliography. Throughout my research, I depended upon the kindness of strangers as well as friends. Many people, some now deceased, furnished me with information that found its way into my notes. They are listed in the Acknowledgments, but when my debt to a particular individual is especially keen I have cited his or her name in the note itself.

For the sake of convenience, consistency, and economy, I have used abbreviations to denote the nature and provenance of each item (e.g., TLS/PU = "typed letter, signed/Princeton University"). The key to these abbreviations is as follows:

ALS	autograph letter, signed
APC	autograph postcard
TLS	typed letter, signed
TLU	typed letter, unsigned

BU	Special Collections, Boston University Library
Col	Rare Book and Manuscript Library, Columbia University
Emory	Emory Special Collections, Robert W. Woodruff Library, Emory University
Harv	Houghton Library, Harvard University
Ill	University Archives, University of Illinois at Champaign-Urbana

Ind	Manuscripts Division, Lilly Library, Indiana University, Bloomington
Iowa	University of Iowa Libraries, Iowa City
LC	Manuscripts Division, Library of Congress
LSU	Special Collections, Louisiana State University Libraries
Maryland	Special Collections, University of Maryland Libraries
Minn	Manuscript Division, University of Minnesota Libraries
MissA	Mississippi Department of Archives and History, Jackson
Newb	Newberry Library, Chicago
NYPL	Berg Collection, New York Public Library
Penn	Rare Book and Manuscript Library, University of Pennsylvania
PennS	Rare Books and Manuscripts, Pennsylvania State University Library
PU	Manuscripts Division, Rare Books and Manuscripts, Princeton University Libraries
SUNY-B	Poetry/Rare Books Collection, State University of New York-Buffalo
Syracuse	Special Collections, Syracuse University Library
Tul	Special Collections, Tulane University Library
UArk	Special Collections, University of Arkansas Libraries
UCal	Rare Books and Literary Manuscripts, Bancroft Library, University of California, Berkeley
UChi	Special Collections, University of Chicago Library
UDel	University of Delaware Library, Newark
UNC	Southern Historical Collection, Wilson Library, University of North Carolina at Chapel Hill
UOk	Western History Collections, University of Oklahoma
UTex	Harry Ransom Humanities Research Center, University of Texas at Austin
UWash	Manuscripts and Special Collections, University of Washington Libraries

VU   Special Collections, Heard Library, Vanderbilt University

WashU   Special Collections, Washington University Libraries, St. Louis

YU   Beinecke Rare Book and Manuscript Library, Yale University

SELECTED

LETTERS OF

ROBERT PENN

WARREN

Volume Two

THE "SOUTHERN REVIEW" YEARS

1935–1942

While this second volume of Robert Penn Warren correspondence picks up where my edition of the early letters left off,[1] I have endeavored to make it as self-contained as possible. At the same time, I have worked to ensure its continuity with its predecessor. Both volumes are informed by my conviction that James G. Watson's ideas about an author's letters constituting a kind of "second canon" are not only substantively correct but also provide editor and reader alike with a vital and integrated way of coming at a writer's epistolary output on its own generic terms, all the while preserving a traditional respect for the unique role "letterly" writing plays by virtue of its autobiographical and historical dimensions. First and last, the letters that appear here provide us with a running documentary account of what was arguably the most crucial period in Robert Penn Warren's long and increasingly distinguished career. Indeed, at times a given sequence of letters may be said to offer us a virtual daily log rich in its vivid representation of people, places, and events. In that regard, it would be accurate enough to regard this selection of correspondence as a confirmation and (with due modesty) a further fleshing out of previous work like Joseph Blotner's masterful *Robert Penn Warren: A Biography* and Thomas W. Cutrer's superb excursion into literary and institutional history, *Parnassus on the Mississippi*.[2] Yet not infrequently, an isolated letter, from Mon-

---

1. *Selected Letters of Robert Penn Warren*, vol. 1, *The Apprentice Years, 1924–1934* (Baton Rouge: Louisiana State University Press, 2000).
2. Again I welcome the chance to acknowledge my pervasive debt to Blotner's indis-

tana, Mexico, Italy, or Iowa City, amounts to a surprisingly well-crafted set piece, and this serves to remind us of Watson's insightful and highly useful contention that letters occupy a place "midway between life and art." They somehow "span time and distance" and "measure the distances between actual experience and imaginative re-creation, between the life of the man writing and his written self-image."[3] The letter, whatever its intention or occasion, is by its very nature a literary construction, a *made thing;* and in reading this body of correspondence we would do well to remember Warren's own words in *Democracy and Poetry,* where he insists that "[t]he 'made thing'" (however broadly construed) is "a vital emblem of the struggle toward the achieving of the self."[4]

Even at the most direct and literal level, Warren's letters from his Baton Rouge years have new and important things to tell us about their author and the world—or rather the spiral of ever-expanding concentric worlds—in which he moved and had his being. We catch him in the first flush of enthusiasm as he settles into a congenial academic appointment in an exotic and stimulating corner of the American South altogether different from the Border South of his youth. No less shrewd than brilliant, he immediately begins to pursue its possibilities. Warren's student days at Vanderbilt, Berkeley, Yale, and Oxford and his time teaching in Tennessee constituted a long apprenticeship, albeit an apprenticeship in which he published a notable biography of John Brown, placed poems and reviews in prominent venues, and earned an enviable, if subordinate, spot in the company of many of the most influential literary and academic figures of the 1920s and '30s. But it was at Louisiana State University, against the unsettled backdrop of the Great Depression and America's belated entry into the Second World War, that Warren came into his own and established himself as a compelling new voice, perhaps the most versatile writer of his generation. To be sure, his editing of the *Southern Review* in collaboration with Cleanth Brooks (and initially

---

pensable biography (New York: Random House, 1997). I likewise owe a great deal to Cutrer's *Parnassus on the Mississippi: The "Southern Review" and the Baton Rouge Literary Community, 1935–1942* (Baton Rouge: Louisiana University Press, 1984). Cutrer's meticulous research lightened my own labors considerably.

3. James G. Watson, *William Faulkner: Letters and Fictions* (Austin: University of Texas Press, 1987), xiii.

4. Robert Penn Warren, *Democracy and Poetry* (Cambridge: Harvard University Press, 1975), 69.

Charles W. Pipkin) offered an immediate springboard to prominence on both sides of the Atlantic, and Warren's letters to friends, allies, contributors, and would-be contributors alike testify to both the inspired vision and quotidian drudgery he brought to that task, even as they serve to chronicle the birth, maturation, and sudden demise of that most distinguished of quarterlies.

Indeed, the now-legendary tale of the rise and fall of the original series of the *Review* may be said to provide whatever overarching narrative cohesion this book might claim, but that story, however central, is but one of many these letters have to tell, for the relative security of his appointment at LSU enabled Warren to explore and test the boundaries of his genius on a number of simultaneous fronts as never before, and the range and sheer diversity of his correspondence, whether with old friends, established literary figures, hopeful younger writers, recalcitrant academic administrators, or occasionally troublesome publishers, reveals an extraordinarily keen mind and heightened imagination operating in concert with optimum efficiency. What any number of commentators have called Warren's "protean" energy is fully in evidence in these letters, which document his steady rise to national—and indeed international—stature. During his tenure at LSU, Warren not only emerged as a celebrated poet (his long-delayed first volume of verse, *Thirty-Six Poems* [1936], was accepted for publication shortly after he came to Baton Rouge, and the even more striking *Eleven Poems on the Same Theme* [1942] came out just before he left for the University of Minnesota), he also published his first major fiction, the novel *Night Rider* (1939)—to high praise from Kenneth Burke and equally astute critics—and effectively completed work on a second, radically different book, *At Heaven's Gate* (1943). From scattered references throughout his letters, we can see how seriously Warren took his role as a teacher (burdensome though it could be), and once again one is struck by the "protean" quality that characterized his pattern of sustained and varied productivity, as Warren and Cleanth Brooks draw directly upon classroom challenges to design and launch a series of textbooks that gradually transform the teaching of poetry and fiction in American colleges and universities.

They engage along the way in some hard-nosed negotiation with textbook publishers, and this same practical and businesslike streak in Warren's personality is one important aspect of his character to emerge from a close reading of his correspondence. Even so, it coexists with what can only be regarded as a recurring countertendency to act precipitously—if not recklessly—at certain crucial junctures. While Warren is more than capable of ascertaining and insisting upon his own best interests when he bargains with his former Vanderbilt classmate David M. Clay over the possibility of signing with the firm of Harcourt Brace, he is equally capable of buying a farmhouse and acreage outside Baton Rouge on a last-minute impulse, even as he and his wife Cinina are leaving town for an extended stay in Mexico. Earlier, an even more dramatic disregard for conventional prudence nearly ended in disaster when the couple determined to remain in Italy after the outbreak of World War II, as Europe crumbled around them. Yet in his criticism and creative work, Warren proved himself to be no less than Herman Melville or Dostoevski a lover of paradox, so it is little wonder that his letters, like his life, are often rife with ambiguities, ambivalence, and apparent contradictions. He was, after all, a very complicated man. As a case in point, I would direct the reader to the sequence of hurried notes he wrote Cinina in the spring of 1939, as she traveled to California for her father's funeral. Here passion, compassion, and pragmatic cost-accounting share center stage.[5]

Some two decades after he left Louisiana, Warren described his time there in these terms:

> Melodrama was the breath of life. There had been melodrama in the life I had known in Tennessee, but with a difference: in Tennessee the melodrama seemed to be different from the stuff of life, something superimposed upon life, but in Louisiana people lived melodrama, seemed to live, in fact, for it, for this strange combination of philosophy, humor, and violence. Life was a tale you happened to be living. . . . And all the while I was reading Elizabethan tragedy, Machiavelli, William James, and American history—and all

5. These letters are part of an immensely rich and varied collection of Warren-related materials presented to the Mitchell College Library by Burton Hathaway Gardner, Emma "Cinina" Brescia Warren's second husband, after her death in 1969. (She had headed the languages department there from 1963 to 1967.) The collection languished in the basement and sustained minor water damage until it was rediscovered by a new library director, Barbara van der Lyke, who immediately took steps to preserve it and maintain its integrity. The materials have since been acquired by the Woodruff Library at Emory University.

that I was reading seemed to come alive, in shadowy distortions and sudden clarities, in what I saw around me.[6]

These observations are part of a retrospective account Warren gave of the role his years in Louisiana had played in the writing of his greatest novel, *All the King's Men,* without doubt the most lasting product of his time there. That novel was written after the fact, as it were, once Warren had left the South for a new life in the North (though a number of the letters in this volume do concern the verse play *Proud Flesh,* out of which *All the King's Men* mysteriously evolved). In closing, I would suggest that Warren's correspondence from his *Southern Review* years reflects precisely the same kind of highly sensitized consciousness he described above and that his letters do in fact constitute what James G. Watson calls a "second canon."

6. Robert Penn Warren, "*All the King's Men:* The Matrix of Experience," *Yale Review* 53 (1963), 166.

1935

*hen Robert Penn Warren and his
wife Emma (Cinina) Brescia arrived in Baton Rouge in the fall of 1934,
they had reason to celebrate. His appointment to the English faculty at
Louisiana State University must have seemed nothing less than a godsend,
for in the months prior to the offer from LSU the long string of good fortune
that had characterized his professional life seemed to have played itself out.
During the preceding decade, Warren had enjoyed an enviable series of
opportunities and mounting accomplishments. As a Vanderbilt undergraduate still in his teens, he had participated actively in the Fugitive group,
thus assuming a role (however junior) in an important contingent of the
modernist vanguard. He had gone on to take an M.A. at the University of
California in 1927 and briefly pursued doctoral study at Yale before accepting a much-coveted Rhodes Scholarship in 1928. While at Oxford, Warren
had emerged as a creditable man of letters, finishing his first book,* John
Brown: The Making of a Martyr, *and contributing an important (and
controversial) essay to the Fugitive/Agrarian symposium* I'll Take My
Stand, *even as he worked toward the successful completion of his degree.
When Warren returned to the United States in 1930, he found a nation
hard hit by the Depression, but nevertheless his own luck had held. There
was a job waiting for him at Southwestern College in Memphis, though he
found that relatively humble institution less than congenial and after a year
welcomed the chance to return to his alma mater Vanderbilt as a visiting
professor on a renewable basis. By early 1934, however, Warren's career
seemed stalled. His attempts to place a novel had been frustrated, and he
had been denied a Guggenheim grant. Then Warren was faced with the
grim prospect of unemployment. Despite the tenuousness of his position at*

6

Vanderbilt, he had hoped somehow to settle in the Nashville area perma-
nently, but his contract was not renewed for the fall term. His calculated
gamble had not paid off, and for a time things appeared desperate indeed.
Though the possibility of returning, chastened, to Southwestern eventually
presented itself, Warren's morale had reached a nadir when, rather like a
deus ex machina, the "old boy" network came to his rescue in the person of
Charles W. Pipkin, himself a former Rhodes scholar and now a dean at
LSU, who recognized Warren's remarkably varied gifts and valued them
accordingly. Pipkin had already brought another Vanderbilt alumnus and
Rhodes man, Cleanth Brooks, to Baton Rouge, and he arranged for Warren
to join them there. Warren was, in effect, entering upon a new life. He was
intrigued by the exotic landscape and culture of Louisiana and pleased by
his classes and schedule. Louisiana State University, a major priority of
Huey P. Long's regime, was enjoying a relative boom in the midst of the
Depression, and Cinina soon found a teaching position as well. Another
opportunity arose. Pipkin enlisted Warren and Brooks to help him handle
the Southwest Review, *headquartered at Southern Methodist University*
but partially underwritten by LSU, which had thereby acquired an editorial
interest in its production. Warren recognized the potential of such an ar-
rangement immediately and began to focus a good deal of energy and
thought on how a primarily regional quarterly might be expanded and im-
proved. At year's end, three of his closest literary friends, Allen Tate, Caro-
line Gordon, and Andrew Lytle, came down from Tennessee to visit for the
holidays and help bring 1934 to a triumphant close. As 1935 began, Warren
had every reason to be optimistic about the future, but things were soon to
take an even more auspicious turn when the university decided to fund a
new journal of its own. The Southern Review *was born, and under the*
guidance of Brooks and Warren it was destined to alter the course of Ameri-
can letters.

TO ALLEN TATE

TLS/PU   Southwest Review
                                              Louisiana State University
                                                         Baton Rouge
                                                       [Early 1935][1]

Dear Allen:
    Here is a new piece, just finished this morning. How does it strike you?
This poem is my only news. I hope you have survived the difficult

7

transition between your past condition and your present sobriety. It has taken me all this time to conquer the impulse to start drinking after breakfast. And even yet the impulse to drink in the middle of the afternoon is recalcitrant.[2]

It looks as if Manson quite definitely has a place here after the first of February if he wants it. I believe he is going to take it. I feel fairly confident that Rose will get a straight faculty job too.[3]

I am working pretty hard now with my courses, the *Review,* some poems, and odds and ends. I plan to launch the baseball story[4] tomorrow afternoon unless something unexpected occurs. [I]t feels rather hot to me now. I have sent Davis[5] another story, but haven't heard from him about it although he has had it three weeks. That may be a good sign. But I want to get the new one done in time for consideration for the anniversary issue in case he turns the one down that he already has.

Your visit was a tremendous pleasure. I have missed seeing you all a great deal this fall, and shall miss you this winter and spring. Give Caroline my love.

As ever,

Red

1. Tate's bracketed date on the original reads "late 1934 or early '35," but clearly this letter was written after the first of the year.

2. Warren alludes to the extended period of celebration the Warrens, Tates, and Andrew Lytle had enjoyed in New Orleans over the Christmas holidays.

3. The poet Manson Radford and his wife, the artist Rose Chavanne, were living in New Orleans at this time.

4. An early version of "Goodwood Comes Back," a story based on Warren's childhood friend Kent Greenfield, who had played in the major leagues. It would eventually be published in the *Southern Review* (Winter 1941).

5. Lambert Davis, editor of the *Virginia Quarterly Review* from 1933 to 1938. He later joined the editorial staff at Harcourt Brace and worked with Warren to bring out *All the King's Men* (1946), then moved on to serve as director of the University of North Carolina Press.

TO FRANK LAWRENCE OWSLEY

TLS/VU   Southwest Review
                                            Louisiana State University
                                                      Baton Rouge
                                                    January 8, 1935

Dear Frank:[1]

We have not recovered as yet from a disappointment that you and Harriet could not come; but I congratulate you on the honor which made it impossible. Your absence was a topic for much sorrowful discourse both here and in the French Quarter.

I shall not be able to write you the long letter now that I should write, for I am busy trying to clear up a deskful of unanswered letters dealing with my poor affairs. But I do want to raise the question of an essay for the Spring or Summer issue of the Southwest Review. If it is published you will be paid for it at the rate we discussed. I say, if it is published, because at the last moment the money to pay for it might not be forthcoming. And I say that only because I am in the habit of crossing my fingers. Pipkin, Brooks, and I went to Shreveport before Christmas for a conference with the Texas editors.[2] It was a very amiable and I think, on the whole, a successful meeting. Henry Smith is a smart young man and very likable. So is McGinnis, for that matter, but he is a scion of Henry Grady[3] if I ever saw one. Let me know about the essay. Of course it is best for the reply to Mencken to go in the Virginia Quarterly,[4] but how about the one on the Machine?[5] Have you revised it yet?

Our best wishes to you all for the New Year, and all our love. Cinina is answering Harriet's fine letter immediately.

As ever,
Red

1. The southern historian Owsley and his wife, Harriet, became fast friends of the Warrens during the early 1930s, when Warren taught at Vanderbilt. A committed adherent to the Agrarian cause, he was among the contributors to the symposium *I'll Take My Stand* (1930).

2. Henry Nash Smith (later a major force in the field of American studies) and John H. McGinnis of Southern Methodist University, who had rather reluctantly agreed

to the collaborative arrangement with LSU whereby the more "conservative" team of Pipkin, Brooks, and Warren shared editorial responsibilities.

3. Henry W. Grady (1850–1889) had been a pioneering spokesman for the "New South" agenda that favored industrialism and liberalization—and thus anathema to Agrarians like Owsley, Tate, and Donald Davidson.

4. H. L. Mencken's essay "The South Astir," in which he attacked the Agrarian program, had appeared in the *Virginia Quarterly Review* (January 1935). Owsley's principled response, "The Pillars of Agrarianism," would run in the March 1935 *American Review*.

5. "Man or Machine," never published.

TO ALLEN TATE AND CAROLINE GORDON

TLS/PU

Southwest Review
Louisiana State University
Baton Rouge
February 4, 1935

Dear Allen and Caroline:

I have been prevented from making an earlier answer to your letters by the tumult of examinations and some other distractions. One of the distractions, however, has been a pleasant one. Father is here,[1] and will probably be here for five or six days more. He arrived with a very bad cold, which prevented our intended trip. Thank you for your services in intercepting Fletcher.[2] He wrote me that he was coming down early in February, and wrote Pipkin at the same time to ask if a lecture or two could be arranged. I saw the reply from Pipkin to the effect that he could get a lecture if he would postpone his trip down here. I assumed that that would take care of the situation until I could get around to writing. Therefore, I was completely astonished when he wired me that he would be here the next morning. Nobody could take care of him: I was leaving, Pipkin had given up his house and was staying with some friends until he found a new one, and Brooks had a house full and a sick father.[3] I hope Fletcher will take it all right. Certainly, he ought to be glad to wait until he can get something out of the effort. I shall be sincerely glad to see him when he comes; last Tuesday I should have been sincerely distressed.

I am delighted that the story about Luke pleased you.[4] I feel, and have been told by others, that the first part is a little too long; but I haven't been able to do anything about it. I don't believe that the principle is wrong; but the detail work does seem to need some compression. I sent the thing to Perkins[5] and have had a letter from Wheelock[6] about it, a rather long letter. I had the slight consolation that several of the people in the office liked it. But, naturally, they found it unsuitable for the magazine. I just can't keep bad language out my stories. Meanwhile I have sent it to *Esquire* in the hope that the baseball element may recommend it to them. And God knows, nobody knows less about baseball than I do. They have had it three weeks now, but I am scarcely encouraged by that fact. Perhaps I wrote you in my last letter that Lambert Davis was using a story in the anniversary issue: *Her Own People.*[7]

I am pleased that a solution for the *Fathers* has at last appeared.[8] That book really ought to be finished. The part I have read is fine in every respect. Lately I have read again the section in the *Yale Review*[9] and find that it stands up beautifully. And when will The *Cup of Fury*[10] begin to brim? Speaking of *Furies;* Caroline, would you undertake to do a moderately long review of Mrs. Agar's book?[11] Say about 800–1200 words? It would be for the spring issue. I shall send a copy to you immediately if you haven't one. The review copy has come in.

About the poems: I find nothing in your list of comments with which to disagree.[12] In the case of the suggestion to change a line or two, I shall have to wait until I find something better. I agree with you about the "Cold Musket barrels glittering with frost," and am striking it out. At first I thought of reversing the lines, that with the mustaches line; but that doesn't seem to work. Out comes the *Wrestling Match,* the *Limited, Admonition to the Dead,* and *Pro Sua Vita.*[13] I am still debating with myself over *To One Awake,*[14] probably because forty makes such a good round number for the poems of a book. Your suggestion for making a new arrangement for the poems se[e]ms to be a good one. I was trying for something more complicated, but it now appears quite empty to me; and I can scarcely remember what principle I was working on. I am enclosing a new table of contents. How does it look to you?

I owe you a vote of thanks for the pains you have taken in going over the thing. And I feel somewhat encouraged in my own judgment, for every poem that you nominate for immediate oblivion was put in the manuscript with the greatest doubt. It is pretty depressing when you begin to put poems together and see the number you simply can't face.

Right now I haven't any notion whether or not a single line is worth a god damn.

I have sent the poetry manuscript to Bobbs-Merrill along with the novels.[15] The first novel, I am told, has gone through the hands of six readers and they, apparently, are still undecided what they are going to do. They have had it about two months, but have had the first eight chapters of the new novel (which they requested in its unfinished condition) only about three weeks. I hope something comes of it. Chambers[16] wrote me that they would be inclined to publish the poetry as well as the novels if they published anything of mine, but that means nothing; at least, I have little optimism about the novels.

(About the failure in dramatic situation in many of my poems, which I recognize as a fact, and the barbarous ladies of my fiction: They may be related, as the feminine half of your brain suggests. I know that the ladies in the fiction are pretty barbarous, but I had never thought of connecting the two facts. And I did have a mystical experience of a field full of folk, sitting in a movie palace in San Francisco, watching Mick[e]y Mouse, after I have drunk a lot of licker for lunch. I wish to God you had a ready-made formula for making the poems more dramatic and the ladies more ladylike, or more human, or something.)

I am crossing my fingers about the magazine with Agar.[17] It sounds too good to be true. If I were a Catholic I should take the matter up with the proper saint im[m]ediately; but I don't know the name of the saint who supervises such matters. Do you?[18] You say Andrew is going with you? I had a letter from Frank Owsley two days ago with the news that Andrew is not at all well. I am writing him immediately.[19] I hope that your news is as recent as Frank's.

No further news occurs to me. The new term began today and I expect to be busy with the matter of courses by Wednesday. Write me about the Cincinnatti [sic] trip, for I am burning with impatience.

Love to all from us both,
Red

P.S. I meant for the *Owl*[20] to come out too. That leaves thirty-nine poems instead of the good round number of forty, doesn't it? And have you any suggestion about a title?

But with the new *Letter from a Coward to a Hero*[21] there are forty poems . . . like forty days and forty nights and forty thieves, etc. By the way, how do you like that one, the *Coward*?

I've just read proof on the review of *Alec[k] Maury.*[22] It sounds pretty terrible to me. I'm sorry I did such a job!

1. Robert Franklin Warren, subject of the moving memoir *Portrait of a Father* (1988).

2. The poet John Gould Fletcher, who had been a contributor to *I'll Take My Stand* and had visited Warren and Cinina in Nashville. Fletcher had lived abroad for many years and been part of the Imagist movement presided over by Ezra Pound and Amy Lowell, but he was now back in his native Arkansas.

3. Cleanth Brooks Sr., a prominent Methodist minister and administrator, came to live with his son following a debilitating stroke.

4. The "baseball story" ("Goodwood Comes Back") alluded to in the first letter in this volume.

5. Maxwell Perkins, celebrated editor-in-chief at Scribner's, who counted among his authors Hemingway, Fitzgerald, Thomas Wolfe, and Caroline Gordon herself.

6. John Hall Wheelock, poet and editor at Scribner's.

7. *Virginia Quarterly Review* (April 1935). This story signaled an important departure in Warren's career: a growing concern with the relationship between race and the problem of identity.

8. Tate's only novel, *The Fathers,* would come out in 1938.

9. "The Migration," *Yale Review* (September 1934).

10. The working title of Gordon's third novel, *None Shall Look Back* (1937).

11. The novelist Eleanor Carroll Chilton was married to Herbert Agar (see n. 17 below). Her *Follow the Furies* would be reviewed by Andrew Lytle in the inaugural issue of the *Southern Review* (Summer 1935).

12. Warren, following a practice he repeated throughout his career, had submitted the manuscript for a volume of his verse to Tate for advice and criticism. *Thirty-Six Poems,* his first collection, went to press later in the year.

13. Early poems dating from the period 1924–1933.

14. Another early poem; Warren decided to include it.

15. During the first half of the 1930s, Warren worked on two novels, *God's Own Time* and a shorter, untitled work. Neither was published.

16. David Laurence Chambers, editor at Bobbs-Merrill.

17. Herbert Agar, journalist, historian, and social critic, had won a Pulitzer in 1933. He and Tate were planning to travel to Cincinnati to secure financial backing for a new journal from Tate's wealthy brother Ben. Though the publication never appeared, their collaboration did bear fruit: the 1936 volume *Who Owns America?: A New Declaration of Independence,* often regarded as a sequel to *I'll Take My Stand.*

18. Warren takes a good-natured dig at the Tates' increasing interest in Catholicism.

19. Andrew Lytle had been one of Warren's closest friends since their days as undergraduates at Vanderbilt. At first attracted to a career in the theater, he published

a biography of Nathan Bedford Forrest (1931) and soon turned his efforts toward fiction.

20. *Poetry* (May 1932). It had originally been part of the "Kentucky Mountain Farm" sequence.

21. Published in the first issue of the *Southern Review* (Summer 1935).

22. *Aleck Maury, Sportsman* (1934), Gordon's second novel, was based on her father, an inveterate outdoorsman. Warren's assessment appeared in the Winter 1935 number of the *Southwest Review*.

TO FRANK LAWRENCE OWSLEY

TLS/VU   L.S.U.

                                                        February 11, 1935

Dear Frank:

You must pardon my delay in answering your letter, but I have had examinations on my hands and then a visit from my father. He was here about two weeks, and se[e]med to enjoy himself. We made two trips to New Orleans during that time and one down to Pass Christian and Bay St. Louis. Further, we drove up to Rosedowns [*sic*] and the plantation country around St. Francisville.[1]

I have just had a long session about the spring issue of the *Review*. I am enclosing the manuscript of the *Machine* essay for your revision. I have just read it carefully twice today. It fal[l]s, of course, in the section of the magazine that falls properly under P[i]pkin's jurisdiction; he says that he wants it i[n] the revised form for the April issue. Can you conveniently put it in the new form you mentioned in the letter in that time? You say you are going to use the material as a basis for another essay; but I suppose it will be substantially the same with material to bring it more up to date. In any case, the magazine should feel honored to get it. (The money has *not* run out; I asked again point-blank today. All seems to be set. There will be a set sum put aside for the purpose to be divided. It should run about a cent a word.)

I have been terribly busy since Christmas. Besides my work for courses I've done a short story (the one about my baseball player) of about 5000 words, a longish poem, and a review of Caroline's book. The review is to appear in the winter issue of the *Southwest Review*. It isn't as good a review as it should be, but it was the best I could do at the time and in the space I had. With fingers crossed I am telling you that Bobbs-Merrill will probably bring out my novels and poems. At least, it seems about as definite now as it could be without a contract signed. They say that they are now trying to decide which to bring out first with no *ifs* about it. But, after all, the fingers are crossed. And I am knocking on wood. I am getting back to the new novel toward the end of the week. I still have two chapters to write.

When Pipkin gets back from Atlanta next week I shall see definitely about your lecture here, the date, etc.[2] I am terribly anxious to see you and Harriet; and I believe Cinina would pop her buttons if she thought you all would be here next week.

I am distressed to hear about Andrew. He has had a hell of a time in the last few years, really worse than the rest of us, I suppose. I gathered from your letter that he should be all right by summer. Is that the case? Where is he now? Has he been able to do any work?

I am pleased to know that you have been so productive lately. If you get any more hot ideas, please let the *Review* have a shot at them if the price can be compared with what you can get elsewhere for the same piece of work.

I must close this now and get on some work. Ah! I almost forgot to mention that Fletcher will arrive tomorrow morning at ten. So we are in for a few days of what might be termed conversation.

And I forgot to say that Cinina's Italian classes here seem to be a considerable success.[3] In conjunction with the Music School the Italian classes gave a recital the other night which was very successful. The Consul came up from New Orleans to attend and appeared to be very pleased. As a result it seems that the library will get a large gift of books from the Italian Government and possibly a student exchange with one of the leading Italian Universities. She has worked like a dog at the business, coaching singers, coaching grammar and everything else. I'm pleased that she seems to be doing well. Besides she has been reading on her damned thesis.[4] She has done four or five times more work than is customary or necessary for it already.

Goodnight, and our best love to you all. Albert[5] sends his regards.

As ever,
Red

---

1. Rosedown is an antebellum plantation house dating from 1835. Nearby is Oakley, where the subject of Warren's *Audubon: A Vision* (1969) stayed for a time. The St.

Francisville area exerted an evocative influence over Warren's imagination throughout his career.

2. Owsley's lecture at LSU would be scheduled to coincide with the university's seventy-fifth anniversary celebration in April and was handled in a rather creative manner, as becomes evident in Cinina Warren's letter of March 21 below.

3. Cinina had been hired to teach in the Romance languages department.

4. Cinina was completing her M.A. thesis, a study of Marcel Proust, and would receive the degree from Vanderbilt in 1936. (My sincere gratitude to Jami Awalt.)

5. Albert Russell Erskine had been a student of Warren's at Southwestern College (now Rhodes College) in Memphis and had followed him to LSU. He acted as business manager once the *Southern Review* was launched and went on to a distinguished career as an editor, eventually working with leading writers on the Random House list—including Robert Penn Warren.

TO ANDREW LYTLE

TLS/VU
                                                       Southwest Review
                                            Louisiana State University
                                                           Baton Rouge
                                                     February 19, 1935

Dear Andrew:

I was cussing you for not writing to me until I heard from the Tates that you are ill.[1] I am terribly sorry, and anxious to know exactly how you are. Cinina and I shall be greatly alarmed until we hear. Do make Miss May or Polly[2] write to us, at least a line, to tell how you are.

There is little news here. I teach my classes and tend to odds and ends and try to get back into my novel. I have a promising prospect for publication of them both, but my fingers are well crossed.

On April 11 and 12 there will be a conference here of Southern and Southwestern editors, directors of University presses, and writers.[3] It is part of the celebration of the seventy-fifth anniversary of the University. Since I am attending to the writers, you may regard this as an official invitation to be present as a guest of the University for those days and the two following days. The 13 and 14 will be devoted to expeditions into the Teche country and to New Orleans. Now get yourself in good shape to argue with Texas industrialists, Georgia communists, and New Mexico folklore-ists.[4] I am counting on you!

But seriously, do take care of yourself! You are a very valuable adjunct to my happiness; and I take your illness as a personal affront from both you and destiny.

My regards and best wishes to all your kin there. And tell someone to write me a note.

Albert (who has measles) and Cinina send love.

As ever,

Red

1. Lytle had fallen seriously ill on the trip home to Tennessee following the Christmas visit he and the Tates had paid the Warrens in Louisiana. The precise nature of his illness remains vague, but it appears to have been related to the prostate troubles that would plague him later in life. (My thanks to Thomas "Tam" Carlson.)

2. "Miss May" was the affectionate nickname of Lytle's aunt Mary Nelson; Polly was his sister.

3. The actual dates were April 10–11. This conference turned out to be a significant event, the occasion for announcing officially the start of the *Southern Review*. Among those in attendance were Tate, Gordon, John Peale Bishop, Lyle Saxon, John Gould Fletcher, Lambert Davis, and the legendary British novelist Ford Madox Ford.

4. A letter (now at Emory University) from A. L. Campa of the New Mexico Folklore Society indicates that he had been invited through the good offices of Fletcher and John Crowe Ransom. He told Warren he would have to decline if travel funds were unavailable.

TO CAROLINE GORDON

TLS/PU

Southwest Review
Louisiana State University
Baton Rouge
February 19, 1935

Dear Caroline:

This is just a note to thank you for the story. I have read it several times and like it very much. If Texas vetoes it, they will do it over my dead body.[1] (And several of their dead bodies.)

The official date for the editors and writers conference here is April 11 and 12, with the 13 and 14 devoted to excursions into the Teche country. Yo[u] all must save those dates. We are looking forward to having you both then. Please don't let anything interfere. I saw Bishop[2] last week end, and he has definitely accepted. There are a number of other acceptances in already, and a number of invitations have just gone out today. In fact, that is the way I have spent the day. Please suggest any names that occur to you all. And you might, if you will be so kind, mention the matter to people who are invited. I'll send you a list of those who are invited.

Fletcher stayed here from Tuesday to Saturday and behaved like an angel. He was very charming, talked wel[l], ate his meals on time, never interfered with anyone, and took us to Arnaud's[3] on Saturday. He is fatter now; that probably accounts for it all.

Love to all,

Red

1. "A Morning's Favor" would not depend upon the verdict of Smith and McGinnis. Brooks and Warren appropriated it for the *Southern Review* (Autumn 1935).

2. John Peale Bishop, now living in New Orleans and a novelist as well as a poet, had first met Warren in Paris in the late 1920s. Warren was an early champion of his work.

3. A fashionable French Quarter restaurant in a class with Antoine's and Galatoire's.

TO DONALD DAVIDSON

TLS/VU

Southwest Review
Louisiana State University
Baton Rouge
February 28, 1935

Dear Don:[1]

I have been intending to write you for several weeks, but my intentions have been consistently defeated by some immediate chore here or pure lethargy.

I shall dispose of my business first. On April 11 and 12 there will be held here a conference of Editors of Southern and Southwestern magazines, Directors of University Presses, and writers. You must come. You, John, and Frank are on the list from Vanderbilt . . . by far the most imposing contingent. You simply must come. Why couldn't the lot of you drive down together? Of course, all those who come will be guests of the University during their stay here. On April 13 and 14 some excursions are planned to New Orleans and the Teche country for various groups; but we might make up a private excursion. A number of people have accepted, and I believe that the thing will be a success. Come and bring your fighting clothes.[2]

Things are going very nicely here, and I like the place more and more. The fact that I only teach three days a week gives me an opportunity to do a considerable amount of reading and writing. I only lack two chapters of the new novel now, and hope to finish that within a month. I've managed to do seven poems, three of them longish, two reviews, and a short story of some 6000 words in the last few months. Two of the new poems will be in the *V.Q.* anniversary number;[3] and a story, too, but not a very new one. I am sticking some of the shorter poems in this letter. What do you think of them? I've been occupied recently in making up a syllabus and analytical anthology of a modest order to be mimeographed for use in the sophomore poetry term here.[4] For the most part the thing is a chore, but it offers moments of interest. I'll send you a copy when the entire thing is run off; only a part has been mimeographed yet. I've got a good deal of material together for the spring issue of the *Southwest Review:* essays by Dixon Wecter,[5] Andrew Corry,[6] John Ransom,[7] Frank Owsley, Cleanth Brooks; stories by Caroline Gordon, John Bishop, Edward Donahoe;[8] reviews by Caroline Gordon, John Gould Fletcher, Cleanth Brooks, Randall Jarrell;[9] poetry by John Bishop and Raymond Dannenbaum.[10] In addition there is some stuff already in, or pledged, for the summer and fall issues. How does that seem to you? And this is important . . . when are you going to be able to do something for the *Review*? Could you undertake a long review of Thomas Wolfe's *Of Time and the River* which has just come in? Or of Bishop's new novel, *Act of Darkness*? Will you wire me collect? The manuscript should be here just after the middle of March. That is a rush order, but the books have just come in.[11]

Do write me something about yourself. I am anxious to hear from you. And do come down in April! Give our love to Theresa.[12]

As ever,
Red

P.S. I neglected to say that contributions will be paid for.

1. Davidson had been a senior figure in the Fugitive group and a faculty mentor to Warren during his undergraduate days at Vanderbilt. A committed regionalist in both his poetry and prose, he was to remain among the most "unreconstructed" of the Agrarians. For all their later ideological differences, especially regarding the race issue, Warren tended to treat Davidson with a measure of respectful deference.

2. Warren anticipates verbal fireworks between Agrarian traditionalists and more "progressive" attendees like Lambert Davis and the *Southwest Review* contingent. As it turned out, neither Davidson nor Ransom came to the conference.

3. "Resolution" and "History," *Virginia Quarterly Review* (July 1935).

4. This relatively modest pedagogical aid would provide the germ for the first of Brooks and Warren's influential textbooks, *An Approach to Literature* (1936).

5. A native of Texas, Wecter met Warren in graduate school at Yale and was among his closest friends at Oxford. He became a cultural historian of considerable note.

6. Corry had been a fellow Rhodes scholar with Warren at Oxford. A man of immense and varied talents, he became a mining engineer and noted public servant as well as a writer.

7. It was John Crowe Ransom's class at Vanderbilt that had turned the young Warren toward literature as a vocation. If the Fugitives and Agrarians may be said to have had an identifiable "leader," Ransom was the man. Warren regarded him as something of a father figure, though they would have their disagreements.

8. A gifted but highly erratic Oklahoman from a wealthy family, Donahoe was a close friend of both Warrens during the 1930s and early '40s. His one novel is *Madness in the Heart* (1937), based in part on the career of oilman and Oklahoma governor Ernest W. Marland, a fellow citizen of Ponca City.

9. Jarrell had been a student of Warren's at Vanderbilt. A brilliant poet and acerbic reviewer, he owed much to the sponsorship of Brooks and Warren.

10. A poet and Hollywood writer Warren had met in California.

11. Davidson must have declined. Vanderbilt English professor John Donald Wade (a contributor to *I'll Take My Stand*) reviewed Wolfe's novel in the Summer 1935 *Southern Review*, and Manson Radford addressed Bishop's book in the same issue.

12. Davidson's wife, a native of Oberlin, Ohio.

TO FRANK LAWRENCE OWSLEY

TLS/VU   Southwest Review
                                          Louisiana State University
                                                      Baton Rouge
                                                February 28, 1935

Dear Frank:

This is a long overdue letter; but it is not going to be a good one.

First, I want to ask you to attend the conference of Editors of Southern and Southwestern Magazines, Directors of University Presses, and writers which will be held on April 11 and 12. This, of course, is one feature of the celebration of the 75th anniversary of the University. All those invited will be guests of the University while in Baton Rouge; but, I may say, that you would be taken care of a bit more privately. You must plan to come. Don and John are the other two being invited from Vanderbilt. Why couldn't you all drive down together? A number of people have accepted already, among them W. T. Couch,[1] Brandt of the Oklahoma Press,[2] A. [*sic*] Botkin,[3] John Gould Fletcher, the Tates, John Bishop, Henry Smith of S.M.U., and McGinnis. Andrew, whom I wrote last week, isn't sure whether he can make it or not, but I am certain that he would join a party. And when you come, come prepared to show a little spirit! And to absorb some spirits. On the 13 and 14 of April some excursions are planned to N.O. and into the Teche country for the guests. We might get up something more private. You must, naturally, bring Harriet.

I am going to try to get your lecture here set in a few weeks, but I fear that the two things could not be combined. I'll let you know more definitely in the near future.

What about the Machine essay[?] I want it as soon as you can get it to me, for we want the spring issue out on April 10. Here is the set-up for that issue: Essays by Owsley, Ransom, Dixon Wecter, Andrew Corry, Cleanth Brooks; stories by John Bishop, Caroline Gordon, Edward Donahoe; reviews by Caroline Gordon, John Gould Fletcher, Cleanth Brooks; poetry by John Bishop and Raymond Dannenbaum. I forgot to mention an article by Pipkin, a long review of books from the present Cabinet, and another political article by Manning of Kentucky State.[4] We have a pretty good lot of stuff committed for the summer and fall issues too. How does that look to you?

I have been mighty busy since Christmas and the attendant depravities . . . which, I am sorry to say, you missed. I'm trying to dig out now, but a slight cold for the past two days has set me back some. I've been doing my class work all right, but I feel pretty fagged out by the time I get home and not good for much more than lying down and reading. We have been to N.O. for flying trips a few times since Christmas, but it scarcely looks the way it did in that tumultuous week. I had a beautiful garden, too, until night before last. My corn was well up, and lots of other stuff. But we got a frost! So now I must start over on some of the produce.

Give my love to Harriet and Larry.[5] We have missed you all no end all year; and, I suppose, we'll go on missing you just as much for a long time to come.

As ever,

Red

P.S. I'm putting in a poem I've done since Christmas.

1. Director of the University of North Carolina Press.
2. Joseph A. Brandt had founded the press in 1929. (He later directed the Princeton University Press before returning to Norman to serve as president of the University of Oklahoma in the 1940s. [Special thanks to Yvonne C. Evans.]) The success of the University of Oklahoma Press under Brandt's leadership provided Warren and his friends with a useful model for regional publishing.
3. B. A. Botkin, folklorist at the University of Oklahoma, whose relationship with the state was rocky at best. He is best remembered for the *Treasury of American Folklore* (1944).
4. "The County in the United States," by John W. Manning (*Southwest Review* [April 1935]).
5. The Owsleys' son Frank Lawrence Owsley Jr. He was a favorite of Warren, whose natural affinity for children was warm and spontaneous and repaid in kind.

TO SEWARD COLLINS

TLS/YU

Southwest Review
Louisiana State University
Baton Rouge
March 12, 1935

American Review
218 Madison Avenue
New York

Dear Collins:[1]

Thank you for replying so promptly to my suggestion about the review on Thomas Wolfe.[2] I am working on it now, and find that it will run in the neighborhood of 5000 words, really a sort of short essay. I shall be able to get i[t] off to you within a week, if all goes well.

There is another matter I want to raise. On April 11 and 12 there will be held here, under the auspices of the University, a conference of Southern and Southwestern Editors, Directors of University Presses, and Writers. I am very anxious to have you come, for I believe the meetings might be a good index to a number of things you are interested in. Some of your Southern friends will be here at the time, Owsley and Tate, for instance. All those invited will, of course, be guests of the University during their stay in Baton Rouge. On the days following the conference there will several excursions into the Teche country for those who are interested. I am enclosing a program for the Diamond Jubilee Celebration of which the conference is a part. You must come down! This is an extraordinarily interesting part of the country in more ways than one.

Please let me hear from you at your earliest convenience.

Very sincerely yours,
Robert Penn Warren

[Handwritten] P.S. Any suggestion you have about persons to be invited to the conference would be appreciated.

1. Seward Collins was editor of the *American Review,* and his magazine was a major outlet for the Agrarians and like-minded traditionalists. Warren and company distanced themselves from Collins when his politics took a sharp turn toward fascism in the later 1930s.
2. Warren's "A Note on the Hamlet of Thomas Wolfe" ran in the May 1935 issue of the *American Review.*

TO ALLEN TATE

TLS/PU
Southwest Review
Louisiana State University
Baton Rouge
March 20, 1935

Dear Allen:

Here is a tidbit of news. Sunday afternoon President Smith[1] took me for an automobile ride and asked if a literary quarterly could be edited here if he could get the jack in large quantities. I was not coy. He asked that a project be detailed by Monday afternoon. I got Pip and Cleanth Monday morning and by 3:30 P.M. the whole matter had been approved with a minimum guarantee of $10,000; we are instructed to ask for more if we need it. That sum of course is not supposed to be drawn on for office equipment, etc. The set-up is this: Pipkin, Editor-in-chief, Brooks and Warren, Managing Editors. The first issue must appear June 1.[2] Naturally, there is a terrible rush to get proper material, and to get the publicity arranged. I shall be very grateful for a lot of advice on the matter, and even more grateful for contributions from you and Caroline. (We are posting prizes of $100 for poetry, not to exceed 150 lines, and $150 for a story, plus the usual rate on publication.[)] The magazine will be called the *Southern Review* (no connection of any kind with the *Southwest Review*). It will run about 200 pages the issue and will pay about $5.00 a page for prose contributions. You all have got to help us on this. Do think about it and write me; or better, have a lot of suggestions on hand in April. About April: It is now possible for me to offer expense money to some of the guests. Obviously, it is impossible to pay expenses of all whom we invited. I simply must have you both here by the evening of April 9. The first meeting is April 10 at 10:00 A.M. A letter is being sent to Diehl immediately,[3] and I want you to insist on coming. It is urgent.

I am greatly rushed, and cannot write more now. Ford,[4] I believe, will be here for the conference.

Brooks showed me the letter you wrote him. He did a good job, didn't he?

Love to all,
Red

P.S. I forgot to say that the scale of the *Review*'s ambitions is large. We are aiming at a national distribution and have a considerable sum for promotion. Hold that in mind for your suggestions. The iron is hot here, and I feel that we can get whatever we ask for.

When do you leave for Cincinatti [*sic*]? Wire me *yes* or *no* from there as soon as you know. (over)

I am sending a letter to Elizabeth M. Roberts[5] in your care. Will you please forward it immediately, and if you will be so good, urge her independently to come to the conference here April 10 and 11. We are offering her transportation.

[Handwritten] I have got her address in Springfield. But urge her to come if you will. She has her expenses too, and I hope will come.

1. James Monroe Smith had been handpicked by Huey P. Long to preside over the university, one of the governor's most cherished projects. Smith later spent time in prison for speculating with university funds.

2. Not surprisingly, the new editors missed this deadline.

3. Charles E. Diehl was president of Southwestern College, where Tate was teaching.

4. Ford Madox Ford (1873–1939) had played a major role in the shaping of modern British fiction. Caroline Gordon had worked as his secretary in the mid-1920s, and he had loaned his Paris apartment to the Tates during their first stay abroad. A lover of tradition, Ford was sympathetic to Agrarian ideas.

5. Elizabeth Madox Roberts (1886–1941), Kentucky novelist and significant figure in the southern literary renascence. Her best-known book, *The Great Meadow,* came out in 1930.

TO THE EDITORS, *CONTEMPO*

TLS/UTex

Southwest Review
Louisiana State University
Baton Rouge
March 20, 1935

The Editors,[1]
CONTEMPO
Chapel Hill,
North Carolina

Gentlemen:

On April 10 and 11 there will be held under the auspices of Louisiana State University a conference of Editors of Southern Magazines, Directors of University Presses, and Writers. I wish to urge your presence on this occasion.

The leading question for discussion will be that of reading in the South. This question, of course, has many ramifications and should lead to fairly spirited and interesting discussion. We feel that your experience will enable you to make a contribution of tremendous value to the success of the conference.

All persons who attend the conference will, of course, be guests of the University during their stay in Baton Rouge. I shall be very grateful for an answer at your earliest convenience, since hotel reservations and other arrangements must be completed in the near future.

I hope to have the great pleasure of seeing you here in April.

Very sincerely yours,
Robert Penn Warren

P.S. Under separate cover you will receive a program of the Diamond Jubilee of the University and of the conferences that will be held in connection with that event.

1. *Contempo* was a short-lived but highly respected little magazine edited in Chapel Hill by various hands, including A. J. Buttitta. It had published its final issue (devoted to Joyce) a year earlier.

TO JOHN GOULD FLETCHER

TLS/UArk
Southwest Review
Louisiana State University
Baton Rouge
March 20, 1935

Dear Fletcher:

We shall expect you in Baton Rouge on the 9th of April. I am making hotel reservations for you on that date. There will be no formal papers or addresses at the conference, but I hope that you will present the same ideas more informally.

About the *Virginia Quarterly*.[1] I did contribute a story to it and I have some poetry appearing there in the July issue. I do not know the details of the treatment of Davidson, and so have no opinion about that matter. In general, however, I may say this:

(1) Literary integrity, as I conceive it, is simply this: a man puts down what he thinks to be true in the best form he can command.

(2) The matter of publication appears to be a purely practical matter. If we should only publish in magazines that conduct their business strictly in sympathy with our ideas, we should never publish anywhere, except, perhaps, the *American Review* . . . and I have some grave qualifications there.

I think that the Mencken essay was disgraceful and ill-written, but that reflects simply on the editors of the magazine and not on us. No magazine in its routine performance is entirely blameless in such matters. Further, as regards the sympathy with agrarianism, I can remark on this. The *Westminster Review* [*sic*], cheek by jowl with your essay[2] (which I think was splendid and for which I am very grateful), published an essay by Knickerbocker[3] that was, in my opinion, far worse than the Mencken essay because it was more personal, more motivated by spite and envy, and essentially more confused. Yet I do not feel that that reflects in any sense on you. I do not even feel inclined to ask whether you knew that Knickerbocker was going to contribute to the magazine. I took your essay for what it was: a thoughtful and generous exercise of your great critical gifts.

I appreciate your second letter in which you remarked that you had meant nothing personal by the first. You know, I am sure, that I have the greatest personal esteem for you and have admired your work for a long time. It is probably unnecessary for me to say that. And I hope that you will accept the foregoing remarks in the spirit in which they are intended: the spirit of one friend answering frankly the query of another on a fairly important issue.

I look forward with great pleasure to seeing you in April. We must have you here then. And I hope that you can make arrangements in Little Rock for proper newspaper publicity for the conference. I can provide you in a few days with a list of acceptances.

And I hope that the other people from Arkansas will come. I have written them urging that they do so. Any other suggestions concerning the conference will be greatly appreciated. Who is the last man you name at Fayetteville? I can't make out his name. I have written Thomas and Jones,[4] but there is a third.

As ever,
Warren

[Handwritten] P.S. You remember, of course, that your expense[s] here are paid. Cinina sends her best regards.

1. Fletcher, like Owsley, was upset over Mencken's attack on the Agrarians in the January 1935 issue of the *Virginia Quarterly Review* (see n. 4, letter to Owsley [January 8, 1935] above). He wanted Warren to boycott the journal.

2. Fletcher's "The Modern Southern Poets" had appeared in the *Westminster Magazine* (January–March 1935).

3. William S. Knickerbocker, editor of the *Sewanee Review,* was skeptical of Agrarian principles and had publicly challenged Davidson and Ransom in debates.

4. David Yancey Thomas taught history and political science at the University of Arkansas, and Virgil L. Jones was a professor of English there. (I am grateful to Ethel C. Simpson, curator of the Fletcher papers.)

CININA WARREN TO FRANK LAWRENCE OWSLEY

TLU/VU

Southwest Review
Louisiana State University
Baton Rouge, Louisiana
March 21, 1935

Dear Frank,

I suppose that you will receive letters from the University with the details of your performance on the twelfth of April, but I thought that I had better tell you something about it.[1] You are to please send an account for your transportation charges, and you will have a check forwarded to you before you leave. All expense[s] here are to be paid by them. This is the official item. Of course we expect you as our guests. Just the same, if you want to you might accept the Hotel Reservations if you so wish, just in case of emergency where to put Andrew or somebody else [*sic*]. Do just as you please about this matter.

The Ambassador arrives here at 11.00 A.M. He pays official call to Gov.[2]—watches military parade, and receives 19 gun salute. Luncheon is at one o'clock, and the Ambassador will speak then. In the afternoon at two o'clock we have a distinguished lecture from the well known historian, Prof. F. L. Owsley—a talk from the Ambassador—a talk from the Royal Italian Consul—one from Comm. Prof. Roselli of New York—and a few words from yours truly—a few more from the Head of the Romance Language Department here.[3] There is going to be a tea later on at the President's house. In the evening—late, about eight, there is [a] convocation, and later the Ambassador receives an honorary degree from the University and he speaks. The idea for you is a speech of about 20 minutes. I would have written sooner but I've really been standing on my head, since to date I've had charge of the arrangements for that day.

Tell Harriet I'm certainly looking forward to her coming. Would you please explain to Dr. Cabeen[4] why I haven't been able to write and thank him for having the library books sent to me, and tell him I've done some work[?] We have our garden well up and there is summer heat here already.

I am delighted that you decided to come, and am really looking forward to hearing you and seeing you. The speech might concern some phase of Italian history that you consider brilliant from *our side,* but then I know your sentiments regarding my well beloved Italy!

I hope your health continues to improve. Tell Harriet that I'll write her as soon as the buzz around here stops a little. I have never seen such stewing! I'm part of the stew by now.

> Love to you all from us, and a big
> kiss for Larry,
> [Unsigned]

[Typed note from Warren to Owsley at bottom of page]

Dear Frank:

I am so glad that you are coming. And Harriet. I can scarcely wait until you all drive up.

I have a little news for you. At last we have got the money to found a large quarterly. It will be called the *Southern Review,* with absolutely *no* connection with the *Southwest Review.* Pipkin, Brooks, and I are editing it. The first issue appears June 1. It will be formally announced at the Writers' conference, but we are busy as beavers in a woodpile now working on it. It is all set. It will be very large and handsome, if money can make it so, and will be introduced with a publicity campaign of considerable proportions. Meanwhile, we have withdrawn your essay from the *Southwest Review,* and are holding it for one of the early issues of the new thing. The whole thing has been pushed through this week, and so you can see what a week we have had to spend.

Is Andrew coming down with you? And Don? There is some money

now available for expenses of some of the people invited to the conference, and of course, money for expenses will go to them.

I have to get back to work. Don't fail to come!

Love to all.

As ever,

Red

P.S. It looks as if we might get the series of little books started in conjunction with the *Review,* beginning next year.[5] Cross your fingers and
pray that Louisiana doesn't go broke!

1. As becomes clear from context, Cinina had arranged for Owsley's lecture to take
place under the partial auspices of the Italian consulate in New Orleans.
2. Oscar K. Allen, who succeeded Huey Long when the latter became a U.S. senator.
The building that has long housed the English department at LSU bears his name.
3. James F. Broussard, who became an antagonist of Warren, Brooks, and other reformers in the subsequent internecine wars that plagued the campus.
4. David C. Cabeen, professor of French at Vanderbilt, who was directing Cinina's
thesis.
5. The "Southern Review Series" never quite materialized as Warren had hoped.

TO SHERWOOD ANDERSON

TLS/Newb
The Southern Review[1]
Louisiana State University
Baton Rouge
March 23, 1935

Mr. Sherwood Anderson
Troutdale,
Virginia

Dear Mr. Anderson:[2]

On June 1 the first issue of the *Southern Review* will appear. Despite its
title this quarterly does not aim, especially in its literary aspect, at a
sectional program, nor will it have an academic bias. We hope to provide
a large quarterly which will be a real index to the most vital contempo-

rary activities in fiction, poetry, criticism, and social thought, with an adequate representation in each of these departments. Since we are writing you almost immediately after the inception of this project, we can not, at this time, give you a precise statement in regard to rate of payment for contributions; but our budget will certainly permit something better than a cent a word for prose and about thirty-five or forty cents a line for verse.

We are extremely anxious to have some of your work in the first issue. Have you a story or sketch which you could submit at once? The first and second issues will carry work by John Peale Bishop, Herbert Agar, John Crowe Ransom, Katherine Ann[e] Porter, Caroline Gordon, Ford Madox Ford, Andrew Lytle, and Allen Tate. I give you this list, which is not inclusive, to indicate something of the character of our contributors.

Since the time for the preparation of the first issue is so short, we are anxious to have a reply at your earliest possible convenience. If it is impossible for you to send us any manuscript immediately, we shall be glad to know whether you will be willing to do so for the second issue.

Very sincerely yours,
Robert Penn Warren

1. Warren uses the letterhead of the new quarterly, apparently for the first time.
2. The celebrated author of *Winesburg, Ohio* (1919) was well past his prime, but still a force to be reckoned on the American literary scene. (A virtually identical letter went out to Thomas Wolfe the day before.)

TO SEWARD COLLINS

TLS/YU   *The Southern Review*
Louisiana State University
Baton Rouge
March 24, 1935

Dear Collins:

Did you get the Wolfe essay? And if so, how do you like it? Please let me know whether you are going to use it. I discovered today that there is a small error, which could easily be corrected in proof. "Professor

Thatcher," as it appears in your copy, should read "Professor Hatcher."[1] It's not of much consequence, but it might be better to have it right.

You may observe that a new magazine is in progress. We have just managed to get funds to found a large quarterly, which will pay well for contributions and which will have a decent budget for publicity. The first issue appears June 1. It will be largely literary but will carry a body of material dealing with social topics. I shall greatly appreciate any advice you may be willing to give me, or any assistance of any other kind. We are going to run fiction and poetry in considerable quantity, as well as critical material.

Will you be able to come to Louisiana for April 10 and 11? I do hope that you will be present. Please let me know, for hotel reservations, etc. must be made in the near future.

Very sincerely yours,

R. P. Warren

1. A character in Wolfe's *Of Time and the River* inspired by the influential professor of playwriting George Pierce Baker. (The mistake went uncorrected and was replicated when "The Hamlet of Thomas Wolfe" was reprinted in Warren's *Selected Essays* [1958].)

TO JOHN GOULD FLETCHER

TLS/UArk

The Southern Review
Louisiana State University
Baton Rouge
March 25, 1935

Dear Fletcher:

As you may observe from the letter head, the University has embarked on a new project. The *Southern Review* will be a large quarterly, well financed, which will aim at a national distribution from the first. This has all happened within the last week, and so we are extremely busy trying to put together the first issue for publication by June 1. I believe that this is a fine step, for it gives us a great deal more scope for our activities. I want you, if you will do so, to do the review of Moore's poems[1] for this paper [*sic*], unless you have already sent it in for the

Southwest Review. Can you do this? We shall be able to pay a fairly good rate for work of all kinds, something better than the *American Review, Nation,* etc.

I hope to see you in April, when we can talk further about plans for the new venture.

Very sincerely yours,
Warren

1. The psychiatrist and prolific sonneteer Merrill Moore had been an undergraduate with Warren at Vanderbilt and a fellow member of the Fugitive group. His *Six Sides to a Man* had just been published. Kenneth Burke would review it for the inaugural issue of the *Southern Review.*

TO SHERWOOD ANDERSON

TLS/Newb
The Southern Review
Louisiana State University
Baton Rouge
March 30 [1935]

Dear Mr. Anderson:

Many thanks for your prompt reply. And I hope that you will be able to get something to us in time for the first issue.[1] Tentatively, our deadline will be about May 10, but we might be able to stretch it a little. Meanwhile I am making out a list of contributors for the next few issues for publicity purposes. I am encouraged by your willingness to contribute to ask you to permit me to use your name in that connection.

Probably you have never received two letters from me concerning the Conference of Editors of Southern Magazines, Directors of University Presses, and Writers that will be held here April 10 and 11. I am very anxious for you to be present. The Conference will be highly informal, with no prepared papers or addresses. All those invited to the Conference will, of course, be guests of the University during their stay in Baton Rouge. And further, the University will be happy to defray your transportation expenses. This last, I may say, applies whether you are in New Orleans or elsewhere.

The following people, among a good many others, will be present for the Conference: W. T. Couch, Director of the University of North Carolina Press; Allen Tate and Caroline Gordon; Donald Davidson; Frank Owsley; Donald Joseph;[2] Andrew Lytle; Ford Madox Ford; Irita Van Doren;[3] S. D. Myres, Henry Smith, and John McGinnis, of the *Southwest Review;* Lambert Davis; Edward Donahoe; Manson Radford; John Wade; George Milburn;[4] B. A. Botkin, of *Space;* J. Brandt, of the University of Oklahoma Press; and a large number of the New Orleans group.[5]

Since the time is drawing near when hotel reservations and other arrangements must be completed, I shall be grateful if you will wire me, collect, in care of the University, concerning the possibility of your being here. I shall be greatly disappointed if you cannot come.

Very sincerely yours,
Robert Penn Warren

1. Anderson did not come through, though Howard Baker did address his book *Puzzled America* (1935) in the inaugural issue.

2. A Texas writer whose works include *October's Child* (1929), *Long Bondage* (1930), and *Four Blind Mice* (1932).

3. Wife of Carl Van Doren and a prominent figure on the New York scene. She edited the New York *Herald Tribune*'s weekly book review section from 1926 to 1963. (Special thanks to Charles East.)

4. An Oklahoma author whose books include *Oklahoma Town* (1931), *No More Trumpets and Other Stories* (1933), and *Catalogue* (1936).

5. Most notably Lyle Saxon and Roark Bradford. The latter's *Ol' Man Adam an' His Chillun* (1928) became the basis for Marc Connelly's successful play *Green Pastures.*

The Conference on Literature and Reading in the South and Southwest had provided the perfect occasion for announcing the birth of the Southern Review, *and immediately afterward Warren went to work to ensure the new quarterly's success. From the beginning, his correspondence with contributors and would-be contributors alike reveals his insistence upon the highest standards and his rigorous commitment to editorial integrity. Things were clearly breaking in Warren's favor, and the following month he received additional good news when he was offered a contract for a book of poems—his first.*

TO JOHN GOULD FLETCHER

TLS/UArk   *The Southern Review*
                                        Louisiana State University
                                                  Baton Rouge
                                              April 29, 1935

Mr. John Gould Fletcher
411 East Seventh Street
Little Rock, Arkansas

Dear Fletcher:

I should have replied earlier to your note, but this is really my first opportunity. Cinina is well from the cold at last, and I am beginning to settle down to something like my ordinary routine.

About the SOUTHERN REVIEW and Haniel Long's book:[1] you know that we are all sympathetic with such a project for publishing as the Writers' Editions of Santa Fe, and that we feel this endeavor to be one of real importance. But this attitude toward the Writers' Editions as a publishing project and a commitment to approve sight-unseen the literary performance in a given item on their list seem to be two different things. Brooks has not read Long's other book of poems,[2] and neither he nor I has any notion of what the second will be like. As far as we can go with an assurance of a favorable review is to say that we shall place it, along with some other books of the quarter, in the hands of a reviewer in whose intelligence and integrity we have some confidence. We intend to select our reviewers with the greatest possible care, but we also intend never to indicate what special line of treatment they shall adopt toward an individual book (I, myself, have declined to do reviewing for certain magazines because they undertook beforehand to indicate whether a review should be favorable or unfavorable). I know that this policy of non-interference may involve us in certain difficulties, but I also know that the contrary policy would involve us in greater difficulties. I hope that you will see this position and sympathize with it.

It is true that I reviewed ATLANTIDES unfavorably,[3] and do not like the other work I have seen by Long; but this no way qualifies my own sympathy with the publishing project as such.

We are busy now putting the transcript of the conference in shape.

It should reach you by the middle of this week. We used Botkin's notes as a basis, but they are very good and, I hope, may prove generally satisfactory.[4] I mailed you the other day a copy of Yeats' plays for review in either the spring or fall issue, but preferably in the first.[5] If it does not appeal to you, express it back to us collect. In the end we decided to put Merrill Moore's poems in the general poetry review, which Kenneth Burke is doing.[6] The Yeats' [sic] plays seem to give a better basis for a single review. I hope you will see fit to do it.

Write to us soon.

As ever,
Warren

1. *Pittsburgh Memoranda* (1935).

2. *Atlantides* (1933).

3. Warren's review had appeared in *Poetry* (January 1935).

4. The transcript of the conference proceedings, edited by Thomas W. Cutrer, has been printed in *The "Southern Review" and Modern Literature,* ed. Lewis P. Simpson et al. (38–78).

5. Fletcher did review Yeats's *Wheels and Butterflies* in the inaugural issue.

6. "Recent Poetry," *Southern Review* (Summer 1935). Despite his leftist political orientation, Burke shared a deep mutual respect with Warren.

TO RONALD LANE LATIMER

TLS/UChi

Louisiana State University
Baton Rouge, Louisiana
May 2, 1935

Mr. Ronald Lane Latimer
The Alcestis Press
551 Fifth Avenue
New York City

Dear Mr. Latimer:[1]

I am greatly honored that you would consider a volume of my verse for inclusion in your series. I gather that each volume in the series will be guaranteed by the author, although you do not definitely say so. Unfortunately, I probably could not afford the luxury of printing my own work. But I should be glad to know precisely what your arrangement is.[2]

Thank you for forwarding the letters to E. E. Cummings;[3] and again my thanks for your invitation.

Very sincerely yours,
Robert Penn Warren

P.S. I am enclosing some of our preliminary publicity for the SOUTHERN REVIEW . . . a rather hastily prepared and entirely horrid folder. But it may interest you. Our regular announcements will be out in the near future.

1. Latimer was also known as J. Ronald Latimer and James G. Leippert. It is clear from the published correspondence of Tate and Bishop that they regarded him as somewhat suspect, which may have colored Warren's attitude toward him.

2. Latimer's terms proved to be a far cry from the vanity press arrangement Warren feared, as would soon become evident.

3. Cummings and other prominent poets like William Carlos Williams and Wallace Stevens had published work in *Alcestis,* the little magazine edited by Latimer. Warren may have asked Latimer to forward cummings an invitation to contribute to the *Southern Review.*

TO W. S. CAMPBELL

TLS/UOk

The Southern Review
Louisiana State University
Baton Rouge
May 10, 1935

Mr. W. S. Campbell
University of Oklahoma
Norman, Oklahoma

Dear Mr. Campbell:[1]

It is with regret that we are returning THEY DANCE IN OKLAHOMA,[2] but the piece does not seem to be exactly suited to our present plans for the magazine. The topic you treat appears to us to be a little too special for a quarterly such as we are projecting. It is not the fact that it deals with a local matter, but that it deals with a fairly restricted aspect of the subject. May we have a chance at something else of yours in the near future?

Thank you for your interest in the REVIEW. We have some hope at present of making it a rather important publication; but we must wait the event [*sic*]. Botkin and Lottinville[3] added greatly to the Conference, and we are very grateful to them for coming. We still regret that you were unable to be here.

Very sincerely yours,
Robert Penn Warren

1. A faculty member at the University of Oklahoma, Campbell was much better known as Stanley Vestal, the prolific author of books and articles about the American West and a recognized authority on the Plains Indians.

2. Campbell/Vestal's essay on Native American dance was picked up by Smith and McGinnis for the July 1935 *Southwest Review*.

3. Savoie Lottinville of the University of Oklahoma Press was eventually Brandt's successor and served as director until 1967.

TO RONALD LANE LATIMER

TLS/UChi

The Southern Review
Louisiana State University
Baton Rouge
May 10, 1935

Mr. Ronald Lane Latimer
The Alcestis Press
551 Fifth Avenue
New York City

Dear Mr. Latimer:

Your offer is surprising and magnificent. Of course, on this basis I shall be delighted to have my work appear in your series.[1] I am greatly pleased with the other names in the group, and am looking forward with a great deal of interest to seeing the volumes as they appear. The SOUTHERN

REVIEW will be definitely interested in reviewing the series. We are hoping to make the reviewing section of the magazine of some importance, concentrating on long studies of a closely selected list. In our first issue Kenneth Burke is doing an essay on the poetry of the quarter, Howard Baker[2] on the fiction, John Wade a study of Thomas Wolfe, Manson Radford a shorter paper on John Bishop's novel etc. All of these will run from 3500 to 6000 words, except the Radford item. Further, we are planning to publish longer poems than ordinary magazines are able to accom[m]odate; for instance, we have a very fine piece by [Wallace] Stevens[3] in the June issue. Do let us have review copies of your series. I shall not be here this summer, for I am lecturing at the University of Colorado Writers' Conference;[4] review copies should be addressed to Cleanth Brooks, the SOUTHERN REVIEW, at the University here.

I am expressing my manuscript to you this afternoon. I have just put it in shape and was preparing to offer it to a publisher, but for the present your arrangement pleases me more than an ordinary publishing arrangement. I am sending forty poems, which I believe are the best and which, at least, are more consistent in tone. I have discarded other pieces, because they were really incidental and had no definite relation to the rest of my work. As the matter stands now it might be better to print the work up in two sections, the second beginning with *Pacific Gazer*. This second group is essentially more miscellaneous than the rest and it might be best to make an arbitrary separation. There is another matter in connection with the manuscript: I have included four sonnets at the very end, not mentioned in the table of contents, *Images on the Tomb*, which are very early work. I'm not certain that I want them in the volume at all; I am sending them merely because they have received a modest amount of mention. What do you think about them? I have no title for the collection. In the last few weeks I have been flirting with *Kentucky Mountain Farm* or *Cold Colloquy,* but something seems wrong with both. The first is pretty well occupied now by my friend Jesse Stuart,[5] and the second seems a bit fancy. I have about decided to use *Thirty-Six Poems* (or Forty, as the case may be). What do you think? Although the poems are not arranged in chronological order, I believe that the dates on the poems might be of some interest.

Again my thanks to you, and my best wishes for your ventures, the series and the magazine.[6] I have seen one issue of the magazine and found it ex[t]remely interesting. I shall be among your subscribers in a few days.

Very sincerely yours,
Robert Penn Warren

1. Warren's decade-long dream of publishing a volume of his selected verse was finally realized when the Alcestis Press brought out *Thirty-Six Poems.*

2. Warren's friendship with Baker, a poet, novelist, and protégé of Yvor Winters, dated from his days as a graduate student at Berkeley.

3. "The Old Woman and the Statue," *Southern Review* (Summer 1935).

4. The Colorado conference and workshops were under the direction of the British-born poet Edward Davison.

5. Stuart had been Warren's student at Vanderbilt, where they had formed a warm relationship. His *Man with a Bull-Tongue Plow* had been published in 1934.

6. *Alcestis,* which ceased publication in 1935.

TO KATHERINE ANNE PORTER

TLS/Maryland

The Southern Review
Louisiana State University
Baton Rouge
May 10, 1935

Dear Katherine Anne:[1]

Thank you very much for sending us the story by your husband.[2] We think that it is very good and are still debating the matter of using it. But we shall let you have a definite decision in the near future. How is the PALE HORSE coming on?[3] We keep watching the mails for it. Do let us have it as soon as you can. I am anxious to see it myself, for I have never read a line of yours that didn't move me to admiration. We are using the CIRCUS in the June issue.[4] May we keep the rest of the manuscript you sent us a little longer?

I hope that you are feeling well again. Do take good care of yourself.

I am distressed that we may not see you this summer, after all. I am leaving Louisiana early in June to go West, where I have some scattered jobs lecturing and teaching. I shall be in Montana[5] in June and early July and then at the University of Colorado Writers' Conference (a school run there in the summer for three weeks by Edward Davison, Robert Frost, De Voto,[6] Whit Burnett,[7] and a few others) until early August, and then in Oakland and San Francisco, California.[8] But we shall be back in the South again by the middle of September. Could you all be in Tennessee or Louisiana then? I certainly hope so. Cinina and I both are very anxious to see you again.

Let us hear from you soon.

As ever,

Red

1. Warren had met Porter through the Tates in New York during the late 1920s, and she remained one of his most cherished friends. Warren and his second wife, the novelist Eleanor Clark, asked Porter to be the godmother of their daughter Rosanna.
2. The diplomat Eugene D. Pressly; they divorced in 1938.
3. Porter was a notoriously deliberate writer. Her novelette "Pale Horse, Pale Rider" eventually appeared in the Winter 1938 issue of the *Review*.
4. "The Circus," one of Porter's quasi-autobiographical "Miranda" stories, added distinction to the first issue of the *Review*.
5. Warren went to the University of Montana through the good offices of his Oxford friend Andrew Corry, who had taken a job teaching Latin and history there.
6. Bernard De Voto, Utah-born critic and novelist and authority on Mark Twain and the American West, would become editor of the *Saturday Review of Literature* in 1936.
7. Coeditor, with Martha Foley, of *Story* magazine.
8. To visit Cinina's father, Domenico Brescia, a composer and professor of music at Mills College.

TO GEORGE MARION O'DONNELL

TLS/WashU

The Southern Review
Louisiana State University
Baton Rouge
May 16, 1935

Mr. George Marion O'Donnell
Box 43, Calhoun Building
Vanderbilt University
Nashville, Tennessee

Dear Mr. O'Donnell:[1]

Thank you for your note. Your copy of the magazine and your check will be sent to the address specified.[2] The checks for the first issue will be sent out two weeks after publication; after that, on the date of publication.

We are interested very much in publishing longer poems than most magazines are able to accommodate. Would it then be possible for us to have a look at the long poem you mention? I imagine from my own experience with the *American Caravan*[3] that our rates for publication in the magazine will compare favorably with those of FOREGROUND; and we can assure you of a considerable publicity.

Very sincerely yours,

Robert Penn Warren

1. O'Donnell was a native Mississippian and a vocal advocate of Agrarian ideals. He contributed the essay "Looking Down the Cotton Row" to Tate and Agar's *Who Owns America?*

2. O'Donnell had two poems in the first issue of the *Review*.

3. An annual edited by Alfred Kreymborg, Lewis Mumford, and Paul Rosenfeld. Some of Warren's best early work had appeared in the series.

Summer teaching and participation in writers' conferences would become necessary fixtures of Warren's professional life over the years, and his trips to the West in 1935 and 1936 in particular were to exert a powerful influence over his creative imagination, as works as varied as Night Rider *(1939) and* Chief Joseph of the Nez Perce *(1983) attest. Even when he was away from Baton Rouge, the* Southern Review *remained very much on his mind.*

TO FRANK LAWRENCE OWSLEY

TLS/VU

The University of Montana
Missoula
June 13, 1935

[Note at top of page] Unofficial (as you termed it): destroy.

Dear Frank:

We finally got here. And it is a long way from Baton Rouge or from anywhere else. But it is a wonderful spot, and from present prospects we shall have a nice time here. When we struck Colorado both Cinina and I almost felt like running into the nearest house of God to offer up a little prayer that we were safely out of Kansas. You have no notion what has happened in that part of the world in the last two years. The people in the western half of the state are like survivors of a shipwreck. The drouths and the dust storms have really done them in. When we were there last the people were merely surly; now they want to tell you all about their troubles. From Dodge City west it is worse, of course. There are abandoned houses along the road. People are getting out we were told. We met old cars on the road with six or seven people in them, chairs tied on the back, and a mattress on top. It rained the day we passed through (for which thank God), but even then you could see a man plowing or harrowing ten miles off from the cloud of dust raised. Don was right; God is wroth. There had been a bad dust storm three days before we passed through. And, of course, we had detours in Colorado because of the floods. But the drive up from Denver, which took in itself two and a half days, was fine. The northern section of Wyoming where we crossed is lovely, especially the Wind River district: a very deep, winding canyon through the mountains with the road running beside a very vigorous mountain river for miles. Southern Montana is rather dreary, but once we crossed the Divide, just east of Butte, things are rather grand. Missoula is a pretty, prosperous town of about 12000, set right in the middle of the mountains. A fine little river and a creek run through the town. On three sides of town we can see the snow-caps. A mountain begins two hundred yards back of the main building of the University. (Needlessly to say, it is not too hot here; we have the windows down tonight and the steam heat turned on.) The University is a nice place, and people have been very agreeable. We got an apartment within an hour after arriving, for Corry had one picked out, and, since is was Sunday, immediately set out for Flathead Lake, which is about a hundred miles north of Missoula. We spent the night in a cabin there, and got up the next morning in time to be back here for nine o'clock registration. (That was rather heroic, don't you think, after a 2600 mile trip?) But Flathead was worth the effort. It really is a splendid place. And it is one place where they don't know that a depression exists. All around this thirty-mile long lake there are tight pleasant little cottages with sheep ranges in the hills behind them, and gardens and orchards, chiefly cherry, in front. We had supper up there with a mining engineer, a friend of Corry; he told us that only bread and luxuries are brought in from the outside, and that the cherry crop, even in the worst years, has made enough to keep everybody comfortably, educate the children, and improve the houses and land. All the places are tight, comfortable, well-painted, and attractive. They have brought in a power line lately. There seems to be a real community life there, too. (By the way, that day was the first time I have ever seen a lot of real sheep dogs work. We saw an enormous flock being handled by four dogs. It is a fine sight!) My classes are good. The people seem unusually well prepared, and the writing they have turned in so far is well above average. I have already received one novel, have read it twice, and have had a two hour session with the author. There are five other novels in that class, either finished already, or about half finished. So I shall have to earn my money during my little stay here. The verse isn't up to the fiction in so far as I can tell from the stuff already in hand. We shall leave here about the middle of July to go to the University of Colorado. (We spent the night there on the way up, and liked the place.) After three weeks there, we shall go on to California for a month. I have been trying to get some work done all week, but reading seems to be all I can put my self to so far. I see that I shall have to put myself through a new discipline if I am to get anything done this summer. I still have the Colorado lectures to write, because I didn't have a chance to do anything on them in Baton Rouge except some reading. I am trying to revise a novel this summer too, and I hope to do some verse I have in mind. God knows how much of that program I can put through. Not much, I imagine. (Did I tell you that my poems are coming out this summer? The Alcestis Press, a new publishing house to handle only poetry, is bringing out a series of six limited editions, one by Bishop, by Allen, by William Carlos Williams, Wallace Stevens, Willard Maas, and myself.[1] The arrangement is very liberal: 33% royalty to the author, copyright vested in author, seven copies free to author. Two hundred will be for sale at $7.50 a copy. God only knows who would buy a book at that price. Now this may blow up at the last minute. I've got my fingers crossed again.)

I suppose you have received a card I mailed you while on the road. I've forgotten what I said precisely, but the idea was this: I mentioned to Pipkin that you were rewriting your essay and would let us have it in the fall. I told him that it would be a study of technological unemployment in relation to the present capitalistic system, socialism, and agrarianism.

He said "good," or "yes," or some phrase of assent, but we did not discuss the matter, for it was in one of our very abrupt and hurried sessions toward the end of term. Cleanth was present at the time. I suppose that if Pipkin had objected on *a priori* grounds to the essay he would have voiced his disapproval then. I don't mean to imply that he would necessarily agree with the essay in its entirety, but that, of course, is beside the point. (Neither Cleanth nor I agree with Kenneth Burke's poetry review, which we are publishing, in its entirety, but we want to publish it, for it is an acute and intelligent analysis of its kind.) What will happen I can't predict for the fall; but Pipkin was perfectly innocent on the earlier count. Apparently I was less innocent than I had imagined. I have been trying to reconstruct our conversation at Wilkinson's [*sic*] party[2] without any great success, for fatigue and licker were then having their way with me. But the impression I carried away with me certainly was that you still intended to withdraw the essay. Otherwise I should not have sent it back. The irresponsibility in delaying to send it back was great; I didn't realize when I had your first letter that there was a greater black mark involved. All I can ask is that you understand that there was nothing malignant in the situation.[3]

Naturally, your letter, the second one, contained an alarming item. And I am anxious to know what it is. I have speculated wildly, but fruitlessly, for yet I haven't the slightest notion. If it is something you can't write, or prefer not to write, I hope to have my mind cleared when we come through Nashville in the fall. (That is our present plan, though something may arise to change it.) You can imagine that the matter is disturbing. I showed the letter to Cleanth, since you gave your leave and since he is equally involved in the general situation. He was at as great a loss as I.

I want to thank you for your full and good letter in answer to the joint one. It made me feel a lot better. Cleanth was worried badly about the matter, and, needless to say, I was tremendously disturbed.

The magazine will appear about July 1, a letter from Cleanth tells me. There is a lot of good stuff in it and a lot of stuff I wish were not in it. I am not entirely happy about some of the poetry and I don't like the tone in part of Vance's review.[4] But what we have to do now is to try to buck up later issues. The problem of distribution is going to be a hard one too. If you think of any people who might be interested, will you please jot them on a piece of paper and send them to Albert? We are having to ask our friends to do that in order to build up a promising list of our own.

John Ransom wrote me a short note which I received a day or two ago. In it he mentioned that Don had received a good offer at Alabama, and that Don was in a stew about making up his mind.[5] I am simply delighted about the offer. The fact itself is fine, no matter what Don decides to do.

Give our love to Harriet and Larry. You all are always in our conversations, and we miss you as much in Montana as we did in Louisiana.

Write me here until the middle of July. After that until August 10 at Boulder, care of Edward Davison.

> As ever,
> Red

P.S. I am enclosing two items of greatly dissimilar nature. The more important one is a check for $4.00, the sum I borrowed from Harriet in Baton Rouge during the last day of the Conference. The other is a recent poem, one I did just before leaving. How do you like it?

[Postscript in Cinina Warren's hand]

Dear Harriet:

Am beginning to regenerate after the long trip & am getting busy on learning Latin & doing thesis & housework. This is glorious country & I can't think of anything nicer than for all of us to take that Western trip—so long planned—then up to Canada & down west to Calif. Try to count on it for some future date. It's cool & we can see snow from here. Love to all of you—More later. X Cinina

1. Bishop's *Minute Particulars*, Williams' *An Early Martyr*, Stevens' *Ideas of Order*, and Maas's *Fire Testament* came out in 1935. Tate's *The Mediterranean* was issued in 1936.

2. Warren probably means Marcus Wilkerson, director of the nascent Louisiana State University Press.

3. The substance of this cryptic passage is unclear, but it may have to do with confusion over the handling of Owsley's "Man or Machine" essay.

4. Rupert B. Vance's "Is Agrarianism for Farmers?" reflected his "progressive" views.

5. Davidson remained at Vanderbilt.

TO DONALD DAVIDSON

TLS/VU

The Southern Review[1]
Louisiana State University
Baton Rouge
July 8, 1935

Dear Don:

I am writing you from Missoula, Montana, which I find a very fine place for a summer visit. We had a good trip out, always just in the wake of dust storms, floods, and tornadoes, but always escaping them. Since getting here we have taken some kind of a trip every week end. The other day we took a trip to Glacier Park, which is superb. I've never seen anything like it. But all this end of Montana is fine, especially Flathead Lake, about seventy miles north of Missoula; we have been up to the lake several times. We leave in ten days for the University of Colorado. On the way up we spent the night there, and found the place very good. We shall be there until August 10, and then to California. My address there will be 478 Vernon Street, Oakland, California, care of Domenico Brescia.

Brooks and Erskine write me that the REVIEW is almost through the press despite all sorts of delays about getting type, etc. A local printer is doing it for us, following, we trust, the design laid out by Paul Johnston [*sic*][2] of the Van Rees Press. Working out a design by correspondence, of course, caused a lot of delay. But the design looks mighty handsome. Your copy should reach you in a few days after this letter. Your poem is in it, of course.[3] And a nice one it is, too! Have you got any essays in mind for coming issues? Do try to get something to us this fall anyway. I have asked Cleanth and Erskine to send you several copies to drop in strategic places. There will be people at Breadloaf [*sic*][4] who should know about the thing, and people who might contribute. Give us a lift there if you can. And could you provide us with a list of a few names of people who should receive sample copies or publicity? You might star the ones on the list to receive copies. If you have time, such a list would be of great value to us. We have more formal lists, of course, but we are trying to build up a very active one by soliciting our friends in this way.

I hope that your summer is proving very fine. Recently we have met a very enthusiastic admirer of yours, a Miss Merrilies [*sic*],[5] who teaches here, and who knew you at Breadloaf [*sic*]. She gives glowing reports of the place. And of you.

Give our love to Theresa and Mary.[6] And let me have a word from you during the summer.

As ever,

Red

P.S. If you can make out a list, please send it to Cleanth or to Albert Erskine at Louisiana State.

1. Warren occasionally used *Southern Review* letterhead when he was away from Baton Rouge.
2. The name is Johnson; he was a highly respected print designer.
3. "On a Replica of the Parthenon at Nashville."
4. Davidson had been on the summer faculty of the Bread Loaf School of English in Vermont since 1931.
5. Lucia B. Mirrielees had a long and distinguished career at Montana and, like Davidson, taught at Bread Loaf. The author of several textbooks, she served a term as president of the National Conference of Teachers of English. (My gratitude to Jodi Allison-Bunnell.)
6. Davidson's daughter.

TO GEORGE MARION O'DONNELL

TLS/WashU   [*Southern Review* letterhead]
                                                         July 18, 1935

Dear Mr. O'Donnell:

Your letter was forwarded to me here in Montana. I suppose, since it had been opened at Baton Rouge, that you have already received an answer to your request. You have not received a copy of the REVIEW only because the REVIEW is not yet out. We ran into all kinds of delays in getting type, etc. But I hear in the last note from Louisiana that the proof has been finished and that the covers are off [the] press; so by the time you get this you may have the magazine itself. In the future we should be able to keep our schedule.

Your poems are in the files at Baton Rouge. I suppose they have been mailed to you by this time.

I shall probably be in Nashville during the fall, and look forward with great pleasure to seeing you then.

> Very sincerely yours,
> Warren

[Handwritten] P.S. Have you got any new poems or stories? Or an essay?

[Typing resumes] My address until August 9 will be University of Colorado, Boulder, Colorado.

By the fall of 1935, Warren's life had assumed the varied and hectic rhythm that would characterize his years at LSU. He balanced the demands of a heavy teaching schedule with his own writing of poetry, fiction, and criticism; accepted speaking engagements and summer teaching when they arose; and began his fruitful collaboration with Cleanth Brooks on a series of highly influential textbooks. He continued to support the Agrarian cause in principle, though with waning enthusiasm, but at the center of his working life was the Southern Review. *Pipkin was the* Review's *official editor, but Brooks and Warren, the managing editors, gradually assumed responsibility for the quarterly and its contents. The seriousness and care Warren brought to his editorial duties were evident from the outset, and he was determined to establish and maintain the stature of the quarterly even as he systematically nurtured the talent of a younger generation of writers that included Eudora Welty, Randall Jarrell, Peter Taylor, and John Berryman.*

TO GEORGE MARION O'DONNELL

TLS/WashU

> *The Southern Review*
> Louisiana State University
> Baton Rouge, Louisiana
> Oct. 4, 1935

Mr. George Marion O'Donnell
Vanderbilt University
Nashville, Tenn.

Dear O'Donnell:

We have kept your poems for a disgraceful period, but during that period we have read them many times. Our policy for publishing the poetry raises a special question about a group of poems like this. Some of them we like, and like very much, but that number is not so great that we could consider them as a group for presentation. I am making the following suggestion, which may work to some disadvantage for you, but which I hope you will accept. Judging from the quality of the work we have seen, we have hopes that in the not too distant future we might be able to arrange a real display for your poems, such as the display we are giving Bishop in the fall issue.[1] If you wish to hold these poems and others you may write in what I hope will be a productive year, we shall be happy to reopen the question of publicat[i]on for a group. If this plan does not suit you, please let us know in full candor.

I am very anxious to see the essay on Southern poets which you mentioned, and hope (as you might guess) that Collins will publish it.[2] Whatever the quality of the essay, it certainly could not be used in THE SOUTHERN REVIEW very gracefully.

Another matter: Would you be interested in doing a review for us during the course of the year?

Very sincerely yours,
Warren

1. Bishop's cluster of verse "Experience of the West and Other Poems" was included in the Autumn 1935 number.
2. The *American Review* did not publish the essay in question, though Collins did run two of O'Donnell's Agrarian pieces.

TO HUBERT CREEKMORE

TLS/BU

The Southern Review
Louisiana State University
Baton Rouge, Louisiana
October 15, 1935

Mr. Hubert Creekmore[1]
1607 Pinehurst St.
Jackson, Miss.

Dear Mr. Creekmore:

We found all of this interesting, especially A PUBLIC SQUARE, WITH MEN and PRELIMINARY, but could not quite make up our minds to use it.

As far as the story is concerned, it seems to us that there is too much rationalization of the action. The end, however, comes off. We shall be happy to see some more.

Very sincerely yours,
Robert Penn Warren

1. A Mississippian, Creekmore had made an auspicious literary debut the previous year, when his verse appeared in *Poetry* and his fiction in *Story*. He went on to become a poet, novelist, and translator of some note.

TO ANDREW LYTLE

TLS/VU

The Southern Review
Louisiana State University
Baton Rouge, Louisiana
October 15, 1935

Mr. Andrew Lytle
Guntersville, Ala.

Dear Andrew:

We have a book here that might interest you for review, ADVENTURES OF GENERAL MARBOT, by Captain Thomason.[1] In the winter issue we are planning to run, in addition to the regular review section, a series of selected short reviews, about a paragraph or so each. Would you be interested in doing such a note on this book?

We have just finished looking over the galleys on your Lee review.[2] I have not yet had a chance to read Freeman's book, but I have read all of the major treatments of it. You, I think, have raised the fundamental point, and I wish to applaud you. By the way, I want to borrow the book from you some time this winter and read it myself. Give my best love to your family. When you finish your novel,[3] try to come to Louisiana for a visit.

We are terribly busy and don't see the light yet, but by Christmas, I suppose things will slack up. Let me hear from you.

As ever,
Red

1. John W. Thomason, the military historian; Lytle must have declined Warren's invitation.

2. Lytle's review of Douglas Southall Freeman's monumental *R. E. Lee,* in the *Southern Review* (Autumn 1935).

3. *The Long Night* (1936).

TO MORTON DAUWEN ZABEL

TLS/UChi

The Southern Review
Louisiana State University
Baton Rouge, Louisiana
October 15, 1935

Mr. Morton Zabel
c/o POETRY: A MAGAZINE OF VERSE
232 East Erie St.
Chicago, Ill.

Dear Mr. Zabel:[1]

Thank you for your letter. I am truly delighted that you like the little essay on Wolfe,[2] and I am equally delighted that you find something to please you in the first issue of THE SOUTHERN REVIEW. We put a good deal of effort into the thing, and are gratified when someone whose verdict we really respect finds it not too bad. Something else: we are very anxious to get positive suggestions and opinions from people like you who have had a so much wider experience with the problems of editing.

I don't believe that I am going to be able to do any reviewing this fall, except one piece which I have already taken. As a matter of fact, I have also committed myself to writing an essay which must be done by January 1 and which will mean a good deal of work.[3] But in the winter, say after the first of the year, I shall be delighted to undertake some reviews of books of verse. Thank you for the invitation.

Very sincerely yours,
Robert Penn Warren

1. The poet-critic Zabel taught at Loyola and was associate editor of *Poetry* under its founder, Harriet Monroe. He assumed the editorship in 1936. Warren began review-

ing for the magazine at Zabel's invitation in 1931 (letter of Zabel to Warren [October 9, 1931], Emory University).

2. "A Note on the Hamlet of Thomas Wolfe," *American Review* (May 1935).

3. Presumably the omnibus review "Some Recent Novels," *Southern Review* (Winter 1936).

TO THOMAS WOLFE

TLS/Harv

The Southern Review
Louisiana State University
Baton Rouge, Louisiana
October 16, 1935

Mr. Thomas Wolfe
Charles Scribner's Sons
597 Fifth Ave.
New York, N.Y.

Dear Tom:[1]

Thanks for the note. I am sorry that my letter struck you at such a bad time, and hope that you have finished the proofs and won the law-suits by the time you get this.[2] If you have assembled yourself by the time this reaches you, let me know whether you would be able to give the talk at the University here this winter and how much your fee would be. I am anxious to see you, and so my interest in this matter is selfish to a large extent. And I don't want to let the budget for such matters be used up before your appearance can be arranged. Do try to make it.

Sincerely,
Red

1. Warren and Wolfe had met and established friendly relations at the Colorado Writers' Conference in August, despite Warren's public reservations about *Of Time and the River* in his *American Review* piece.

2. Wolfe was reading proof on the collection of stories *From Death to Morning;* he was being sued by his former agent, Madeleine Boyd.

TO JOHN GOULD FLETCHER

TLS/UArk

The Southern Review
Louisiana State University
Baton Rouge, Louisiana
Nov. 8, 1935

Mr. John Gould Fletcher
411 East 7th St.
Little Rock, Ark.

Dear Fletcher:

Would you consider doing an essay or long review on Damon's AMY LOWELL[1] for our spring issue? I know that this might be in some respects an embarrassing project because you yourself play such a prominent part in the biography and in the Imagist Movement itself, but I also know that you would be able to command enough detachment to obviate this difficulty. Perhaps the review might take up matters of fact in the biography and interpretations of fact, and present, in addition[,] your portrait of Amy Lowell and a criticism of her principles and practice. There is no one who is better able to speak on this general subject than you, and we shall consider ourselves fortunate if you will undertake this task. Do not limit yourself in space, but do let us know at your earliest convenience, if you do decide to write the piece, approximately how much space you will require. Our deadline for the spring issue will probably fall in early February. Would that be rushing you too much?

About the poems, which we have had in hand so long: we have decided, after all, not to use these. I do like very much the central section of LIVEOAK, but neither Brooks nor I believe that these three, taken as a group, are among your best or more representative pieces.

Cinina and I did indeed have an agreeable summer, going to Montana, Colorado, and California. I hope that yours was pleasant, and I hope that we shall see you this winter. Meanwhile my best wishes and regards to you.

Warren

1. Fletcher's "Herald of Imagism," occasioned by S. Foster Damon's biography of Lowell, was included in the Spring 1936 number.

TO GEORGE MARION O'DONNELL

TLS/WashU

The Southern Review
Louisiana State University
Baton Rouge, Louisiana
Nov. 11, 1935

Mr. George Marion O'Donnell
Box 43, Calhoun Building
Vanderbilt University
Nashville, Tenn.

Dear Mr. O'Donnell:

We like these poems and certainly intend to publish a number of them at some time in the future.[1] We are sending them back to you now for two reasons. First, we do not think that there are enough pieces here to make a fully rounded exhibit and to justify an accompanying critical note. In the second place, if they were published now, these poems would be eliminated from competition in THE SOUTHERN REVIEW Poetry Contest, which may be of interest to you since the prize is $250 plus the usual publication rates. We are intending, of course, to use in the magazine a large number of poems submitted for the contest. I hope that you will compete, and I certainly believe that you would have a strong chance for first place.

Very sincerely yours,
Robert Penn Warren

1. O'Donnell's verse cluster "Return and Other Poems" came out in the Spring 1936 issue.

TO ANDREW LYTLE

TLS/VU

The Southern Review
Louisiana State University
Baton Rouge, Louisiana
Nov. 12, 1935

Mr. Andrew Lytle
Monteagle, Tenn.

Dear Andrew:

We want to impose upon you again for a paragraph review, this time for the spring issue if you cannot do the book before November 28. The book is MULES AND MEN, by Zora Hurston, a sort of negro folklore and anecdote collection.[1] We are so sure that this will interest you that we are sending the book on now. If you will need more than 150 words, take it.

Best love,
Red

1. Regrettably, Lytle must have declined, and no review of this African American classic appeared. It would have been interesting to know what Lytle would have made of it.

TO GEORGE MARION O'DONNELL

TLS/WashU

The Southern Review
Louisiana State University
Baton Rouge, Louisiana
Nov. 25, 1935

Mr. George Marion O'Donnell
Vanderbilt University
Nashville, Tenn.

Dear O'Donnell:

Mr. Ransom writes me that a collection of your poems will be Number 7 in the Alcestis Press series.[1] This, I suppose, will eliminate you in competition in our Poetry Contest. Since we want to use some of your work, may we have it all back again with the idea of working out a group for our spring issue, which will appear in early March? We had hoped that you would be one of our strongest contenders for the prize and regret to lose you in that capacity, but I know that you are glad to have your book brought out. And I hope that you will be glad to let us run some of your pieces in the spring.

With best wishes,
Robert Penn Warren

1. The volume was never published, though Charles East notes that James Laughlin of New Directions included a number of O'Donnell's poems in *Five Young American Poets* (1940).

TO ALLEN TATE

TLU/PU   [Baton Rouge]
                                                 [Autumn 1935][1]

Dear Allen:

Your essay came this afternoon and I have only had time to give it a single hasty reading before leaving the office. But it strikes me as very good indeed—exactly the line that I, personally, had hoped that you would take. I am delighted that we have it for winter.[2] The only thing that struck me as needing a possible revision was the section on payments, which seems somewhat out of proportion. Cleanth has taken the essay home with him to read, and in our telephone conversation about it a few minutes ago he said that he felt as I do about the paragraph or two in question. He says that he will write you about it in the morning when he goes to the office. (I shan't go in tomorrow until noon.)

I am working like hell on the fiction review for the winter issue. I have read innumerable novels, most of them bad, and am not quite half through with the actual writing. Aside from my own effort, I believe that the winter issue is the one that will really take us to town. We have a good essay by Don on American Heroes,[3] a marvelous analysis of Erskine Caldwell by Wade,[4] an essay on Yeats by Blackmur,[5] your piece, Agar's Pareto (not in yet),[6] Kendrick on Dubois' [*sic*] BLACK RECONSTRUCTION,[7]

Baker on Van Doren,[8] William Moses on Lindsay (Masters' biography—
in, and good enough),[9] four stories,[10] which, at the moment please us,
John on poetry of the quarter[11] (exclusive of the Alcestis books, which
Flint[12] is reviewing), and Van Doren's poems.[13] These are the high
points. There are some other items, including Vance on Agar's book,[14]
which is not in yet and which is quite unpredictable; I pray that it will
be really good. (By the way, have you seen the little book on the South
by Kendrick and Arnett?[15] It is far better than I had hoped, really on the
good side. Of course, he can't quite make the grade in some respects,
but he has come a long way, and the book is a mine of valuable statistics.
It ought to [be] put in every freshman's hand.)

I am putting in a new poem, the only one I have had time to write
lately. I have several others in various stages and can finish them if I can
take out the time from the day-to-day pressure. What do you think of
this one?

By the way, I forgot to say that Cleanth's Part III is far better than
the preceding parts.[16] He is doing the thing up brown in this installment—and the first two were fine enough. Now it seems that we may
get our series of critical books and anthologies—the SOUTHERN REVIEW
SERIES, nicely printed (we hope to get Paul Johnson to design them
uniformly with the magazine), numbered in series, etc. Cleanth's would
form one of the first two books, perhaps the first, with John closely
following. We would want to get you, Don, Wade (who ought to have a
batch of fine e[s]says assembled by now—I can name a good many off-
hand), perhaps Blackmur, Frank (if he writes the short book he is considering). My essays would probably form number three or four in the
series.[17]

I have been at work for a week now on the estimates, etc., and hope
that we can push the matter to completion soon. *Do not discuss the matter with anyone,* for I cried "wolf!" once before. But I am even more
confident now. Please write me all that you can think of in the way of
advice about possible contributors to the series, promotion, distribution,
etc. We want to make the books range in price from $1.00 to $2.00,
according to size. A person could subscribe for the series, which, we
hope, would run indefinitely (Subscription by the year, titles and prices
announced a year in advance). Do you think we could run this on a
small deficit? Or no deficit? [Handwritten in margin] The Oklahoma
Press is self-supporting. [Typing resumes] The series would contain one

anthology of poetry a year from the REVIEW, with the accompanying critical notes and an introduction. We might even get around to bringing out a collection of our best fiction at the end of a period of several years.[18] This is rather ambitious, but it *may* come off. Meanwhile, my fingers are crossed.

I must sign off now and do something on my review. I'll write in a day or so.

Love to you all from us,

RED

1. Tate's date.

2. "The Function of the Literary Quarterly," *Southern Review* (Winter 1936).

3. "A Note on American Heroes."

4. "Sweet Are the Uses of Degeneracy."

5. The brilliant autodidact R. P. Blackmur dealt with Yeats's later poetry in the Autumn 1936 number.

6. Vilfredo Pareto (1848–1923) was an Italian economist and social theorist whose ideas were embraced by Mussolini. A posthumous translation of his most important work had just appeared in English under the title *The Mind and Society.* Evidently, Agar failed to submit his review.

7. Benjamin B. Kendrick's review of W. E. B. Du Bois' daring revisionist study was entitled "History as a Curative."

8. Howard Baker, "A Note on the Poetry of Mark Van Doren."

9. The poet W. R. Moses reviewed Edgar Lee Masters' study of Vachel Lindsay under the title "Ferment of the Poet's Mind."

10. S. S. Field, "Goodbye to Cap'm John"; Allen McGinnis, "Let Nothing You Dismay"; Katherine Anne Porter, "The Old Order"; and Harriette Simpson, "The Washerwoman's Day."

11. Ransom reviewed volumes by Daniel Whitehead Hicky, Edgar Lee Masters, Archibald Fleming, Edwin Arlington Robinson, Ruth Pitter, T. S. Eliot, Forrest Anderson, Muriel Rukeyser, and Ann Winslow.

12. The critic F. Cudworth Flint.

13. Mark Van Doren, "Winter Tryst and Other Poems."

14. Vance's review of Agar's *Land of the Free* was entitled "Little Man, What Now?"

15. *The South Looks at Its Past,* by Benjamin B. Kendrick and Alex M. Arnett. It was reviewed in the Winter 1936 issue by the social scientist H. C. Nixon, who had an essay in *I'll Take My Stand.*

16. "Metaphysical Poetry and the Ivory Tower," the third and final installment in Brooks's series of groundbreaking *Southern Review* essays that included "Metaphor and the Tradition" and "Wit and High Seriousness."

17. Again, Warren's plans were disappointed. The series never materialized.

18. Long after the *Review* had ceased publication and they had both left LSU, Brooks and Warren, reunited at Yale, did bring out *An Anthology of Stories from the "Southern Review"* (1953).

1936

TO MORTON DAUWEN ZABEL

TLS/UChi

The Southern Review
Louisiana State University
Baton Rouge,
Louisiana
Jan. 15, 1936

Mr. Morton Zabel
POETRY: A MAGAZINE OF VERSE
232 East Erie St.
Chicago, Ill.

Dear Mr. Zabel:

I am enclosing three poems by a young man whom I know here.[1] I hope that you may like one or more of them well enough for publication. These poems have not been rejected by THE SOUTHERN REVIEW, as I feel I should explain to you. If we could get a group as good as a couple of these, we would certainly publish them, but we have given up publishing miscellaneous selections—perhaps misguidedly. In any case, let me know what you think of them, for I am interested in Mr. Palmer's work.[2]

Very sincerely yours,
Robert Penn Warren

1. John Ellis Palmer, a student at LSU who would later serve as managing editor of the *Southern Review* after Albert Erskine's departure. Following meritorious naval service during World War II and a stint at the *Sewanee Review,* he went on to edit the *Yale Review* for many years.

2. Zabel did not publish Palmer's poetry.

TO MORTON DAUWEN ZABEL

TLS/UChi

The Southern Review
Louisiana State University
Baton Rouge,
Louisiana
Jan. 27, 1936

Mr. Morton Zabel
POETRY: A MAGAZINE OF VERSE
232 East Erie St.
Chicago, Ill.

Dear Zabel:

I am delighted that you find it possible to make an exchange with us. And I hope that the quality of the Review will not disappoint you. I gather from your letter that you have in hand a copy of our first issue. We are sending immediately copies of the second and the third, in which our policy of long groups of poems by single authors is put into practice. It is very kind of you to give us a notice in your March number,[1] and I hope you will make some mention of our Poetry Contest. The date of closing for the contest has been postponed from May until October, 1936.

You ask whether the Review is restricted to Southern persons. Decidedly not, as a glance at any table of contents will show you. As a matter of fact, we have already decided to ask you to write some criticism for us in the near future. Would you be willing to undertake a long review of the poetry of a quarter for us? If so, we shall put you down for one in a near issue.[2]

Thank you for the review books.[3] I shall undertake to get the reviews to you on time, even though I am pretty busy trying to finish a new volume of poems,[4] edit the Review, teach, and write a text book. (It sounds as if nothing could be well done under those circumstances, and that it just about the way it is.)

Did you get the poems by the young man named Palmer? What did you think of them?

Thanks again on all accounts.

Very sincerely yours,
Robert Penn Warren

1. The notice actually ran in the April 1936 issue of *Poetry.*

2. Zabel's "Poets of Five Decades" appeared in the Summer 1936 number.

3. Presumably Ann Winslow's *Trial Balances* and Robinson Jeffers' *Solstice and Other Poems.* Warren's reviews of these books appeared in the June and November 1936 issues of *Poetry* respectively.

4. A somewhat confusing observation, since Warren's second volume of poetry (*Eleven Poems on the Same Theme*) would not be published until 1942. However, though 1935 is the "official" date of publication for *Thirty-Six Poems,* Warren's bibliographer James A. Grimshaw Jr. lists the actual date as February 15, 1936. Thus Warren may have been making some last minute adjustments to his manuscript. (Here as elsewhere in this edition, my debt to Grimshaw's authoritative *Robert Penn Warren: A Descriptive Bibliography* is obvious.)

TO LOUIS UNTERMEYER

TLS/UDel

The Southern Review
Louisiana State University
Baton Rouge,
Louisiana
Feb. 3, 1936

Mr. Louis Untermeyer
21 Birckhead Place
Toledo, Ohio

Dear Mr. Untermeyer:[1]

I am greatly pleased to know that you will be in Louisiana in March, and am anxious that you come up to Baton Rouge and pay us a visit. If you will let me know when you will be in New Orleans, I shall meet you there and drive you back to Baton Rouge. Don't fail to let me know.

Needless to say I am grateful for the sentiments you expressed in your letter and in the review.[2] Many thanks.

I shall expect you in March!

Very sincerely,
Red Warren

P.S. I am enclosing some new ones. How do you like them?

1. Poet, critic, and pioneering champion of modern verse, Untermeyer (1885–1977) is best remembered as an anthologist. He included eight of Warren's poems in the fifth edition of his *Modern American Poetry* (1936).
2. Most likely a reference to Untermeyer's brief critical introduction to the Warren selections in his anthology.

TO SEWARD COLLINS

TLS/YU

The Southern Review
Louisiana State University
Baton Rouge,
Louisiana
Feb. 12, 1936

Mr. Seward B. Collins
231 W. 58th St.
New York, N.Y.

Dear Collins:

Here is a little paper that Brooks and I have done in answer to a very silly essay which appeared in the MERCURY this month.[1] The essay by Mrs. Gerould is in itself not important, but it is important, it strikes us, as a symptom of a fashion. We have tried to make our piece comprehensible for a reader who has not actually seen the piece we are answering; and we have tried to cast it in a tone not too pontifical.

Since Mrs. Gerould's essay appeared in the MERCURY, we have send a copy to Palmer[2] on the off-chance that he would rather run the answer in his own magazine. That accounts for the carbon copy. But we are fairly certain that Palmer will not see fit to use this, and so are sending this copy almost simultaneously. Since our piece has some topical reference, being an answer, we shall be very grateful if you will wire either of us about your decision on the matter.

Very sincerely yours,
Robert Penn Warren

1. Katherine Fullerton Gerould, "A Yankee Looks at Dixie," *American Mercury* (February 1936); Brooks and Warren's response, "Dixie Looks at Mrs. Gerould," ran in the March 1936 *American Review.*
2. Paul Palmer, editor of the *American Mercury* and an associate of Mencken.

TO MURIEL RUKEYSER

TLS/NYPL

The Southern Review
Louisiana State University
Baton Rouge,
Louisiana
March 10, 1936

Miss Muriel Rukeyser
313 West 4th St.
New York, N.Y.

Dear Miss Rukeyser:[1]

Enclosed you will find an announcement of THE SOUTHERN REVIEW Poetry Prize, for which we hope you will make an entry.[2] The date of closing for the contest has been postponed until August 1, 1936.

The rates for poetry in THE SOUTHERN REVIEW are 35¢ a line.

Very sincerely yours,
Robert Penn Warren

1. Rukeyser had made an auspicious debut the previous year when her first volume, *Theory of Flight,* appeared in the Yale Younger Poets series.
2. Rukeyser may or may not have responded; her sole poem in the *Southern Review* would not appear until the Autumn 1939 issue.

TO GEORGE MARION O'DONNELL

TLS/WashU

The Southern Review
Louisiana State University
Baton Rouge,
Louisiana
March 19, 1936

Mr. George Marion O'Donnell
Vanderbilt University
Nashville, Tenn.

Dear O'Donnell:

I understand that you are being recommended for a fellowship here, which will pay $40 a month. There will be no tuition. You ask about the nature of your connection with THE SOUTHERN REVIEW. Your duties will be to assist us in handling the proof. We shall, however, profit by your literary judgment—but we see no way to get any money to reimburse you for that. We hope you will be with us next year.[1]

Dr. Pipkin says not to fill out the application blank, for he is attending to that matter here by his recommendation. It will not be necessary for you to come down this spring, but I shall be more than glad for you to come visit me if you can do so.

I shall write again in a day or two about ELEGY. The matter is not settled yet.[2]

Very sincerely yours,
Robert Penn Warren

1. O'Donnell appears to have declined the fellowship, but he later taught at LSU.
2. "Elegy" was not accepted.

WARREN AND BROOKS TO ALLEN TATE

TLS/PU

[Baton Rouge]
[March 1936][1]

Dear Allen:

Here is [a] clipping from the New Orleans [MORNING] TRIBUNE, March 17, 1936.[2] We were in N.O. last night to talk to a club and accidentally discovered this item. Driving home we did a great deal of talking about the matter, and are sending on the result of our conversation. It may be merely late evening fuzziness, but again it may not. At any rate we wanted to send you the clipping at once, as a matter of interest if not importance.

Has the lady any right to quote you as saying: "the people must be pushed back to medieval times, that there shall be lords and kings, and a few masters to rule an abject and hopeless mass of workers"[?] (At any rate, the quotation marks in the paper seem to imply that.) It seemed to us that here, if ever, is a clear and dramatic opportunity to call the hand of some of our loose-thinking and loose-talking friends. We don't know whether there is a damage suit here or not, but the two elements, one falsehood and two damaging falsehood, certainly seem to be present. This matter, of course, would have to be determined by some one who knows more law than we do. And, of course, if there is a case the chance of your collecting any damages is remote. On the other hand, a suit, skillfully argued, would, it seems to us, start a wave on which WHO OWNS AMERICA would ride in. In addition that book would make perfectly clear what you do *believe;* and it contains definite remarks on the possibility of American fascism.

What do you think about this?

The order for your requisition went in yesterday.[3] We pray that it will reach you promptly. The amount is $86.00.

> As ever,
> Red
> &
> Cleanth

1. Tate's notation.
2. Charles East has located the item in question: "Sharecroppers in Distress, Novelist Says," in which the Georgia writer Grace Lumpkin is quoted regarding the *Southern Review* and the Agrarian agendas. (Brooks and Warren later accepted her story "The Treasure" for the Spring 1940 *Southern Review*.)
3. Payment for "The Function of the Literary Quarterly."

TO MALCOLM COWLEY

TLS/Newb

The Southern Review
Louisiana State University
Baton Rouge,
Louisiana
April 8, 1936

Mr. Malcolm Cowley
THE NEW REPUBLIC
40 East 49th St.
New York, N.Y.

Dear Malcolm:[1]

This is to ask you to do a long review of the FLOWERING OF NEW EN-
GLAND, 1815–1865, by Van Wyck Brooks.[2] Will you do it for us? I suppose
that the book will demand a fairly long treatment, say about five thousand words. And could you let us have the manuscript, if you do write
the piece, before August 1?

The last number of our first volume came off the press yesterday.
One will be on its way to you shortly. Let me know what you think of it.

As ever,
Red

1. Warren's acquaintanceship with Cowley, an early admirer of his work, went back
to the late 1920s, and despite Cowley's communist leanings the two became increasingly friendly. They played complementary roles in the resurrection of Faulkner's
reputation in the 1940s, and Cowley dedicated his memoir *The Dream of the Golden
Mountains* (1980) to Warren.
2. John Donald Wade reviewed the book in the Spring 1937 issue.

TO HUBERT CREEKMORE

TLS/BU

The Southern Review
Louisiana State University
Baton Rouge,
Louisiana
April 25, 1936

Mr. Hubert Creekmore
1607 Pinehurst St.
Jackson, Miss.

Dear Mr. Creekmore:

We think this story is essentially good, but we have some objection to the detail. In the first place, it may be too long. Second, the conclusion, it seems to us, should come on page 19, before the conversation with the father begins. All the points of the story could be made with more subtlety and indirection by such a process. Third, some of the dialogue, particularly on pages 8, 9, 10[,] seems rather routine and mechanical. You might be able to compress that into half the space and avoid such flat interpolations as "George was a little crestfallen," and "the joy of having an aggie was working strangely in George." We have made this criticism to try to explain to you why we are not using a story which you yourself must know is good, and which we know is good. It is possible that we would be able to use this story if it were revised, though we cannot make a definite commitment about it.[1] Certainly we are interested in what you are doing and want to see more.

Very sincerely yours,
Robert Penn Warren

1. None of Creekmore's stories were published in the *Southern Review*. His neighbor in Jackson, Mississippi, Eudora Welty, would do much better.

TO CATHERINE WILDS

TLS/VU
The Southern Review
Louisiana State University
Baton Rouge,
Louisiana
May 25, 1936

Miss Catherine Wilds
252 South Crest Road
Chattanooga, Tenn.

Dear Cath:[1]

Here is the stuff. Your letter just about covers the case, but in a rather disorderly fashion I'll develop some of the points. (It is a rare opportunity to be able to write a review for yourself.)

The magazine was founded a little more than a year ago, its announcement being one of the features of the Jubilee celebration of the Louisiana State University. The magazine is published by the Louisiana State University Press, quarterly, at Baton Rouge. Charles W. Pipkin is the editor, and Cleanth Brooks and I are the managing editors. I am enclosing one of the original announcements, which may be of some interest to you. The departments of the magazine, as you will see from the announcement, are essays, fiction, poetry, and reviews. The essays deal primarily with [current] affairs and literary criticism, though such essays as Donald Davidson's AMERICAN HEROES and J. M. Dabbs' Religion[2] have appeared and will appear. Among the most effective and distinguished of the essays of THE SOUTHERN REVIEW—those that have been most mentioned, quoted, or reprinted—are CULTURE AND COLONIALISM, by Herbert Agar, TECHNIQUES, by Ford Madox Ford, AMERICAN HEROES, by Donald Davidson, FOUNDATIONS OF DEMOCRACY, by Frank Owsley, SWEET ARE THE USES OF DEGENERACY (an essay on Erskine Caldwell), by John Wade, THE TENSE OF POETRY, by John Crowe Ransom, THREE REVOLUTIONS IN POETRY (a very important series of essays for those interested in modern poetry), by Cleanth Brooks.

Among the stories special attention should probably be called to the ones by Katherine Anne Porter, Caroline Gordon, Jesse Stuart,[3] and George Milburn[4]—among the established writers; and S. S. Field, K. C.

Shelby,[5] Allen McGinnis among writers who [have] published for the first or second time.

The policy for the publication of poetry (except in the first issue) is to publish long groups of poems by a single author, so that the reader may get a real opportunity to appreciate a poet's work, and is not compelled to pick up a fragment here and a fragment there from different magazines or anthologies. In this way each issue of the magazine really contains the equivalent of a small volume of the work of a single poet. Poets whose work in large groups has appeared in THE SOUTHERN RE-VIEW are John Peale Bishop, Mark Van Doren, and George Marion O'Donnell. (You may say of course if you like, and I think with some proof, that the work of these people which has appeared in the Review is extremely fine, at their best level, etc.) In addition to these groups several rather long poems of special distinction have appeared[:] THE OLD WOMAN AND THE STATUE by Wallace Stevens (author of the extremely well known volume HARMONIUM), FRAGMENT OF A MEDITA-TION, by Allen Tate,[6] and THIS LAKE IS MINE, by Thomas Hornsby Ferril[7] (winner of the NATION prize and of the Yale University Press prize for poetry.) In each issue an essay appears on the work of the poet who is featured in that issue of THE SOUTHERN REVIEW.

The reviews are in general rather long discussions of a very restricted number of books, rather than mere description of what the books are about. You can check some of these. Many of the reviews are of essay length and might really be classified as essays. THE SOUTHERN REVIEW is really trying to make reviewing, once more, a department of criticism, rather than a department of sales promotion.

Perhaps some word should be said about the regional aspect of THE SOUTHERN REVIEW. You ask whether the editors have any odd theories about literature in the South or anywhere else. I don't suppose they have. You might simply say that THE SOUTHERN REVIEW is attempting to provide a kind of focus for literary activity in the South, but holds that its purpose can best be served by maintaining the highest standard possible, rather than by publishing something merely because its author happens to be a Southerner. But, as a matter of fact, a very high percentage of the contributors are from the South.

You ask about the editor. Charles W. Pipkin is a native of Arkansas, educated at Henderson Brown, Vanderbilt, Harvard, and Oxford; he is an extremely well-known writer on government and politics; at present

Dean of the Graduate School at Louisiana State University. [Handwritten in margin] See *Who's Who.*

[Typing resumes] You may say indeed that the magazine is simply marvelous and should be on the table as sunshades should be at the windows. (You will notice that it is a very pretty magazine.) But the enclosed list of remarks from reviews and articles about THE SOUTHERN REVIEW will give you an idea of the reception it has had. Privately I may point out to you that some of this applause has come from the most unlikely quarters.

The files of the magazine are being mailed to you today. I hope after you read them that you will not feel that you are perjuring yourself to give us a favorable display. I think the general line you take in your letter is quite right. We are all very grateful to you for what you are doing. If you have the time, will you please drop us a note about the most likely people to handle THE SOUTHERN REVIEW in Chattanooga[?] I have forgotten what you said about that.

Very best regards. Cinina joins me in this, or would do so if she were here, for she has gone to Nashville.

Very sincerely,

Red

P.S. I am enclosing a proof of the announcements for the summer issue, which would be number 1 of our volume 2. I am starring the especially interesting articles with a pencil. I am sorry that some of the copies of the magazine we are sending you have been slightly faded by exposure to sunlight. We are getting very low on our reserves, because of the increasing demand for back issues, and so have to preserve our stock of perfect copies. You see we hope to have our first numbers become collector's items in the not so remote future.

Other picture will follow.

1. Catherine Wilds was a cousin of Caroline Gordon. Warren was enlisting her aid in publicizing the *Southern Review* in the Chattanooga area.
2. "Religion without Poetry" (Winter 1936); James McBride Dabbs later distinguished himself with his analyses of southern race relations from a liberal Christian perspective.
3. "Woman in the House" (Summer 1935).
4. "The Wish Book" (Autumn 1935).

5. "Picnic at Hamburg" (Summer 1936).

6. Autumn 1935.

7. Spring 1936. Ferril was a Colorado poet Warren may have met at the Summer Writers' Conference in Boulder the previous year.

TO THE ALCESTIS PRESS

TLS/UChi

The Southern Review
Louisiana State University
Baton Rouge,
Louisiana
July 6, 1936

Alcestis Press
170 Broadway
New York, N.Y.

Gentlemen:

Mr. Edward Davison, the director of the Writers' Conference at the University of Colorado, Boulder, Colorado, where I shall be for three weeks this summer on the staff, has asked me to arrange, if possible, for several copies of my volume of poems to be on sale there. It is customary for books by the lecturers to be offered for sale by the university bookstore; and last year I observed that there was a very considerable number of copies sold. They take such books on *consignment*. Can you undertake to make this arrangement with them? In any case, will you please write to Mr. Edward Davison, Department of English, University of Colorado, Boulder, Colorado, *and* to me concerning your decision in this matter? I shall be leaving for the West in nine days.

Very sincerely yours,
Robert Penn Warren

TO SEWARD COLLINS

TLS/YU   Nashville, Tennessee
                                    Care of John Crowe Ransom
                                    Vanderbilt University
                                    September 6, 1936

Dear Collins:

This note is to ask you for an advance on the work which I am doing for the [American] Review and to discover whether you would be interested in an essay on which I did the work this summer. As for the first item: I ran into some unexpected expense returning from the University of Colorado, where I was giving some lectures for three weeks, and don't see a clear financial path until pay day. If you can make me an advance on the work already arranged for,[1] and perhaps on the essay which I shall describe to you, I shall be bound in great gratitude. The essay is called "The Dilemma of the Modern Poet," or at least, that is the idea. A poet always has the problem of making a resolution of the forces of, as it were, two poles of force, which we might call the absolute and the relative. The demand of the absolute is that his work embody the primary aesthetic fact that makes us call all sorts of different kinds of work poetry; the demand of the relative is that the machinery for the embodiment of this effect, the central artistic fact, be conditioned by the flux of his immediate time and environment.[2] That is the starting point of the thing, which is developed now as lectures but can easily be compressed into essay form. (It is the Colorado lectures.) Would you be interested? I can let you have it very promptly.

I hope that your vacation has been a successful one. I can scarcely say that mine has been.

                                    Very sincerely yours,
                                    Warren

P.S. Whatever your decision is, I shall be grateful for a prompt reply in care of Ransom, preferably a telegram collect.

1. Warren's "Some Don'ts for Literary Regionalists" would run in the December 1936 *American Review*.

2. Warren seems to be describing an early version of what would become his seminal essay "Pure and Impure Poetry" (1943).

TO PETER TAYLOR

TLS/VU
The Southern Review
Louisiana State University
Baton Rouge,
Louisiana
Sept. 21, 1936

Mr. Peter Taylor
Department of English
Vanderbilt University
Nashville, Tenn.

Dear Mr. Taylor:[1]

My absence from Baton Rouge for the past two or three months and a great press of work on both Brooks and me have prevented our proper acknowledgment of your stories. Both Brooks and I feel that Tate's enthusiasm for your work is entirely justified, and we are certain that we shall be able to use some of it in the near future.[2] We debated a long time the use of "The Lady is Civilized," and finally decided against it on the grounds of the conclusion. That seems to us to have a rather too obvious irony—at least, that is the only way we can frame our dissatisfaction with the conclusion. Perhaps some line of revision may occur to you.

   Meanwhile, please let us see anything you have on hand.

Very sincerely yours,
Robert Penn Warren

1. Taylor had studied briefly with Tate at Southwestern College in Memphis before transferring to Vanderbilt to work with Ransom. The presence of Brooks and Warren brought him to Baton Rouge as a student in 1940, but he soon left to serve in the army.

2. Taylor's work would not appear in the *Southern Review* until the Autumn 1940 number, which carried his stories "A Spinster's Tale" and "Sky Line."

TO EUDORA WELTY

TLS/MissA

The Southern Review
Louisiana State University
Baton Rouge,
Louisiana
Sept. 23, 1936

Miss Eudora Welty
1119 Pinehurst St.
Jackson, Miss.

Dear Miss Welty:[1]

The absence of the editors from Baton Rouge has delayed decision on many manuscripts during the past several weeks. We find much to interest us in your verse, but have decided against immediate publication. May we see more of your work?

Very sincerely yours,
Robert Penn Warren

1. Welty was a virtually unknown writer when she began submitting her work to the *Southern Review,* where in time seven of her finest stories would appear. She became one of Brooks and Warren's most celebrated "discoveries" and has expressed her gratitude to them repeatedly throughout her career.

TO RANDALL JARRELL

TLS/NYPL

The Southern Review
Louisiana State University
Baton Rouge,
Louisiana
Sept. 23, 1936

Mr. Randall Jarrell
2524 Westwood Ave.
Nashville, Tenn.

Dear Randall:

Can you let us have immediately a slick finished photograph of yourself for newspaper use? We shall greatly appreciate it.

The requisition for your contribution, etc., has gone in, and you should get your check before the week is out. I like the poems very much—better than ever after seeing them in print.[1] The magazine is just off the press.

Please remember me to your mother.

Very sincerely yours,
Red
By B.[2]

1. Jarrell's group "Seven Poems" ran in the Autumn 1936 issue.

2. Bessie Barnett (Turpin), the *Review*'s secretary, may have signed Warren's name and initialed the signature; the handwriting does not appear to be Brooks's.

TO WILLIAM CARLOS WILLIAMS

TLS/SUNY-B

The Southern Review
Louisiana State University
Baton Rouge,
Louisiana
Sept. 24, 1936

Dr. William C. Williams
9 Ridge Road
Rutherford, N.J.

Dear Dr. Williams:[1]

Please accept our apologies for the length of time this poem has been in our hands. My colleagues and I have been out of the city most of the time the second half of the summer, and, in addition, have been greatly overworked. I am sorry to report that we shall be unable to publish your present piece. But will you be kind enough to let us have a chance at something of yours in the future?

Very sincerely yours,
Robert Penn Warren

1. Pioneering modernist and friend of Ezra Pound and H. D. (Hilda Doolittle), Williams was already a noted poet. In declining his work to make space available for lesser known writers, Brooks and Warren proved they were no respecters of persons.

TO HUBERT CREEKMORE

TLS/BU

The Southern Review
Louisiana State University
Baton Rouge,
Louisiana
Sept. 26, 1936

Mr. Hubert Creekmore
1723 N St., N.W.
Washington, D.C.

Dear Mr. Creekmore:

We have debated the matter of your story a long time, because there is a great deal in it that we like very much. But we are not finally satisfied with it and so are returning it to you now. We are very definitely interested in your work and hope that the next manuscript you send us—if you will be so good as to send us more—will suit our purposes somewhat better. Thank you very much.

Sincerely yours,
Robert Penn Warren

TO JOHN BERRYMAN

TLS/Minn

The Southern Review
Louisiana State University
Baton Rouge,
Louisiana
Oct. 7, 1936

Mr. John Berryman
Clare College
Cambridge, England

Dear Mr. Berryman:[1]

Although your poem did not receive THE SOUTHERN REVIEW prize,[2] the judges were enormously interested in it; and so are we. We do not feel, however, that we can publish it as it stands. We think that certain sections resemble too closely, even to the point of imitation, Tate's "Ode to the Confederate Dead." We admire that poem very much, but at times it seems that you have not assimilated the actual influence which, apparently, that poem has had on your work. We also feel that at times the effect of your poem, especially since it is a very long piece, could be improved by a freer and more sweeping movement. At times the composition appears to be choppy and crabbed.

Please take these remarks in the spirit in which they are meant. We simply feel that because your work is so good we owe you an explanation for not publishing it as it stands. We are positive that in the near future we shall be able to arrange a large display for you in THE SOUTHERN REVIEW,[3] if your present poem can be taken as a fair sample of your general performance. We beg you to keep us in mind and to let us see as soon as possible anything else you may have on hand.

Very sincerely yours,
Robert Penn Warren

1. After studying at Columbia with Mark Van Doren (who may have suggested that he send work to the *Southern Review*), Berryman had embarked on what would prove to be a formative period of study abroad.
2. The *Southern Review*'s first poetry prize went to Randall Jarrell. The judges were Allen Tate and Mark Van Doren. (My thanks to Charles East.)
3. The *Southern Review* published a collection of Berryman's poems under the title "Night City and Other Poems" in the Summer 1938 edition.

TO R. P. BLACKMUR

TLS/PU

The Southern Review
Louisiana State University
Baton Rouge,
Louisiana
Oct. 13, 1936

Mr. R. P. Blackmur
Harrington, Maine

Dear Mr. Blackmur:[1]

We are delighted that you will do the poetry for us this time,[2] and shall have the publishers send you [the] books immediately. I now want to raise another question, in which I hope you may be interested.

There is strong probability that the Louisiana State University may undertake a publishing program of a nature somewhat different from the ordinary program of university presses. One feature of this program would be the establishment of a series of critical books. Among those who have been discussed as possible contributors in the series are John Crowe Ransom, Allen Tate, John Donald Wade, F. Cudworth Flint, Howard Baker, and yourself. Some of these people have already been approached and are favorably disposed to the project. The publication will be on a straight commercial basis, and the series will be properly promoted. The books would probably be published in uniform or in similar format and would be numbered in the series. They would be attractively made. It has been suggested here that the series of essays on which you are now working (Hardy, Emily Dickinson, Yeats, etc.) would make an extremely valuable book and would be a great ornament to such a series as is now being projected. The advantages of publishing such books in a series seem to be considerable, since each item will support the other items and would serve as an advertising [sic] for them. Will you let me know how you feel about such a project, and I shall put the information in the proper hands here. It seems to me that a concentrated program of such publication would be a valuable service for the University Press to perform, because of the difficulties at present in the path of both writers and readers of criticism. Such a series might become a kind of clearing house for the better type of such writing. I am anxiously looking forward to your reply.

> Very sincerely yours,
> Robert Penn Warren

P.S. I have just received your letter of October 10. Have you already signed the book on Henry Adams?[3] If you have not, would you consider it for the series as well as your essays?

1. Lacking conventional academic credentials, Blackmur was nonetheless one of the most brilliant critics of his generation and would eventually merit an appointment at Princeton.

2. Blackmur reviewed volumes by Frederick Prokosch, Arthur Guiterman, Wallace Stevens, A. E. Housman, Carl Sandburg, Edgar Lee Masters, Witter Bynner, and Conrad Aiken and a translation of Euripides by Dudley Fitts and Robert Fitzgerald in the Winter 1937 *Southern Review*.

3. Though Blackmur would receive a Guggenheim in 1937 to complete this study, it remained unpublished during his lifetime.

TO MORTON DAUWEN ZABEL

TLS/UChi

The Southern Review
Louisiana State University
Baton Rouge,
Louisiana
Nov. 4, 1936

Mr. Morton D. Zabel
POETRY: A MAGAZINE OF VERSE
232 E. Erie St.
Chicago, Ill.

Dear Mr. Zabel:

With the greatest surprise and with great pleasure I discovered several days ago that I had received the Levinson prize.[1] I wish to express to you and to your staff my very great appreciation.

I want to tell you how pleased I am that you are now the editor of POETRY—though I regret, of course, the occasion.[2]

I am enclosing the review of Robinson Jeffers' poems.[3] I have made several false starts on this and set up a number of psychological hurdles in the way of getting the thing done. My feelings are very mixed about Jeffers, and I found that every time I started a piece about him it promised to run well outside the bounds of a review for you. I hope that the present offering will be adequate, and I regret this unseeming [*sic*] delay. This fall, illness, a necessity of traveling, and more work than I have been able to do have conspired to delay even further this piece.

I am sending back to you the Jeffers' [*sic*] book.

With most sincere best
wishes,
Warren
By B.[4]

1. The Helen Haire Levinson Prize for the best poem published in *Poetry* during a given year carried a cash award of $100. Warren took the prize with his Marvellian lyric "The Garden" (October 1935).
2. Harriet Monroe had died suddenly while on a trip to South America.

3. "Jeffers on the Age," *Poetry* (November 1936).

4. See September 23, 1936, letter to Randall Jarrell, n. 2, above.

TO MORTON DAUWEN ZABEL

TLS/Newb

The Southern Review
Louisiana State University
Baton Rouge,
Louisiana
Nov. 10, 1936

Mr. Morton D. Zabel
POETRY: A MAGAZINE OF VERSE
232 E. Erie St.
Chicago, Ill.

Dear Zabel:

I am delighted that you wish to use "A Hamlet of Thomas Wolfe" in your book.[1] You have my permission, of course. It first appeared, as you know, in THE AMERICAN REVIEW, but I am sure that Collins will gladly grant permission. You ask about possible suggestions. I suppose that the two others I am most nearly satisfied with are "T. S. Stribling: A Paragraph in the History of Critical Realism" (AMERICAN REVIEW)[2] and "John Crowe Ransom: A Study in Irony" (THE VIRGINIA QUARTERLY).[3] My essay in WHO OWNS AMERICA (Houghton Mifflin)[4] might, however, serve your purpose better than either of these two if you decide that you have space and inclination for an additional exhibit.

I am glad that Holt is bringing out your book,[5] for that firm is publishing the book on poetry which I am doing in collaboration with Brooks.[6]

I am sending you today a copy of another book done in collaboration with Brooks and another friend.[7] I hope that you will find time to glance at it, even though it is a textbook. The method of the Poetry Section might interest you. We have tried to work from a broad simple base toward more difficult poems and difficult critical questions. Any criticism or suggestions you have concerning it will be received very gratefully and respectfully. If the Poetry Section seems worthy of any notice in POETRY, either in editorial or in review, we shall be pleased.

About the Spender review: if you can use the double review as late as January 15, I can promise to get it done.[8] Perhaps incautiously, I have undertaken to work at a paper for the Modern Language Association for December,[9] and find it such slow going that I hesitate, even with my optimistic nature, to promise anything by the middle of December. If January is too late, please let me know, and I shall return the book to you with a flood of apologies for my procrastination.

I may have a batch of poems on hand soon—only revision remains to be done. Would you be interested?[10]

Very sincerely yours,

Warren

1. Zabel's anthology of contemporary criticism *Literary Opinion in America* (1937).

2. February 1934. Zabel did indeed reprint this piece along with the essay on Wolfe.

3. January 1935.

4. Warren's contribution to the Agar and Tate symposium was "Literature as a Symptom."

5. Zabel's book was in fact published by Harper and Brothers.

6. The influential textbook *Understanding Poetry* (1938), which would go through four editions and revolutionize the teaching of literature in college classrooms.

7. Brooks and Warren's first textbook, *An Approach to Literature* (1936), had been undertaken in collaboration with John Thibaut Purser.

8. Warren had been asked to review Stephen Spender's *The Destructive Element* and *Forward from Liberalism,* both published in 1936. He eventually passed the task on to Brooks.

9. At the 1936 meeting of the Modern Language Association, Brooks and Warren presented a joint paper entitled "The Reading of Modern Poetry." The panel also included Tate and Mark Van Doren. All three papers were published in the *American Review* (February 1937).

10. The identity of these poems remains an intriguing mystery, but "Bearded Oaks," one of Warren's most admired lyrics, would run in the October 1937 issue of *Poetry.*

TO ALLEN TATE AND CAROLINE GORDON

TLS/PU   [Baton Rouge]
                                                 [Autumn 1936][1]

Dear Allen and Caroline:

We are setting up the novel section today.[2] It is a beautiful piece of writing, without question. If this, with the other parts we have seen, is a fair sample of the novel, the book will be a stem-winder. We'll pray that proof will get off press early enough for you to pass on it yourself, Caroline, and try to save yourself from the regular plight of your old man. But if we can't get the proof early enough, please bear with us.

I am enclosing some poem[s], Allen, by the young man named Palmer, whom you met this summer. He seems to me to be the best writer around here, and I hope that you will feel that he is talented. He is twenty-one years old. The immediate purpose of sending the poems is this: the boy is applying for a Rhodes Scholarship,[3] and I want you, if you can see your way clear to it on the basis of these pieces, to write a letter to the Selection Committee about them. Palmer's academic record is first-rate, but some comment on his poems would probably be decisive. And no one on the committee, probably, would be able to reach an independent judgment. What Palmer really needs is a chance to do some uninterrupted reading and writing, and the scholarship would give him a better opportunity than he has here with his job. Will you send the letter to me to be forwarded (I haven't the name of the chairman by me)—if you feel agreeably disposed toward the work[?]

We are swamped with work here. I have just finished a hundred-line poem and am almost through with a story.[4] This was self-indulgence, for other stuff is riding my neck. I'll send the story and poem as soon as I can make some copies. Cinina is almost through with the second novelette.[5] I hope all projects there, you all and Andrew, are going well. I long sometimes for a mountain fastness of my own.[6] I have a class this minute.

As ever,
Red

[P.S.] Hurrah for the third edition of Long Night. . . . I hope it goes twenty before the Modern Library[7] gets it.

P.S.—If you decide to write the letter concerning the poems, please send it without delay, since the time is very short.

1. Tate's notation.
2. "The Women on the Battlefield" (Winter 1937), excerpted from Gordon's novel *None Shall Look Back.*

3. John Palmer completed his master's degree at LSU in 1937 before leaving for Oxford, where he took the bachelor of letters degree in 1940.

4. The identity of the long poem remains uncertain, but the story was undoubtedly "Christmas Gift," *Virginia Quarterly Review* (Winter 1937).

5. Joseph Blotner and others have suggested that Cinina's frustrated literary ambitions may have been a source of marital tensions. Her papers at Emory University attest to her persistent attempts to place her work.

6. The Tates were in residence at the resort settlement of Monteagle, Tennessee, where the Lytle family maintained a home.

7. Inclusion of one's work in the relatively inexpensive but prestigious Modern Library series conferred a measure of "canonicity" on an author.

1937

TO EUDORA WELTY

TLS/MissA

The Southern Review
Louisiana State University
Baton Rouge,
Louisiana
Jan. 13, 1937

Miss Eudora Welty
1119 Pinehurst St.
Jackson, Miss.

Dear Miss Welty:

We have been extremely interested in these stories and several times have been on the verge of publishing two of them, "The Petrified Man" and "Flowers for Marjorie." We think that both of them are extremely well done. "Flowers for Marjorie," we feel, is somewhat conventional in subject matter, and in its general effect perhaps too closely resembles a story we have previously published. But we like the writing in it enormously. Many of the comic effects in "The Petrified Man" struck us absolutely first-rate, but we were not quite satisfied in the way it held together as a story.[1] About many aspects of your work we are enthusiastic, and we are absolutely confident that, if you are good enough to submit other work to us, we can publish your things in THE SOUTHERN REVIEW. Please let us hear from you again.

> Very sincerely yours,
> Robert Penn Warren

1. Brooks and Warren reversed their decision on "Petrified Man," and it was published in the Spring 1939 issue. (See the letter to Welty of February 4, 1937, below.)

TO T. J. WILSON FROM WARREN AND BROOKS

TLS/PU

> *The Southern Review*
> Louisiana State University
> Baton Rouge,
> Louisiana
> January 27, 1937

Mr. T. J. Wilson
Henry Holt and Co.
257 Fourth Ave.
New York City

Dear Mr. Wilson:

Here are copies of the analyses to be included in the textbook.[1] We are very anxious that the analyses be read in the order indicated and with a consideration of the general emphasis in which any given analysis falls. The analyses are numbered in pencil in sequence. A list according to group is also included for your guidance. Each section is preceded by a note indicating the nature of the poems to be included in that section and the amount [sic] of the analyses. (The notes in the textbook itself will state the purpose of each section at considerable length.) The list of analyses sent is altogether complete, particularly in regard to Section V. All the analyses here will be revised to insure [a] greater degree of coordination and to direct the building up of a critical vocabulary.

We are sending this to you so that you can have some ground for any specific suggestions. We hope that you will return these at your earliest convenience, since they are our clearest copy of material.

The introduction will follow in a few days. We hope very much that you will find the work thoroughly satisfactory. If it proves so, we can push the book to an immediate conclusion.

Very sincerely yours,
Robert Penn Warren
Cleanth Brooks, Jr.

1. *Understanding Poetry,* published in 1938.

TO EUDORA WELTY

TLS/MissA

The Southern Review
Louisiana State University
Baton Rouge,
Louisiana
Feb. 4, 1937

Miss Eudora Welty
1119 Pinehurst St.
Jackson, Miss.

Dear Miss Welty:

We do not like the present story—as a story—as much as we liked your previous one. But there is certainly a touch of distinction in the writing of the present piece. We are beginning to regret that we rejected "The Petrified Man," and we might like to reopen the question of publication some time in the near future.[1] But if you have anything else on hand, will you please let us see it[?]—I just learned that two more manuscripts of yours came in this morning. I shall read them immediately and let you hear early next week concerning them.

No, THE SOUTHERN REVIEW does not publish photographs.[2] That is a very expensive business, and we feel that our budget is better devoted to paying as well as we can for contributions.

Very sincerely yours,
Robert Penn Warren

1. In her dejection over Brooks and Warren's original decision to reject this story, one of her finest, Welty had destroyed the manuscript and had to reconstruct it from memory.

2. In her travels throughout Mississippi, Welty had recorded her impressions in a series of photographs reminiscent of the Farm Security Administration work of Dorothea Lange, Arthur Rothstein, and others. She had exhibited these photographs in New York in 1936.

TO HARPER AND BROTHERS

TLS/NYPL

The Southern Review
Louisiana State University
Baton Rouge,
Louisiana
March 3, 1937

Harper and Brothers
49 E. 33rd St.
New York City

Gentlemen:

In a long review of *Edna St. Vincent Millay and Her Times* (Elizabeth Atkins, University of Chicago Press) which John Crowe Ransom has done for THE SOUTHERN REVIEW[1] three quotations from Miss Millay's works appear: "The Return," and two sonnets ("Heart Have No Pity on This House of Bone" and "Oh, Sleep Forever in the Latmian Cave"). We wish to retain these quotations in printing the review in order to make clear the critic's argument, and should greatly appreciate your permission to this effect.

Thank you very much for your attention in this matter.

Very sincerely yours,
Robert Penn Warren

1. "The Woman as Poet" (Spring 1937).

TO FRANK LAWRENCE OWSLEY

TLS/VU

The Southern Review
Louisiana State University
Baton Rouge,
Louisiana
March 22, 1937

Mr. Frank Lawrence Owsley
712 8th Ave., W.
Birmingham, Ala.[1]

Dear Frank:

This is a long overdue letter with thanks for [the] Christmas present and [a] request for future favors. The most immediate future favor on hand is this: will you do an article on Judge Robert Winston's autobiography for our Summer issue?[2] The book, of course, isn't worth much as a book. But it does set out to be a kind of social history and commentary for the period since the Civil War. I can give you, for instance, a tidbit that will make your hackles rise and the ink churn in your fountain pen: "Chambers of Commerce, Rotary clubs, and Kiwanians are moving heaven and earth—building hard-surface roads, erecting winter resorts, constructing school houses, all this to bring in desirable settlers. But Civil War societies are just as busy undoing this work, creating such an atmosphere of sectionalism that practically no Northern families come down. We have many tourists, we have winter visitors, but we have no permanent residents, no citizens to help us pay taxes and bear the enormous overhead which we have imposed upon ourselves in the race of life."

We hope that you will also make an appraisal of Winston's historical writing,[3] and relate it to the general point of view of this book. If you will do it, but cannot get it done in time for the Summer issue (deadline May 15) how about the Fall? And when do you think you will be able to work up a longish essay based on your researches of this winter? I can't think of anything more important or appropriate for THE SOUTHERN REVIEW than that.

Life here today resembles that of yesterday. I am very busy and so is Cinina. Since Christmas, Cleanth and I have been trying to push to completion the book of poetry that we should have finished in January. But it's not done yet. In January Houghton Mifflin notified me that they wanted several chapters of my novel by May 1—and that, as you may guess, caused some consternation in my bosom.[4] The thing had been on the verge of getting started for several months, but I couldn't find the exact center for it, somehow. But it is, however, underway now—some two chapters, rather long ones, already finished. I have lost the last week from work, but expect to be back at it tomorrow. One day, when I read over what I have done, I get rather complacent; the next, I get suicidal. I haven't showed it to anybody yet, but I hope to soon. And to you.

Which brings up another matter. We want to urge you all to come down in the very near future. The weather should be fine here for another six weeks, not too hot. Your room is ready, and you can have a quiet place to work every day in the house. We insist on this, because there is a good chance, or rather a bad chance, that we will not have the opportunity of seeing you next summer. I have resigned the Colorado job,[5] because I must devote all summer to the novel, even if I eat honey and wild locusts. I don't know where we shall go, but there is some talk of Mexico, if the favorable exchange holds out.[6] Do come down now. You might even get in a little fishing, and certainly we can scout the country side looking at parish records. Cinina enthusiastically joins me in these recommendations. And so do Albert and Cleanth. We are terribly anxious to see you all and to spend some moonlit evenings over a julep. Come soon—the sooner the better. There is a great deal more I should like to say to you now. But I prefer to say it face to face. When will it be? Give my best love to Harriet and Larry. Cinina sends love to you all.

As ever,

Red

---

1. Owsley, on leave from Vanderbilt, was in Alabama doing research for his ground-breaking *Plain Folk of the Old South* (1949).

2. "A Key to Southern Liberalism," Owsley's review of Robert W. Winston's *It's a Far Cry*, appeared in the Summer 1937 issue.

3. Winston had written biographies of Andrew Johnson, Jefferson Davis, and Robert E. Lee.

4. Two early novels had gone unpublished, but now Warren was at work on *Night Rider*, encouraged by a fellowship from Houghton Mifflin.

5. The Summer Writers' Conferences, under the direction of Edward Davison.

6. The trip to Mexico would be postponed until the summer of 1940.

TO MORTON DAUWEN ZABEL

TLS/Newb

The Southern Review
Louisiana State University
Baton Rouge,
Louisiana
March 23, 1937

Mr. Morton D. Zabel
POETRY: A MAGAZINE OF VERSE
232 E. Erie St.
Chicago, Ill.

Dear Zabel:

Here are the facts you requested for your book on literary opinion.[1]

1. Born 1905, Todd County, Kentucky.

2. Educated at Vanderbilt University, University of California, Yale University, and Oxford.

3. Taught at Southwestern College, Vanderbilt University, and at present Louisiana State University; managing editor with Cleanth Brooks of THE SOUTHERN REVIEW.

4. Essays: "T. S. Stribling: A Paragraph in the History of Critical Realism" (THE AMERICAN REVIEW, Feb. 1934); "John Crowe Ransom: A Study in Irony" (THE VIRGINIA QUARTERLY REVIEW); "Modern Poetry: Its Audience" (with Cleanth Brooks, THE AMERICAN REVIEW, March, 1937); "The Briar Patch" in *I'll Take My Stand* (Harper's, 1930); "Literature as Symptom" in *Who Owns America* (Houghton Mifflin, 1936); *Thirty-Six Poems* (Alcestis Press, 1936).

I suppose that this is full enough for your purposes. I haven't a way to check up on the page numbers of these articles, for I have lost my copies of the magazines in question. I hope that this does not inconvenience you too much.

I shall definitely save the time for the Spender review. And I shall send the poem soon.

Most sincerely,
Warren

1. *Literary Opinion in America* (1937).

TO ALLEN TATE

TLS/PU   [Baton Rouge]
                                            [Spring 1937][1]

Dear Allen:

This is merely to assure myself that you all are still alive and active. I had a note recently from Sam Monk,[2] who said that he expected to see you all in Monteagle soon. I wish I could have that pleasure—in Monteagle or elsewhere. We had hoped, a little, to have some time this Easter for a trip, perhaps to Nashville, but in the end I had to stick to my knitting. Cleanth and I are on the verge of finishing the book for Holt (and on the verge of nervous prostration because of the vacillation and stupidity of that editorial department—they settle a thing one day and the next day have hysterics which they communicate to us). I am pretty well into my novel, and have hope that it is moving fairly well. In any case, the pages are accumulating beside my typewriter. Soon I shall send you all what I have—when I get a copy made and a little revision done.

Howe,[3] of Scribner's, was through here recently, as I believe I wrote in the letter to Caroline. He is very anxious to have some assurance about the modern poetry book.[4] Do you think that we could get it to him in the summer of 1938? We could devote next winter solidly to it. Walsh[5] followed a little later than Howe, and said that the thing would be a gold mine and that he had rather have it than a $10,000 bond apiece. (For mine, I'll take the bond, but still, that sounds encouraging.) We really have a large part of the stuff on hand, and our primary job is simply to put it in order and sequence. Walsh went on to say that he was sure Scribner's, after we actually got on the job, would be willing to finance a trip for us to Chicago, or elsewhere to work up the bibliographies, etc. (I say Chicago because of the collection *Poetry* owns.) How do you feel about the business?

How is The Fathers? We are extremely anxious to see some of it. Can we announce some of it for fall, perhaps? And how is None Shall Back going? Beautifully, I hope. The Lord knows it deserves to, for it's a damned fine book, easily the best novel I ever read on the Civil War. A note from Dixon Wecter, just received, asks about the novel and goes on to say: "the manifestation of Caroline's genius always makes me feel humble indeed." Which is pretty handsome, but thoroughly justified by the present event.

Forgive this haste. Our best to you all.

As ever,
Red

P.S. It now seems that the critical series by the L.S.U. Press is off to a start. Wade has consented to have a book of essays published here, and the Press has written for the manuscript. They also want Ransom; and you once said that you would be willing for your next book of essays to appear here. Does that still hold? I hope so.

1. Tate's notation.
2. Samuel Monk, an eighteenth-century literature specialist, taught at Southwestern College and was thus not only a friend but a former colleague of both Warren and Tate. He eventually moved on to the University of Minnesota.
3. W. D. Howe was in charge of the textbook division at Scribner's.
4. Warren and Tate had discussed the possibility of coediting a collection of modern verse for several years, but their plans never materialized.
5. Thomas Walsh, a Scribner's representative.

TO MORTON DAUWEN ZABEL

TLS/UChi

The Southern Review
Louisiana State University
Baton Rouge,
Louisiana
April 26, 1937

Mr. Morton D. Zabel
POETRY: A MAGAZINE OF VERSE
232 E. Erie St.
Chicago, Ill.

Dear Zabel:

The book by Spender has not come yet. I shall start work on it as soon as it arrives.

Thank you very much for your very flattering interest in the new poems. The only available one that seems to be moderately satisfactory, I shall send tomorrow—as soon as I can make a copy. My absence from town for several days accounts for this delay in answering your note. Forgive my present haste—but I am nursing an ailing tooth and will leave this note to start off to the dentist's.

Most cordially,
Warren

TO MORTON DAUWEN ZABEL

TLS/UChi

The Southern Review
Louisiana State University
Baton Rouge,
Louisiana
[Spring 1937]

Mr. Morton D. Zabel
POETRY: A MAGAZINE OF VERSE
232 E. Erie St.
Chicago, Ill.

Dear Zabel:

The book has just come in, and your note. If the book had arrived here a week earlier I could have done the review by the day you specify, but we are now in the middle of examinations. I am on several examining committees in the graduate school, have my own examinations to give, must read a great pile of term papers and one thesis, and must keep an almost innumerable list of student conferences. I don't see any time out for the next ten days or so except for eating and sleeping. I hate like the devil to let you down on this, but I don't see how I can touch the job until around June 1. I have read the other book, of course, but normally I work rather slowly, and in my present harried condition I would not be able to work at all.

I am sending a poem now, and hope that it will please you. I delayed sending it because, from day to day, I felt I could retouch it a little here and there. I did get some slight changes made; now it will have to stand or fall as it is. Stand, I hope you will decide. I may be able to get another one, a good deal longer, to you early in June—that is, as soon as I can take the day off and work at some revisions without having students charging in and out and my telephone ringing. Meanwhile, I hope you like this one.

I have seen a prospectus of your book on criticism. It looks very interesting indeed. I am pleased to have the Wolfe in.

I saw from the kind letter you wrote Shirley Forgotson[1] here that you had been ill. I hope you are completely recovered now.

Most cordially yours,
Warren

P.S. It has just occurred to me that Brooks might be able to do the Spender piece for you by May 25,[2] since he has already finished most of his committee and conference work. You are probably familiar with his critical articles in the New Republic, American Review, Virginia Quarterly, Southern Review, etc. If you will wire me on this point I can turn the books over to Brooks immediately. I know he is very familiar already with Spender's work.

1. E. Shirley Forgotson, a student from Alexandria, Louisiana, enjoyed Warren's considerable confidence and perennial support, as is clear from subsequent letters. Unfortunately, he later succumbed to a debilitating mental illness, and his early promise was never fulfilled. (My special thanks to Leonard and Sherley Unger.)

2. Brooks's review of Spender's *The Destructive Element* and *Forward from Liberalism* was published in the August 1937 issue of *Poetry*.

TO EUDORA WELTY

TLS/MissA

The Southern Review
Louisiana State University
Baton Rouge,
May 17, 1937

Miss Eudora Welty
1119 Pinehurst St.
Jackson, Miss.

Dear Miss Welty:

We are going to use your story, "A Piece of News," probably in the Summer issue.[1] The other one is here enclosed. May we see more of your work soon?

Very sincerely yours,
Robert Penn Warren

1. The story appeared on schedule.

TO C. D. ABBOTT

TLS/SUNY-B

The Southern Review
Louisiana State University
Baton Rouge,
Louisiana
May 26, 1937

Mr. C. D. Abbott
Lockwood Memorial Library
University of Buffalo
Buffalo, N.Y.

Dear Mr. Abbott:

I am, of course, greatly pleased by your interest in my work; and I shall be glad to do what is possible to fulfill your request.[1] I do not make a practice of keeping manuscript[s], for, God knows, I never sold any, for the simple reason that nobody ever wanted to buy any. You are more than welcome to anything which I can find. I don't suppose that you want merely typed copies or clean copies written out. But if that is what you want, I can very easily provide you with either. As a matter of fact, I do most of my writing directly on the typewriter. If you will let me know precisely what you want, I shall be very happy to try to provide you with it.

Very sincerely yours,
Robert Penn Warren

1. Charles David Abbott, professor of English and director of libraries at what is now the State University of New York at Buffalo, was assembling an impressive modern poetry collection and had asked Warren to deposit samples of his work.

TO MORTON DAUWEN ZABEL

TLS/UChi

The Southern Review
Louisiana State University
Baton Rouge,
Louisiana
May 26, 1937

Mr. Morton D. Zabel
232 E. Erie St.
Chicago, Ill.

Dear Zabel:

I am delighted that you like the poem.[1] If I had even a few hours, I think that I might get the other one in some sort of shape. It is quite long (some 120 lines).[2] It has some places which are rather rough, but if I should get a few hours alone with it I might be able to get it in shape within the next few days. I will certainly send it to you when it looks half decent.

I don't see how I could do an honest piece of work on the Spender between now and June 10. I probably could get it ready for you by the 20th or 25th of that month. I suppose this means that I should turn the books over to Brooks. He is going to read them anyway, he says. I am really distressed over this confusion about the matter, but things will be so piled up until a week or so after Commencement here that I don't see how I could do a piece of work that wouldn't disgrace both you and me.

Most sincerely,
Warren

1. Presumably "Bearded Oaks," *Poetry* (October 1937).
2. This longish poem may have taken a fateful turn toward verse drama later in the year. (See the letter to Tate [December 1937] below.)

TO KATHERINE ANNE PORTER

TLS/Maryland

The Southern Review
Louisiana State University
Baton Rouge,
Louisiana
May 26, 1937

Miss Katherine Anne Porter
67 Perry St.
New York City

Dear Katherine Anne:

I have been intending almost daily to write you. Now when my more amiable impulses are fortified by a small piece of brutal self-interest, I do write. Houghton Mifflin has asked me to prepare a collection of short stories by Southern writers.[1] Naturally, I want to include something of yours, and something that will make as big a showing as possible— probably "Noon Wine" or "Old Mortality." Does a publisher hold a copyright on either of these? (I imagine that they are included in your forthcoming book with Harcourt Brace).[2] If so, I shall, of course, take up the matter of permissions with the publisher. But if no publisher does hold a copyright, can I get a permission from you? There will be a fee, of course, for reprinting. I am simply taking the amount suggested by the publishers and dividing it among the contributors. So much for the brutal self-interest.

I was delighted at your prize and know that nothing was ever more richly deserved.[3] I am extremely anxious to see the book that is coming out. And anxious to see you. Are you ever going to make the trip to Louisiana which you have now promised for so long? I don't suppose there is any chance for Cinina and me to get East again for some time. We managed to go as far as Richmond last Christmas.[4] This summer we shall probably go to California again. I am trying to finish up my novel, which *Houghton Mifflin,* with childish optimism, expects next January. We shall probably be in Lake County in northern California until the middle of September. If the book isn't well in hand by that time, my bones will probably be found bleaching there by some wandering deer hunter or prospector.

Do let us have some more stories soon. I was green with envy when I found "Noon Wine" in STORY. And let us hear from you.

Cinina sends warmest regards; and so do I.

Red

1. *A Southern Harvest* (1937).

2. *Pale Horse, Pale Rider: Three Short Novels* (1939).

3. Porter had received a Book-of-the-Month Club award ($2,500) for "best writer, unduly neglected."

4. For the Modern Language Association meeting.

Cinina Warren was especially close to her father, the composer Domenico Brescia, who taught at Mills College, and the surviving evidence suggests that her husband likewise enjoyed a pleasant (albeit respectful) relationship with his father-in-law. Warren had come to know the San Francisco Bay area well during his graduate school days at Berkeley and always found California, with its varied climate and striking landscapes, a stimulating place, so from the start of their life together the couple tried to include a trip to the West Coast in their summer travels whenever possible. Warren's vacations, then and later, were invariably working affairs, and the summer of 1937 was no exception. He was hard at work on his new novel, Night Rider, *and preoccupied with editorial and contractual matters related to his anthology* A Southern Harvest *and a second textbook he was doing with Brooks,* Understanding Poetry.

TO KATHERINE ANNE PORTER

TLS/Maryland [California]

[Early Summer 1937]

Dear Katherine Anne:

Many thanks for your long and fine letter. But why, in God's name, do things have to fall out so that you make your trip South exactly at the time when we have to be away? We are terribly disappointed—and urge you to repeat the visit soon, and when we are in Baton Rouge. Or perhaps you really will settle in Louisiana or Kentucky or Tennessee, and we can see you often.

I am enclosing a copy of a note from Harcourt Brace concerning my use of "Old Mortality." They feel that publication of the piece in the anthology could hurt the sale of your book. I just can't see any logic to that. Nobody would take the piece in the anthology as a substitute for the complete collection of your novelettes. The only possible effect, it seems, would be to encourage someone who was not acquainted with the rest of your work to get acquainted with it. I am writing them again to urge them to let me have the piece, or "Noon Wine." They are perfectly representative of your best work and give me a type of thing perfectly adapted to the use I have in mind. If they won't let me have either, they won't, I suppose, and that is that. In that case I shall have to use one of your shorter pieces.[1] But I want to ask you, if you have any influence with Harcourt Brace, to use some of it to persuade them about the stories. I say stories, because I haven't really decided which one of the two I like better. I know publishers don't like to have authors meddling in really serious matters such as permissions, etc. But they might forgive you.

This whole business of making an anthology is a miserable occupation, one I shall never undertake again.[2] I undertook this with the notion that I could put some stories which I liked between covers, and that that would be that. But every goddamned thing comes up, and here I am spending time badly needed for something else. The only pleasure is in getting a few of the things into the book that seem permanent and important. Not that it will do the things any good—for things like "Old Mortality" or Caroline's "Old Red" don't need any help. But there is a sort of pleasure in recording my admiration.

I hope that this letter will reach you soon; but it will probably wander about the Union until early autumn. We shall be in San Francisco for several days more, and then shall go to one of the more remote counties in northern California, where I shall undertake to wrestle with the angel for a couple of months. With luck, I hope. At your leisure I hope to hear from you. Things will be forwarded to me from 478 Vernon Street, Oakland, California.[3] Or if you forget that, anything in care of the Southern Review will eventually reach me.

Your trip, I hope, will be a great pleasure to you.[4]

> With all best wishes,
> Red

1. In the end, Warren had to content himself with reprinting Porter's story "He."

2. Warren did not keep this promise to himself.

3. The address of his father-in-law, Domenico Brescia.

4. Porter's biographer Joan Givner notes that she spent part of the summer visiting family in Houston and then joined the Tates at Olivet College, returning with them to Benfolly, their home outside Clarksville, Tennessee. There Porter met Brooks and Warren's assistant Albert Erskine and commenced a romance that ultimately led to her fourth marriage (*Katherine Anne Porter: A Life*, 303–4).

TO PAUL GREEN

TLS/UNC   [Southern Review letterhead]
                                             Care of Worthen Bradley
                                               Sulfur Bank Mine
                                               Clearlake Park,
                                                   California[1]
                                                  [Summer 1937]

Dear Mr. Green:[2]

I am using "A Tempered Fellow" in the anthology. I have asked Houghton Mifflin to let you know whether or not there is time for revision. I hope that there will be. In any case, there should be opportunity to make a few changes in the proof if you feel that any are necessary. The story, I think, is very fine and moving.

By the way, I hope that you will let us see some stories for the Southern Review in the not distant future. Will you be that kind? (Our rate of payment is not very high, however: about a cent and a half a word for prose).

Very sincerely yours,
Robert Penn Warren

1. The Warrens were vacationing with Berkeley professor Bertrand H. Bronson and his wife.

2. Though a gifted writer of fiction, the North Carolinian Paul Green was best known as a playwright, his *In Abraham's Bosom* having taken the Pulitzer in 1927. In the later 1930s, he turned his attention to full-scale regional pageants he called "symphonic dramas."

TO GEORGE MARION O'DONNELL

TLS/WashU   [Southern Review letterhead]

Sept. 8, 1937

Mr. George M. O'Donnell
120 Church St.
Belzoni, Miss.

Dear O'Donnell:

The fact that I am in California, and in fact, have been cut off for the last two weeks from regular mail, explains the somewhat tardy reply to your note.

I am sorry to write that it is going to be a rejection for the essay on poetry. The situation isn't that we aren't sympathetic with your basic view or don't like the handling of the particular essay; the primary trouble is that we have already accepted a long piece on *Primitivism and Decadence*[1] which touches on a good many of the same issues you have raised. And we do run into the problem Davis[2] hints at, to this extent—we are more heavily stocked up on literary criticism than anything else.

Forgive the brevity of this note. I am just preparing to start back home, and a thousand last-minute obligations have descended upon me here. And don't be puzzled at the Baton Rouge postmark you will see on this. I am putting this note and your essay in a bundle of manuscripts which are being sent back to the office today.

Let us hear from you again soon, and with other contributions. And I hope that I shall see you this fall or winter.

Very sincerely yours,
Red

1. By Yvor Winters; Delmore Schwartz reviewed it for the Winter 1938 number.
2. Possibly Lambert Davis at the *Virginia Quarterly Review*.

TO T. J. WILSON FROM BROOKS AND WARREN

TLS/PU

The Southern Review
Louisiana State University
Baton Rouge,
Louisiana
Sept. 8, 1937

Mr. T. J. Wilson
Henry Holt and Co.
257 Fourth Ave.
New York City

Dear Mr. Wilson:

We are somewhat surprised and disturbed to hear that you did not think the book would support the advance requested. The real cause of our distress is not primarily the fact in itself that the advance was refused, but that the refusal of a $600 advance on a book which has involved as much work as this one, it seems to us, indicates a lack of confidence in the project.

But the matter of permissions surprises us even more. There seems to be no reference in the contract to our responsibility for them, and no reference in the correspondence. In our previous experience with books involving permissions, the publisher has either assumed the responsibility or has clearly specified the conditions before the work was undertaken. Fortunately, in the present case the permissions will not cost a great amount. Our *estimates* have run between $450 and $500, but the higher figure is probably the more accurate. We tried to hold down the amount of modern material, but a book that is to compete successfully must have a fairly liberal selection. It will probably be impossible to reduce substantially the number of selections at present indicated. We might, for instance, cut the one poem by Millay, probably one of the most expensive poems, but hers is a name which the average teacher looks for in the table of contents.[1]

We probably ought to tell you that we would not have been disposed to undertake the present book with the obligation of handling the permissions. In the case of an ordinary anthology it is probably just for the anthologist to assume the expense, but in the case of a book like the present, in which the investment of labor and original material is quite large, the matter, we feel, is somewhat different. Needless to say, however, we know that abstract justice does not necessarily offer the only consideration in such circumstances.

We are anxious to hear from you. We don't want to be cantankerous, but we think that we ought to let you know the worst.

Very sincerely yours,
Cleanth Brooks, Jr.
Robert Penn Warren B.[2]

P.S. You aren't, by any chance, planning another trip South in the near future?

1. Millay, hardly a favorite of Warren and Brooks, was dropped from the first edition of *Understanding Poetry*.

2. The secretary, Bess Barnett, apparently signed Warren's name in his absence.

TO KATHERINE ANNE PORTER

TLS/Maryland   Dallas, Texas
                                                      September 13, 1937

Dear Katherine Anne:

Your note reached me just as I was leaving California. I wrote immediately, air mail, to Houghton Mifflin asking them to hold printing on your story ("He") until the matter of permission on "Old Mortality" was set too. They were to wire me in Amarillo, which, as you may recollect[,] is the capital of the cow country. They did wire me there, saying that they would like to have "Old Mortality" and would hold up the printing, but would have to have a clean bill of health from Harcourt on it. If you can, without embarrassment to yourself, secure this, I'll be jubilant. If you can't, I'll be content with "He," which is a great story anyway. Now simply consult your own desires and your own convenience in the matter. I mean this. But I shall be enormously grateful to you if you'll wire me at Baton Rouge the final word on the matter, and will let me know from whom I am to get the documentary permission.

Meanwhile, I am asking Houghton Mifflin to hold off until I get final word. But I am sending them copy of "Old Mortality" so that they can start printing immediately upon receiving word from me.

Good bye, and forgive the present haste and incoherence. We have just arrived here after a day in the saddle. Many thanks, really, for all your trouble about the story. Cinina joins me in very best wishes.

As ever,
Red

Settled once more into their routine in Baton Rouge, the Warrens would look back on their time in California wistfully. The academic year 1937–1938 would prove busy indeed, as the Southern Review *blossomed into an increasingly important (and correspondingly demanding) concern and Warren worked toward completing* Night Rider, *dealt with vexatious textbook publishers, and planned an array of new projects.*

TO JOSEPHINE MILES

TLS/UCal

The Southern Review
Louisiana State University
Baton Rouge,
Louisiana
Sept. 21, 1937

Miss Josephine Miles
2672 Hilgard Ave.
Berkeley, Calif.

Dear Miss Miles:[1]

Some time ago I saw in *The New Republic* your poem "Approach," and admired it very much. I later got copies of some of your poems from Howard Baker. I am returning that manuscript to you now. We hope to persuade you to submit some of your work to *The Southern Review,* perhaps some of the poems in this manuscript. Would you be willing to do so? In fact, since *The Southern Review* publishes rather long groups of poems, we should like to have a shot at all of the unpublished stuff you now have on hand.[2] But perhaps this is asking too much. In any case, we hope to hear from you in the near future.

Very sincerely yours,
Robert Penn Warren

1. At this point a graduate student at the University of California, Miles joined the faculty there in 1940.
2. Five of Miles's poems appeared in the Winter 1940 *Southern Review*.

TO EUDORA WELTY

TLS/MissA

The Southern Review
Louisiana State University
Baton Rouge
Sept. 23, 1937

Miss Eudora Welty
1119 Pinehurst St.
Jackson, Miss.

Dear Miss Welty:

I am happy to say that we are using your story "A Memory" in the Fall issue, which will be out soon. May we see some other pieces?

Very cordially yours,
Robert Penn Warren

TO T. J. WILSON

TLS/PU

The Southern Review
Louisiana State University
Baton Rouge,
Louisiana
Sept. 29, 1937

Mr. T. J. Wilson
Henry Holt and Co.
257 Fourth Ave.
New York City

Dear Mr. Wilson:

We hope that you will pardon the considerable delay in answering your last letter, but the business of registration and of opening term has forced everything else out of hand. But here the answer is.

It certainly seems that Clause II covers the question of responsibility for permissions, and so that is that. But the telegram which you quote in your letter and which stated explicitly the matter of responsibility for permissions failed, somehow, to get into our files; and whichever one of us received the telegram failed, apparently, to grasp the point at the moment. Since we did have the opportunity to get the information from the telegram, one, or both of us, probably should accept the responsibility for the misunderstanding. And, of course, we should have asked for a clear statement of the matter in the beginning.

But there is another matter—one, however, of no practical importance—which should be cleared up. The question is raised in the following extract from your letter: "You state in your last letter that you would not have been disposed to undertake the present book with the obligation of handling the permissions. Isn't it true that a great deal of the work had been done when I first talked with you, and that the whole scheme of the book had been laid out at that time? In other words, isn't it true that the book had actually been undertaken?" First, you seem to understand that the manuscript you have was completed in large part before the contract was signed. This is not the case. Actually, *all of the following material was written entirely after the contract was signed:* all of the General Introduction and the Introductions to the various sections;

all of the Glossary; all of the individual analyses with the exception of *Trees*[1] and the possible exception of *Portrait, A Litany,*[2] and *In Church,*[3] that is, thirty-five out of a total of thirty-nine; and all of the questions. In addition to this work there was the work of assembling the manuscript. It is true that the scheme of the book had been laid out when we first talked to you, but it is also true that the main body of the work has been done since, partly because we rejected some material then in hand, and partly because the scale of the book changed as we proceeded with work on it. So much for the merely mechanical fact of the amount of work done since the signing of the contract. Second, it is obviously true that the project had been *undertaken* before we talked to you, but the full implication, or intended implication, of our remark is this: We would have not been disposed *to undertake the completion* of the book on the terms specified, for we had, or thought we had, a concrete reason to believe that better terms would be obtained. All of this is now really irrelevant, and we say this simply because it is not true that we misstated the facts. The actual statement in our letter of September 8 is this: ". . . disposed to undertake the present book. . . ." The word *present* seemed to cover the case—the book for Henry Holt and Company. But, as we said, this is irrelevant to the practical question.

You very kindly say in your last letter that you don't want us to be dissatisfied with our bargain. Although the advance would still be convenient to us, it is not of as much concern to us now as it was toward the end of summer; and Clause II settles the other matter. But we want to feel that you are pleased with the book and have faith in its possibilities. In other words, we want you to be satisfied with your bargain.

Within the last month or so, several ideas for revision have occurred to us. We should like to make these revisions now, rather than in proof. Can you let us have the manuscript? It would be possible to make the revisions if we merely had all of Section IV, the analysis of "The Main Deep,"[4] and all of the General Introduction, but it is probably better to keep the stuff all together.

Very sincerely yours,
Robert Penn Warren

1. A highly sentimental, much-beloved poem by Joyce Kilmer; Warren vigorously detested it.
2. Poems by e. e. cummings and Sir Philip Sidney respectively.

3. This title does not appear in the published textbook.

4. A poem by James Stephens.

TO MORTON DAUWEN ZABEL

TLS/Newb

The Southern Review
Louisiana State University
Baton Rouge,
Louisiana
Oct. 11, 1937

Mr. Morton Zabel
POETRY
232 E. Erie St.
Chicago, Ill.

Dear Zabel:

Can we get you to do the poetry review for our winter issue? The main things in the group will be the *Selected Poems,* by Tate, and the *Collected Poems,* by James Joyce. There is also the book by Katherine [*sic*] Worth,[1] and then two or three others, which seem negligible. If you can do these in the neighborhood of three thousand words or very little over, we shall appreciate it. We are more and more crowded for space all the time. And could you get it done by something [*sic*] near the middle of November?[2]

I still have not finished the poem I have written to you so often about. It's now one hundred or so lines, but I can't quite bring it to proper focus. I'll submit it to you as soon as it is in a decent shape— if ever.

We do hope that you will do the review for us, and, by the way, what has become of the essay you said you were working on?

Sincerely,
Warren
By B.[3]

1. Kathryn Worth, *Sign of Capricornus.*

2. When it finally appeared in the Spring 1938 issue, Zabel's omnibus review not only addressed the books by Tate, Joyce, and Worth, but volumes by St.-John Perse, Marya Zaturenska, Sara Teasdale, Ezra Pound, Edgar Lee Masters, and Padraic Collum—hardly the "negligible" roster Warren envisioned.

3. Apparently signed and initialed by Miss Barnett, the *Review*'s secretary.

TO MORTON DAUWEN ZABEL

TLS/Newb

The Southern Review
Louisiana State University
Baton Rouge,
Louisiana
Oct. 13, 1937

Mr. Morton Zabel
POETRY
232 E. Erie St.
Chicago, Ill.

Dear Zabel:

This morning I have heard that you are resigning from the editorship of POETRY.[1] The first thought that Brooks and I had was, well who will be able to run the thing now? I am very sorry indeed that you are giving up the place, for I have fears for the future of the magazine. It has occurred to us that you out of your experience might want to say something on the question of editing a poetry magazine. If you are interested in doing a piece on this, we shall certainly be interested in publishing it. We do not wish this substituted for the poetry review (which I wrote you about the other day) but would like to have both.

Let us hear from you soon.

Very sincerely,
Warren

1. Zabel was summarily replaced by George Dillon and Peter DeVries.

TO ALLEN TATE

TLS/PU   [Baton Rouge]
                                               [Fall 1937][1]

Dear Allen:

Here is the MS.,[2] which I should, God knows, have returned sooner. I have read it twice, once rapidly and head-on, the way you ordinarily read a novel you pick up, and once more slowly and carefully. It will stand either kind of reading. It certainly has the real stuff, I think—a strong narrative drive (you are fine at managing the leads and holding suspense), and yet an almost constant closeness of observation. There is a very subtle texture to the writing. I have very little to offer in the way of suggestions. But a few things have occurred to me. I wouldn't want to go to the mat on any of these questions, but you might let me know what you think about them. I'll number them.

(1) I don't think that the first few pages get off on the right foot—or rather, I think I see a way to sharpen the effect. Particularly, the opening paragraph strikes me as a fairly stereotyped way of opening: the business of the smell of herring seems to be a kind of a dodge for getting into the story, and an unnecessary dodge. It seems to me that the novel should begin, probably, with the second sentence of the first full paragraph on page 4: "I have a story to tell, but I cannot explain the story. I cannot say, etc. . . ." Then, when you get down to the mention of the coffin on page 4, near the bottom, you can begin to build in what is now the second paragraph on page 2, and the other family stuff a little later, getting it all in before the second paragraph on page 5, the one that begins: "I remember George Posey coming out. . . ."

(2) The transition between the section on page 49 does not seem quite right to me. I feel fairly certain that an ordinary reader will have lost his bearings at the point and will need a different point of reference when he moves into the new section. More formality, perhaps, in the transition; and since you have established your narrator you have some ground for working it out.

(3) The section from page 45, about, to 76 seems not quite right to me. It gives me a little the impression that you feel under an

obligation to build in some social examples and are trying to conceal the intention by treating those items as if they were properly part of your narrative. Since you have a narrator who would, conceivably, take a deliberative course for building in the social picture and for commenting directly on it, it strikes me that here you might throw forward the character of the narrator and present such materials in an anecdotal form, indicating quite overtly the intention to give illustrations. Now there is an attempt to appear casual about the matter, but the thing doesn't quite come off—for me, that is. And I especially object to the speech, which seems arbitrary, more so than the rest of the section.

I haven't any other specific suggestions, but I believe that my objection under (3) could apply to one or two incidental matters elsewhere in the book.

I attach very little importance to these objections and suggestions, and, as I said, I certainly shouldn't want to go to the mat with anyone who felt differently. These sections don't impair the main effect, even for me. I am terribly anxious to see the rest—for one thing, just to see how the story itself goes on. You told me in June you weren't really satisfied with the thing. I can see no possible justification for that.

The Selected Poems have come—a review copy and the two personal ones. Many thanks. If this isn't the Pulitzer, the bastards are even worse than I thought.[3]

Too bad the Dollard makes you want to *vomick*.[4] Or rather, too bad you can't get your sentiments on paper. We'll have to hunt up somebody with a stronger stomach.

We've managed to settle down now and get at our usual chores. I have some poems going, and hope to wrestle one or two of them to completion during the next month. And I've got about 80,000 words done on the novel. But the scale of the thing has been increasing chapter by chapter, and now I'm not half through. I'm jittery about the thing, one minute thinking I've really got something by the tail and the next thinking it's a bust. I've been laying off for several weeks now, but like you, I feel that the pause may have been profitable. I'm having a copy made now of what is done, and I'll ask for a reading on it from you and Caroline, if you all can take time off. When is Caroline's book due out?[5] And what is she doing now?

The news about New Orleans is fine. I do hope that it works out that way. Meanwhile, our best.

As ever,
Red

1. Tate's bracketed date "[Spring 1937]" seems inaccurate.
2. Of Tate's novel in progress, *The Fathers.*
3. Scribner's had just brought out Tate's *Selected Poems.* The Pulitzer went to Robert Frost's *A Further Range* that year.
4. John Dollard's *Caste and Class in a Southern Town* was precisely the kind of book that would rankle southern traditionalists. Lyle Lanier, a psychologist and close friend from Warren's student days at Vanderbilt, reviewed it in the Spring 1938 issue.
5. *The Garden of Adonis* (1937).

TO ALLEN TATE

TLS/PU

The Southern Review
Louisiana State University
Baton Rouge,
Louisiana
Nov. 2, 1937

Dear Allen:

We are very depressed about the fact that we can't have your piece on the "Ode."[1] You specified in your note accompanying the essay that you needed the money bad, but you made the serious mistake of not specifying how bad or when. It's uncertain, but we might have been able to do something. And as for our tardiness in letting you have a reply, we can only say that our machinery is a little cumbersome at times. We like the piece very much indeed and feel that we have lost a scoop to [Lambert] Davis. We do wish that you had wired us when you received our answer or had wired us when you submitted the piece to Davis. That would have saved a little confusion—but it is really no great matter. Our real grief is that we haven't got the article.

Spencer[2] is not doing the review of your book. Zabel is. Spencer claimed that he can't get enough time for several months to do anything except his teaching. Zabel is not the most penetrating critic in the world, but I suppose his heart is in the right place. As a matter of fact, we have abandoned the critical commentaries with the poem groups, simply because we can't find people to do them. What you say about the matter of scale is, of course, true.

How is Nancy[3] now? Well, we all hope.

Tell Caroline that "The Enemy" sounds fine for a title[4] and that *The Garden of Adonis* has come in. I have only managed to read about 75 pages so far. What I have read is absolutely first rate, and I am going to take an evening off Thursday and read the thing through as it should be read. It is probable that Katherine Anne will review the book for us as one of our separate novel reviews.[5] I hope that it has a good run.

By the way, we were in New Orleans for an evening Friday and had a very nice time with Katherine Anne. She was up here a week or ten days before that for a short visit, and we are expecting her back some time before Christmas.

Bill Clark is due to drive through on his way to Quantico.[6] He is going to spend the night with us and then going to New Orleans to see Cannon.[7] I haven't seen him for ten years and naturally am pretty excited about the prospect.

Business: what about the Dollard book? Remember we wrote you again trying to persuade you to do the thing. But if you won't do that—or even if you will—we have another project to put to you. Several college textbooks on contemporary literature and on poetry have come out in the past few years. One of the most offensive—a book by a professor at Columbia on modern literature—has just been released. We had thought that a very good article could be done on this subject of what such people "teach," and certainly you are the man to do the article. What we want is a long, thorough piece, taking a few of these books as examples. Would you consider doing this? And fairly soon, say for spring or summer? Anyway, let us hear how you feel about it.[8]

By the way, what did you think of the poem I put in my last note to you? Or did I put it in?

I wish I could see you but it doesn't seem probable we will be taking any trips soon. I am pretty busy and pretty broke. Meanwhile our best all around.

As ever,
Red

P.S. I am sticking in some poems by a lad named Shirley Forgotson, who is applying, as John Palmer did, for a Rhodes Scholarship. He is twenty years old and is extremely intelligent. I don't expect him to get it this year, but should like to see his case presented as strongly as possible before the Committee. If you really like the poems, do you mind writing a note to the Committee of Selection[?] You can just send the note to me. If this is too much of a chore or if you don't like the poems, just chuck them in the wastebasket.

1. "Narcissus as Narcissus," Tate's discussion of his poem "Ode to the Confederate Dead," would appear in the *Virginia Quarterly Review* (Winter 1938).

2. The critic and Harvard professor Theodore Spencer.

3. The Tates' daughter.

4. Gordon's story ran in the Spring 1938 number.

5. Porter must have declined; Howard Baker reviewed *The Garden of Adonis* for the Spring 1939 issue.

6. Saville T. "Bill" Clark was a valued friend from Warren's undergraduate days at Vanderbilt and was pursuing a notably successful career in the marines.

7. Bill Clark's brother.

8. Tate did not accept the assignment.

TO MORTON DAUWEN ZABEL

TLS/Newb

The Southern Review
Louisiana State University
Baton Rouge,
Louisiana
Nov. 15, 1937

Mr. Morton Dauwen Zabel
1100 Pratt Blvd
Chicago, Ill.

Dear Zabel:

I am sorry to hear of the illness, very sorry. I hope that it is over now and that you are now in possession of your usual energies.

It's too bad that the extra burden of the review for us had to come at this time.

About the review: we do want you to include the Stevens and Teasdale if you feel disposed to do it. We should especially like to have you comment on the Stevens. Leave out the Masters if you wish, for we can send it on to the next man. It reached us late.

We didn't realize that the situation concerning POETRY was of the precise nature which you describe.[1] We still, however, would like to have your piece if you can be persuaded to write it. We are not interested in any mudraking [*sic*] for mudraking's sake, and our original proposal for the piece was innocent of any such motivation—but what you call the "therapeutic value" of such a piece ought to be very great. Of course, we can understand certain obvious reasons why you would hesitate. But if you bring yourself to do it, even if the account, for any reason, must be incomplete, we shall be glad to handle the article. Anyway, it is too damn bad.

I am sticking in a few poems by a young man named Shirley Forgotson, for you to look at. If you feel disposed, merely on the possible merits of the work, to write a statement of a few lines to the Committee on Selection for the Rhodes Scholarship in my care, I shall be very grateful. Forgotson is twenty years old and badly needs some sort of a subsidy to go on with his work. He is a senior here this year. But please do not do this unless the work itself seems to merit it.

We are looking forward with the greatest interest to your essay on the novel.[2]

With warmest regards,
Warren

P.S. By the way, was it Harper's or Holt that published your anthology of American criticism?[3] We should like to get a review copy, and, of course, I am interested in seeing one. [Handwritten] We'll do the ordering.[4]

1. A reference to the unpleasantness leading to Zabel's resignation as editor.
2. No such essay appeared in the *Southern Review*.
3. It was Harper's.
4. Herbert J. Muller reviewed Zabel's book in the Summer 1938 number.

TO T. J. WILSON

TLS/PU

The Southern Review
Louisiana State University
Baton Rouge,
Louisiana
Nov. 24, 1937

Mr. T. J. Wilson
Henry Holt and Co.
257 Fourth Ave.
New York City

Dear Mr. Wilson:

Thank you for your note. We are, of course, very grateful that your office can assist us in the matter of permission[s] for the poetry selections. We have written to the owners of the copyrights of the prose selections included in the book. I am sorry to say that we neglected to include in our list for you a poem for which permission must be obtained: "The Man He Killed," by Thomas Hardy. Macmillan, of course, holds the rights on this.

We have now completed our revisions on the manuscript, and it will come to you immediately. Of course, some changes may be necessary after we hear from the permissions. I suppose that could be settled by correspondence.

Very sincerely yours,
Robert Penn Warren

TO T. J. WILSON

TLS/PU

The Southern Review
Louisiana State University
Baton Rouge,
Louisiana
Nov. 30, 1937

Mr. T. J. Wilson
Henry Holt and Co.
257 Fourth Ave.
New York City

Dear Mr. Wilson:

We are sending you the revised manuscript. Now I believe we have caught everything that we can think of for the present. There may, of course, be a few minor revisions after the proof is prepared. You will notice that the Table of Contents is not included in the bundle. We shall send a revised Table of Content[s] to you in a few days. By the way, I believe that there are some loose sheets stuck in one of the folders—sheets with poems listed according to types. These sheets are notes for a classified index of types which we are also preparing for the appendix. Will you please return any such material to us?

With warm regards,
Robert Penn Warren

TO FRANK LAWRENCE OWSLEY

TLS/VU

The Southern Review
Louisiana State University
Baton Rouge,
Louisiana
Nov. 30, 1937

Mr. Frank L. Owsley
Vanderbilt University
Nashville, Tenn.

Dear Frank:

I have been planning a long letter just for a long letter's sake, but I have as usual postponed it until a piece of business created a pressing occasion. So, not to be disingenuous, I'll attend to business first. The business is this:

Will you do us a piece on McElroy's new *Jefferson Davis*, say, for the Summer issue?[1] The biography, as you probably know, is a big, pretentious two-volume affair, and, I suppose, aims at polishing off the job for once and for all. I haven't the slightest idea what is it like, for I have read only a few pages of it. Cleanth has taken it home, however, and doesn't give a too glowing report. We are all very anxious to have you do this. You are certainly the man for it. If you find that you cannot do the job for the Summer issue, we should control our impatience until fall.

We had talked a little bit about coming by Nashville Christmas, but now that possibility seems very remote. I am running so far behind on my novel that I see no hope for me if I do not take full advantage of the holidays for work. I did manage to get a lot done this summer, up to some 80,000 words, but the fall was so cluttered that I have only done a chapter and a half since my return. And here it is almost December. To make matters worse, Cleanth and I got a little dissatisfied with some of the things in the poetry book we had done for Holt and recalled the copy for revision. We have just finished that now. In fact, it is now lying on the table, wrapped for mailing. And thank God for that. It is supposed to be out sometime in the spring.

Have you done anything further about your farm?[2] I am sorry that we did not get to go by the place last June and take a look at it. Now probably we shan't be able to satisfy our friendly curiosity until some-time in the late spring. I am planning a trip up into Kentucky and per-haps into Ohio when I get the novel finished. I am simply going to take an arbitrary vacation then. We haven't done anything further on our project for a place except cut brush and do a little heavier clearing.³ Lord knows when anything more substantial will materialize. For the present I am simply taking my hour a day exercise with a brush hook or axe.

The general temper of existence remains uncharged. The big event of the fall has been a visit by Katherine Anne. By the way, we have a swell story by her in the Winter issue of the Review.⁴ Don't forget to look for it. Meanwhile, we hope that a visit from the Owsleys will be the big event of, say, February. How about it? Meanwhile, let us hear from you in some detail. We hope that everything is going happily with you all now. Cinina sends love to you all, and, of course, I join her.

As ever,
Red

[Handwritten P.S.] You must do the piece for us!

1. Owsley's review of Robert McElroy's biography came out in the Spring 1938 issue.
2. The Owsleys had purchased a one-hundred-acre farm outside Nashville.
3. The Warrens had decided to build a small house of their own on a piece of prop-erty off the Old Hammond Highway.
4. Porter's "Pale Horse, Pale Rider."

TO FRANK LAWRENCE OWSLEY

TLS/VU
The Southern Review
Louisiana State University
Baton Rouge,
Louisiana
Dec. 7, 1937

Mr. Frank L. Owsley
Vanderbilt University
Nashville, Tenn.

Dear Frank:

This is a hurried answer to your very welcome letter. Your news is fine, and we'll abide your injunction to secrecy. All best wishes to you both.

And we are delighted that you will do the Davis. Of course, we want the long piece, as complete a study of the subject and book as you care to make. If you are prepared to write the longer piece on the topic of Davis we'll certainly find the space for it. We had intended, as a matter of fact, to specify an article length review in the first place, and it was only by accident that we omitted to do so.

I gravely fear that you are right about the war situation.[1] I am still an isolationist, and only hope that I can remain one.

Forgive my rush, and let me have another letter from you soon. I am terribly sorry that the chances of a visit to Louisiana in the immediate future are not very good, but we are hoping to come to Nashville sometime during the year. Cinina joins me in love to you both.

As ever,

Red

P.S. By the way, you remember that I asked you about the possibility of putting the result of your researches on the nonslaveholding farmer into an article for us. How do you feel about that now? When could we hope for such a piece?[2] And when can we expect the Davis? [Handwritten] April 15? May 1?

1. Japan had invaded China, and in Europe the alliance between Mussolini and Hitler was an increasing cause for concern.
2. Owsley must have declined Warren's invitation, though he would review Charles Morrow Wilson's *Corn Bread and Creek Water* for the Spring 1941 issue.

TO EDWARD DAVISON

TLS/YU

The Southern Review
Baton Rouge, Louisiana
Dec. 8, 1937

Mr. Edward Davison
University of Colorado
Boulder, Colorado

Dear Ted:

Cinina and I still grieve that you did not come to California for your vacation. We had almost counted on that, and the place is a good place.[1]

We both enjoyed it tremendously. There was good swimming and boating and hiking, and plenty of undisturbed time for work. I gained some fifteen pounds during the summer and have been a new man ever since. But I can imagine that after another spell of writers' conference that you were probably hating the sight of a human face and wanted to take refuge in a cave to lick your wounds. (By the way, I have heard practically nothing about the Conference. I haven't seen Ransom, and the two days we spent in Amarillo were so full that Thompson[2] didn't talk about the matter much—except to say that he got a lot out of some of the comments on his work. Bishop seems to have been particularly helpful to him.)

I have been intending to write you for weeks, but the usual disorder prevails in my affairs, and the usual pressure of work. I want to tell you among other things that I did get in touch with Priestly [sic] as soon as I got Natalie's letter.[3] I talked to him by telephone and tried to persuade him to come up and go to Natchez the next day. But he had a series of engagements in New Orleans which held him until the very moment of his departure. I hope you will tell him to look me up if he ever comes this way again. And, as a matter of fact, Robert Frost's daughter did stop over a week or ten days ago and gave us a very pleasant evening. Now, we are looking forward to a visit from you, or better—much better—you and Natalie. They have asked me to write you to get a list of dates that might be convenient for your lecture here. Personally, I think it would be nice if you could come around Mardi Gras. If we can get the date soon enough, we might be able to arrange for some other appearances in this neighborhood—perhaps Tulane, or Loyola, or Centenary in Shreveport, or some of the other state colleges.

I'm still sunk in the novel, which now, scarcely only half finished, is almost as long as a novel already. I completely miscalculated the scale of the thing in the early chapters. Now I'll probably have to go back and try to do a lot of compressing when the first draft is finished. I have only been able to do two rather long chapters this fall, but I have managed to do a couple of poems, one of them rather long. I am going to dig in for Christmas and try to get a couple of more chapters by January. Both the publishers and I have given up hope of early spring publication, but I do hope to have enough done by the end of January to take time off for some carefree jollification. Dammit, I'll take it off anyway. We are anxious for news of you all. Let us have some soon. Cinina joins me in love to the lot of you.

As ever,
Red

1. The Warrens had vacationed in the Clear Lake region.

2. Warren's student Thomas H. Thompson, who gave up creative writing for a career in journalism, ultimately leading to a Pulitzer Prize.

3. Davison and his wife, Natalie, were close friends of the popular British novelist and playwright J. B. Priestley.

TO ALLEN TATE

TLS/PU   [Baton Rouge]
                                    [December 1937][1]

Dear Allen:

We had already seen the Walton review.[2] It is one of the most infuriating things I've ever come across. It is, however, so obviously inspired by malice—and the logic of her argument about revision is so insane—that there is no plausibility about the review. And she made the mistake of quoting some of the best lines. The review almost confirmed us in a decision—which we have debated for some time—to run a series of articles on N.Y. critics. Thoroughly documented articles.

I believe that you will get the seventy-five bucks, though I don't know exactly when. Getting money in advance has been recently impossible, but Pip took this request to the president's office and, I think, got an OK there.[3]

I am mighty pleased that you liked the new poem. I have done a few revisions, and shall send the new version to you soon. You are right about the dramatic element. I have been aware of that question, and especially aware of it in the last several poems. I have been trying in the last couple of years to get at a greater fluidity and ease of movement and at a less constrained manner. But whether I have gained any ground or not, I know that I have lost some—or at least, I have passed up certain poetic resources. The long poem, or rather, the play, which I talked to you about, interests me more and more.[4] I have done a few fragments, but I shan't get seriously at it until I finish the novel. Now I've got 90,000 words on it, but I can't see an end before 155,000 or 160,000 words. I believe that I have solved some of the questions of a style that would be adequate to such a subject—but, of course, I can't know yet.

We are delighted at the prospect of getting the Harvard piece, and delighted that you have the lecture.[5] It pays something pretty substantial, doesn't it? Are you going to Greensboro for a lecture?[6] And on what? If you are going.

By the way, we have written to Lyle about the Dollard book. That was a fine suggestion. We have some other pretty promising things lined up for the next few issues. Don on Caldwell's new book,[7] Hollis on Prescott Webb's *Divided We Stand*,[8] Webb on a batch of reconstruction books,[9] Owsley on McElroy's *Davis*, etc. In the coming issue we have a novelette by Katherine Anne,[10] and another of Wade's biographies.[11] In fact, he is going to do a CCC [*sic*]. Jones and a Lanier for us.[12] The press here is bringing out his book on some Southerners.[13] And by the way, have you any suggestions for articles?

I know that I am leaving unsaid a lot of things that I should take up, but I've had a hard morning and my mind is fuzzy as hell.

Let me hear from you all.

As ever,

Red

1. Tate's original date was "Autumn 1937," but a subsequent correction was made, apparently in Tate's hand.

2. Eda Lou Walton's review of Tate's *Selected Poems* in the New York *Times Book Review* (December 5, 1937).

3. It seems likely that Tate had asked for an advance on his essay "Tension in Poetry" (Summer 1938).

4. The first stirrings of what would become *Proud Flesh*, the verse-drama prototype for *All the King's Men* (1946).

5. Tate spoke at Harvard in early 1938.

6. Tate would accept a job at the Women's College of North Carolina (now the University of North Carolina at Greensboro) the following year.

7. Davidson reviewed Erskine Caldwell and Margaret Bourke-White's classic of photojournalism *You Have Seen Their Faces* in the Summer 1938 issue.

8. Christopher Hollis' review was in the Spring 1938 issue.

9. The Texas historian Walter Prescott Webb would not be among the *Review*'s contributors.

10. Porter's "Pale Horse, Pale Rider" (Winter 1938).

11. "Henry W. Grady" (Winter 1938).

12. Neither essay appeared.

13. The book never appeared.

TO T. J. WILSON

TLS/PU

The Southern Review
Louisiana State University
Baton Rouge,
Louisiana
Dec. 16, 1937

Mr. T. J. Wilson
Henry Holt and Co.
257 Fourth Ave.
New York City

Dear Mr. Wilson:

Here is a revised Table of Contents. But it is possible, of course, that further changes may be made after all data on permissions has been assembled. For instance, we may add "Bryan, Bryan, and Bryan," by [Vachel] Lindsay.[1] We have also prepared a rather long sort of preface or "Letter to the Teacher,"[2] which we shall send you a copy of in a day or two. It attempts to analyze the organization of the book and to give some leads for its use. Perhaps mistakenly we also included in that preface our attack on the conventional organization and method of dealing with similar material. We shall be anxious to have word of your reaction to the preface.

With best wishes for a good Christmas from us both,

Sincerely,
Robert Penn Warren

P.S. The note with the question concerning the identification of "Portrait," by E. E. Cummings, has come in. The poem is the well known one on Buffalo Bill, which begins, "Buffalo Bill's defunct. . . ." Thank you very much for the information concerning permission on the other poems.

1. They did not.

2. This crucial feature of the textbook delineated the New Critical principles that informed it and served to underscore its essentially polemical nature.

1938

TO HERBERT J. MULLER

TLS/Ind

The Southern Review
Louisiana State University
Baton Rouge,
Louisiana
Jan. 4, 1938

Mr. H. J. Muller
248 Marstellar St.
W. Lafayette, Ind.

Dear Professor Muller:[1]

We have read your essay with the greatest interest, and like it. We have very heavy commitments for the next three or four issues in literary criticism and do not see a possible opening in the near future, especially since we have to attach so much of our literary criticism to the excuse of reviewing. Perhaps, however, we can persuade you to do some essay length review for us.[2] Certainly, we should like to have you nominate some book, or groups of books, in which you might be interested. Again, let me say that I am sorry we can't find a place for this, for it certainly deserves a serious hearing.

Very sincerely yours,
Robert Penn Warren

1. Muller, who taught at Purdue (and later Indiana University), emerged as an influential critic with the publication of his *Modern Fiction: A Study of Values* (1937).

2. Muller's "Pathways in Recent Criticism" would appear in the Summer 1938 issue of the *Southern Review*.

TO GEORGE MARION O'DONNELL

TLS/WashU

The Southern Review
Louisiana State University
Baton Rouge,
Louisiana
Jan. 4, 1938

Mr. George Marion O'Donnell
120 Church St.
Belzoni, Miss.

Dear O'Donnell:

Thank you very much for letting us see the poems by Harry Brown.[1] Some things we like very much, but we do not feel that we can get an exhibit out of the present lot. It is needless to say that we are interested in his work and hope to see more of it. We especially like "Tailpiece for a Pamphlet."

And how is your own work coming?

Sincerely yours,
Warren

1. It would appear that O'Donnell had submitted work of the young poet Harry Brown, whose first book of verse would appear in 1940 and who would go on to be a successful novelist and screenwriter, best remembered for *A Walk in the Sun* (1944). (I am grateful to Charles East for this suggestion.)

TO JAMES T. FARRELL

TLS/Penn

The Southern Review
Louisiana State University
Baton Rouge,
Louisiana
Jan. 5, 1938

Mr. James T. Farrell
336 Lexington Ave.
New York City

Dear Mr. Farrell:[1]

We should like for you to do the review of *Famine* at the length you specify.[2] We cannot promise, however, that we can publish it before summer. But we should like to have it in time for the spring just in case there is an opening. The deadline for spring would be about February 15.

Very sincerely yours,
Robert Penn Warren

P.S. We should, of course, be greatly interested in seeing sections from the novel on which you are working.[3] Please do instruct your agent to let us have a look, even though it has been our policy in the past to insist that pieces of fiction be complete in themselves.

1. Farrell had achieved considerable notoriety for his Studs Lonigan trilogy (1932–1935).
2. *Famine* (1937), a novel by Liam O'Flaherty, was not reviewed in the *Southern Review,* but Farrell's essay on Ignazio Silone's *Bread and Wine, The School for Dictators,* and *Fontamara* appeared in the Spring 1938 issue.
3. Probably *No Star Is Lost* (1938); none of Farrell's fiction appeared in the *Review.*

TO WILLARD MAAS

TLS/UTex

The Southern Review
Louisiana State University
Baton Rouge,
Louisiana
Jan. 14, 1938

Mr. Willard Maas
62 Montague St.
Brooklyn, N.Y.

Dear Mr. Maas:[1]

Although you ask for an early consideration of your poems, we have only recently reached a final decision on them. Perhaps you do not have as much difficulty as we do in making up your mind about poems which suddenly appear before you. We feel more and more timidity about making quick decisions on this subject.

We like many things about these poems but, with some dubiety, have decided against their publication. However, we are very anxious to see more of your work.

Very cordially yours,
Robert Penn Warren

1. Willard Maas, like Warren, had a book of poems published by the Alcestis Press in 1935. His second volume, *Concerning the Young,* came out in 1938.

TO JOSEPHINE MILES

TLS/UCal

The Southern Review
Louisiana State University
Baton Rouge,
Louisiana
Jan. 14, 1938

Miss Josephine Miles
1140 Keniston Ave.
Los Angeles, Calif.

Dear Miss Miles:

We are greatly pleased with some of these poems and could have told you that some time back. But we have held the complete manuscript in hope of having a change of heart about some of the others, so that we might make out a full exhibit from those on hand. At present we are holding only those which we think are the very best. The ones which we also considered for publication you will find indicated by a check mark or a question mark. What do you think of this proposal? We shall hold the following pieces: "Hospice," "Sound Track," "Prospectus," and "Equinox" and shall definitely want to publish them. Will you give us a shot at other things you have on hand or may write in the next few months? We are previously committed for the poetry for the next several issues. If this is an unreasonable request on your part and you wish us to relinquish the poems named, we shall do so, though regretfully. We are very anxious to have your response to this suggestion.

Very sincerely yours,
Robert Penn Warren

TO ALLEN NEVINS

TLS/Col   *The Southern Review*
                                      Louisiana State University
                                                Baton Rouge,
                                                    Louisiana
                                               Jan. 18, 1938

Mr. Allen Nevins
Dept. of History
Columbia University
New York City

Dear Mr. Nevins:[1]

We hope to persuade you to do an essay length review of *Jackson* (entire), by Marquis James, for THE SOUTHERN REVIEW, at a length of some four or five thousand words.[2] We shall not be able to use it in our next issue, and could, if necessary, postpone publication until the Fall issue. We find it impossible to present our reviews immediately after the date of publication of books, but we do hope that some of our reviews will have more than the value of a notice. And we are certain that your treatment of the Jackson book would have such a value. Will you consent to do this for us?

   THE SOUTHERN REVIEW rate for prose is $1^{1}/_{2}$¢ a word, payment on publication.

                                       Very sincerely yours,
                                       Robert Penn Warren

1. Years before, Nevins had written a complimentary review of Warren's first book, *John Brown: The Making of a Martyr* (1929), for the *New Republic* (March 19, 1930).
2. The proposed review never appeared.

TO JOHN PEALE BISHOP

TLS/PU

The Southern Review
Louisiana State University
Baton Rouge,
Louisiana
Jan. 28, 1938

Mr. John Peale Bishop
South Chatham, Mass.

Dear John:

The notion of a piece on Cummings is good. But we want to suggest a rider. Cummings' collected poems are coming out this spring. Why don't you treat him as both poet and novelist, attaching your piece to the occasion of a review? You could, of course, treat the poems with as little space as you desired and concentrate your interest on the fiction. Would something in the neighborhood of 4,000 words serve your purpose?[1] That is on the short side, I know, but our general commitments are heavier and heavier.

Try to think up another proposal to make to us in the near future. By the way, could this piece be ready by May 1?

We are hoping to follow your example and build a house some time in the near future. But how near, I don't know. All I am doing now is working over six and a half acres of relatively untouched woodland with an ax and brush hook. I wish you were here so you could give me some advantages of your experience in the matter. I am glad yours is surviving the gale.

Our best regards to you
both,
Red

1. Bishop's "The Poems and Prose of E. E. Cummings" would appear in the Summer 1938 issue of the *Southern Review.*

TO T. J. WILSON

TLS/PU

The Southern Review
Louisiana State University
Baton Rouge,
Louisiana
Feb. 7, 1938

Mr. T. J. Wilson
257 Fourth Ave.
New York City

Dear Mr. Wilson:

From the total of $675 you name subtract $40 for Masters, $25 for Millay, and $50 for Lindsay—$115. This would leave a total permissions fee of $560. In place of the Masters' poems we wish to insert "The Tailor," by De la Mare. At the end of Section II just after "Corinna's Going A-Maying," by Robert Herrick, we wish to insert "King David," by De la Mare. Copies of these two poems are enclosed. Just after "The Tailor" we wish to insert one of Housman's poems, "Farewell to Barn and Stack and Tree," a copy of which is enclosed.[1] This will ease the permissions situation a little bit, since you hold copyrights on De la Mare and Housman. We have carefully worked over the other poems and would find it very hard to confront the necessity of cutting any more of them. Naturally, we are anxious to make as much money as possible out of the book, and are sympathetic with your own desire to hold down permission expenses, but, frankly, we don't see how we can get below $560 and still do the job properly. We hope that this sews up the sack. And we know that you hope so, too, because you must be pretty well fed up with the whole matter by this time. We look forward to your Monday letter.

Sincerely yours,
Robert Penn Warren

P.S. By the way, may we have the following books for review in THE SOUTHERN REVIEW: *The Shelley Letters*, edited by George S. Gordon; *The Past Must Alter*, by Albert Guerard; *Natural History*, by Raymond

Holden; *American Regionalism,* by Howard W. Odum and Harry E. Moore[?]

1. Brooks and Warren were still tinkering with the contents of *Understanding Poetry,* and adjustments to the order specified here were subsequently made. Walter de la Mare's "The Tailor" was not included.

TO HUBERT CREEKMORE

TLS/BU

The Southern Review
Louisiana State University
Baton Rouge,
Louisiana
Feb. 8, 1938

Mr. Hubert Creekmore
1607 Pinehurst St.
Jackson, Miss.

Dear Mr. Creekmore:

It was a close thing on all of these. We especially liked "Overnight." May we see more?

Sincerely yours,
Robert Penn Warren

TO EUDORA WELTY

TLS/MissA

The Southern Review
Louisiana State University
Baton Rouge,
Louisiana
Feb. 22, 1938

Miss Eudora Welty
1119 Pinehurst St.
Jackson, Miss.

Dear Miss Welty:

We are using "Old Mr. Grenada" in our forthcoming issue.[1] Here is the other story, which we should have sent back to you before this. But have you any more handy? If so, please let us have a shot at them. By the way, I may say that I think "Old Mr. Grenada" very brilliantly done.

Very sincerely yours,
Robert Penn Warren

1. Spring 1938.

TO FRANK LAWRENCE OWSLEY

TLS/VU

The Southern Review
Louisiana State University
Baton Rouge,
Louisiana
Feb. 22, 1938

Dear Frank:

Your piece on Davis came yesterday (Sunday). Cleanth and I have already had time to read it, and now wish to say that we like it very much indeed. We are sorry, as a matter of fact, that you were so bored with the subject that you couldn't do a long, full dress piece, but this certainly accomplishes all that could be expected within its limits. We do, however, want to take up with you one paragraph, not with regard to what you have said so much as with regard to possible misinterpretation. The paragraph follows:

> "Perhaps it is not doing Mr. McElroy an injustice to say that he is not sufficiently familiar with the trend of thought in the North and in the South during the thirty years preceding the Civil War, to understand the position taken by his protagonist. Had the author made a systematic study of the antislavery attack upon the South during these years, Davis' attitude and that of almost all Southerners would have been more intelligible: certainly their attitudes would have needed no apology. These attitudes were but the normal psychological reactions of individuals and groups subjected to sustained attacks from the outside. They were a defense mechanism and the social psychologist would doubtless deal with such a defense mechanism as a natural phenomenon, neither to be defended nor

condemned. Not so Mr. McElroy. In so much as Davis defended slavery, despite the fact that the author finally discovers that he was a patient abolitionist, Davis was a sinner. (After all is it the business of the historian to pass ethical judgments? Is it not rather the duty of the historian to explain why individuals and peoples have conducted themselves in a certain fashion or have thought as they have?)"

The sentence here which is underscored [*sic*] would remove all valued judgments from historical matters, as it might be interpreted by some readers who would take it to say that there should not be such valued judgments as you make, for example, in your discussion of the crusades in [*sic*] the South in THE AMERICAN REVIEW article or in the last paragraph, by implication, in the present article. Isn't what you wish to say something like this: that McElroy takes an absolute view of the moral question without relating his valued judgments to the whole pattern with which he is dealing[?] This might tie in, then, with the sentence about "defense mechanism." We don't wish to seem pedantic in raising the question, as perhaps we ourselves have misinterpreted your paragraph.

Meanwhile, we are setting up the rest of the essay.[1]

By the way, may we have a look at the two papers which you read at Georgia? And what's the news about your work on the nonslaveholding farmer?

It's fine news that you will probably be in New Orleans in March. Certainly, you can't get back to Tennessee without coming by for a stop here. Do let us know what your plans are.

Meanwhile, our best love to you all.

As ever,
Red

[Handwritten P.S.] You'll probably want to kick us in the pants for presumption—but I recall some of the words you've said to me on the matter of science and history.

1. The problematic passage does not appear in the published version of the Owsley review.

TO EDMUND WILSON

TLS/YU

The Southern Review
Louisiana State University
Baton Rouge,
Louisiana
March 23, 1938

Mr. Edmund Wilson
Harcourt, Brace
383 Madison Ave.
New York City

Dear Wilson:[1]

I am writing in the hope that you can be persuaded to do some work for THE SOUTHERN REVIEW. Would you be interested in doing a group review of several recent European novels, *Claude,* by Genevieve Fauconnier, *The Song of the World,* by Jean Giono, and the last books by Kafka and Malraux? Or could we persuade you to do a review of one of these, preferably Kafka or Malraux, independently?[2] And in addition, we hope that you will make some proposal to us for an essay or essays.

I am just now reading *The Triple Thinkers,*[3] and reading it with great admiration.

I haven't been East in several years, but it is possible that I shall be able to make a visit there this year. If so, I can hope that I shall be able to see you.

Very sincerely yours,
Robert Penn Warren

P.S. I am sending a copy of our Spring issue. It has several items that might be of interest to you: Bamford Parkes on Kenneth Burke and Burke on Thurman Arnold.[4] By the way, take a look at the story by Eudora Welty.[5]

1. Warren had known Wilson from the late 1920s and had reviewed books for him in the *New Republic.*
2. Wilson never published in the *Review,* but Howard Baker addressed Fauconnier's

novel in the Spring 1939 issue, and Philip Rahv, the maverick Marxist critic and coeditor of the *Partisan Review,* subsequently reviewed Kafka's *The Trial* (Summer 1939).

3. Subtitled *Ten Essays on Literature* (1938).

4. "Attitudes Toward History" and "The Virtues and Limitations of Debunking" respectively.

5. "Old Mr. Grenada."

TO EUDORA WELTY

TLS/MissA   *The Southern Review*
                                                Louisiana State University
                                                            Baton Rouge,
                                                                Louisiana
                                                          March 23, 1938

Miss Eudora Welty
1119 Pinehurst St.
Jackson, Miss.

Dear Miss Welty:

Mr. Paul Brooks, of Houghton Mifflin, has sent me the enclosed material with the suggestion that we ask you to compete for their fiction award this year. If you are interested in doing this, THE SOUTHERN REVIEW will certainly do everything it can to push your case. For your sponsors you might name Cleanth Brooks, and myself, and Katherine Anne Porter, who, I happen to know, likes your work. Of course, these might be in addition to any one else you have in mind.

    "Old Mr. Grenada" is appearing in our Spring issue. I like it better all the time. Have you any more stories on hand? And may we have another look at "The Petrified Man" some time?

                                                Very sincerely yours,
                                                Robert Penn Warren

TO EUDORA WELTY

TLS/MissA

The Southern Review
Louisiana State University
Baton Rouge,
Louisiana
April 5, 1938

Miss Eudora Welty
1119 Pinehurst St.
Jackson, Miss.

Dear Miss Welty:

I think that your statement of the plan and the sample of treatment [are] excellent, and I have high hopes that Houghton Mifflin will think so too. Certainly, they already admire your writing, and the only question would be, I am sure, the matter of the plan of this particular novel. But that seems highly satisfactory to me. Since April 1 was the closing date for applications, I wired Houghton Mifflin an application for you, and have received an acknowledgment. However, it will probably be best if you get your blank in to them as soon as possible. Meanwhile, I am sending this other material to them direct. I hope that these arrangements will suit you.

With all best wishes for the award.[1]

Very sincerely yours,
Robert Penn Warren

1. Welty did not receive the fellowship.

TO LYLE SAXON

TLS/Tul

The Southern Review
Louisiana State University
Baton Rouge,
Louisiana
May 10, 1938

Mr. Lyle Saxon
St. Charles Hotel
New Orleans, La.

Dear Mr. Saxon:[1]

I greatly appreciated your kindness in sending me the clipping of the review of *Southern Harvest*. And I appreciate your remark concerning the collection of stories.

Next time I am in New Orleans I shall certainly take you up on your invitation to drop in on you at the St. Charles. And I hope that when you are next in Baton Rouge you will give me a ring and let me mix one for you.

Very sincerely yours,
Robert Penn Warren

1. Saxon had just brought out *Children of Strangers;* Baker would include it in his omnibus review of new fiction for the Spring 1939 number.

TO CAROLINE GORDON

TLS/PU

[Late Spring 1938]

Dear Caroline:

I'm taking advantage of the fact that I'm on a train and don't have to attend to classes and papers and things to write you a note which I've been wanting to write for some time. I've read the *Garden of Adonis* a couple of times now, once pretty fast, and again at a more ruminative pace. When the novel is in the country, it's absolutely at your best level—

which is certainly anybody's best level. The whole handling of the story of the croppers is very strong and moving, and the countryside is rendered as well as possible. But I am unable to escape the feeling that when the novel comes to town there is a falling off, a certain sketchiness. I wish that you had expanded the novel to give a more detailed treatment of the people in town. It's a relatively short novel, and I have the feeling that it should be considerably longer. (Were they pressing you for publication?) But the whole matter of Ote,[1] etc., is enough to make the book important.

We've had an unsatisfactory time in getting reviewing done on it. Two people have fallen down, for one reason and a[n]other, Mark Van Doren the last man. But Baker will handle it, we've decided.

What are you writing now? Is there a chance for a short piece any time soon? And could we interest you in doing any reviewing?

Night Rider (the only passable title I've been able to strike on for my novel) is about to wind up. I've got to do a little more than one chapter, before I settle to the business of revision. I hope to have a carbon [of] the thing in its present condition, and, if you can spare the time, I want you all to give it a reading before I finish the business of revision. Will you be able to take the time? I know that there are a lot of changes to be made (if it's worth making any changes—I simply have no idea now whether the thing is coming off at all), and I'd like to get suggestions while there's still a chance of taking advantage of them. This request is an imposition, but I'm making it anyhow.

We went down, as you probably know, and saw Albert and Katherine Anne married a little time back.[2] They now have an apartment opposite the University and almost next door to the apartment house where we are temporarily living. (We had a chance to sell our contract on the house where we were at an attractive figure—which I think is the term real estate dealers use for such matters—and are in an apartment until we can make more permanent arrangements. The apartment has been a convenience during the last two months, which has been a period of considerable pressure for both of us.) I suppose that Albert and Katherine Anne will build a house this summer or in the early fall. They have a place on the road opposite the location where we may build.[3] Getting a place to live in Baton Rouge is so difficult that one is almost forced to build. And the FHA terms are so liberal that one can build a modest but satisfactory place for something decidedly less than our contract-rental on the other house which we were in.

How do you like the teaching? If by any chance you discover a young genius please steer her to the SR. And is Greensboro an agreeable place to stay?

How is Nancy? We haven't had a word about her in a long time. Give her our love.

I must wind this up now, and get at a long overdue note to Allen, to enclose with this.

> Our best,
> Red

1. A tenant farmer in Gordon's novel.

2. Porter and Erskine (much her junior) had been married in New Orleans in April, as soon as her divorce from Eugene Pressly was finalized.

3. Off the Old Hammond Highway in what was then the outskirts of Baton Rouge. Porter and Erskine never built on the property. (Special thanks to Charles East.)

TO ALLEN TATE

TLS/PU   [Late Spring 1938]

Dear Allen:

I've been trying to get at a letter for some time, but the time has gone more rapidly than ever this spring, and I seem to have found less and less [o]pportunity to do such things—even things that ought to be done or that I want to do.

First, a few pieces of business. We are glad to have the piece on criticism, John [Ransom] and [Edmund] Wilson, but could you make mention of a few more books and give us a piece that would stand as a survey of the critical books of a half year, or so?[1] Since we are running a long review of some recent books of criticism in the summer issue (by a fellow named Muller, whom we asked to do the job on the strength of an essay he submitted to us and a very good book on contemporary fiction—at least, the chapters we read were very good), how about counting on your criticism piece for the winter issue? Then if you get a chance to do the text book piece in between, well and good. We can get some sample books to you at any time you ask. I suppose by this time you have proof on your other essay, the "tension" one, which will appear in the summer issue. By the way, I don't remember whether I even said how good I think that essay is. Perhaps it's not as important as the three types of poetry essays or the Phi Beta Kappa piece, but close to them, certainly. I wish that we had seen it early enough to incorporate the little piece of Dante analysis in our poetry book.

How is the *Fathers* coming? And will there be a section that could stand as an independent story?[2] Or that could be made into a story? And has Caroline done any stories recently? (I remember her vow never to do another, but I hope she won't remember it, and don't think for a moment that she will.)

There's something else about the SR I wanted to say, but can't recall what it is. But this does occur to me: we've had two other references to the rumor that the magazine was on its way out, one from Blackmur. That sort of talk certainly isn't doing us any good—I remember now what the other thing was: the book of criticism you are going to do for Scribners.[3] How about giving us a shot at some of it for the magazine? And when will your piece for the *Purpose-SR* series be ready?[4]

We have finished all the proof on the poetry text book and expect to [have] a copy in about ten days. I know that we have been able to get results by using that system of teaching, but I don't know whether we've been able to put the system persuasively on the printed page. And I'm not elated about some of the writing in the book. But maybe—and my fingers are crossed—it'll make us a little money. We are very grateful to you for the reading you gave the thing. It was of very considerable use to us, and your remarks did a lot to lift our then flagging spirits.

I'm just finishing the next to the last chapter of my novel. If HM[5] will give me a little extra time, I'm going to impose on you all for a reading—even though I know how little you like to read novels. I hope to be through in about two weeks and to [h]ave a carbon copy shortly after that. The thing has run a good deal longer than I had anticipated— about 150,000 words, I guess. I'm anxious to be through with it now, and get at the long poem. I've been composing a few scattering [*sic*] fragments of that. By the end of the summer I hope to have something consolidated and be able to judge whether it's worth pushing to the conclusion.

Cleanth is about ready to push his book of essays through.[6] He has been reorganizing a lot of the material in those already published, and has only one more complete piece to write. The Yeats piece will appear in our summer issue as a review of the *Vision*.[7] He hasn't got a publisher yet, but he hasn't submitted the manuscript—he has merely sounded out one or two on the possibility.

Something I was trying to think of above: Zabel is reviewing your *Poems* as part of the group review in the Summer issue, but we are trying to pick somebody to do an essay length analysis for fall or winter. And we can't think of anybody, except, perhaps, Blackmur who is up to the close kind of treatment which we want. And since you reviewed Blackmur not so long ago for the SR we feel a little hesitant about asking him to write the piece. We have also talked a little about Matthiessen.[8] Have you any suggestions?

How is North Carolina? I saw Vance[9] a few weeks ago when he was here and he reported that he had seen you all just before he left NC. Don[ald Davidson] writes me that [W. T.] Couch has been making ingratiating gestures in the direction of the agrarians, chiefly to you and to him. But we received a cordial note the other day—much to our surprise, after some sharp words about an article of his which was turned down last year, the article he read at Nashville.

By the way, wasn't Lyle's piece on *Class and Caste* a stem-winder? In the summer issue, Don has a review of Caldwell's picture book. It's one of the sharpest pieces of writing Don has ever done. Did you see Couch's review of it in the VQ?[10] A very good review, I felt. Don interprets that as [a] gesture in the agrarian direction. And I guess it is.

What's the news with Andrew? I haven't had any for some time. As much my fault as his, however. And what do you hear from Manson [Radford]? You all probably saw him in NY. We had a note a time back, but it really didn't tell us how they are making out.

There's a lot more I'll want to say as soon as this is in the mails. This train is juggling so that it's almost impossible to type. (I am on my way back from the University of Oklahoma, where I gave the Phi Beta Kappa talk. I was there two days, and got practically no sleep, and can scarcely hold my head up now. And I've got six more hours to go before getting home.) But I suppose you can make out the sense of all this. Let me hear from you soon. With some account of how things are panning out in Greensboro.

> Our best to you all.
> As ever,
> Red

1. Tate must have declined. Although Warren mentions Tate's piece on Ransom and Wilson in several subsequent letters, the article never materialized.

2. Tate published no fiction in the *Southern Review*.

3. Scribner's had brought out Tate's *Reactionary Essays on Poetry and Ideas* in 1936; his next book of criticism, *Reason and Madness,* would be published by Putnam in 1941.

4. "The Reading of Modern Poetry," *Purpose* 10 (January–March 1938).

5. Houghton Mifflin.

6. *Modern Poetry and the Tradition* (1939).

7. "The Vision of William Butler Yeats."

8. F. O. Matthiessen of Harvard was already at work on his monumental *American Renaissance* (1941). He contributed with some regularity to the *Southern Review*, but the job of critiquing Tate's poetry at length fell to Delmore Schwartz (Winter 1940).

9. Rupert B. Vance, the Chapel Hill sociologist with a New South bent.

10. "Landlord and Tenant," *Virginia Quarterly Review* (Spring 1938).

In the summer of 1938, the Warrens broke with their usual custom. Rather than drive west across the continent, they sailed for Italy. Cinina's ancestral pride in her Italian heritage and personal and professional devotion to the country's language and culture were among her defining traits, but it was Warren who ultimately profited most from their stay abroad. He was, in the last analysis, no less American a writer than Whitman or Sandburg, and to be sure he was by training and temperament intimately connected with the British tradition from the sixteenth century on. But Italy, its landscape and literature, would increasingly play a formative role in his imagination.

TO ALBERT ERSKINE

TLS/Maryland

[Perugia, Italy]
[Summer 1938]

Dear Albert:

We took somewhat longer to reach Genoa than we had anticipated, because as it developed the ship had a twisted propeller as a result of backing into a mudbank at Tampa—the work of the Tampa pilot, we were told. We got to Genoa June 26, found John[1] already there—we spotted him on a bus, as a matter of fact, just after we got on, going to the shipping office to try to get word of us. That evening we went to Rapallo, just about twenty miles south down the coast, where John had been staying for several days. We had a fine evening there, a swim, a good meal, and comfortable beds, and scotch and soda and bourbon and water—the last the result of the kind offices of yourself. (A good hotel, fronting the bay, about thirty-five feet from the beach, a dinner and breakfast, etc., for $1.60.) The next day we spent in getting to Perugia, going through Pisa and Florence, but not stopping except to change trains. We got to Perugia last night, took a walk and went to bed. I was a little too done up to write last night. Perugia is absolutely on top of a very high hill, a magnificent spot, and the most completely medieval town in Italy, they say—and I am prepared to believe them—with the Etruscan walls and gates still standing. We know nothing yet about plans, except for a short conversation this morning with the lady at the government tourist agency. She says we can get a house on the lake or on the Tiber for $15.00 a month. Travelling terribly expense [sic], relatively and almost absolutely, especially when you have a lot of baggage (a high price for handling at every stop), and so we shall hole up as promptly as possible. I'll write as soon as there is anything definite. I've finished the revision of the novel except for two or three minor details. HM writes me that they are postponing publication until January, for the problem of promotion on such short notice is too great. (I gather that they didn't actually believe me when I told them the MS would be delivered in early July.)

John is in fine shape, hasn't got an English accent, has gained about fifteen pounds and grown about two inches, and sends his best to you and Cleanth.

I am looking forward to a communication from you and Cleanth, but I know that summer school and the summer issue have been bearing down. But will you ask Miss Barnett[2] to see that our bank statements for June 1, and for July 1, are forwarded promptly to us[?] And the story by Pasinetti,[3] with the comments and suggestions which you all may have for revision. Of course, if you all don't think the thing has enough life in it, that is another matter. And I look forward to receiving a big bundle of SR. MS soon.

And when you write, send me both the size and measurement in inches (length and width) of your foot, and ask Cleanth to do the same.

Cinina sends love to you and Katherine Anne. We shore [sic] wish you were with us. That's something we'll have to do at some not very distant date.

Affectionately,

Red

1. Palmer, who was abroad on his Rhodes Scholarship.

2. Bessie Barnett (Turpin), the first secretary of the *Southern Review*, who served from 1935 to 1939, when she moved to LSU Press.

3. Pier Maria Pasinetti, a young Italian graduate student at LSU who in time became a celebrated author in his own right. His story "Home-Coming" had run in the Spring 1937 number, and "Family History" would appear in Spring 1939. Warren would be instrumental in arranging for his reentry into the United States following World War II.

TO H. T. STUART

TLS/UChi

Poste restante

Perugia,

Italy

[Summer 1938]

Mr. H. T. Stuart
The Alcestis Press
174 West 4th Street
New York City

Dear Mr. Stuart:[1]

Your very kind letter reached me after considerable delay, and now, after a little further delay, I am able to answer it.

First, let me thank you heartily for the statement and the money order, and second let me thank you for the very generous offer concerning the unsold copies. I deeply regret that the Alcestis Press has burned its fingers by publishing my work—though I could have predicted it. Of course, I should be happy to have the copies and should undertake to provide you with any of them at any time, if call should come to you.

This is not the most propitious time, I imagine, to reopen the matter of another volume, which I mentioned to you last February. You very kindly replied at that time that the Alcestis Press might be interested. If, now that you know the worst about XXXVI POEMS, you still wish to have a shot at the other MS, I shall send a copy to you as soon as I'm back in Louisiana, that is, in September.

There is a chance that I shall be coming back by way of New York, arriving on the Rex about September 9 or 10. It would be a great pleasure to me to have a word with you and your colleagues.

I shall be in Italy and can be reached at the above address until August 25. Perhaps you will let me have a word from you before that time.

Very sincerely yours,
Robert Penn Warren

1. Apparently Latimer's assistant at Alcestis.

TO ALBERT ERSKINE

TLS/Maryland   [Perugia]
                                                            [July 1938]

Dear Albert:

There's not a great deal of news here, except that I'm getting anxious to hear from you all. First, how are the Erskines? Second, how are the Brooks? Third, how is the SR[?] Four, has any MS been sent to me and been lost? Five, have any leopards changed any spots lately[?] Etc.

I must say that the one piece of American news which we have had since reaching Perugia was sensational enough to satisfy the most thrill-jaded palate, Andrew's marriage.[1] That was one to the solar plexus after a Thanksgiving dinner.

Lately we've made several little excursions into the surrounding country. One to Assisi was the most satisfying. That, I must say, is quite a place. Their chamber of commerce, if they had one, couldn't do much to overstate the claims of that little city. And we've been to Lake Trasimene for a day of swimming, etc., and several times to a little town on the Tiber, five miles from here. But I am taking four hours of lessons a day, and have been trying to do some writing; so we haven't been entirely foot-loose. John is working on some poems. I am putting a copy of one he just finished into a letter to Cleanth. Take a look at it. I feel that he's coming along pretty fast.

Have you all started the actual process on your house? How are the orchards? Has Katherine Anne finished her story yet? I hope so. Tell her to hurry and get it done and write another for us. Let us hear how things are with you all.

We shall probably leave Perugia in early August and go to Lake Garda for about three weeks. We think that we have an apartment waiting for us there, on the lake, with direct access to it for swimming, etc. At present we have a cook, a good one, and are quite comfortable. At Garda we'll probably only have one meal in the apartment, for the time will be too short to make it worthwhile setting up the mechanics. We'll probably sail about September 1, but we shan't know definitely until another week is up.

Cinina sends love to you all. And so do I.

As ever,
Red

P.S. Thanks for the items forwarded from the review, the bank statement, etc. I'll be enormously grateful if you'll find out about August 2, if Cinina's check for $100.00 has been deposited along with mine ($225.00 should be the total amount deposited then, for the rest of my check is made over to the bank as a salary assignment). The request for Cinina's salary to be put on a twelve-month basis was approved by the President's office, and so if there's any slip a word there ought to fix matters up. And, my friend, it would be a word well spoken, too.

[Typed at top of page] P.S. Don't forget the foot measurements.

1. Lytle had married Edna Langdon Barker in June.

TO ALLEN TATE

TLS/PU

Poste restante
Perugia,
Italy
[July 1938]

[Warren's note] This will serve for the duration of our stay in Italy.

Dear Allen:

I should have written you a few days ago that Houghton Mifflin has decided to postpone publication of NIGHT RIDER until January. They say that fall wouldn't give them enough time for promotion. The delay, as a matter of fact, will give me an opportunity to do a little last-minute retouching. I sent the MS to them about a week or so ago. I am not waiving my request for you to read the proof. I shall be tremendously grateful if you all will do so (for general criticism, as I said, and not for typographical errors), for that will give me a chance to take advantage of your suggestions. I am a lot up in the air about the thing now, as it cools off. I just don't know whether it's any good or not.

Your novel must be about done by this time. When does it appear? And if it doesn't get to press until September, I'll be mighty glad to do proofreading on it, if that will be of any use to you.

We have been settled here for more than two weeks now. It is a fine place, really, I am sure, one of the most beautiful in the world. The Vanucci gallery, a very good one, is here, and Assisi is in the neighborhood. We've made one trip to Assisi. Palmer and I walked over, and Cinina went on the train. There's a strong probability that we'll go back a time or two more before we leave this neighborhood. At present we are planning to go to Lake Garda early in August for three weeks or so. We shall sail about the end of August or early in September.

I'm getting a certain amount of writing done and a lot of studying. A long poem, book length, is moving now[1]—in what direction I can't be too sure—and I'm trying to get the plans worked out in some detail for another novel.[2] But it promises to be so long, much longer than NIGHT RIDER, which runs about 160,000 words, that I shudder at the thought of settling down to the grind of it. In any case, I shan't start actual writing until the poem is finished or abandoned.

An announcement came a few days ago of Andrew's marriage. At last. But it rocked me on my heels, and I'm still a little punch-drunk.

I haven't had any news since June 26th, when we reached Genoa and picked up the mail there. Let me have a letter when you can. How are things going in Connecticut?[3] Are you down yet at the criticism book?[4] How are the Indians coming?[5] Etc.

> Our best to you all.
> As ever,
> Red

1. Possibly an early version of the verse play *Proud Flesh,* which Warren would later say had been colored by his observations in Mussolini's Italy.
2. Most likely *At Heaven's Gate* (1943), with its Dantean echoes.
3. The Tates were summering in West Cornwall.
4. Tate's *Reason and Madness: Critical Essays* (1941).
5. Gordon was at work on her frontier novel, *Green Centuries* (1941).

TO ANDREW LYTLE

TLS/VU   Venice
                                                             August 23, 1938

Dear Andrew:

It is great news. Our warmest wishes to you for all kinds of happiness. When did it happen, where, and a dozen other questions? John Palmer joins us in congratulations and felicitations and all appropriate sentiments.

I am anxious for further news from you all, and hope to find a letter waiting for me in Baton Rouge when I get back. How is the book coming?[1] When will you be able to begin actual composition? How long a book are you planning? Is it a biography or a novel? Etc. Let me have a little salve for my very considerable curiosity. And how is Hollywood?[2]

We up and tore out for Europe on less than a week's notice, catching a freighter out of Savannah, after a bus ride of a day and a night. And a freighter is certainly the way to come, much more comfortable and with better food than I have found in my inadequate experience with tourist class on other boats. We had two large cabins and a bath shared only with the captain. We had our meals with the captain and chief engineer. It is a perfect arrangement if you have to do a little work during the trip [Handwritten in margin] no other passengers [Typing resumes]—as I had to, for the novel required a lot of retouching. (And by the way, do you know Savannah? It is a grand place, with first rate food, an easy rival to New Orleans in that respect.) In Genoa we met John Palmer, Albert's room-mate whom you may recall, and then proceeded to Perugia, where we stayed a month, having part of that time in a villa with a magnificent garden and a view of Assisi and part in an apartment in town. Sin[c]e we set up house-keeping, our living expenses were mighty near to nothing, and Perugia is, according to all reports, the finest example of a mediaeval town anywhere. I'm prepared to believe it, and to say that there is probably no city anywhere more beautiful—on the very top of a mountain. We took a few days in Rome visiting some distant cousins of Cinina; they made the trip to Rome, for they know the city cold and are fine company. Then a three-week stay at Sirmione on Lake Garda—which is up to all expectations—and now in Venice where we are staying with Pier Pasinetti,[3] the young man who was at LSU and who had a story and will have another in the SR. His hospitality is unexcelled and Venice is entirely to my satisfaction—so thus far the trip has been a first-rate success. I cross my fingers when I say this, as one always should. We sail in a day or two now, from Genoa.

As for work, I've managed to get a smattering of Italian, working at it several hours a day while in Perugia, but less after, and I've managed to write a good deal of verse, part of a long poem, book-length, which I hope to have finished by next summer. The novel has been in the hands of the publishers since middle July. They are not bringing it out until January or a little later, though they had originally scheduled it for November. That is probably just as well, for now I can do a little more tinkering in the proof. I wish that I could get you to do a reading on the proof, for the thing in general (the story, etc.) and for the dialect and dialogue in particular.

I've about exhausted my supply of news, all of which pales into insignificance beside your own. In regard to that news, again our very best wishes! Let us hear from you all.

As ever,
Red

1. *At the Moon's Inn* (1941).

2. Lytle had gone to California earlier under the sponsorship of his close friend, the screenwriter George Haight, and returned there for a few months following his marriage.

3. Pasinetti was the son of a distinguished Venetian family.

Back from Europe and having resumed his duties at LSU, Warren immediately made plans to return to Italy for an extended stay, all the while balancing his own writing with classroom and editorial responsibilities.

TO ALLEN TATE

TLS/PU   [Baton Rouge]
                                                    [Fall 1938][1]

Dear Allen:

The other day, a week or so back now, the letter you wrote me from Connecticut to Perugia finally caught up with me, along with a lot of other mail that had been forwarded from Perugia to Sirmione to Venice, and from Venice to Genoa. Which accounts for my expression of astonishment when I saw you at the dock.[2]

We got back here without mishap and are now settled in our place in the country. It is proving more pleasant than we had anticipated, even, despite the domestic set-back of Mayme's going home for a couple of weeks to be with her mother, who was very sick.[3] I suppose you all, too, are now trying to get the harness to sit comfortably again on the old calluses. Mine isn't quite easy yet.

I haven't had time yet to tinker much with the play [*Proud Flesh*], but I shall get a copy off to you within the next few days. On my return here I got sidetracked on a short story which is now finished for better or for worse, but, I fear, for the latter. Aside from that, the class work, and the SR, things have been as usual.

By the way, Van Doren is also applying for a Guggenheim, and so can't stand as a reference for my application.[4] So that leaves my former references with the addition of two new ones. K. A. [Porter] and Zabel. I suppose that you will get a request from the Foundation, but—and I say this because, you remember, that in 1935 they did not write you—will you give them a letter even if they do not write you[?] That is, after you've had a chance to read the novel and the other stuff? I'll be, as ever, deeply obliged. Maybe it'll work out this time. I certainly hope so, for with a free year, I believe I could get something accomplished. Certainly, the last two free summers have been fine.

Cleanth is reworking part of his book, and is planning, I believe, on making certain enlargements. I have recently been reading the thing consecutively for the first time. I'm mighty impressed with the thing. We haven't yet been able to get to the table of contents for the Scribners text book, but will have one to you before very long. And we'll expect yours.[5]

The two girls from the Wom[e]n's College are here, and look promising. The Arnett girl[6] is helping on the SR. An enthusiastic proof reader, that pearl above price.

(And in connection with the SR, don't forget your piece on Ransom and [Edmund] Wilson for the winter issue. And in connection with Ransom: I've just had a letter from him asking me to do a review for the first issue[7]—which I can't do if I'm to do the MLA paper.)[8]

I don't suppose the W[omen]'s College has a football team. But LSU may have one this year. We lost the first game to Mississippi, God knows how, but came back with something that looks like a bone-crusher last Saturday, making mincemeat of Texas. But it's too early to tell much yet. The Vanderbilt game, by the way, is here this year. I'll treat myself to that one anyway.

At the moment, no news of great moment comes to mind.

Our best to you both.

As ever,
Red

[Handwritten P.S.] The Atlantic *almost* serialized *Night Rider,* but the publication date got underfoot—*too bad.* That would have been nice financially.

1. Tate's notation.

2. The Tates had come down from Connecticut to meet the Warrens on their return.

3. The Warrens' servant Mayme Welch had accompanied them from Tennessee to Louisiana three years before. In the Cinina Warren papers at Emory University there

is a letter from her reporting on her mother's condition and thanking the Warrens for their generosity and support.

4. Warren wanted a Guggenheim fellowship to return to Italy the following year. The application was successful.

5. A confusing reference, but it may be that Brooks had now joined Warren and Tate in their longstanding (but ultimately abortive) plans to bring out an anthology of modern verse for Scribner's. See Alphonse Vinh's *Cleanth Brooks and Allen Tate: Collected Letters, 1933–1976* (p. 28).

6. Georgianna Arnett (Bonds), a newly arrived graduate student assigned to the *Review* who would eventually write her M.A. thesis on Ransom, Tate, and Warren.

7. After much controversy, John Crowe Ransom had left Vanderbilt and the South for Kenyon College in Ohio, where he founded the *Kenyon Review.*

8. Warren's paper for the 1938 meeting of the Modern Language Association was "Tradition and Environment: A Restatement."

TO ALLEN TATE

TLS/PU   [Baton Rouge]
                                                          [Fall 1938][1]

Dear Allen:

I've just read *The Fathers* for the second time. On the train, coming down, I read it, but the circumstances weren't the most favorable. Now, I'm even more sure than I was then that it is a damned fine book. And it's a very exciting book. The handling of the suspense, and the narrative thrust, are extremely effective. I still feel that a few little bits of the earlier part aren't quite up to the rest of the book—especially the stuff just at the tournament—the political speech, etc. But my objections there are very mild, much milder even now than they were when I read the MS last year. One thing is clear on almost every page—there's a really enormous skill in just the matter of putting the thing on paper.

How is the thing going? Is the promise of sales holding up? I haven't seen any reviews yet, except the one in the New Yorker, by Fadiman, I suppose.[2] You must have seen it, but in case you didn't, it was extremely favorable, concluding with this: "A fine novel by a fine poet." Which sounds like a slogan—and is the sort of remark, I imagine, that publishers love to put on jackets and in advertising.

There are no new developments here since my note of the other day. Have you read Herbert's new book?[3] If so, what do you think of it? I haven't had a chance at it yet, but am planning on this week end.

Let me hear from you soon.

Love,
Red

1. Tate's notation.

2. The unsigned review in the *New Yorker* (October 1938) may or may not have been the work of the prominent critic Clifton Fadiman, the magazine's literary editor.

3. Herbert Agar's *Pursuit of Happiness: The Story of American Democracy* (1938).

TO FRANK LAWRENCE OWSLEY

TLS/VU

The Southern Review
Louisiana State University
Baton Rouge,
Louisiana
[Fall 1938]

Dear Frank:

A long overdue letter: but you mustn't believe that the poverty of this correspondence is any index to the number of times you enter the thoughts of your humble correspondent. That number is very large.

Our summer was, on the whole, an eminently satisfactory one, certainly the most pleasant one we've had in a long time. We didn't travel about much, spending a month at Perugia, three days at Rome, three weeks at Sirmione at Lake Garda, and about ten days at Venice. We both worked pretty hard, for Cinina was taking some work at the University for a month, and I was studying Italian some four or five hours a day. I also got a good running start on a long poem—which doesn't go to say that the poem's any good but that a good part of it is done. It'll be finished next May, I hope. Back here things jog along as usual. The SR had a lot of unfinished business accumulating during August, and the customary rush of the term-opening almost got us all down. We're about to simmer down to normal now, in the office at least, although Cleanth is putting the finishing touches on his book on poetry and the Warrens are trying to settle into a new house in the brush.[1]

As for the house, it's tiny, a living room, bedroom (10 by 12), bath, and kitchen. But, anyway, we aren't paying rent and we're where we have all the privacy we want. We're enjoying the place very much, even if we're doing most of the work about it ourselves, or perhaps because of that fact. You must come down soon and see us, and even take a few whacks with a brush hook yourself or do a little spading, while Harriet advises Cinina on domestic problems. (I forgot to say in describing the place, that we can, and hope to, accom[m]odate guests—or rather, certain guests.)

A little business: can we get you to do an essay-review of J. Daniels' *A Southerner Looks at the South* [*sic*]? For our winter issue, if convenient, or for spring.[2] We had been thinking about another piece for you, if you would consent to do it, but this seems to have a little more life in it. Or perhaps you have something else in mind you could do for a near issue. Of course, we still want the essay that would interpret your research of the past several years. Let us have a word about your feelings on these matters. And better, some actual work for the SR in the very near future.

There's a bare chance we'll get to Nashville before the year is out, perhaps in February between terms. Christmas will probably find us in New York, for I have a paper at the Modern Language Association and think that the university will stand me the trip. We're awfully anxious to see the Owsleys we knew, and anxious to see the new Owsley.[3] Meanwhile, our love all around.

Let us hear from you all. And pass on any local news.

As ever,
Red

[Handwritten] P.S. Forgive this vile typewriter!

1. The house off the Old Hammond Highway Warren put together with the help of an "unemployed carpenter."
2. Owsley's review of Jonathan Daniels' *A Southerner Discovers the South* would run in the Spring 1939 issue.
3. The Owsleys' daughter Margaret, born the previous March.

TO GEORGE MARION O'DONNELL

TLS/WashU

The Southern Review
Louisiana State University
Baton Rouge,
Louisiana
Sept. 15, 1938

Mr. George Marion O'Donnell
129 Church St.
Belzoni, Miss.

Dear O'Donnell:

It just looks like we can't get together. As for the story our reactions are something like this: there is a lot of good writing in it paragraph by paragraph, but we just don't like the story as a story. The poems raise a more complicated issue. If your book were not coming out,[1] we should probably be disposed to discuss the matter of a group at some time in the future, with one or two of these as a nucleus. But since the book is coming out this winter, it seems to be useless to discuss this matter now. But we are anxious to have a shot at the next poems that you do.[2]

I hope that everything is going well with you, and that this year you will be able to come by to see us.

With warmest regards,
Robert Penn Warren

1. The National Union Catalog lists no such book.
2. None of O'Donnell's subsequent work appeared in the *Southern Review*.

TO EUDORA WELTY

TLS/MissA

The Southern Review
Louisiana State University
Baton Rouge,
Louisiana
Sept. 28, 1938

Miss Eudora Welty
1119 Pinehurst St.
Jackson, Miss.

Dear Miss Welty:

We are very much interested in "A Curtain of Green," but want to have the revision which you mentioned in your letter of August 16, before making a final decision. Can you get this to us by return air mail? Haste is necessary here, because we are considering using it in our Fall issue.[1] Also, have you a copy of "The Petrified Man" to send along with it? "Keela"[2] interests us a lot, but we can't quite see it as a story. If you have anything else on hand, please send it along, too.

I am disappointed—and surprised—that nothing more came out of the Houghton Mifflin business. But if it isn't that, it will be something else, and soon.

Very sincerely yours,
Robert Penn Warren

1. The story did indeed appear in the Autumn 1938 number.
2. Welty's story "Keela, the Outcast Indian Maiden."

TO MERRILL MOORE

TLS/LC

The Southern Review
Louisiana State University
Baton Rouge,
Louisiana
Oct. 7, 1938

Dr. Merrill Moore
384 Commonwealth Ave.
Boston, Mass.

Dear Merrill:

I was away all summer, and the present batch of your poems was among the things left over for conversation this fall. I feel—and the others are in agreement with me on this—that this batch is well under your best level. But how about making up another batch some time?

The news about the Harcourt, Brace volume[1] is extremely interesting. I am looking forward with the greatest pleasure to getting my hands on it. When is it scheduled for publication?

Please give my regards to Ann Leslie.[2]

As ever,
Red

P.S. Are you by any chance going to be in New York around Christmas?

1. Moore's *M: One Thousand Autobiographical Sonnets.*
2. Moore's wife.

TO JO SINCLAIR

TLS/BU

The Southern Review
Louisiana State University
Baton Rouge,
Louisiana
Oct. 27, 1938

Miss Jo Sinclair
3386 East 145
Cleveland, Ohio

Dear Miss Sinclair:[1]

"The First Clean Grief" is a close call with us. We'll be very glad to see some other pieces.

Very sincerely yours,
Robert Penn Warren

1. Jo Sinclair was the pen name of the Jewish American novelist Ruth Seid. Though Brooks and Warren did not print any of her stories, she valued the encouragement they provided at the start of her career.

TO ALLEN TATE

TLS/PU

[Baton Rouge]
[Fall 1938][1]

Dear Allen:

I'm sorry about the boils. It sounds pretty damned uncomfortable. But even with boils you ought to have some comfort in the way the novel seems to be going. The Baton Rouge book stores have big dummies in cardboard in the windows and nice little stacks of books. And people are talking a lot about it. I am enclosing two clippings which you may not have seen—the sort of review, I imagine, which really sells books.

About the Guggenheim recommendation: I was wanting you to read the novel proofs as a preliminary to the recommendation, except [sic] in so far as concrete references to new work might keep your remarks from looking like a mere rehash of your previous ones. The same goes for the two scenes of the play which I shall send in a few days. (I'm still tinkering with the first part, but I am getting on into the third scene, too. But I want you to read the first two scenes as soon as I can get them into some sort of shape.) I am taking your advice and not submitting any part of a work in progress. For the project I simply say that I am doing some preliminary work on a novel—which is true—and hope to be at the actual composition in early summer. With luck, I shall finish the play by that time, for the place where we are living now is proving to be ideal for work—real quiet and no casual callers. Moe² suggested that I merely bring my old application up to date by a supplement of publications and additional references, if any. I simply added Katherine Anne and Zabel, leaving you and Caroline, John Ransom, etc. standing on the old application. If you have no word from Moe, I'd like to know—unless of course you write before he has a chance to write you—for I want to have a line as to whether he actually consults the references. You recall that he didn't consult you in 1935 when I last applied.

Have you definitely deci[d]ed about the New York Christmas?³ Will your college come across, or do you know yet? It seems that LSU will put up the money, all right, but I can't be absolutely positive quite yet.

Our new issue will be out in a few days. It looks pretty good, especially on the critical side. How about your piece on John [Ransom] and [Edmund] Wilson for Christmas? Will you be able to do it?

What's the news in the other department in your household? Our best all around.

As ever,
Red

1. Tate's notation.
2. Henry Allen Moe of the Guggenheim Foundation.
3. The Modern Language Association was meeting in New York.

TO MORTON DAUWEN ZABEL

TLS/Newb

The Southern Review
Louisiana State University
Baton Rouge,
Louisiana
[Fall 1938]

Dear Zabel:

I want to ask a favor of you. Though I have not yet definitely made up my mind, I am thinking about applying for a Guggenheim. I want to know whether you would be willing to sponsor the application. I am encouraged to ask you because of your very kind review of my poems in POETRY,[1] but I want to warn you of the amount of reading that would be entailed by you[r] granting of my request. There is a novel (which doesn't get published until January or February, but which I can get to you in proof sheets early this fall) and some scenes from a play (in manuscript). The play is a mixture of verse and prose—but I'll give you a synopsis and description in addition to the finished parts, if I hear favorably from you.

I know that you have not been in the best of health, and I don't want to burden you with this reading if you don't feel up to it. Furthermore, I don't want you to do this if you are already committed to support another application or if you feel that the case isn't worthy of your support.

I hope that your summer has been a good one, and a productive one. If it has been productive, please remember the SR.

With thanks and best
regards,
Robert Penn Warren

1. Zabel's "Problems of Knowledge" (*Poetry* [April 1936]) is an early classic in Warren criticism.

TO JO SINCLAIR

TLS/BU

The Southern Review
Louisiana State University
Baton Rouge,
Louisiana
Dec. 5, 1938

Miss Jo Sinclair:

Although we are interested in your writing, we cannot use the present piece. But please do not forget us when you send manuscript out again.

Very sincerely yours,
Robert Penn Warren

TO DONALD DAVIDSON

TLS/VU

The Southern Review
Louisiana State University
Baton Rouge,
Louisiana
Dec. 6, 1938

Dear Don:

Please do not believe that my delay in thanking you for the copy of the poems[1] is any indication of the [*sic*] lack of appreciation. It's simply that I have been snowed under even a little more than usual, for I have had the proofs of my novel on hand for the last several weeks. The poems have given me a great deal of real pleasure. I particularly like "The Horde" and "Aunt Maria and the Gourds" among the new pieces. You already know what I think of the section from *The Tall Men*. "Lee in the Mountains," I may say, couldn't be better. It's a great poem. On the other side of the ledger, honesty compels me to remark that "The Running of Streight" rings no bells. I don't believe that that kind of material can be presented directly without falling into unfortunate comparison with the resources possible to the prose writer. A novelist or historia[n] could never do what is done in "Lee and the Mountains," but it seems to me that a novelist or historian has the jump when it comes to treating Streight right.

I wrote to Miss Enid Morgan and suggested that she apply for a graduate fellowship here. She has replied that she is considering this course and will probably do so. I feel fairly confident that she will be able to get one. I certainly hope so.

It is almost certain that I shall be in Nashville during Christmas vacation for a couple of days on my way to the Modern Language Association. Are you going to be there? I devoutly hope so, for we are behind on our conversation.

Cinina joins me in warmest regards to Mary and Theresa.

As ever,
Red

1. Davidson's *Lee in the Mountains and Other Poems* (1938).

Warren at LSU, ca. 1935

Source: The "Southern Review," Original Series, 1935–1942: A Commemoration; *courtesy LSU University Relations*

Cinina Warren (second from right, back row) and members of her
beloved Italian Club at LSU

Source: Gumbo, *1936 (detail); courtesy Charles East*

The Campanile, heart of the LSU campus.
The North Administration (Thomas D. Boyd) Building at far right
housed the offices of the *Southern Review.*

Courtesy Charles East

Allen Tate at Benfolly, his home in Clarksville, Tennessee, ca. 1937

Papers of Katherine Anne Porter, Special Collections,
University of Maryland Libraries

Andrew Lytle at Benfolly, ca. 1937

Papers of Katherine Anne Porter, Special Collections,
University of Maryland Libraries

Warren and T. S. Stribling

Source: LSU Alumni News, *April 1937; courtesy*
LSU University Relations and Charles East

Albert Erskine in Baton Rouge, 1938

Papers of Katherine Anne Porter, Special Collections, University of Maryland Libraries

Caroline Gordon, Allen Tate, and their daughter Nancy
in Greensboro, North Carolina, 1939

Papers of Katherine Anne Porter, Special Collections, University of Maryland Libraries

"Red" Warren the year *Night Rider* was published

Source: LSU Alumni News, *February 1939; courtesy Charles East*

Charles W. Pipkin

Courtesy LSU University Relations and Charles East

Cleanth Brooks in the 1940s

Courtesy Cleanth Brooks's estate

1939

The early months of 1939 would hold good news for the Warrens. After frantic last-minute adjustments, Night Rider *would finally appear, and word soon followed that Warren's application for a Guggenheim had been funded. But there would be sad news as well. Even as she convalesced from surgery, Cinina would learn that her father, Domenico Brescia, had died unexpectedly in California.*

TO ALLEN TATE

TLU/PU   [Baton Rouge]
                                                  [Early January 1939][1]

Dear Allen:

At last I have time to write more in detail in answer to your letter about the novel.[2] But first, I'll say again how glad I am that you all liked it and felt that it hadn't entirely missed the boat. I had some pretty black moments in the course of writing the last half, and then after the thing was done. Now I'm just putting the thing from mind and am back at the play.

As I wrote you in my last hurried note, HM sent the thing back to me with a request for some cutting. The BMC had turned the thing down on the grounds that it needed cutting by considerable "chunks." The HM sales department was of the same opinion. And Linscott[3] himself agreed. He made some suggested cuts, amounting to about 30,000 words in all. I put in most of my time before Christmas on the thing and a few days after Christmas. I managed to cut 18,000 words. All in all, I feel that the cuts improved the novel. I used something over half of Linscott's suggested cuts and then made some cuts of my own. You, you recall, suggested a cut, or drastic reduction, of the Proudfit story; so did Linscott. With grave misgivings, I finally left the thing in, although I reduced it some. I had hoped that the thing would have some organic reference to the total meaning of the novel and would, really, make a contribution to the effect of the last chapter.[4] I'll try to say what I had hoped would come across. First, the thing you mentioned, the exhausting, on psychological grounds, of the possibility of going West, etc. Second, the reference, almost as in terms of oblique fable, of the "ghost dance" to the night-riding, a kind of dancing of the buffalo back by the ritual—outmoded, too—of personal violence. Third, the reference to Munn's private situation in general. This may be stated along these lines: Proudfit is a man who has been able to pass beyond his period of "slaughter" into a state of self knowledge. If he is not at home in the world, practically (losing his place, etc.), he is at least at home with himself, has had his vision. It is an incommunicable vision, and is no solution for anyone but himself. He is, in a way, a foil for Munn, who has tried to embrace his vision by violence (discovery of humanity leading him into the act, murder, which is the cancellation of humanity, the act which defines isolation). But more specifically, as the tale relates to Munn's decision: Munn feels, as it were, that though he cannot achieve the vision, he can, perhaps, by a last act of violence, inject some rationality into his experience, he can round it out in terms that on mechanical grounds at least would be comprehensible—that is, by committing his murder, he can in a way justify his present situation, for he is on the run for a murder he did not commit and the murder of the Senator would be the first completely personal and private murder for him. Fourth, the Indian business, obliquely again, implies the tribal loyalties, the conflict within the tribe (Lone Wolf and Mamanti against the idea of Kicking Bird, who would grasp the white man's hand and not beat his head on a stone, etc.); all of this has some extensions into the situation among the people involved in the tobacco troubles. This stuff—all of these points—may be mistakenly developed in the novel, but this may indicate some of the reasons why I felt I had to keep the section. But I did write in, in the last chapter when Munn goes up to the bluff for the last day, a clue for his own basic relation to Proudfit's narrative. I hope it will do something to tie the thing together.

I took your advice about Sukie's narrative, reducing that to an almost casual reference to the riding instructor, and cutting out all reference to the doctors, etc. This, I feel, was a very decided improvement, for I have never been very happy in my own mind about the scene. I also cut such purely secondary scenes as that of the sheriff who found the note on his own post oak, and the scenes with the old negro and the sheriff.

I spent a day in Boston, most of the time with Linscott, who impressed me very considerably. I have the feeling that he knows what he is about. Besides, he is an awfully pleasant man. The only concrete fact coming out of the talks, however, is this: the sales department doesn't know what audience to go after, adventure readers or "high brow"—the choice lying apparently between those groups, other groups not coming into the picture at all.

At this point I had to knock off, and now, as you see, I'm starting on another typewriter.

I had a pretty good time in NY, especially at a lunch with Burke.[5] He seems to be a fine fellow, and God knows, he's sharp. I wish that I could see more of him. I saw Rosenfeld,[6] Cowley, Zabel, Spencer, Dixon [Wecter], and one or two other people, but no one for long. I was only in NY a little over two days, and I had several meetings to attend, and some work on my MS still hanging over me. Spencer's paper was interesting, but the other two papers on my program were pretty dull.[7] I'm afraid mine was dull, too, but I'd like to send it to you for a glance, if you care to see it. It's not that the paper itself is much—it's that I'm interested in your reaction to one or two of the things I used as illustrations, a comparison of the *Wasteland* [*sic*] and the *Ancient Mariner*,[8] for instance.

The visit with John [Ransom] was fine. He seems to be in good shape—better than I've seen him in some years. But he doesn't really seem to feel settled there. While I was there, your letter about the Kenyon Review came, and John read it to me. It is in substantial agreement with my own reactions, except on the point of the Auden piece.[9] I think that [Delmore] Schwartz has a pretty sound analysis—which might be better without the Freudian stuff. I'd like to hear you at more length on this.

Today, we just remembered that Hardy's birth was in 1840. We are talking about an issue of the SR devoted to analyses and assessments of his work, say by fifteen American and English writers.[10] Not tributes, but critical articles. What do you think? And would you be interested in doing a piece? Deadline January 1, 1940. Meanwhile, what about that piece on [Edmund] Wilson and John?

There's been another lapse here. I've had a wire from HM asking me to get a statement from you about the novel, if possible. I didn't send Linscott your letter even though you suggested it, because I felt that the long-standing personal relationship would adversely affect the use of the thing for publicity purposes, even in the minds of the HM people. But I did tell Linscott about your criticism, some of which agreed with his own, and he asked me how you feel about the thing as a whole. I the[n] told him about your suggestion. He asked me to send him the letter, and then I couldn't find the damned thing. So could you knock off a few sentences for it and send them on directly to him? He says that haste is imperative.

Don't forget to let me have your reaction to the idea of the Hardy issue. And word about your other essay.

Again, many thanks for the letters on the novel, yours and Caroline's.

Best wishes for 1939!

P.S. How is Andrew getting on?

1. Tate's bracketed notation ("Late 1938") is clearly inaccurate.
2. *Night Rider.*
3. Robert N. Linscott, Warren's editor at Houghton Mifflin, and later an editor at Random House.
4. Most readers of *Night Rider* will agree that Warren's decision to retain the self-contained narrative of Willie Proudfit contributed much to the novel's success.
5. Kenneth Burke, who greatly admired *Night Rider.*
6. Paul Rosenfeld, who as one of the editors of the *American Caravan* series had published Warren's earliest fiction.
7. Theodore Spencer's paper for Warren's panel at the Modern Language Association meeting was "Tradition and T. S. Eliot"; the other papers were Willis Wager's "The American Background of T. S. Eliot" and J. B. Harrison's "Robert Frost and Contemporary America."
8. James Justus and other Warren critics have long noted the centrality of Coleridge's text to the Warren canon.

9. Delmore Schwartz's essay "The Two Audens" had appeared in the inaugural issue of Ransom's *Kenyon Review* (Winter 1939).

10. The Thomas Hardy issue (Summer 1940) would feature pieces by Ransom, Blackmur, Baker, Schwartz, Auden, F. R. Leavis, Tate, Bonamy Dobree, Zabel, Porter, Davidson, Jacques Barzun, Arthur Mizener, and Muller.

TO MERRILL MOORE

TLS/LC

The Southern Review
Louisiana State University
Baton Rouge,
Louisiana
Jan. 9, 1939

Dr. Merrill Moore
384 Commonwealth Ave.
Boston, Mass.

Dear Merrill:

It was fine to see you, even for that few minutes. Perhaps some day, not too far off, I shall be in Boston for a real visit.

About the sonnets we have had: it's our feeling that only one in the present group, "Dark Dying Faces," approaches your best work. But perhaps you'll give us a reading on another batch some time soon? We shop [*sic*] so.[1]

Again, my best thanks for *M*. You are right, it will take more than a weekend to read it.

Sincerely,
Red

1. None of Moore's poetry appeared in the *Southern Review*.

TO JOSEPHINE MILES

TLS/UCal

The Southern Review
Louisiana State University
Baton Rouge,
Louisiana
Jan. 10, 1939

Miss Josephine Miles
1140 Keniston
Los Angeles, Calif.

Dear Miss Miles:

We are holding the following poems for publication: "Hospice," "Sound Track," "Prospectus," "Equinox," "Corinthian," "Joshua," "Now That April's There," and "Solo." That is, if you will let THE SOUTHERN REVIEW have them. This group could be published in our Spring or Summer issue, but more probably in our Summer issue. Meanwhile, if you have any other poems on hand we should like to have a look at them with the idea of possibly adding one or two or perhaps of making a substitution since one of the poems, "Prospectus," seems definitely inferior to the others.[1]

We do hope that this arrangement meets with your approval and that you will in the future let us see much of your work.

Very sincerely yours,
Robert Penn Warren

1. Miles's poems, minus "Joshua" and "Solo," were published in the Winter 1940 issue.

TO W. S. CAMPBELL (STANLEY VESTAL)

TLS/UOk

The Southern Review
Louisiana State University
Baton Rouge,
Louisiana
Jan. 12, 1939

Mr. W. S. Campbell
University of Oklahoma
Norman, Okla.

Dear Mr. Campbell:

Lord knows how it happened, but this morning for the first time I have seen the note you sent me about the Willie Proudfit chapter of my novel. I don't know how the slip happened, but somehow it got sidetracked in the office. I do wish that I had been able to make the corrections you suggest.[1] But sad to say it's too late now, for the book is on the press, the last proofs having been turned in at Christmas. But I am encouraged to know that you didn't find too many holes in the chapter. And I hope you will find the book readable. I'll see that you get a copy as soon as any are available.

I hope that our paths will cross soon.

Very sincerely yours,
Robert Penn Warren

1. Campbell, under his pseudonym Stanley Vestal, had published on the mountain men and on the ghost dance among Plains Indian tribes, an important element in the Willie Proudfit story.

TO JOHN BERRYMAN

TLS/Minn

The Southern Review
Louisiana State University
Baton Rouge,
Louisiana
Jan. 13, 1939

Mr. John Berryman
41 Park Ave.
New York City

Dear Mr. Berryman:

At last—and with sincere regret for our long delay—here is a decision on the poems. We should like very much to add "The Translation" (or "Myth") and the second song from *Cleopatra* ("From Pharos I have seen her white") to "Film," which we already had. Also, we are greatly interested in "Meditation," but we have not been able to make up our minds to take it as it stands, despite our very great admiration for most of the poem. Perhaps you might be interested to know our objections to it as it now stands. The first five stanzas please us greatly, but the sixth stanza, which does not seem to advance the poem, reads almost too much like an echo from Yeats. The last line of the eighth stanza raises the same question for us. But the ninth, we believe, doesn't really bring the prom [*sic*] to focus. We do not have, of course, any specific suggestions to make for revision of the poem. That would, indeed, be a piece of presumption. But we do hope that if you ever find it necessary to do any more work on "Meditation," you will let us have another reading on it. Meanwhile, we are very anxious to see more of your poems so that we can fill out another and, we hope, a larger group.[1]

Very sincerely yours,
Robert Penn Warren

1. "Meditation" would be among the "Five Poems" by Berryman in the Spring 1940 number.

TO C. A. MADISON

TLS/PU

The Southern Review
Louisiana State University
Baton Rouge,
Louisiana
Jan. 16, 1939

Mr. C. A. Madison
Henry Holt and Co.
257 Fourth Ave.
New York City

Dear Mr. Madison:

We wish to ask a great favor of you. Would it be possibly to get copies of the various letters written to you about *Understanding Poetry* and to get a list of adoptions up to date and of adoptions for the second term of this year in so far as they can now be determined[?] We shall, of course, be very happy to pay for the clerical work involved in this matter. And, in addition, may we have a little packet of the green folders which you prepared for the book? I think we can find some use for them.

I greatly enjoyed my conversation with you, and I hope it will not be long until we can have another. Please give my very warm regards to Mr. Wilson and tell him we hope to see him here this spring.

Very sincerely yours,
Robert Penn Warren

TO LIONEL TRILLING

TLS/Col

The Southern Review
Louisiana State University
Baton Rouge,
Louisiana
Jan. 25, 1939

Mr. Lionel Trilling[1]
c/o W. W. Norton and Co.
70 Fifth Ave.
New York City

Dear Mr. Trilling:[1]

I have just finished reading your book on Arnold, and want to tell you how much I admire it. I hope to be able to communicate something of my admiration to others, for I am now doing a review of it.[2]

Can we interest you in doing an essay-review for THE SOUTHERN REVIEW of the following books: *Victorian Critics of Democracy,* by Benjamin E. Lippincott, and *Lord Macaulay,* by Richmond Croom Beatty?[3]

Or perhaps you have something else in mind which would interest you more? But I do not offer this as an either-or proposition. Perhaps you will make us a suggestion in addition to the review we are requesting.

Our rate of payment is $1\frac{1}{2}$¢ a word for prose.

Very sincerely yours,
Robert Penn Warren

1. As a Columbia professor and (along with his wife, Diana) a quintessential "New York intellectual," Trilling represented a significant countertradition to the "new critical" stance of Brooks and Warren.

2. Warren's review of Trilling's *Matthew Arnold* ("Arnold vs. the 19th Century") was published in the Spring 1939 *Kenyon Review.*

3. Trilling's "The Victorians and Democracy" would be included in the Spring 1940 number.

TO LIONEL TRILLING

TLS/Col

The Southern Review
Louisiana State University
Baton Rouge,
Louisiana
Feb. 7, 1939

Mr. Lionel Trilling
620 W. 116 St.
New York City

Dear Mr. Trilling:

Even though you have done a review of the Lippincott book, *Victorian Critics of Democracy*, perhaps you can find another approach to the book and could treat it with Beatty's book on Lord Macaulay. Will that work out for you? If so, please proceed with the review, say, at a length of about 2500 to 3000 words. In any case, will you do the piece on the Macaulay book? We are sending it to you immediately. If you can think of any other related book which might profitably be treated at the same time, please go ahead with it.

Very sincerely yours,
Robert Penn Warren

TO JOHN BERRYMAN

TLS/Minn

The Southern Review
Louisiana State University
Baton Rouge,
Louisiana
Feb. 7, 1939

Mr. John Berryman
41 Park Ave.
New York City

Dear Mr. Berryman:

We are sorry to have to strike out "The Translation" for publication. That leaves us with "Film," and "From Pharos I have seen her white." And we are sorry to say that we do not feel that we can use any of the present batch of poems. We do like "The Trial" best of all, but we don't think it's up to your best. Please let us see some others, for we are, as we have said before, anxious to have another and longer group by you.

Brooks and I were, of course, greatly pleased by your comment on *Understanding Poetry.*

Very sincerely yours,
Robert Penn Warren

WARREN AND BROOKS TO FRANK LAWRENCE OWSLEY

TLS/VU

The Southern Review
Louisiana State University
Baton Rouge,
Louisiana
Feb. 16, 1939

Mr. Frank L. Owsley
Vanderbilt University
Nashville, Tenn.

Dear Frank:

Your account of Daniels' book is excellent, in fact, one of the best pieces of writing that you have done. We admire in particular your pointing out what is the weakness of the book—Daniels' consistent vacillation between a sensible view of the South and a distorted view. It occurs to us, however, that the indictment might be pointed up even more perhaps by giving Daniels full credit for having seen the light in the places where he has—say in the chapter on Davidson [Handwritten in margin] and more especially toward the end of the book [Typing resumes]. Particularly, we should like to call attention to the paragraph at the top of sheet 3 of the galley. We may be wrong, but a return to the chapter on Davidson, which you discuss there, does not seem to give the impression that Daniels is "irritated." Certainly, we do not mean to imply that he accepts Don's attitudes and interpretations, but he does seem to respect Don. We agree with you, of course, that his attitude toward the interview does seem to be a confused one. We suggest the deletion of the last seven lines of that paragraph, as being somewhat out of tone [*sic*] with the rest of the piece. You have made the point purposely specific when you say that Daniels accepts Amberson's account of the incident at Chattanooga but rejects Tate's. That is, to rest a case on a factual matter such as that may be more effective than to rest it on a matter of a general impression which could not be so definitely documented.

We have one other suggestion. Would it, for the casual reader, clarify your basic objection to the book, to add a sentence such as the following at the end of the first paragraph of section IV: "It is a pity that Mr.

Daniels has not clarified the intention of his book by relating such excellent discussions as these to some general social philosophy."

We repeat that we think that the piece is first-rate, and it will certainly be a big asset to our Spring number. And may we repeat, also, that our suggestions are offered in all appropriate humility.

> Our very best to you all,
> Red and Cleanth

TO DOMENICO BRESCIA

TLS/Emory

[Baton Rouge]
[Early March 1939]

Dear Mr. Brescia:

Everything is going great for Cinina.[1] She says that even now she feels better than she has felt for the past month. And certainly she is looking very well indeed. I don't believe that she has lost any weight, incredible as that may seem. They will let her have broth, tea, and coca cola tomorrow, that is, the third day after the operation.

She had very little pain, and little nausea. I shall keep on a private nurse through tomorrow night, simply to be on the safe side, but then Mayme will spend part of the day with her everyday to wait on her. I have been staying in town at the home of a friend, so that I could be near the hospital; but Tuesday I shall move back out to our house.

By the way, two or three days before Cinina went to the hospital she and I made a couple of trips into the swamps for plants. We put out quite a few pines and magnolias, all of which seem to be taking. We get more and more attached to this place; and, in fact, to Louisiana.

The Houghton Mifflin salesman was through here the other day, and reported to me that the advance sales of *Night Rider* are very satisfactory. What, precisely, that will mean, I don't yet know. But it is encouraging. I shan't have the positive advance sales figures until March 14, the date of publication. I'll let you know then.

Please remember me to Bianca.² Cinina asks that I give her love to you both.

As ever,
Red

1. She had undergone an appendectomy.
2. Brescia's second wife; Cinina's mother had died some years before.

TO JAMES T. FARRELL

TLS/Penn
The Southern Review
Louisiana State University
Baton Rouge,
Louisiana
March 7, 1939

Mr. James T. Farrell
185 Lexington Ave.
New York City

Dear Mr. Farrell:

We asked the publishers some time ago to send you a copy of GLAD-STONE AND THE IRISH NATION, but have recently been informed that they could not do so. We are terribly sorry about this, but if you happen to have access to the book we shall be very glad to have the review.¹ It is certainly not possible to use it before the summer issue, deadline May 1, and it is likely that we could not use it until fall. I am sorry all this has to be so unsatisfactory but I am afraid there is no help for it. But if you can do the piece let us have it.

Very sincerely yours,
Robert Penn Warren

P.S. How about a few remarks on KING OF THE BEGGARS² in conjunction with the other book in question? Wouldn't this work in? If you think so we will send you a copy right away.

1. Farrell did not review J. L. Hammond's book.
2. A biography of the Irish hero Daniel O'Connell by Sean O'Faolain.

TO FRANK LAWRENCE OWSLEY

TLS/VU

The Southern Review
Louisiana State University
Baton Rouge,
Louisiana
[March 1939]

Mr. Frank L. Owsley
Vanderbilt University
Nashville, Tenn.

Dear Frank:

I've been very remiss about writing you, but things have been on the whole rather topsy-turvy since our return here. Cinina hasn't been at all well—several attacks of appendicitis—and so about ten days ago the doctor decided to operate. He did so last Saturday morning. Cinina has had an unusually easy time of it, and is looking fine. She will probably come home this week-end, that is, the day after tomorrow. But the appendix was a bad one, full of stones, and so we are very glad that things have gone by as well as they have. At least, that is off the books.

Your essay, which was received with cheers, is on [sic] press. We can probably have proofs to you within the next few days, early enough for you to give the thing a leisurely reading. Start thinking of something else to do for us. By the way, confidentially, there's a damned silly review of Nixon's book, by Woodward, the fellow who did what I considered a pretty good biography of Tom Watson.[1] But he has given a very silly and superficial view of Nixon's book, and repeats the usual clichés about agrarianism—plantation system, magnolias, and that bilge. He has either failed to take the trouble to understand, or, in fact, to read, what has been written, or he is deliberately misrepresenting what he does know.

The novel comes out March 14, but I suppose I'll have advance copies before that. I'll get one on to you all as soon as any are available. By the way, Eyre and Spottiswoode bought the English rights, and will bring out an edition there late this spring. I yet have no definite information about advance sales, although I am told they are beginning satisfactorily. Frankly, I anticipate mighty little.

Please let us have a little news from you all. I hope that everything is going well with you, but it wouldn't be bad to have that hope verified in fact.

Again, my thanks to you all for the Christmas present, which I have greatly enjoyed.

Give our best to Isabel.[2] Cinina would—if she knew about this letter—join me in love to you all.

As ever,

Red

1. C. Vann Woodward, author of *Tom Watson: Agrarian Rebel* (1938) and in time the dean of southern historians (and future colleague of Brooks and Warren at Yale), had reviewed Herman Clarence Nixon's *Forty Acres and Steel Mules* for the Spring 1939 issue.

2. Isabel Howell, Nashville librarian and mutual friend.

TO ALLEN TATE

TLS/PU   *The Southern Review*
Louisiana State University
Baton Rouge,
Louisiana
[March 1939][1]

Dear Allen:

We hope you'll be interested in doing a shortish review of the new book by Colonel Burne on Lee, Sherman, and Grant—say about 2000–2500 words.[2] We know you have some other projects for us on hand—for instance, the piece on Edmund Wilson and John Ransom, which we are very anxious to get—but we have thought that you might be able to do the Burne review quickly and it might give you a little vacation from more purely literary endeavors. We hope it'll work out that way. But for God's sake, don't let it stand in the way of the Wilson-Ransom piece, if you are actually working on that. I don't mean the *actually* too ironically, I shall hasten to add.

By the way, are you already embarked on the new novel[?][3] I believe Pipkin said that you were ready to start writing—or something of the sort. What is it to be about? I remember, of course, that in New York you told me it would be on a contemporary subject.

I had word a little while back that Eyre and Spottiswoode is bringing NIGHT RIDER out in England, and more recently I've had direct word from Jerrold.[4] He suggests a few small revisions to make certain things a little clearer for the English reader, but since the matters he mentions are entirely general I don't see how they can very well be brought into the regular exposition of the novel; I have thought of elaborating the little introductory note which the novel now carries. But that may not be the best way. In addition, he is worried about the Proudfit dialect. God knows, Willie is an old man of the sea.[5] I have time—that is, if I get the idea soon enough—to try to rework that whole section, substituting something else for his narrative. But at present I haven't the faintest notion as to what the substitute will be.

We are now in the throes of putting another issue together. [Delmore] Schwartz recently sent in his piece on your poetry, but we shall be compelled, by reason of the excessive length of certain other items which we have to run, to hold it over till June. It isn't his best work, though, I must say, highly complimentary to the poems and prose of Mr. Tate. We believe that he misinterpreted a few poems, and have asked him to reconsider one or two points. For instance, he assumes that the bay "a slingshot wide" means that the bay is the shape of a drawn sling shot, a "nigger-shooter." While we, I hope correctly, read it as meaning the distance which a sling can shoot, etc. Like a *gunshot*, a *musketshot*, wide. There are many good observations in his piece, but I don't feel that he really gets to the center of your work.

We are thinking about bringing out a Hardy issue in June, 1940, the hundredth anniversary of his birth. We hope to have some seven English and the same number of American critics and poets and novelists on various aspects of his work. We aren't interested, naturally, in maintaining a level of pure eulogy, or in trying to found a Hardy circle. How about doing us a piece, say on some aspect of his poetry? In fact, we insist upon it. The dead line is January, 1940. That's giving you fair warning. Do come across with it.

No news here, except that Cinina's appendicitis operation has turned out as successfully as I could have hoped. She is about now, and doing very well indeed. She'll probably be back to work this week.

So long, and our fervent hope that you'll do the Hardy.

As ever,

Red

1. Tate's notation is "Early 1938."

2. No review of Alfred Higgins Burne's *Lee, Grant, and Sherman: A Study in Leadership* appeared.

3. Tate would never complete a second novel.

4. The British writer Douglas Jerrold, a director at Eyre and Spottiswoode.

5. An implicit recognition of the debt Warren owed Coleridge in the Willie Proudfit section of *Night Rider.*

TO DONALD DAVIDSON

TLS/VU   [Baton Rouge]
                                                         [March 1939]

Dear Don:

I'm writing to thank you for your note about the copyright assignment form, and to ask about the state of affairs concerning [Shirley] Forgotson's application for the writing fellowship under you. My immediate interest in the present situation arises from a recent lecturing visit here of Cabell Greet,[1] of Columbia, who said he would be glad to push an application or two from LSU for graduate fellowships at Columbia. Forgotson is applying there, at the suggestion provided by Greet's friendly attitude, but he much prefers to go to Vanderbilt. If there seems to be a lot of life in the Vanderbilt application, the Columbia one won't be pushed, or will be withdrawn. I strongly feel that he would get ten times more of what he wants at Vanderbilt, and would be considerably happier.[2]

You will notice on Forgotson's transcript a notation to the effect that he was suspended last year for several months. Cleanth and I want to explain the situation to you. When Forgotson was a freshman or sophomore, he took some books from the library and kept them around his room for two years, afraid to carry them back. Last year another student reported the matter, and he was called up. The administration did not want to take a stern line, one of the deans told me—for Forgotson was a brilliant student and had a very good record in all other respects. But they had made eleven expulsions that year for the offense of taking books from the library and selling them to second-hand dealers, and they felt that they had to do something to prevent kick-backs [*sic*] from the previous expulsions. He was reinstated in the summer and finishes up his degree this June. The Dean of Administration, you will notice, has attached a letter to the transcript of Forgotson's record, recommending him despite the suspension. Cleanth and I know him extremely well, and feel that he has a very fine character and is a thoroughly good person. But we want you to know the particulars of the case, for many reasons, all of which are, I suppose, sufficiently obvious. [Handwritten in margin] By the way, feel free to use this letter in any way, for instance, to [*sic*] Dean Pomfret,[3] if you think it desirable.

[Typing resumes] By the way, you should receive, in a few days, a copy of NIGHT RIDER. If it doesn't show up, please let me know so that I can take steps in the matter. I do hope that some things in the book will please you.

Everybody in the office here joins me in warm regards to you, and Cinina joins me in greetings to Theresa.

As ever,
Red

P.S. Cinina has recently had an operation for appendicitis, but she is back at school now. She had a pretty easy time of it, on the whole.

1. William Cabell Greet, an authority on American dialects.
2. Forgotson's application for a fellowship was unsuccessful, as later letters make clear.
3. John Pomfret, dean of the graduate school at Vanderbilt.

TO MORTON DAUWEN ZABEL

TLS/Newb

The Southern Review
Louisiana State University
Baton Rouge,
Louisiana
March 22, 1939

Mr. Morton D. Zabel
1100 Pratt Blvd.
Chicago, Ill.

Dear Zabel:

I have just received news of the Guggenheim appointment, and I want to tell you how grateful I am for your support in the matter. My gratitude would not have been less if the application had been refused, but I want you to know how valuable I think your recommendation was.

Very sincerely yours,
Robert Penn Warren

TO HERBERT J. MULLER

TLS/Ind

The Southern Review
Louisiana State University
Baton Rouge,
Louisiana
March 24, 1939

Mr. Herbert J. Muller
Department of English
Purdue University
Lafayette, Ind.

Dear Mr. Muller:

We have received the Arnold piece and like it very much indeed. But, in addition, I want to repeat that we like the long general essay equally well and now can see our way clear, in the light of our commitments, to accepting it. One of the two pieces—we can not say which at the moment—will appear in the summer issue; the other in the fall.[1] And we are damn glad to have both of them.

Very sincerely yours,
Robert Penn Warren

1. Muller's "Humanism in the World of Einstein" and "Matthew Arnold: A Parable for Partisans" appeared in the Summer 1939 and Winter 1940 issues respectively.

TO EMMA "CININA" WARREN

TLS/Emory   [Baton Rouge]
                                    [Postmarked March 28, 1939]

Dearest Cinina:

I've missed you so. And you are on my mind every minute. I'm glad that, at least, you'll get in tomorrow, for being cooped up on the train with nothing to do but go over and over in your mind the whole thing must be pretty awful.[1] I keep wishing that I could be with you, Darling— for I know how I'd want you under such circumstances. And maybe you'd like to have me.

I saw Broussard[2] today and made all [the] arrangements for your work. He was extremely nice about the thing, and when I told him that there was a fairly complicated family situation to handle, he said to tell you not to come back until you had done what was necessary. Josie, Pousson, S[e]rgio, and Ingarammo [sic][3] are dividing up the work. All of the classes were met today except the eight o'clock. And I met that to dismiss the class. As soon as your grades come, I'll attend to handing them in. They aren't due until Wednesday.

I had dinner with Albert and K.A., but came home immediately after, for I wanted to be alone. In a few days I'll get somebody to come out here. Tom[4] came last night. Tomorrow I'll see Ellis[5] and try to get that matter settled. I hope to have the house fixed before you get back.

I had a letter from Andrew Lytle today, enclosing some information from George Haight in Hollywood. He is now the second man in general charge of RKO. He said: "Warren's book is powerful and absorbing and if I can get around the controversial angle I'll take it. I'm working on that now." I don't think he can get around the controversial angle, but he might. I had another pressing letter from Bader of MCA about handling the rights.

Mrs. Wilson[6] had me in today to give her biographical information about your father. I'll send you copies of the papers tomorrow.

I can't think of anything else. Except what I am thinking of all the time—how much I love you and how damned fine and beautiful you are. Baby, Baby, I do love you, and I hate to think of you suffering so.

Goodnight,
Red

1. Cinina's father, the composer Domenico Brescia, had died of a sudden heart attack, and she was en route to Oakland, California, for the funeral.

2. James F. Broussard was head of the Romance languages department at LSU and thus Cinina's immediate supervisor. In the later internecine conflicts among the faculty, he would oppose the interests of Brooks and Warren.

3. Charles East has determined that Josephine Rinaudo, Leon B. Pousson, Sergio Carnalo, and Giovanni Ingaramo were members of Il Circolo Italiano at LSU. They had obviously been recruited to manage Cinina's professional responsibilities during her unexpected absence.

4. Possibly Warren's graduate student Thomas H. (Tommy) Thompson, the future journalist.

5. Charles East has identified this individual as Ellis Burkes, Baton Rouge general contractor.

6. Georgia L. Wilson was in charge of LSU's News Bureau, which issued press releases to the local newspapers. (My gratitude to Charles East.)

TO EMMA "CININA" WARREN

TLS/Emory

[Baton Rouge]
[Postmarked March 30, 1939]

Dearest Cinina:

I had dinner at home tonight and have been working on some Spenser stuff for class. The class is so far behind that I'm having to meet them twice a week instead of once. And Crofts' arrival next Monday is creating a little pressure on that business of the text book revisions.[1] (By the way,

Holt has just put out another big circular, in color and all, on the poetry book.)

I saw Ellis this afternoon and had another session with him. He didn't have his figures in final shape, and so our conversation didn't amount to much, but he promises me something definite in the morning. I'll try to push this whole business through—except perhaps for the plumbing—before your arrival. Or at least, it ought to be in the course of construction by the time you are here. But Ellis is a big-time man now; he is just finishing up a large brick apartment house. And I may have to go after another man. Anyway, I'm getting another bid.

Heidel[2] called tonight to get your California address. He said that he wanted to wire you. Before your letter came today I had already written to Edward [Donahoe], [the] Ted Davisons, Amy Breyer[3] (who had just written me a note), and one or two other people. I shall write to the [Italian] consul right away. And I'll send your papers and roll book tomorrow morning. A lot of people have asked about you here.

But I think about you all the time. And love you all the time. Please hurry back, Darling.

Red

1. F. S. Crofts was the publisher of *An Approach to Literature*.
2. Heidel Brown was a successful realtor and close personal friend.
3. A Nashville friend and sometime sweetheart of Randall Jarrell.

TO EMMA "CININA" WARREN

TLS/Emory   [Baton Rouge]
                                   [Postmarked March 30, 1939]

Dear Baby:

I've just come in—it is now about ten—and am pretty tired. I did a lot of work on papers today, and had a time chasing Ellis down. I brought him out here this afternoon and went over the ground for Mayme's house. It seems that it will be possible to put it down on the lower side and still get the sewerage disposal. That is a better location if the sewerage can be worked out properly. He is to give me his figures on costs tomorrow. I am having him figure it two ways: with a store-room ten by ten plus the closet and the bath, and without the store-room. Then we can see how the extra cost of an unfinished store-room stacks up with our storage fees. It'll probably be pretty expensive, but it might be a saving at that. Please let me know as soon as you have this letter, your precise views on this point. And tomorrow I'll send you the figures.

I had a letter from Crofts today: he will be here next Monday. So Cleanth and I have been getting at the revision tonight in order to have our proposals ready for him. I hate the business, but now it has to be finished up.

I have prepared all your grade cards, and shall turn them in tomorrow. They are not due until tomorrow, for the date has been changed, as I was notified yesterday. The classes seem to be taken care of, or at least are being met.

Darling, all my love and thoughts are to [sic] you. Please take care of yourself, and keep a grip. And hurry back to me, for I miss you and want you with me, and I love you forever and ever and keeps.

> Goodnight,
> Red

P.S. I had a long talk with Palfrey[1] today and fixed up the money business. $200 more, but a hundred of that goes back to Duncan[2] and fifty goes to Lester,[3] who has *not* cashed his check.

1. W. Taylor Palfrey, banker and trust officer for the City National Bank. (My thanks to Charles East.)
2. Most likely Duncan Ferguson, a sculptor in the LSU art school.
3. Probably Lee O. Lester, a general contractor and builder. (My thanks to Charles East.)

TO ANDREW LYTLE

TLS/VU

The Southern Review
Louisiana State University
Baton Rouge,
Louisiana
March 30, 1939[1]

Dear Andrew:

Thanks for the very encouraging note. I'm happy to hear also, from other sources, people who've heard part of De Soty [sic],[2] that it's pretty damned good. But that, in my mind, is to be expected. I can't imagine what the book will be like, but I know it'll be good.

NIGHT RIDER has been having a good press, with the exception of *The Saturday Review*.[3] HM is pleased with the way things are going—or rather, was pleased the last time I heard from them. There was a pretty good advance sale, but it's hard to know what that will mean in the end. Anyway, the Guggenheim has come out of the thing.

We don't yet know what our plans will be. Cinina is in California, where she has gone because of her father's death. Until she returns, there won't be any chance to work things out. It is probable, however, that we shall be in or near Nashville for a while. I'm in the middle of a play—let that rock you on your heels—which I hope to finish by fall. Then, another novel. But I'm going to rely heavily on your experience of the stage and of writing for it to pull me out of some holes as far as the play is concerned.

Cleanth hasn't been very well, apparently as a result of eye-strain. The doctor has just told him that he'll have to cut down drastically on his reading.[4] Well, you know what that means for a fellow in Cleanth's position. Tinkum,[5] too, has been under. Katherine Ann[e] had flu that damned near went into pneumonia, and so did yours truly. Cinina had her appendix out in February. So, God knows, there's been trouble around here. But as a local wit remarked, viewing the scene of carnage, "when you get to thirty or so you'd just as well realize you're a big boy now, and things are going to happen to you."

Well, I hope things are happening to you all. Spring must be pretty nice on the mountain[6] and I envy you your peace of mind and lack of distraction. God knows, I could use some of that.

My best to you both,
Red

1. Date added in what is apparently Lytle's hand.

2. Lytle's *At the Moon's Inn* dealt with the Spanish adventurer Hernando de Soto.

3. Basil Davenport reviewed Warren's novel in the *Saturday Review* (March 18, 1939).

4. Brooks would be plagued by serious eye problems throughout his life.

5. Brooks's wife, the former Edith Blanchard.

6. The Lytles were in residence at the Log Cabin, the family retreat in Monteagle, Tennessee.

TO C. A. MADISON

TLS/PU

The Southern Review
Louisiana State University
Baton Rouge,
Louisiana
March 31, 1939

Mr. Charles A. Madison
Henry Holt and Co.
257 4th Ave.
New York City

Dear Mr. Madison:

We are very glad indeed, that you can review Asch's SONG OF THE VAL-
LEY.[1] We shall ask the publishers to provide you with a copy. If you do
not receive this in a reasonable time, please let us know. Also, I shall
look forward to seeing your long essay on Asch.[2]

Thank you very much for sending us the last information about the
text book. By the way, we have been doing a little thinking on the subject
of revision and would appreciate your letting us know what it costs per
page to renumber the plates. We know, of course, that no immediate
revision is under consideration, but even our tentative work on the matter would naturally be colored by this consideration.

Very sincerely yours,
Robert Penn Warren

1. A novel by the prolific Polish writer Sholem Asch.
2. For whatever reason, neither the review nor the essay appeared.

TO EMMA "CININA" WARREN

ALS/Emory

[Baton Rouge]
[Postmarked April 3, 1939]

Again not much news. I'm missing you, but that isn't news—or
shouldn't be news—but maybe you still feel it's worth commenting
upon.

Conrad[1] came back yesterday. The Wendts,[2] whoever they are, sent a Packard limousine down to get him, so he came back in state. I dropped by to see him for a moment just before dinner, and was surprised to find him looking so husky—good color and weight, but still weak in the voice. But he begins to walk Tuesday. Jean [*sic*][3] is looking pretty well now too.

Shirley [Forgotson] came out with me last night, or rather yesterday afternoon, and helped me set five posts for the front. And this morning we did a little more—three hours—and so are nearly through with that.

Ellis wanted a fortune to fix up the house—$135.00 *without* the store-room. I told him no soap. Lester has agreed to do it for $20.00 plus actual cost of wages to his men, which seems good enough. Monday he'll give me an estimate of what the wages will be. This thing has taken up as much time as getting our house built last May. And everybody's so busy nobody wants a little job like this.

We made some progress in getting ready for the visit of Mr. Crofts. He's supposed to be here tomorrow.

Goodbye, darling, and absolutely all my love to you.—Not even any left for Sukie,[4] who is as big as a tick and has lost her [ferocity?].

> Forever,
> Red

1. Conrad Albrizio, muralist and member of the art faculty at LSU.
2. Charles East suggests that the reference must be to James R. Wendt, a wealthy engineer, and his wife.
3. Gene Albrizio was Conrad's wife; she would have a story in the Winter 1941 *Southern Review.*
4. Obviously a pet.

TO DONALD DAVIDSON

TLS/VU

The Southern Review
Louisiana State University
Baton Rouge,
Louisiana
[Spring 1939]

Dear Don:

I've just had your letter about the fellowship business. And yesterday I learned that Forgotson had been refused, and that Keefe[1] had received an appointment. I have had Keefe in classes, and think that he is a first-rate fellow on all counts. But he isn't the man Forgotson is, despite the better record he has to offer, even on the straight academic side. I don't mean to be criticizing the appointment of Keefe over Forgotson, for I see the logic of it on the grounds which the department there has to go on. But the situation is now this. I have just seen Keefe, who dropped by my office to borrow some books, and he has told me that he is not accepting the Vanderbilt appointment. He received a much better one at Duke. He has authorized me to say this, and is, himself, writing today or tomorrow to decline the place. Since, as your letter indicates, the fact of two L.S.U. applications had some bearing on Forgotson's case, I am in hopes that the refusal by Keefe will reopen the matter. Don't think, Don, I'm trying to steam-roller the thing, but Forgotson is a man with an enormous amount of talent and intelligence, and has had a damned hard time.

I'll write you again tomorrow when Cleanth gets back from a bout with his oculist—about the Haun stories.[2]

Affectionately,

Red

1. D. J. (Dan) Keefe, an English major from Vicksburg. (My thanks to Robert W. Rudnicki.)
2. Mildred Haun was a young writer in whom Davidson had great confidence. Brooks and Warren turned down her stories. She would later serve as business manager of the *Sewanee Review* under Tate.

TO DONALD DAVIDSON

TLS/VU

The Southern Review
Louisiana State University
Baton Rouge,
Louisiana
[Spring 1939]

Dear Don:

It's too bad about Forgotson, but Cleanth and I are grateful to you for your efforts, and I know that Forgotson himself is grateful. By the way, you said that the fact that only one letter of recommendation came from LSU had some bearing on the case; perhaps I didn't emphasize enough that Cleanth was absolutely with me on the recommendation. But I am sure that that wouldn't have altered the final judgment. But one more question: Forgotson wants to know whether next year, if he gets an M.A. in the coming year, he will have a decent chance at the writing fellowship. He is considering the possibility of staying here for the degree.

When are you leaving Nashville this summer? We are expecting to be there through the month of June, for I have some work to do there in connection with my next novel.[1] I hope that you will not leave before our arrival, which will be about June third or fourth.

Again, my thanks for the efforts in Forgotson's behalf. It's a tough world, and situations like this are very saddening.

Goodbye, and best regards.

Red

1. *At Heaven's Gate* (1943).

TO JAMES T. FARRELL

TLS/Penn

The Southern Review
Louisiana State University
Baton Rouge,
Louisiana
April 25, 1939

Mr. James T. Farrell
185 Lexington Ave.
New York City

Dear Mr. Farrell:

Thank you for your very full and encouraging letter about NIGHT RIDER. Certainly, you have beautifully described what I had wished the novel to convey—and I can only hope that too much of your description is not merely the product of your own insight into the material.

Again, my thanks for the letter, and thanks for your writing to the publishers.

>Very sincerely yours,
>Robert Penn Warren

TO LIONEL TRILLING

TLS/Col

>*The Southern Review*
>Louisiana State University
>Baton Rouge,
>Louisiana
>April 25, 1939

Mr. Lionel Trilling
620 East 116 St.
New York City

Dear Mr. Trilling:

I am sincerely delighted that you like NIGHT RIDER and liked it in the special way which you described. I only hope that when you reflect further, something of your first impression will remain. I was interested to know your reaction to the narrative of Willie Proudfit. I have never been certain that the intention which prompted the inclusion of the narrative came through. Some people for whose judgment I have the greatest respect, have felt that it is a clog in the action and an unjustified distraction from the basic business of the story. In preparing the material for the English edition, which will appear in the fall with Eyre and Spottiswood[e], I have tried to make the ties to the body of the novel more explicit, making Willie comment on certain points of application, and making Mr. Munn's reaction to it more definite.

Again my most sincere thanks.

>Sincerely yours,
>Robert Penn Warren

TO EDWARD DAVISON

TLS/YU

The Southern Review
Baton Rouge, Louisiana
[Spring 1939]

Dear Ted:

Cinina got in Saturday, pretty well done in. But she is well, and will, I trust, be herself in a few more days. God knows, the last few months have been an awful mixture of things, and we're just hanging on till summer in the hope of getting a little quiet life. We still don't know what we're going to do. There hasn't been time since Cinina got back to go into the thing. But we'll have to settle the matter within the next few days, for the time is growing short.

A young man here, one of my ex-students, has asked me to speak to you about his application for a fellowship at the Writers' Conference. His name is Joseph Hopkins. He has published one story in *Esquire,* one in the *Southern Review,* and, I think, one in another magazine. I am, at his request, sending you a copy of the SR with his story, "Without Gunfire."[1] He has been on the WPA Writer's Project in this state for the past two years. He is, in a way, one of Hemingway's proteges, for, if I am correctly informed, Hemingway got his first story published for him, and carries on some sort of a correspondence with him. I am giving you the facts of his career, and am enclosing another story of his in manuscript, which he has left with me. Frankly, I don't cotton to the lad, but this shouldn't, I suppose, be of any weight with you. After all, you're not creating a circle of personal friends. And I do feel certain that he would not be a problem or anything like that. He would behave himself all right, and would, I imagine, be in your upper bracket in so far as ability is concerned. But the stories will speak for themselves.

I hope that things are looking bright for the Conference. I feel a positive twinge of homesickness for it—or, to be more accurate, for the Davisons. To whom our best love,

Red

1. In the Winter 1939 number.

TO FRANK LAWRENCE OWSLEY

TLS/VU   [Baton Rouge]
                                                               [Spring 1939]

Dear Frank:

I should have written you long ago in answer to your very heartening
letter—and did want to write, but you know that. But, God help us all,
there hasn't been a single minute, and now it is business, not pleasure,
that brings me to the typewriter.

First, the business: you have, no doubt, read Woodward's piece in
the SR, last issue. We started to ask him to cover himself on some of his
points before publication, and then decided that it might be better to let
him stay uncovered and have the public stroll by, like Noah's sons, to
leer at his nakedness. How about F. L. Owsley as leerer-in-chief? Will
you do a letter, say 500–1000 words, to run in our correspondence section? For the summer issue. If it gets here by May 25 it can go in. We are
very anxious to have you do this if you can find the time.[1] If you can't,
will you let us know right away so that we can get somebody else?

I enormously appreciated your comments on NIGHT RIDER. I am
happy that the book gave you some pleasure. And I want to say that
your analysis of the basic motivation and development is extremely encouraging to me, for it hits the nail on the head as regards my intention—far more accurately than any reviewer has done—and makes me
feel that, after all, I may not have failed to communicate my fundamental
idea. But more of this later. I expect to see you in June, and am looking
forward with the keenest anticipation to some evenings with the Owsleys, even if one of them wets my knee. If it's a little Owsley, it'll be all
right.

Cinina joins me in love to the lot of you.

                                                               As ever,
                                                               Red

1. Owsley must have declined. Davidson took on Woodward at some length in "The
Class Approach to Southern Problems" (Autumn 1939).

TO EDMUND WILSON

TLS/YU

THE SOUTHERN REVIEW
University, La.
May 6, 1939

Mr. Edmund Wilson
233 Stamford Ave.
Stamford, Conn.

Dear Wilson:

Yes, THE SOUTHERN REVIEW does pay for contributions, and I hope that the check for your wife has already reached her.[1] We cannot pay directly, but have to put in a requisition through the business office of the University; the business office then verifies the fact of the publication of the item in question and then mails out a check. But this last month, there was a complete change of system in the business office with the result that all sorts of things were delayed, including THE SOUTHERN REVIEW payments. At least, that's the story we got when we asked what was holding up our payments.

And yes, we would have a great interest in some chapters of your Marxism book.[2] May we have a look?

Please tell your wife how happy I am that she likes my novel.

With best regards,
Robert Penn Warren

1. Wilson had married his third wife, the writer Mary McCarthy, the previous year. Her story "Cruel and Barbarous Treatment" had just been published in the Spring 1939 number.

2. *To the Finland Station: A Study in the Writing and Acting of History* (1940).

TO JOHN BERRYMAN

TLS/Minn

THE SOUTHERN REVIEW
University, La.
May 11, 1939

Mr. John Berryman
41 Park Avenue
New York City

Dear Mr. Berryman:

We liked the revision of "Meditation" very much, and should like to add it to the material which we have on hand as a nucleus for another group. We shall hold it for your o.k. We are also interested in "Conversation." But the last stanza does not satisfy us. If you ever do any further work on this piece, we should be very happy to consider it.[1]

As for the place at L.S.U., I fear that I have nothing very promising to suggest. I understand that there will be no addition to the department next year, and this leaves open only teaching fellowships which are very poorly paid and in which I imagine you would not be interested, especially since you already have the appointment at Columbia. If I hear of anything elsewhere I shall certainly let you know.

Very sincerely yours,
Robert Penn Warren

1. "Conversation" would eventually be included in the Berryman group.

TO ALLEN TATE

TLS/PU

University, Louisiana
May 16, 1939

Dear Allen:

The Chapel Hill Poets sounds fine. Put me down as a subscriber to the series. As for putting a book in the series, I'd be delighted. I'm probably tied up for a new one, though this isn't absolutely definite. The manuscript is out now, and in case HM doesn't want to publish it in the near future, Holt has a promise from me that I'll turn it over to them. After they see it they may not want it, of course.[1] While we're on the subject of poetry, I'd like to ask you what you think about the following line-up for the new book. I've put all the poems written before 1931 as a separate section, a Part II, of the new book, with a note as to the distinction between the parts.[2] For after that date I feel a very positive change in the whole approach, a difference both in basic idea and in method. You've seen all the new stuff in the book, but I've made some fairly positive revisions. For instance, in "Picnic Remembered," which you saw in Ms and which appeared in *Scribners*, I've dropped one stanza—the stanza which, originally, you said was weak, and have touched up a few things here and there. In another piece, "Athenian Death," which appeared in the *Nation*, I've cut a stanza and done some tinkering. I couldn't do anything to "Love's Voice," the rather long poem which you saw in MS and which took the Sinkler prize last year.[3] But if you now have any suggestions for omissions, especially in the earlier poems as they appear in XXXVI POEMS, please let me know. The tentative title is PROBLEM OF KNOWLEDGE, which may be too fancy. What do you think? [Handwritten in margin] I'm expecting to get a lot of poems done this next year and should have a volume ready about spring, 1941.

[Typing resumes] It's good news about Princeton,[4] as I may have insisted in my last note to you, but is it for one or for two years? I've heard both reports. And what do you do?

And by the way, what about the review of Ransom and [Edmund] Wilson? Our deadline for summer is May 25.

And what other news is there with you all?

We're stewing here in the office and are on the last pull as far as teaching is concerned. Albert has just finished up his thesis,[5] and gets his degree this June. And he's within one course of the Ph.D. requirements.

So long, and our best,
Red

1. They did not.
2. Warren outlines the organizational principle that would guide him in all his volumes of selected verse, the placing of the earliest poems at the back of the book.
3. The Carolyn Sinkler Prize was awarded by the Poetry Society of South Carolina.
4. Tate had been offered an appointment at Princeton.

5. Though in residence at LSU, Erskine took the M.A. from Vanderbilt. His thesis was entitled "The Basis of Marxist Literary Criticism." (Special thanks to Judy Bolton and Charles East.)

TO JOHN BERRYMAN

TLS/Minn

THE SOUTHERN REVIEW
University, La.
May 16, 1939

Mr. John Berryman
41 Park Avenue
New York City

Dear Mr. Berryman:

I have been wanting to write to you for almost two months to the day, to thank you for your very greatly appreciated letter on the subject of the novel. I was really delighted that you liked it so well. Whatever happens to it in general, I have the great satisfaction of knowing that some people like you, Mark Van Doren, Tate, Burke, and a few others whom I enormously respect, have liked it—or have perjured themselves.

I am now about to get started on another novel, at least on the winding-up of some background work; I shan't get at the actual writing until fall. I don't know yet where I shall be next year, but I have taken a leave from L.S.U. for one year.

You ask about the chance for a regular trade edition of the poems. It seems probable that an edition will appear this fall or winter, both the set of poems which were in the Alcestis Press volume and some new ones.

Again, let me thank you for the letter.

Very sincerely yours,
Robert Penn Warren

P.S. We did receive CITIES IN THE WILDERNESS,[1] and shall do our best to get a decent review.[2]

1. Subtitled *The First Century of Urban Life in America,* a groundbreaking study by Carl Bridenbaugh.

2. No review appeared.

TO BRAINARD CHENEY

TLS/VU   University, Louisiana
                                                      May 17, 1939

Dear Lon:[1]

I should have written to you a long time back to say that we couldn't see how Chapter 18 of your novel would work out as a short story. I felt that it really belonged as a section in a novel, and couldn't see how, independently, it could be more than an episode. By the way, have you heard anything more from Houghton Mifflin?[2] From the way [Paul] Brooks talked when he was here I gathered that the prospects were pretty damned good. Do let me know when you have news.

It is probable that we shall be in Nashville about June 6, to stay for a month or so. I have some work to do in that part of the world in getting some last-minute stuff together for my new novel. But we are planning to take a little pleasure, too, and we hope to have a good part of that in your company. Will Fanny[3] be in Nashville then? We hope so.

You gave me very cheering news when you said that Frank and Dick Beatty[4] would like to see me back there—but, I must say, I imagine that they are in a very, very small minority. Needless to say, I am open to any reasonable offer, but I would sell my chances on that one for a very dilapidated dime.

Well, goodbye, and our best to you. We're looking forward to the meeting in June. (We leave here June 2, to go to Atlanta, where I have an autographing party, and then direct to Nashville.)

As ever,
Red

1. Brainard (Lon) Cheney was a Tennessee journalist and writer who was well connected politically. He was among Warren's most valued Nashville friends.
2. Houghton Mifflin would publish Cheney's first novel, *Lightwood,* later in the year.
3. Cheney's wife, the former Frances Neel. A librarian, she would be Allen Tate's

assistant when he assumed the Consultancy in Poetry at the Library of Congress in 1943.

4. Richmond Croom Beatty of the Vanderbilt English faculty.

TO WILLIAM SLOANE

TLS/PU

The Southern Review
Louisiana State University
University
Louisiana
June 18, 1939

Mr. William Sloane
Henry Holt & Co.
New York City

Dear Mr. Sloane:[1]

Some time ago you very kindly wrote me to say that you might be interested in publishing a book of my poems. Well, here is the book, and I hope that you will like it enough to publish it. A number of these poems appeared in xxxvi poems, which the Alcestis Press brought out in 1936, in an edition which sold, or rather didn't sell, for $7.50. But I have a copyright release from them, which, of course, can be made over to you if you decide to publish the book. And, as I say, there was a very small circulation of the xxxvi poems. So that publication shouldn't interfere with yours.

You may be interested in what sort of press the earlier book got. I'm sorry that I haven't clippings, but it ran something like this: Zabel in *Poetry,* Untermeyer in the *Mercury,* Matthiessen in the *American Oxonian,* Cudworth Flint in the *Southern Review* and somebody (I can't remember who)[2] in the *New Republic* were highly favorable; Ruth Lechlichtner (is that the way to spell her name?) in the *Herald Tribune* and somebody in an unsigned review in *Nation* were unfavorable. I don't remember how other reviews ran. This ought to be a better book, for it has a good many more recent poems; and I have to feel that the last ones are better than the early ones. I have to feel that or have to stop writing them.

This brings up another question. You will see that the second section of the manuscript contains earlier poems. Perhaps these should not be included at all, but they have been rather widely anthologized and might have some interest for some people who were interested at all in my work. But I do feel that they should definitely be segregated from the work done in the last seven years. So I've made a division on grounds of date and have indicated that in a prefatory note. Perhaps the whole book should be cut some. I've tried to be pretty rigid in excluding stuff, but perhaps I haven't gone far enough. Certainly, if you are interested in publishing the book, I am open to suggestions along that line.

Since I am on leave from LSU on a Guggenheim, I may be going away in July to Europe. If we do go, we shall probably sail from New Orleans about July 15 or 20. Would it be possible to have a decision before that time? I don't want to cause you inconvenience, but it would be a great help to me to have the manuscript in my hands before sailing, in case of rejection—you see I'm taking a gloomy view.[3] Another firm has asked for a reading on it, and I would like to send it to them before sailing, if you don't want it. But I hope you will take it, especially since you all publish UNDERSTANDING POETRY.

My address, until July 5, will be #6 Vanderbilt Campus, Nashville, Tennessee; after that, *The Southern Review*.

Sincerely yours,
Robert Penn Warren

1. Sloane went on to found the publishing house of William Sloane and Associates and later directed the Rutgers University Press. (My gratitude to Charles East.)

2. Robert Lann had reviewed *Thirty-Six Poems* for the *New Republic* (July 15, 1936).

3. Though Warren's second book of verse, *Eleven Poems on the Same Theme*, would appear in 1942, he would have to wait until 1944 to see his first volume of selected poems.

At the start of summer 1939, Warren spent several weeks in Nashville doing research and background reading for his novel in progress, and he and Cinina returned briefly to Baton Rouge before sailing for Europe, where they would encounter more excitement than they had anticipated. The international situation was rapidly deteriorating, and scarcely two weeks after their arrival in Italy, Germany invaded Poland and World War II began. Rashly or not, the Warrens decided to remain abroad while Italy maintained its neutrality, and Warren's letters from this period are filled with vivid details of their uncertain, often tense, circumstances. But even half a globe away and in the midst of mounting wartime chaos, Warren kept a close eye on LSU, rocked by a series of scandals and academic realignments, and he never lost sight of practical considerations—such as his promised promotion to full professor and the likely consequences of university reforms.

TO FRANK LAWRENCE OWSLEY

TLS/VU   [En route to Europe]
                              [Southern Review letterhead]
                                   [August 14, 1939]

Dear Frank:

Again our thanks for the hospitality. It was a fine thing to do for us. But we have one complaint to make to the management: the Owsleys weren't there.¹ Please see that that's remedied next time. The short bit of visiting we had was all too short. But it was nice to have the opportunity to get really acquainted with Gordon.² We enjoyed his company a great deal. The time in Nashville passed very quickly. I worked at the library every day, on the newspaper files.³ And I got just about what I needed, I think. That is, I got all that I could before the actual process of composition begins to show up specific things that I need. That is bound to happen. It's impossible to predict completely what you are going to do in a piece of fiction, I'm sure; you simply can't sit down and draw up a blueprint of the thing.

Speaking of fiction, I got a chance to read the first forty pages of Andrew's novel. It goes mighty well, damned well, in fact. And he explained to me the whole conception; I was very considerably impressed by it. It certainly lifts the whole thing out of the realm of the cloak-and-sword romance into something pretty philosophical. He says that he hopes to finish within six months. I don't see how that will be possible, since he only has one hundred and twenty-five pages written, but maybe he will.

We left Nashville quite suddenly, several days earlier than we had anticipated. We got a wire to the effect that our boat was sailing on July

15, and that we had to make reservations if we we[re] going to go; we had postponed a definite decision as long as possible, because of the international situation, etc. So we left on a twenty-four hour notice. But when we got to Baton Rouge and had been there a day or so, we got word that the boat would not sail until the twentieth. Which was damned lucky, for we had to use every minute of the extra time in order to get our affairs into shape for leaving. And there were lots of faculty meetings, A.A.U.P. meetings, etc. that demanded my attendance—or at least, I wanted to go and see the fur fly. Well, boy, the fur was flying down there.[4] Some of the younger men and a few of the old-timers were raising hell and demanding a pretty thorough over-hauling of the University. Cleanth is one of the ring-leaders. Naturally, Pipkin—I speak in confidence—was pussyfooting all over the place. Things got so rough that a committee of the faculty group howling for reform waited on several of the deans who wanted to say that everything was jake, and wanted to hush everything up, and gave the deans a little heart-to-heart in no uncertain language. In the end the whole thing, if there is any luck, will help the University very definitely. And apparently, there is going to be no curtailment of the University program because of the blow up. And maybe, God knows I hope so, there will be a nice bevy of politicians behind the bars at Atlanta. That cesspool could stand a draining, all right.

The trip, so far, has been very pleasant, more pleasant, in fact, than the trip last year. The people on board are more congenial than those last year. The captain particularly is a hell of a nice fellow, youngish and very humorous and jolly. We had three days of very rough weather, and took a good beating. The sea broke on the top deck for two whole days and nights; so you can imagine what kind of wind we were having. One night I was standing in the bathroom, which opens on a little passage leading to our cabin and the dining salon. Suddenly I saw that someone had left the outside door of the passage open, and just as I saw that, I saw a wave, say neck-high, come strolling into the passage. I yelled for Cinina to throw suitcases on the bunks, but she wasn't quick enough—no human could have been—to get them all up before the wave was in the cabin with her. She says, too, that she couldn't see much point in saving suitcases if the ship was already sinking. Then the wave marched over into the dining salon. Well, for some hours after, the Warrens observed sailors wading about in their cabin and in the dining salon with buckets and pans and mops and shovels, scooping the water out.

Nothing was damaged by pure good luck, except a few books, and those we dried out so promptly that their utility is not impaired. But water did get into several big suitcases so that everything had to be emptied out and dried. That was the high point of our excitement. The rest of the time has been a pleasant routine of working and doing nothing. Cinina has been doing a lot of reading. I've been working on my play, on Italian grammar, and on Dante. I've read some eighteen cantos and notes on the Inferno, and am prepared to admit, even with my halting use of the language, that it isn't over-rated. I'll finish by Christmas at this rate, and then can start over. And I have a couple of games of chess with the radio man after lunch every day. The time has passed very quickly. We get to Genoa Wednesday, August 16—and today is Monday.

We go directly from Genoa to Sirmione, where we were last year. We shall be there until it gets too cold to swim, which will probably be about the early part of November. So let us hear from you all while we are there. Our address will be: Poste restante, Sirmione, Lago di Garda, Italy. After we leave Sirmione we'll probably go to Rome and then South, or the other way round. Unless we come home on a cruiser before.[5] People on the boat are pretty grim and pessimistic; a vast difference from last year. But, of course, you can't tell much from talking to a few people.

Cinina joins me in love to all of you.

Red

1. On the visit to Nashville prior to departing for Europe, the Warrens had stayed at the Owsleys' apartment during their absence.

2. Harriet Owsley's brother, Gordon Thomas Chappell.

3. Warren's new novel, *At Heaven's Gate,* would be loosely based on events surrounding the career of the discredited Tennessee power broker Luke Lea.

4. Scandal was rocking the LSU campus following discovery of widespread fraud on the part of the university's president, his cronies, and high-placed state officials.

5. The outbreak of World War II was less than a month away, and Warren anticipates the recalling of American citizens from Italy.

TO ALBERT ERSKINE

TLS/Maryland   [En route to Europe]
                                                [August 15, 1939]

Dear Albert:

We reach Genoa tomorrow, and naturally, we can scarcely control our curiosity until the moment we can get to the American Express and seize our forwarded news clippings and long letters which we know are wait-ing there for us. The sacred name of LSU hasn't once been mentioned in the news broadcasts which we had on the boat, and the scarcely less sacred name of Leche,[1] or of J. M. Smith,[2] has not come winging to us over the waters. All we hear is that there has been a derailment of an express in Montana, and that there is a certain amount of friction in the city of Danzig.[3] Apparently, NBC and CBS have been discriminating against Baton Rouge. For I am sure that we are not to interpret this silence concerning that little city as an example of the old wheeze that a happy people is a people with no history. I'm damned sure that history is being made there every thirty minutes. Let us know what some of it is.

The trip has been extremely pleasant, except for bad weather for three days, and that was more exciting than uncomfortable except for the fact that when you were in the bunk you were in mortal danger of emulating the handsome young man on the flying trapeze, or the daring young man, or whatever he was. When we shipped about half the Atlan-tic into our cabin one night, because some sea-going half-wit left the outside passage door open in the midst of a storm, when the deck, and the top deck, was awash—well, that was exciting. But no great harm was done.

I've managed to do another scene of the play, and as soon as I have a chance to curry it down a bit and make [a] copy I'll send it to you all for comment. (One minute I think the thing is going all right and the next I'm tempted to chuck the whole project.) And I've been going through Dante, and studying grammar. I've done a lot of the Inferno, and have got the hang of the language pretty well now, so it isn't entirely a chore. And the notes and commentaries I have are good; they really do elucidate some questions of diction and style. It's astonishing, how similar some of the stuff is to some of Shakespeare, the mixture of tone, the same kind of irony—hell like "a washing vat" etc.

Speaking of poetry, I don't know whether I ever told you fully what Allen said about the series of books.[4] He said that [T. S.] Eliot was going to bring out the series in England and would provide the American part-ner with sheets for a book or two every year by some English poet. He said that Couch *might* be interested in working out a partnership with the LSU press, similar to the arrangement which LSU has with Texas on the Southern History project. The fate of the series of books would look brighter, it seems to me, with a pooling of energy for promotion and editing rather than with competition—especially since Couch has the English tie-up. If you all think it advisable, you might ask Marcus[5] about his feelings on the matter. *But* Allen, *not Couch,* should be notified as to the decision; for Allen would be the one to handle the matter with Couch.

I saw Andrew's new novel, or rather some thirty or forty pages of the hundred and twenty-five which he has done. The part I read was really awfully good, and quite different from what I had anticipated. And I heard him discuss his intentions a little. He's got a pretty sound and exciting sort of theme, too.

We go direct to Sirmione from Genoa, and shall stay there until cold weather, which will probably be in early November. Our address there will be: Poste Restante, Sirmione, Lago di Garda, Italy—to be very explicit. And we hope to hear often from you and KA. We want to know how Olivet went, how Bennington goes, and a lot of other things.[6] Meanwhile, I hope The Promised Land is approaching, and that it really will appear in the fall.[7] It would be the perfect time for it, it seems, with all the excitement still in the literary air. And if it does come out this fall, you all will never be forgiven if an advance copy doesn't reach the W's pretty promptly.

Give our best to Brooks's, Duncan, Albrizios. And write to us.

Love to you both, from us both.

As ever,
Red

[Postscript in Cinina Warren's Hand]

Dear K. A. [Katherine Anne Porter]

I've been looking at the French coast this morning—a lovely sight! The trip is better than [the] Keeley cure, rest-cure, etc. . . . put together. A certain goggle-faced gent ought to try it. It's all gone by very fast and has left me feeling as if I'd been completely overhauled. We miss you both—Love, Cinina

1. Richard W. Leche, governor of Louisiana, was implicated in the burgeoning scandals, later indicted, and sent to the federal penitentiary in Atlanta.
2. James Monroe Smith, the president of LSU, had misappropriated university funds and would serve a prison term.

3. Hitler was determined to wrest the "free city" of Danzig from Polish control, and unrest there increased as his invasion of Poland loomed.

4. The poetry series Tate had hoped W. T. Couch of the University of North Carolina Press might inaugurate.

5. Marcus Wilkerson, founding director of the LSU Press.

6. Porter was participating in writers' conferences and giving readings.

7. "Promised Land" was Porter's working title for the manuscript that eventually became her novel *Ship of Fools*. It did not appear until 1962.

TO ALLEN TATE

TLS/PU

Sirmione,
Lago di Garda,
Italy
August 31, 1939

Dear Allen:

Well, it turned out, after all, when we had completed the dash to Louisiana to catch the boat on July 15, that there was, at the last minute, a five-day delay to wait for cargo at New Orleans. But we didn't find that out until July 18. The delay was fortunate, however, for as it was, with the added excitement of the LSU situation, etc., we barely got aboard. Everything worked out beautifully—a very pleasant trip over, except for a three-day storm, good food, and lots of work and rest—until we had the news here last week.[1] It looks bad, I suppose, but we haven't given up all hope, although the American Consuls are ordering Americans out. But the joke is, when you ask them how to get out—as I asked the fellow at the American Consulate at Milan—they say, "We don't know, there aren't any boats. But we are supposed to warn our citizens." And then they say, "Why don't you go back to Sirmione, which is a nice place, and just stay there until you hear from us? But keep your bags packed." So that is what we are doing. But it's hard to get much done when you hang round all day waiting for radio broadcasts. The broadcast today said that the U.S. was sending ships over for Americans here. Well, if she wants us back, she'll have to come get us, because you can't get a passage any other way.

Things were going so damned well, too. This is a very pleasant and very cheap place, very good food and wine, and perfect conditions for working. I have done quite a lot more on the verse-and-prose play. One act is now complete—in first draft, that is—and I've got a lot more done, but not in very consecutive sections. I recently sent a copy of the first act to John [Ransom] at Kenyon, and asked him to send it on to you after you all had had time to settle down at Princeton. If you will, I'll be awfully glad to have some close comments on the thing. My situation is something like this: I have the stuff assembled for the new novel, and have done a little writing on it, but the play seems more immediate to me, probably because I'm really in it, and it was moving so fast while I was on the boat. I would like to push it through, that is, if I can, and then go on with the novel. This means that I am probably going to ask Moe for a renewal on the ground of the play. A renewal would really give me a chance to push the present program to its conclusion, both the play and the novel—or almost all of the novel, for it will be pretty long. What do you think? Both of the play itself and the proposition to Moe?

I hope that Princeton works out beautifully. And I imagine that it is a very fine place for agreeable living. Certainly, it ought to be an improvement over Memphis and Greensboro. Let me hear how things go. The news from LSU, by the way, is encouraging. It seems that the new acting president, Hebert,[2] is going in for a clean-up and a general investigation of the internal affairs of the University. The attempt of one gang of the faculty to block such a move was defeated, it appears, by our side. Hell was sure popping down there when I was there in July. But, for once, justice seems about to be done.

Forgive this lousy typing, but I'm trying to get this off on the afternoon mail boat across the lake. Our best to you all.

As ever,
Red

P.S. Houghton-Mifflin has turned down my book of poems, saying they'd lose money. Which is a way of saying they'd rather lose money on poetry written by somebody else. I'm sending it to James Putnam, at Macmillans [sic], who asked for a reading. But I haven't any optimism for the outcome.

1. Hitler had signed a nonaggression pact with Stalin, paving the way for his invasion of Poland.
2. Paul M. Hebert, the respected dean of the LSU law school, had replaced Smith.

TO ALLEN TATE

TLS/PU

Fermo Posta
Capri,
Golfo di Napoli,
Italy
October 28, 1939

Dear Allen:

A couple of weeks ago, I sent a card from Naples to say that we had decided to try to stay and would be here on Capri for some months. Well, we are settled now, and have a house out in the country, stuck on the edge of a terrific cliff. It's a beautiful spot, but God knows, it is like living in the crows-nest of a ship rounding the Horn, for we catch every wind that blows, being exposed on all sides, and the winds that blow are pretty remarkable. If we don't freeze to death we ought to have a pretty nice time. Unless we have to get a boat out of Naples. But there seems to be no indication that Italy will leave her neutrality, and we hope that the lifting of the Neutrality by Congress will not mean that our boats will be ordered from this area; for that would mean a dash for the Warrens to catch what, I am sure, would be the last one.

How are things panning out at Princeton? I'd like to have word on that? [sic] And have you begun the new novel, the one you got the idea for last summer? And how are the Indians coming along?[1] And try to put other bits of news in the letter which, I hope, you will write upon receiving this. (By the way, the safest address is, probably, the American Express, Naples.)

My work here is moving pretty well—by which I mean that I'm getting a lot of it done. I haven't any idea what it is like. Has John [Ransom] sent you any of the play yet? I've been sending him sections as I finish them, and have asked him to forward them to you. If he hasn't, it is probably because he wanted to get a look at a fairly big hunk at one time. But when the last batch gets to him, which I shall send off in a day or so, all will be in his hands except the last four scenes. When you do get a look at it, please give me your reactions. I shall finish the thing in mid-winter, and can then get at the new novel, which, however, promises to be a pretty long pull. I've been tinkering at it this fall a little, and I put a lot of time on the thing during June and part of July; and I think I see its dimensions. I'm hoping that Moe will give me a renewal; I've applied for one. I feel pretty sure that the University will work out something satisfactory to the Guggenheim people, if the appointment is made; but if they won't cooperate, I'd be strongly tempted to resign and finish the novel on the Guggenheim and then hope for the best.

As for other activities, I'm studying Dante about five hours a day and exploring the island, which is a pretty interesting spot. Now it is, as you might guess, almost completely deserted, for the war has driven off the tourists—the war and the season. Only natives and maniacs, like us, are left. We know not a soul on the island, except our landlord, and so there are no distractions. We haven't even been to the movies, though we may clamber down this evening to see what claims to be a tremendous exposé of espionage—"Alarm at Gibraltar"—a British film, and probably twenty years old. Then after the film we'll scale our eminence again, by flashlight—and *scale* is the proper word. There is no road, and even firewood comes up to us in baskets balanced on the heads of delivery men.

I'll look forward to a letter. And soon, I hope. Best all around.

As ever,
Red

P.S. Please give my very warm regards to Watty—Walter Watkins[2]—and tell him I'm still nursing the regret of having missed him last Christmas.

1. Gordon was still at work on her novel of the frontier, *Green Centuries.*
2. A specialist in eighteenth-century literature, author of books on Johnson and Swift.

TO FRANK LAWRENCE OWSLEY

TLS/VU
American Express
Rome
November 11, 1939

Dear Frank:

I have been hoping with every mail to have some news from you all, and when I come in after going to the Express Company, Cinina frequently asks, "Nothing from Owsleys?" But there is rarely anything from any-body. For instance, the last mail forwarded to me from the SR office was posted August 15, for the boys quite naturally didn't think that we were going to be big enough fools to stay, and only a while back did they manage to get the information that we were going to try to stick it out. And I've only had two or three odd letters mailed from other points in the United States. But a letter from Katherine Anne did come several days ago—posted on September 29—and gave a nice little summary of news among the Louisiana politicos. It strikes me as rather nice that President Smith has two years, and Seymour Weiss,[1] and a few others similar sentences. And it strikes me as very good news that they are, apparently, going to han[g] a lot of other things on Leche, including, I fondly trust, a number at Atlanta. You know, a number such as 43,169, or something like that. And they'll censor his mail. And when he's not a good boy they'll put him in solitary. Katherine Anne also indicates that a pretty nice clean-up of the University was starting. Well, boy, that will be a winter's work, for things were, apparently, much worse than had been supposed. In any case, I hear, the new President, or rather, Acting President,[2] said that he was going to bring in an outstanding academic committee to investigate the whole set-up. But you probably know a lot more than I do about the situation there.

As for the situation here—our own situation, that is—there isn't a great deal to say. As I wrote you from Genoa, we were going to Sirmione, on Lake Garda, where we were last year. We did go there, and had a blissful two weeks before the radio began to give us bad dreams. For two or three weeks we had a very bad time. Everybody was running like rabbits into Switzerland, where lunches were $2.50 and other things in proportion, and where there are no seaports, or back to England, or was sleeping on deck to get back to New York. Well, we just sat quietly, and listened to the radio broadcasts, and occasionally had a moral collapse. Don't take that *quietly* too literally. We did go to Milan and try to get some advice out of the Consul and we did telephone the Consul at Ven-ice, and we did go to Brescia, and we did take a passage. But, anyway, here we still are, in Rome now, where, if things go well, we shall be for the winter and spring. If things blacken up, or if the Mediterranean is declared a war zone by the U.S. Congress, we'll just do the best we can. But it would be pretty tough on us to have to come back now, with the fares much higher, and not a chance of getting a boat back to a Southern port.

But up to date, except for the few bad days, we have had a very nice time. The period at Sirmione, almost two months, was extremely pleasant, even more so than last year. It is a lovely spot, the hotel is good and is in the country, on a cliff, in an olive grove, and it is a fine place to work. Then we went to Rome, where we stayed for a few days, then to Naples, and now back to Rome. We are in pensione now, after some days in a hotel, but we hope to be in an apartment of our own within a few days more. If you are to be here for any length of time at all, an apartment is actually more economical; and certainly, it is a lot more pleasant. I am getting on toward the end of my play, the one in verse and prose which I told you about, and have done a little tinkering with the new novel. My stay in Nashville turned out to be very profitable, and thanks, I must say, to the Owsley apartment and to Gordon, very pleasant. I shall get down to serious writing on the novel in January, as soon as the play is finished. And I've been putting some hours every day on Dante, who, I find, lives up to his reputation, and on grammar. But we have found time to have some fun, too, and certainly, we've seen a lot of things. And although it has been a sad and distressing time to be here, if you can put such considerations out of your mind, it has been a very interesting and instructive time. As far as we can plan for anything under the circumstances, we plan to come home next summer. But don't be surprised to see us rolling in sooner.

Meanwhile, do write to us, you all. We want all sorts of news, and we especially want news of you all. What are you doing, how are the children, what are the activities at Vanderbilt, how has football been, how is Isabel, what about politics, etc.? Please give my love, and Cinina's, to Harriet and the children. Cinina sends her best to you. Do write.

As ever,
Red

P.S. Did you get a letter from me, mailed from Genoa? And I forgot to say that our address is the American Express, Rome, from now on, indefinitely.

[Handwritten] By the way did a young man named Shirley Forgotson, one of my ex-students at L.S.U., ever call on you? He is the lad who,

I think, has such fine promise, as a poet. And I like him very much. But, I grant you, it takes some time to know him. Alfred Starr[3] was trying to arrange some sort of help for him so that he could come to Vanderbilt for graduate work—for he had his heart set on coming there—wanted to work with Don and Curry.[4]

1. A powerful member of the New Orleans political machine who owned the celebrated Roosevelt Hotel. He had been an intimate adviser to Huey P. Long. (My thanks to Charles East.)

2. Paul M. Hebert.

3. A Nashville businessman who had been active in the Fugitive group when Warren was an undergraduate.

4. Walter Clyde Curry, a distinguished member of the Vanderbilt faculty who had been marginally affiliated with the Fugitives.

TO KATHERINE ANNE PORTER

TLS/Maryland
American Express
Rome
November 11, 1939

Dear Katherine Anne:

For the letter and the news, bless you. We haven't had a word in God knows how long, except for a few lines from my Father, which arrived after all the news was stale, and a letter from Cinina's lawyer. (The lawyer's previous *three* letters have not to this day reached us, and they were addressed directly to us here.) It's pretty damned fine that Smith and some of the s.o.b.'s did get a few years, anyway. Two years sounds like mighty little reward for their special talents, but it means, at least, that the trials were not idle gestures. And if they pin a number on the back of that boy Leche, my cup will run over. And Lorio[1] wouldn't hurt my feelings. And what happened to Jackson,[2] the ex-business manager of the institution[?] I hope that he is peeling potatoes in Atlanta? Please say *yes.* But the thought that things are actually being sifted in the internal affairs of the university is very cheering to me. Has the outside committee, which Hebert spoke of at the August Commencement, been appointed? And if so, how is it constituted? And if it has been digging, what has it found? Did John Earl [*sic*][3] pinch any porch furniture or doormats from sorority houses, or did he get any LSU animal serum for making cocktails? Or are they going to fire him simply because he can't read and write? Write again, and earn our undying gratitude by telling everything that happened since your last letter. And, boy! I bet it will be plenty. That is, if they have really taken down the dung-forks out of the gear room and waded into the product which keeps the soils of la belle France so fertile and on a heap of which the rooster stands to crow for the sun on a frosty morning. And when you write the letter, don't forget to say what the Erskines are doing, for there wasn't much news of that sort in your last letter. I imagine that you are on the last lap of the novel now.[4] I do wish that I could have a quiet evening with the MS., for I'm itching to see the thing. And the articles for the magazines sound like some nice velvet. (Speaking of Erskines, you might tell Albert Russell Erskine III, that the opinion which the Warrens now hold of him wouldn't get through Mr. Farley's mails.[5] Not one word from the lug! You were perfectly right when you said that if you didn't write us the news nobody would. For nobody has. Not A.R.E. III, Conrad, Duncan, Cleanth—he did write in the middle of August—nobody. But Skoal to K.A.!)

As for our doings, there isn't a great deal to say. We stayed in Sirmione until the weather turned off on us—and had a lovely time of [it] there except when the radio gave us a turn, as it did almost daily. Then we went to Rome for a week or so, where we saw our friend Pier [Pasinetti] and had a very interesting time. Then we went south for a short time, and are now back in Rome, where we expect to be until we are forced to come home. God help us to remain for some time to come, for if we do have to come back we haven't anyplace to go, and with the steamer fares so high now we would be painfully broke, for the war has played hell with our budget. We are getting into a small apartment soon, where we can live more cheaply than in pensione, where we now are, and can also have a quieter time for work. I am getting into the last lap of the play. (Before long you may expect a package of the thing, not all, for it won't be finished before January, but a pretty big chunk, say about three quarters of it.) And I'm still plugging away at Dante, with great pleasure, and at grammar, with considerably less pleasure. Cinina has been doing a lot of reading and studying. And we both have developed, quite naturally, into ardent readers of the newspapers. (Occasionally we get a *Herald Tribune,* Paris Edition, but we don't find out much about what is going on in American domestic politics, for foreign affairs dominate all the news.) And we have seen some sights, a lot of which have certainly repaid the effort. And a lot of funny things have happened to us. I'm sorry that they will have to wait for the telling. But we'll promise to tell them only *once.* You won't have to live with them.

I don't suppose that this will reach you until you are back from your trip to Bennington. That, I imagine, will be a very pleasant little jaunt. At least, I hope so. So when you write, say how it came out.

Goodbye, and our best love to you and Albert.

As ever,

Red

P.S. How are the faces of Malcolm Cowley, and Mike Gold, and sich [*sic*], in the light of events of the last several months?[6] Red, literally, and not politically?

I forgot to say that our address from now on will be the American Express, Rome.

[Handwritten] Our best to the boys and girls who sit around spitting ambeer and jawing about neutrality.

1. Clarence Lorio, M.D., LSU's medical director.
2. E. N. Jackson. (My thanks to Philip Uzee.)
3. John Earle Uhler, a member of the English faculty, was a supporter of President Smith and a perennial nemesis of Brooks and Warren.
4. Warren was much too optimistic. Porter's lengthy struggle to finish her only full-fledged novel became the stuff of legend.
5. James A. (Jim) Farley was Roosevelt's postmaster general.
6. Many "fellow travelers" had their faith in the Soviet Union shaken by Stalin's nonaggression pact with Hitler and subsequent invasion of Finland.

TO FRANK LAWRENCE OWSLEY

TLU/VU

American Express
Rome
November 13, 1939

Dear Frank:

I want to ask a great favor of you. Somewhere in your house is a book about Sergeant Alvin York,[1] which belongs to the State Library. I had taken out all of their books on York while I was there this summer, and a note from them, which arrived very recently, tells me that one was not returned. The situation was this. On Friday evening I got a wire from the Shipping Agent in New Orleans to the effect that the date of sailing for our boat had been moved forward several days. That meant that we had to leave Nashville that much earlier than we had anticipated. Gordon very kindly volunteered to help by carrying the books back, but I said that that was not necessary, for I would leave the money for a Western Union Messenger to carry them back, if he would call the boy. He did that, but somewhere in the process a cog slipped—and it may have been the first cog, that is, myself, for I stacked the books together for the messenger to call for later. But I do know that the book was there. Anyway, my great favor is for you to ring up another messenger and have him carry the book back to the Library and get a receipt for it—all of this, if you happen to come across it.

I haven't much to add to my letter of the day before yesterday, except that we are both fighting colds and looking out of our window on one of the first gray days we've seen at Rome. The weather has been lovely, quite balmy with lots of sun.[2]

1. A famous World War I hero from the mountains of Tennessee. He provided a model for Private Porsum in *At Heaven's Gate*.

2. The truncated ending of this letter and the lack of a signature suggest that a page or more is missing.

TO BRAINARD CHENEY

TLS/VU

American Express
Rome
November 13, 1939

Dear Lon:

Blessings on you! A letter is a great event in our lives now, for except for one from Katherine Anne Porter a few days ago—posted September 29—we haven't had a damned word for months. The boys at LSU, quite naturally, didn't send or forward any mail, after hell began to pop over here, until they had some definite word of our plans. And since we didn't know for a time what our plans would be, we couldn't give them any word. But now we are expecting, almost any day, a batch of stuff to coming rolling in from Louisiana. But Katherine Anne's letter did bring the jolly tidings that Smith and a lot of his palsie-walsies are going to be picking oakum or breaking rock for a few years. Not enough years to satisfy my vindictive nature, but enough to prove that the courts didn't regard the boyish waywardness of those prime, quadruple-plated, crested and stream-lined sons-of-bitches as deserving merely an indulgent clucking of the tongue. And I was pleased to know that Leche himself is in for more indictments. And that they are going over the internal affairs of the University with a fine-toothed comb—or as the language of this happy land has it, they are going to "de-flea the situation." For instance, already one department there is on probation. Good news! Cleanth and a lot of his pals had given a statement to the press in the summer, making certain accusations and asking for investigation.[1] So it seems that for the time being, which is all you can ask, some justice is being done. I don't know why I, at this distance and to a newspaper man, attempt to give news of Louisiana, but it has come very fresh to me. When you do write again, as I hope you will soon, please tell me what has happened to Leche.

As for our situation, we may be complete idiots. But it is possible that the situation looks more generally black from that distance than it does here. Life here moves much as usual and there is great optimism that Italy may be able to remain neutral. But the first few days, or weeks, after the war broke out, we were in quite a stew. Sirmione is really a wonderful place; our hotel-pensione is a little place out in the country, on the peninsula, in an olive grove overlooking the lake, a wonderful place to work; but we spent a lot of our time gnawing our nails and waiting for the next broadcast. Then we had the problem of seeing that another person got off on a boat, a Spanish lady, whose amiable fatalism and incompetence makes [sic] all the stories one has ever heard about the Spanish fade into pearl-gray understatement. But that story is like this: In the height of the disorders Cinina and I were in the telephone office trying to get a call through to the Consul in Milan. We noticed a very nice lady, quite pretty and on the sunny side of forty-five and very well-preserved, who was trying to convey some idea, in bad Italian with a Spanish accent, to the operator. Cinina thought that she might be of some help to the woman, since she speaks Spanish, and offered her services. Well, she got the woman's call in—also to the Consul. Then the woman said, "Where did you learn your Spanish?" And Cinina said, "In South America." And the woman: "Where in South America?" And Cinina said: "Ecuador." And the woman: "What was your name?" And Cinina told her, and the woman exclaimed: "Oh you are Mita!" In other words, the woman was an old friend of Cinina's mother in South America, and had been a student in the Conservatory there, and had known Cinina when Cinina was a baby. Well, the woman now lives in New York. It was home-coming week for all us Ecuadorians. But the woman was supposed to leave for she had reservations on the Italian Line. It took, ho[w]ever, the combined efforts of the Warrens and a distinguished Italian gentleman who was a friend of the lady to really put her affairs in order. Boy, you never saw anything until you saw a Spaniard think that tomorrow is as good as today and that God will provide railroad tickets and carry you on the wings of the morning to the station. We were so exhausted by our efforts that we didn't have strength enough to face our own problems; so we just stayed on. And after while things looked quieter so we went to Rome and talked to the Consul there, and then we went to Naples, which we didn't like very much, and talked to the Consul there, and then we came back to Rome, where we now are, and where, God willing, we shall remain until we return to America, which, I hope, will be next summer. We are taking a little apartment within the next few days; we have already found it and have arranged for it; and that will mean a welcome relief from hotel and pensione life, and that we can get more work done. But Sirmione was a fine place for work. I have done five complete scenes of my play since leaving America and some work on the new novel. The play will be finished in January, according to the present schedule, and then I can settle more consistently into the traces of the novel. And, speaking of the novel, I want to thank you for your various services of this summer. I think that I now see my way clear—which isn't very encouraging, because it looks to be a very thorny way.

I've just had a letter from Shirley Forgotson, in the same mail as your own, who is singing Fanny's praises in exalted tones, with such phrases as this[:] "as fine and sweet a person as I've ever met" etc. He says that she has been wonderful to him. And Isabel, too, has apparently been awfully nice to him. He has got a terrific lot of stuff on the ball, I am convinced, and he is a very nice fellow. I do hope that he makes out well there. It will mean a great deal to him.

It was good to hear that Jimmy Waller is fixed up at North Caro-lina.[2] I imagine that he will be much happier teaching than with his bond house.

And it is good to know that your book is out by this time. I do wish it a tremendous success. Have you managed to recuperate and start on another? Or are you still taking a blow [*sic*] for the other? Let me know how things go with it, won't you[?] And let me hear again about the local scene. The letter was, as I assure[d] you, a real treat to both of us.

Cinina joins me in affectionate regards to you and Fanny. Say hello to Puryear[3] and his wife, Owsleys, Beattys, Davidsons, but don't be too God-damned promis[c]uous around too many buildings on the Campus.

As ever,

Red

P.S. Did I tell you in the other letter that HM sent me a nice little check for my rather accidental role in putting them in touch with you?

Love from us both to Isabel.

1. Mark Royden Winchell presents a detailed account of Brooks's reformist activities in his biography *Cleanth Brooks and the Rise of Modern Criticism* (177–83).

2. James Muir Waller was a Nashville banker and contributor to Agar and Tate's *Who Owns America?* who became an academic economist. (My thanks to Walter Sullivan.)

3. Puryear Mims, a sculptor, was the son of Edwin Mims, the long-serving head of the English department at Vanderbilt.

TO KENNETH BURKE

TLS/PennS   American Express
                                                            Rome
                                            November 13, 1939

Dear Burke:

Your letter came today, and cheered me greatly. The fact of a letter is in itself a reason for rejoicing for us, for there have been so few of late—my friends at my office, I am sure, didn't forward any mail or write until they had some news as to my plans, and there has scarcely been time yet for them to get anything to me after receiving word from me that I was going to stick it out for another round. But what your letter said was an even greater cause for rejoicing, for your reaction to the play is enormously hearten[ing] to me. Well before you receive this another batch should be in your hands, for I mailed some more to you about two or three weeks back. I have only four more scenes to go in addition to what you will have when the last batch arrives. By the first of January I hope to have the thing done, or rather, to have a draft of it done. I already have patches of the next four scenes written and have the skeleton pretty well articulated. God, I do hope the thing is some good, for I've invested a lot in it. The Guggenheim people gave me their fellowship for doing a new novel, and I have been working on one—last summer I did a lot of work, in fact—but this thing, which had been on my mind for two years, and of which I had done a couple of scenes, started to move, and so, willy-nilly, I began to violate the terms of my appointment. I do hope that they won't take too harsh a view of my situation when I apply for my renewal, for I am applying on the grounds of the same novel for which I was originally appointed, offering the play as my alibi, as it were, for the mis-spent period up to January or February when I get the play finished. I had a letter from Mr. Moe today to the effect that I had until up in January to demonstrate to the Foundation that I hadn't been wasting my time—he couched the thing in less brutal terms than that—and to offer some reason for a renewal. My situation is, of course, complicated by the fact that I have leave from the University for only one year; but I think that they would co-operate by giving me more time off if I did get the renewal. If they won't, well, I'd be strongly tempted to tell them to go to hell, for I want to finish this play and this novel, which promises to be a long and back-breaking project, without having to do it late at night and sandwiched between classes, as I did most of *Night Rider*. Anyway, I am greatly pleased that you will, when the time comes, speak your piece to the Guggenheim people in my behalf. If you don't receive the rest of the play in early January, or some explanation from me as to why you haven't received it, you can know that it has gone astray in the mails; and in that case, will you let them have an opinion on the grounds of what you already have in hand?

I read the newspapers every day and get more and more befuddled.

I haven't even got as nice a slogan as your tropes-tropisms to tide me over, and so I simply brood. Occasionally my wife and I think we ought to pull out home, and sit and lose our appetites with worrying over the next six or eight months, but for the most part, because life seems to move so uneventfully here and because the weather has been so good recently and because the cost of living hasn't risen as much as we had feared it would (though it is much higher than last year and higher than a short while back), we decide to sit tight. I wish I had some notion of what the commentators are making of things and what the newspapers are saying, but I suppose that I'll have to take a week off and go back into the files when I get back to America. But I imagine that my own condition, that of befuddlement, is pretty general.

I wish that I could see the 40,000 words which you sent to the SR; and even at 40,000 words I may yet see it in the SR unless Brooks manages to suppress his customary enthusiasm for what you send in. And I'd be enormously interested in seeing the remarks on *Night Rider*.[1]

Goodbye, and all best wishes. I hope that the drouth breaks before the freeze sets in and that the Five-Months-Old will learn to practice a little self-control. You might try reading him Wordsworth's Ecclesiastical Sonnets before retiring. That might break his spirit.

Again, thanks for the letter.

Sincerely yours,
Warren

1. It would appear that Burke had sent Brooks a version of the manuscript that became *The Philosophy of Literary Form* (1941), which would eventually be published by LSU Press and in which he makes favorable comments on Warren's first novel.

TO ANDREW LYTLE

TLS/VU
American Express
Rome
November 14, 1939

Dear Andrew:

Did you ever receive a letter mailed in August from Genoa? If you never did, I'll forgive you for not writing. And perhaps you didn't, for I have never received an answer to a letter mailed at the same time to Allen and one to Frank. And, by God, I've scarcely received a word from anybody else. The last mail forwarded to me from LSU was sent on August 15— but that is easy to be explained, for the boys there couldn't have thought, when the headlines started to be hot, that we'd be damned enough fools to take the long shot. Well, we did. And there has scarcely been time for them to hear from us that we had definitely determined to stay and for mail to get back to us here. But we did have a letter very recently from Katherine Anne, just a few days ago, a letter mailed on September 29. It brough[t] the fine news that the courts did decide to make a gesture toward rewarding our dear President Smith and some of his boys with a proper sentence. They only got two years each, but that is something. And at the same time Katherine Anne said that Governor Leche had another indictment and that the internal investigation of the affairs of the University would probably turn up another flock of indictments. But I suppose that you now know a lot more about all of this than I do. And Cleanth when he was up at Monteagle must have filled you full of the low-down. (I had a letter from Cheney yesterday, in which he said that he had seen Cleanth at Monteagle.) But it does seem that the clean-up in the University is progressing. And by God! that is good news.

Well, as I remarked above, we were damned enough fools to take the long shot, and up to date have not regretted it. Except for the running back and forth to the radio during the early days and weeks of the war, we had a fine time at Sirmione, which is, certainly, one of the best spots on the globe. We stayed in the same place as last year there, a little hotel-pensione out in the country, in an olive grove, on a cliff overlooking the lake. And all you have to do to go to work is pick up your typewriter and stroll some ninety seconds away and fall on the grass and go to sleep. But despite the war and over-eating and sleeping I did manage to get some things done, and up to date have done five more scenes on the play which I told you about in July; which makes me four scenes from the end. I hope to finish in January. Then I shall get down to consecutive work on the novel, on which I have been doing some work since I came and on which I worked in Nashville. Sometime in January you can expect a copy of the play to come rolling in for your remarks. I wish that I could have had the benefit of personal conferences with you, as a dramatic critic, during the process of composition.

[Handwritten] (At this point I have to abandon the typewriter for fear of disturbing the people next to us, for we are in a pensione.) But maybe I haven't in my innocence done everything wrong in the play and perhaps some of the things which I have done wrong can be put to rights. Anyway, you may recall what I said about the Confederate Navy and my play. Some writer on the subject of the Confederate Navy said that the Southerners, being unhampered by any naval experience, proceeded to develop the torpedo, the ironclad, and the submarine. So all I can hope is that my ignorance of the stage, like their ignorance of the sea, may develop into an asset. This, I grant you, is a rather extreme piece of optimism.

But after Sirmione: When the weather began to turn the corner we went to Rome, being lured there by the invitation of a friend who said that under the special circumstances we would find the place peculiarly interesting. And he was right. We stayed for almost a couple of weeks, digesting the rumors. Then we headed South, and we [were] at Naples and in that neighborhood for a while. But now we are back here, in Rome again, where we expect to stay until we have to come home. When that will be, I shan't predict, but we should like to remain until next summer. I hate to be bullied out of my plans. We shall soon be in an apartment, which will be a good deal more pleasant than hotel and pensione life. (There are, I regret to say, few places as good as the one in Sirmione.)

How are things going with you all? And how is the novel moving? Do let us have word of life on the mountain. And soon, for we are anxious for news. Goodbye and our best to you and Edna.

As ever,
Red

[P.S.] I hope that you, from old experience, will be able to make out this writing. Lon Cheney writes that Jimmy Waller has gone to North Carolina: which sounds like good news. And what do you hear from Allen? Not a line have I had, the dog.

TO JOHN PEALE BISHOP

APC/PU

American Express
Rome
November 15, 1939

Mr. John Peale Bishop
South Harwick [crossed out][1]
Mass.
U.S.A.

Dear John:

We are still hanging on and hoping for the best. If things go well we shall come back next summer; if not, before that, if we can. But it has been very interesting, and I am getting my work done. I hope that everything is going well for you, and that the new house is a proper joy. My wife joins me in warm regards to you both.

As ever,
Red Warren

1. Corrected in another hand: "South Chatham."

TO FRANK LAWRENCE OWSLEY

TLS/VU

American Express
Rome
December 7, 1939

Dear Frank:

Your very kind card came today, having made remarkable time.

I'm sorry to learn that my previous efforts to get in touch with you had come to nothing. But only God knows what happens to mail these days. I yet haven't [sic] received the long-awaited stuff forwarded from my office. And I recently had a note from a friend in England, who said that he had written twice previously. And I had written to him three times in the past several months, and he had only received one letter. By the way, I've written to Don—some time back—and I wonder if that letter went astray.

As for news with us, there isn't much to say. We are now in an apartment, quite adequately comfortable, on one of highest spots in Rome, and about twenty-five minutes from the center of town. We haven't yet settled down to the grim business of sightseeing, but we have been to most of the obvious places here. And we are getting a season pass to the Vatican Museum, which ought to occupy a good deal of our time, if our short experience with it is any indication. As for our occupations, they are the predictable ones. We read a lot, and work some hours every day at our own little projects. I am just about to wind up my play—the one I told you about—and shall be at the novel for consecutive writing in January, if nothing unforeseen comes along. And I'm still grinding away at the Italian. But I begin to suspect, from the expressions which I sometimes surprise [*sic*] on the faces of polite listeners that my accent must be pretty extraordinary. I'm getting a lot of pleasure, however, from the work I've been doing on the Dante and on the chronicles of his time, the Dino Compagni and the Villani.[1] But my God! what an effect I do create when I mix the vocabulary which I acquire from those gents with my attempts at ordinary bread-and-butter Italian.

We see a good deal of our friends here, especially Pasinetti. But through him we've met a good many of the younger journalists and writers—I say a good many, which is an exaggeration, some four or five. (I shall regale your [*sic*] with a full report on our conversations when we can set [*sic*] back some evening; for the present is not the time, I assure you.) But that is the extent of our social life. We wish that we could import a little Owsley social life right now, but it doesn't look like a very practical idea.

A lot of our time and energy now, especially since the Finland business started, is taken up with reading the papers. War is ruining, not only the civilized world, but my morning's work rather often, for I feel that I can't get settled to work until I've run to the corner to get the paper and find out about the latest horror; and then after I get the paper I have a hard time settling down anyway. I don't suppose that you can find many Stalinists at home now, and when they appear in society or in print they don't feel themselves, I imagine, exactly among friends. I had a letter from Burke the other day—who is by all odds, I think, the most intelligent of all the leftist literary people in NY, though he doesn't fit very well with the label of "Stalinist"—and he said that the developments of the autumn have shaken him to the base. He confessed to bewilderment—which means, I suppose, that he now knows that he is where I've known that I was for a long time. But Burke has never mistaken labels for ideas, which is an achievement heroic enough for any man. (Did you ever see the speech he made to the First American Writer's Congress?[2] He flattened back a good many ears on that count.)

Well, enough for this evening. But there would be a lot more to say if we could say it face to face. I'll look forward to a long letter. Meanwhile, our very best wishes for a Merry Christmas and a Happy New Year. Love to the family.

As ever,

Red

1. Compagni (1260–1324) and Giovanni Villani (1275–1348) were Florentine historians.

2. At the First American Writers' Congress (1935), organized and dominated by communists, Burke had delivered a speech entitled "Revolutionary Symbolism in America" in which he argued that imaginative literature should rise above ideological polemic, thus scandalizing the party faithful.

TO KATHERINE ANNE PORTER

TLS/Maryland
American Express
Rome
December 12, 1939

Dear Katherine Anne:

To begin with a little piece of business: Pasinetti—you know, my friend and the friend of Albert and Cleanth, is interested in a new magazine here, the first number of which will appear in February or March, and is especially interested in getting some translations from American writers who are not known here but who should, he feels, be known. In fact, American books are very popular here, extremely popular, even though many are had in French translations, but the picture given by the people who are translated is a rather weird rendering of the American literary scene. For instance, Saroyan is translated everywhere here,[1] Jerome Bahr[2] to some extent, Hemingway is very popular, Morley Callahan [*sic*]³ (I can't seem to remember how to spell his name, but you know the bird) appears rather frequently, etc. Faulkner is greatly admired, which is all to the good, but his short stories have not, I believe, appeared here. It is against the lack of discrimination which lumps Bahr and Hemingway together and puts Saroyan up as a genius that Pier want[s] to do a little crusading. He wants to begin by translating one or two of your short stories, one or two of Caroline's, something from Kay Boyle⁴ and Eudora Welty and George Milburn (some of whose early stories I like). He wants, if possible, to translate one of your pieces for the first issue and is writing immediately—or rather Mondadori, the publisher and backer—is writing to Harcourt about the permission business. There is pay, of course, though I don't know how much, or how, with the existing regulations about currency, the thing is managed. But I imagine that the rate will be about the same as that from French and German translations; anyway, dozens of American books are published here every year, and there must be some standard way for handling the matter. As I said, Pier is writing to Harcourt, but he wanted also to get your blessing on the project, and I told him that I would write you. He has asked me to do a little note to accompany some of the translations, a little comment, and if I can finish my play by January I shall certainly do it, that is, if he doesn't strike any snags about permissions and have to abandon the project. Oh, I almost forgot, do you mind dropping Pier a note, for it is barely possible that we may have to leave before your response could reach Italy? The address is: Pier Maria Pasinetti, 24 Viale di Villa Massimo, Rome.

As I say, it is possible that we may have to leave soon. But we shall know tomorrow, for then I have my appointment with the consul to try to persuade him to give us a special permission. But I shall write air mail as soon as I know anything definite so that there won't be any mix-up about forwarding of mail, etc. But I do hope that we can stay. Work is moving beautifully now, and if we have to be uprooted, it may be weeks, or months, before a routine can again be established.

Cinina joins me in all love to you and a kick on the Fanny for Albert. If a letter from Albert comes on the next boat, make it just half a kick.

As ever,
Red

P.S. I am sending one copy of this air mail and another regular mail so that I can have some assurance that at least one will reach you. To the other, which I am sending regular mail, I shall add a few more words, and, in fact, shall not send it until after the talk with the Consul. So long!

And I forgot to say that Pier himself is going to do the translation of your work, so there will be somebody who will give the thing admiring care and who will have the proper qualifications.

1. William Saroyan's phenomenal popularity began with the publication of *The Daring Young Man on the Flying Trapeze and Other Stories* (1934). He won the Pulitzer Prize in 1939 for his play *The Time of Your Life.*

2. Bahr's *All Good Americans* (1937) featured a foreword by Ernest Hemingway.

3. Morley Edward Callaghan, a Canadian, had been associated with Pound and Hemingway in the 1920s.

4. Expatriate writer of novels and short stories. Her *Monday Night* had appeared the year before.

TO ALLEN TATE

TLS/PU   American Express
                                                                  Rome
                                                      December 14, 1939

Dear Allen:

Your letter came today, having taken, as you can figure out, quite a time in getting here. But it was more than welcome. I had begun to fear that all of my efforts to reach you were in vain. For I had written several times, one letter as long ago as August 16, mailed from Genoa. And there was another note a little later, and a letter from Capri; and one, and perhaps two—I can't remember—post cards. But I had one letter today, one from Albert, mailed as long ago as October 25. It's a slow business, and at times very disheartening. It is really the most immediately unsettling thing about our staying.

We are settled, that is, we are settled in so far as that can be said at all, in Rome, where we have been now for some six weeks. Things farther South didn't work out for reasons too numerous to mention. Except for the war, things are going beautifully for us—except for the war, and, I should add, except for the servant problem. We've just fired one today for high misdemeanors. But we have a very nice little apartment, very small, on top of a hill, only some twenty minutes from the center of the city, by foot, and a few minutes less by street car. Life moves quite casually here. There is no excitement about the war—that is, no obvious excitement—but, of course, it's damned near all people talk about when they get together and unbutton the vest and prop their heels up. Automobiles are back on the streets again, though with limited gasoline rations. Coffee has not come back, but there are rumors that it will be available shortly. I have had a couple of conferences with the Consul, one before the new passport regulations went into effect, and one since. It seems that we shall be permitted to stay for some time, but, of course, a moment may change all of that; and we haven't got the official stamp on our passport yet, for we had to get some letters and documents together before he could do that—some evidence of the Guggenheim grant, some one here to certify to my occupation, and stuff like that. Naturally, I didn't have all that stuff in my pocket when I went there.

Despite the alarums and excursions—and the fact that I can't get to work of a morning until I've gone out for the paper—I have managed to get a lot done. What it's like, I simply don't know. One day I feel pretty good about it, and the next I want to dump the whole thing in the Tiber. In any case, I finished the next to the last scene of the play today, and tomorrow shall start the last one. Since the last one is very short, and since I have large chunks of it already scribbled down, I should be able to finish before Christmas. There will be a good deal of revision, especially in the first three scenes—some shortening and tightening. I shall send copies of the last several scenes direct to you, assuming that John [Ransom] has forwarded the preceding stuff to you. I'll send another copy to John, and I am considering offering it to him, even though I'm pretty sure that it isn't exactly suitable for the KR.[1] And, in addition, I don't know how he likes the thing, [for I] haven't heard a word from him since I left. But, just in case he [might] like it, I want him to have a first crack at it. (By the way, if you happen to know the name of a good agent in New York who might not throw the thing out the window because it happens to be fifty percent verse, I'd like to have the name and address. But I really have no hope that I shall find a producer.) I have got a lot of stuff on the novel, and have done a lot of work toward it and some on it—bits sketched in, etc. I shall begin consecutive writing as soon as the play is finished. And I've been working pretty hard at the Italian; have read a lot of books, the Inferno several times, the Purgatorio. And I've been grinding away at grammar. I've managed to get far enough along to have some pleasure from the poetry, which, by the way, definitely does not seem to be over-rated.

A recent letter from Cleanth brings me good news from LSU. Apparently the boys are winning out in their efforts to have a real clean-up. The acting president has, to all appearances, sided with Cleanth's gang; but it's too early to be certain as to the results. Meanwhile, the jails are bulging. He said that the current SR had been sent to me, but it hasn't arrived yet. I agree with you [Arthur] Mizener is good. You'll probably run into him sooner or later up there, for he is at Yale. And while I'm on the subject of the SR, let me beg you not to fail to get the Hardy piece done. Will that piece be part of the projected program for the next book of criticism? And what is the new book about, the new novel, I mean? The one that was mentioned at Monteagle last summer? I'd like to hear more about the critical book and about it, too, when you write again. It's astonishing about Moe's reply to you!

As for Princeton, your report doesn't make it all appear too jolly; but the situation you describe is very much what I had suspected to exist. But if you really have so much free time and have good students, things ought to be pretty satisfactory. God knows, a little time of your own can make a big difference. I've felt like a new man all fall. And how is Caroline's Carnegie Fellowship coming on? It is Carnegie, isn't it? And how is Nancy's [sic]?

And speaking of Fellowships, I've applied, or rather have written to Moe, for a renewal. Without one, next summer looks mighty blank, and I think that I would be compelled to do some incidental writing right in the middle of the period when I want to be working steadily on the novel. If I should get a renewal, I think that I could strike some arrangement which would be satisfactory to the University and to the Foundation. (If I get the renewal we should go back to Louisiana anyway.) But I would like to have the chance to finish the novel, which promises to be a long pull—a several pounder, it now seems—without having to sandwich it in between classes. I suppose the Guggenheim reaction will be based largely on the opinion received about the play from the adviser, or advisers, who happen to get it—and you have, in your letter, already named three mighty likely candidates—Canby,[2] Cowley, Millay. (By the way, do you all get to New York much? And have you seen the Radfords?

I wrote Manson some time back but haven't had a reply. If you get this letter, you might ask Manson if he ever got my letter, which was sent in care of the SR.)

I'm going to knock off. I'm in a daze, I'm so tired tonight, for I had to stand in a line for three hours this afternoon at an office down town. Do write as soon as you can. Our very best to you all.

As ever,

Red

P.S. The Kenyon Review has just come, and I've had a glance at my piece. It makes me [look] pretty bad. But I must say that Read's piece is not a hell of a lot better.[3]

1. No excerpt from *Proud Flesh* appeared in the *Kenyon Review*.

2. Henry Seidel Canby, a founding editor of the *Saturday Review of Literature* and a leading figure in the American literary establishment.

3. The Autumn 1939 issue of the *Kenyon Review* featured a symposium on "The Present State of Poetry." Warren addressed the situation in the United States, while Herbert Read surveyed developments in England and Justin O'Brien dealt with France.

TO ALBERT ERSKINE AND KATHERINE ANNE PORTER

TLS/Maryland

American Express
Rome
December 16, 1939

Dear Albert and Katherine Anne:

And as for you, Albert, all is forgiven. Your letter of October 26th came a couple of days ago. To our great joy. Along with several other letters of approximately the same vintage. And a copy of the SR itself, at long last. How this particular batch of stuff got held up will probably remain a mystery, since we have received letters and magazines, mailed at much later dates. But the letter is here, and we are happy to have it. And, I shall add, are touched by the note of avuncular concern which dominates several paragraphs. You are probably right, and we may reform before long. Or we may be forced to reform by another uncle whose name is Samuel.¹ But he seems, for the present, to be willing to let us to have our rope, and, to mix metaphors, eat it too, for that matter. Anyway, he has postponed a decision to such a distant date that the question is academic.

There is very little news with us. The biggest thing in our lives for the day was a morning trip to Saint Peter's, so you can see that the day has been one round of frivolity and excitement. And it has been raining. Cinina has been sunk in her reading of Stendhal all the day—she spends all her time these days reading Stendhal, and only grunts at me when I try to establish some sort of communication. She has read all his stuff which our friend PMP [Pier Maria Pasinetti] has and is going down to buy up all in the city tomorrow morning, or threatens to do so. And I went to bed this afternoon and read the Purgatorio, and having a particularly dull section on hand, could have been lured out by any pretext. I had had an engagement to go to a football game, but the weather was so bad that there was no soap.

How is this for a New Yorker cartoon? The other day we went to the Consulate and during our visit had a talk with little Mister Jones, who, it seems, is the lad who puts his thumb print on passport renewals—that is the truth. I don't know why. Perhaps he has the most elegant whorls in the office. But, anyway, he is the lad who handles that business now. He is a stage version of the American College PRIZE PRODUCT. He is very dressy. He clears his throat frequently, and never says, "I think," but only "We—humph, humph—think." He has a very clear face and somewhat staring blue eyes. I told him about our situation and desires, and he shook his head gravely, and said that he must have some documents. "What kind of documents?" says I. "Anything," says he, "get somebody to write us a letter." "That's easy," says I. "We must have something to show," he said, "we must have—humph, humph—something to show, for if any thing should happen to you, what would Washington say to me?" I was compelled to confess that I didn't have the answer to that little poser. So Cinina and I, for the past several days, have been demanding of each other: "If anything should happen to you, what would Washington say to me[?]" I forgot to say, that he has a habit of whirling his swivel chair round and round, for obviously he is very new to it and the novelty is entrancing. [Handwritten in margin] Twenty-seven years of age if a day—and not precocious.

[Typing resumes] I haven't yet read all of the SR, but find the Teacher's College article[2] more than up to expectations. Has Ives[3] yet called by [sic]? If any of those boys read it, it ought to raise carbuncles, and not goose flesh. And I imagine that somebody will call their attention to it. It's cunning, especially the part that juggles them into the position of village atheists. I would not be surprised to see some reprints of this article, sooner or later, in other places. You know, we ought to hammer that line, [Handwritten at top of page] T. C. not reprints [Typing resumes] and sooner or later, probably, we'd get, if not results, at least some stink. It falls pat, too, with the news Cleanth wrote me about Phi Beta Kappa. It looks as if it might fall too God-damned pat. It begins to look like conspiracy.

By the way, our friend who is interested in family history,[4] and on whose work we spent some time on [sic] last spring doing Ms and proof, has applied for a place, any kind of a place, with Brewer[5] and with some other people. His credentials, which were sent a long time back, are enormously impressive. If either, or both of you, can find it in your hearts to clarify Brewer's mind on any essential points or to speak on our friend's capacities, it would be a chore done in a very good and almost imperative cause. I leave this to your powers of divination. I wrote to Joe, too, but it was not possible for me to explain certain matters which are important.

The political news from Louisiana is encouraging. I hope that they get Earl,[6] too, whether he has or has not rustled cattle. I don't like his face. And I'm glad to think that I don't have to look at the Leche face every time I cross the campus. What are they going to do with the bronze? Or do they just chisel off the face and leave the bronze in place[?] It begins to look as though the architect who wouldn't let Conrad paint in his face next to that of Leche in the fresco of the State Office Building was not modest but just damned cagey. Did Conrad ever tell you that tale?

By the way, speaking of Conrad, do you know whether he and Jean [sic] have received any of our letters? Or has Duncan? I gathered from a letter from Mrs. Daggett[7] that the Albrizios has [sic] not. And I am writing again immediately, but I have written several times in the past, twice, to be exact, and Cinina once, and then, I think, a card. But everything is a mystery. We haven't heard a word from the A's or from Duncan.

It's good news that you are knocking off the work, Katherine Anne, and something else in addition, for the HB stuff sounds like that.[8] Louisiana excitement is probably greater than our own, to judge from the letters we've had from the Erskines and from Mr. Brooks, and so you deserve all credit for snatching a little self possession from the midst of the general tumult. We snatch a little, now and then.

Do write again, and very soon. The letters are big doings for us. Meanwhile, be good and be assured of our best love.

As ever,

Red

P.S. I hope to have the completed MS of the play off to you within a week or ten days. I am on the last scene now. God help me! By the way, I think that the Welty story is better than the King.[9] But, Albert, is not the case with you [sic]. But both are very, very good. And Mizener is quite a hot shot.[10] The oil article is all right, if you have to have that sort of thing. I have tried to read Rogers,[11] and shall, when I am stronger. Haven't tackled Lindley.[12] Give me time.

1. "Uncle Sam," i.e., the United States government.

2. Howard Dykema Roelofs, "Democracy and the Curriculum" (Autumn 1939).

3. Clarence A. Ives, dean of education at LSU. (My thanks to Charles East and Bessie Barnett Turpin.)

4. Pasinetti, whose story "Family History" was in the Summer 1939 issue. As a critic of fascism, he was in a sensitive position, and Warren, aware of the Italian censors, frequently alludes to him in a circumlocutious way.

5. Joseph Brewer, whose publishing firm Payson & Clarke had brought out Warren's first book (*John Brown* [1929]), had shifted careers and was now president of Olivet College.

6. The lieutenant governor, Earl K. Long, brother of Huey, had assumed the governorship after Leche's resignation.

7. Harriet Spiller Daggett was professor of constitutional law at LSU. (My thanks to Robert B. Heilman and Robert W. Rudnicki.)

8. Harcourt Brace had brought out Porter's *Pale Horse, Pale Rider: Three Short Novels* and may have offered her an advance on "Promised Land."

9. Welty's "The Hitch-Hikers" and Mary King's "The Honey House" were both in the Autumn 1939 issue.

10. Arthur Mizener had written on "Recent Fiction" for the Autumn number.

11. Lindsay Rogers, "England and France at 'White War'" (Autumn 1939).

12. Ernest K. Lindley, "Roosevelt in Print" (Autumn 1939).

TO JOHN PEALE BISHOP

TLS/PU

American Express
Piazza di Spagna
Rome
December 27, 1939

Dear John:

Your two letters arrived almost simultaneously—the one of the fall, sent to Baton Rouge, and the one December 9, sent here. My friends at Baton Rouge did not get my letter telling them that we had decided to stay, despite the war, until toward the end of October, and so had forwarded no mail. The package with your letter was sent from Baton Rouge on October 26, but only reached me just before Christmas. I don't know what the answer is, but I am inclined to think that the American Express at Naples had mislaid my address, or just didn't give a damn. I want you to know why you never received an answer to that first letter, especially since you had spoken about the matter of payment on the article.[1] Brooks and Erskine, thinking that the thing was a personal letter purely, had not opened it; but I hope that you did, after not hearing from me, write to them directly. God knows, even if you did, whether the thing was possible. A long time back we managed to pay for a few things on acceptance, when it was requested, but later the business office stopped us, because there is, or was, some law that no state materials can be paid for before delivery—and the office insisted on defining delivery for the SR as publication. But some of those boys are in the soup now—the business manager of the University, included—and the new administration may take a more humane view of arts and letters.

Things were, and to judge from letters, still are at fever heat down there. The president in jail for a long term—the bastard had some forty-odd indictments running from using the mails to defraud to forgery. The governor, Leche, is under several Federal indictments—and may God grant that they nail him. And dozens of lesser birds are already convicted or indicted. It's all damned good news. And the reform seems to be going beautifully inside the university, too, to judge from latest reports from my operatives there.

Things have been going very well with us here. We have a little apartment in a very pleasant section of the city, a very quiet place but only twenty minutes on foot from the Corso. And, after some bad luck, we have managed to get a good servant. We do some sight-seeing, and a lot of work. I have finished my play—by the way, if you happen to know the name of a good dramatic agent, one who won't throw the manuscript out of the window because he sees a lot of verse—I'd appreciate you giving it to me. And I've been at my new novel. And Italian and Dante take a lot of time, some hours every day. Cinina stays pretty busy, too. But we have some friends here, and have some rather nice evenings, now and then.

The war has, up to the present, made very little difference in life here, except of course, for higher prices, the absence of coffee, and the rationing of gasoline. The general feeling is that the country will remain neutral, at least for a long time to come. But I live from one newspaper to the next.

Goodbye, and best luck. I look forward to seeing the piece on Joyce. Cinina joins me in warmest regards to you both.

As ever,
Red

---

1. Bishop may have requested advance payment for his article on Joyce's *Finnegans Wake* (Winter 1940).

1940

TO CLEANTH BROOKS

TLS/YU
Rome
January 11, 1940¹

Dear Cleanth,

The new SR came today,² and that is something like what a magazine
ought to be. I've read it damned near from cover to cover, with pleasure,
even if I was acquainted with nearly everything in it. I hadn't seen the
Bishop, of course, or the Zabel.³ I didn't give Bishop a careful reading,
and am not entitled to an opinion, but it seems OK, and the Zabel,
which I did read carefully, seems to be exactly what you said it was: the
best thing he has done. The job on Millay is not half bad.⁴ Has Mrs.
Stopher been Vashti-ing round over that little item?⁵ And Edna M. herself is going to commence to believe that Louisiana is not a good place
for cultural lectures—after the essays by Brooks, Ransom, and Zabel
which have been financed by the State University at one time and another. Ransom throttled her with one of her own silk garters;⁶ Zabel has
choked her with some of her own taffy. I fear that you, my pal, resorted
to the homely old cleaver, without compliments.⁷ But,—as the lady in
the old New Yorker cartoon remarked to the psychiatrist—"I have a
feeling that my feet are trying to tell me something"—she [Millay] may
be having the feeling that her feet are trying to tell her something—not
to take them to Louisiana on any more lecture tours. I forgot—I haven't

read the revolutionary piece.[8] But the issue looks damned good, with less dead wood than we have had for a long time. And the order of the stuff is nice, huh?

I received a few days ago a very handsome volume recently published by the North Carolina Press.[9] For it, both Cinina and I say a large *thank you.* They did do a very nice job of manufacture for you, I feel. And I have reread the book. It is all that I thought it was. Certainly, nobody has done a cleaner job of getting at the very central situation in modern poetry. And the individual analyses still strike me as extraordinarily keen. And, may I say again, that I am deeply gratified by your comments on my own stuff. I can make this even more emphatic at this distance than when I said it across the litter of our desk. I only hope that a little amiable perjury didn't creep into the book about the point.

And today the mails brought Mr. Crofts' statement. One hundred and ninety-nine berries. Which, you know, could be a lot worse. And was it welcome news! If he can make a fair success of the book during the next couple of years, so that he has something in the bank on it, I imagine that with another revision, and perhaps a change in format and an enlargement, we can put out the book that will sweep the field. (By the way, I suppose our labors of last spring have paid for the twins which I have heard Purser now has. That ought to be our church-work for the year. And, don't forget to tell me when you write next, did he do proofs? If he didn't, there ought to be a damned show-down on this whole affair. If he did do proofs, and he will do the proofs on the next revision, all right. But if not.)[10] I have been doing a little on the story text book,[11] not much, but something. But I shall get something substantial done this spring, I hope.

I shall have your MS of *Proud Flesh* in the mail next Monday or Tuesday. It has been ready for some days, but I discovered that the copy I had for you all was the only copy left which had in it a number of revisions, and so I had to hang on to it, or try to go back and remake the revisions. So I hung on to it, and made another copy. When you have time, please write me in detail about it, all your suggestions and criticisms. For I don't regard this draft as final. In fact, I am almost certain that if the thing is produced—which I am sure, is quite unlikely—I shall have to do some heavy cutting in the second and third scenes of the first act. And I imagine that there will be other important revisions to make. But for the time being I am going to lay it by, so that

I can have the benefit of the comments of a few people and the benefit of a little perspective.

By the way, I have heard from a reliable source, which you may surmise, that you all may be seeing our friend who is interested in family history much sooner than you ever suspected, and for an indefinite period.[12] He is, I hear from the same most reliable sources, making desperate efforts to change his whole plan of life. The motives are, I am sure, easily grasped by you, and are motives with which you would have the deepest sympathy. I hear that he simply can't take any more of what he has been taking.

To take up the ever fascinating subject of life in Louisiana, what is the dope about Bryan?[13] Has anything been decided? Lately I've been watching the mails, day by day, with hope that the announcement of the great event would appear. I'll draw a deep breath when I do hear that.

And as for our own little fortunes, what is the dope about the promotions? I don't suppose that there is any yet. Hebert, during the talk which I had with him last summer, suggested that I write him in the early spring about the matter, referring to the conversation. I shall do that, say in February. Meanwhile, let me know what you get out of Read.[14] I have the feeling that, if Read doesn't go to the bat this spring, things may be indefinitely postponed. And you are the man to put the burr under that saddle. Let me have word as soon as you know anything.

I'm beginning to feel my way into the new novel. I can't be anything but nervous at this stage—but not as nervous, probably, as I'll be toward the end. And I'm tinkering with some short poems, which I'll send you as soon as there's anything to send. At present they look pretty amorphous.

The weather here has been frightful lately. A terrific snow just after Christmas, the heaviest in nearly a hundred years. And now the weather is damp and cold, with a very nasty wind which, I am told by dolorous natives, is the tramontana. Which name is far too good for it. I can't think of any name which wouldn't be. I am just pulling out of a bad cold, which had me sort of in bed for a couple of days, and now Cinina and the cook seem to be getting it. But the official spring should be here soon. And not too soon.

We still spend a lot of time reading papers. Now I've found a German beer place, where the Munich beer is still good and only costs eleven cents, American, the stein, and a big one and where—don't gasp—you get the leading French newspapers only thirty-six hours late, and the Paris edition of the *Herald Tribune*. So I go there about every other day for a little beer—I find that it is only American and Italian beer which disagrees with me,[15] or rather I don't give a damn if the German beer does disagree with me—and there I read the papers. But the reports are almost word for word what we get in the local press. And not as hot on the Finnish and Balkan situation. And occasionally I see the American papers, very late at the Consulate. Don't you boys let the New Deal get us into the war while I'm here. Or after I get back. But you can sell all the planes you want. And I'm damned near getting to be a big navy man. By the way, I recently saw a very impressive news reel here of American gunnery, coast defense and naval. Very, very interesting, from several points of view.

There isn't any news with us. Which, on the whole, is a comforting thing to remark. There must be a lot with you all. Please give me a full account of New Orleans and the goings-on there during the MLA.

Give our love to Tinkum. And KA and Albert, and the boys and girls. We look forward to the reunion.

As ever,

Red

1. As Grimshaw notes in his edition of the Brooks-Warren correspondence, the date on the original reads "January 11, 1939," an obvious error (*Cleanth Brooks and Robert Penn Warren: A Literary Correspondence*, 29).

2. The Winter 1940 issue.

3. Bishop's essay "Finnegans Wake" and Zabel's omnibus review "Two Years of Poetry, 1937–1939" appeared in the Winter issue.

4. Zabel had criticized Millay's *Huntsman, What Quarry?* (1939).

5. The wife of Henry Stopher, who headed the School of Music at LSU. (Special thanks to John Edward Hardy.)

6. Ransom condescended to Millay in his essay "The Poet as Woman," *Southern Review* (Spring 1937).

7. In "Edna Millay's Maturity" (*Southwest Review* [January 1935]), Brooks had in fact given her work balanced treatment.

8. Presumably Crane Brinton's "The Study of Revolutions."

9. Brooks's first major work, *Modern Poetry and the Tradition* (1939).

10. John Thibaut Purser continued to be listed as coeditor on subsequent editions of *An Approach to Literature*.

11. F. S. Crofts would bring out Brooks and Warren's *Understanding Fiction* in 1943.

12. A veiled reference to Pier Pasinetti, written with an eye toward Fascist inspection of the mails. Pasinetti hoped to leave Italy for the United States.

13. Adolphus Jerome Bryan, who ran the freshman writing program, was the candidate Brooks favored to head the Department of English. He was not chosen. (My thanks to Robert B. Heilman.)

14. William A. Read had headed the English department since 1912. His pending retirement presented opportunities and possible liabilities to Brooks, Warren, and their allies. An amputee, Read was irreverently known as "Corky" among junior faculty. (My gratitude to Cleanth Brooks for this information.)

15. At various points in his life, Warren suffered from allergies to beer and pork.

TO KATHERINE ANNE PORTER

TLS/Maryland   American Express
                                                           Rome
                                                January 15, 1940

Dear Katherine Anne:

Your snapshots haven't come yet, and we look forward to them. We're getting awfully soft about such things, and a pressed violet from your backyard would probably make us burst into tears. I have a feeling that we'll be ripe for coming home when we do come home. But here are some snapshots of us taken on the terraces of our little snuggery-on-the-cliff at Capri during those innocent days before the wind shook the whole island as a madman shakes a dead geranium[1] or Caesar[2] Cleanth's handkerchief, and before Mare Nostrum[3] decided to ascend to the crystalline sphere and then collapse back into its normal posture, passing the Warrens on both the ascent and descent, and before snow came to Naples and there was an earthquake in Sicily, and before the blessings of Stalinism overtook the Finns, and before the Warrens came to Rome and caught cold. The place was called the "Falconara," but any falcon who stayed up there would have to be a brass falcon with brass you-know-whats, and they'd get frozen off. But, to give the little guide-book touch, the distant line of coast which you can see in front of Cinina in the photograph of her sitting on the wall of the terrace, is the mainland south of Sorrento, and the coast up which Ulysses dawdled. On a good day the Falconara was a blissful spot, but when there wasn't a good day, it was simply the cosmic cesspool.

The good news about you all is very good new[s] to us. Harper's Bazaar ought to be as good as an endowment[4]—and a few articles now and then are a lot easier to write than stories aren't they? And they don't interfere with the fiction, do they?

The social life of Baton Rouge sounds pretty gay with the streams of distinguished visitors, and the archery field and Chinese checkers and dart board and penny ante and Wednesday night bowling. Doesn't anybody ever drink anymore, asks one small voice plaintively? I sometimes wake up in the night and think of a great big slug of bourbon with a few chunks of ice and a dash of tap water—not soda, mind you. Or in my more ambitious fantasies, one of Albert's juleps. Don't let all this virtue and Robert Browning athleticism kill all argument and alcohol, for I'm coming back with a great thirst for old red-eye and an itch to go to the mat with anybody who isn't an isolationist. (I don't mind stuff for the Finns, too much.)

As I remarked in the letter to Albert, I have finished the play and have put copies in the mail, registered, addressed to him. I also asked him to do a lot of chores about the thing, chores which will not, I hope, prove too onerous—but chores nevertheless. And I hope that you will read the thing; and hope, devoutly, that you will like it. And I'd certainly be grateful for as full a body of comment and suggestion as you have time to give me.

I have sent a copy off to Moe to try to prove to him that his little investment in me hasn't been entirely thrown away; or to prove, failing the other, that I'm leading a virtuous and laborious life. And to try to persuade him to give me a renewal of the fellowship. The situation is a funny one. I've played hookey to some extent from the novel—though I have got a lot done toward and some on it—and I suppose that I have to justify the hookey-playing by the quality of the product. But the novel for which I got the appointment originally—if it was good twelve months ago, it ought to be good now. But as for my personal situation, I would come back to Baton Rouge, work on the SR, and get as big a reduction of teaching as the university would allow—two courses less out of the three and no theses would be my hope—with a corresponding reduction in salary. Of course, I haven't the remotest idea that the university would accept such an arrangement, or that Moe will give me the renewal, but I'm not saying a word to the University until I know something from Moe, and I simply applied to Moe with the remark that I hoped that an arrangement satisfactory to the Foundation and the University could be worked out in case of the reappointment. I simply want to be able to finish this novel without having to do too much of it late at night and in between classes, as I did Night Rider; and this one promises to be a mighty long, tough haul. Moe may write to you and ask your opinion of the play, and so I want you to have read the thing, in case he does; or in case, you feel, after reading it, that you just have to write to Henry Allen [Moe]. But I am not breathing anything about the matter to *anybody except you and Albert* until the matter is settled definitely one way or the other. For those things have a way of getting out, and the rumor around the University could, conceivably, cause me some difficulties, especially since I'm not there on the spot. I'm not counting on Mr. Moe's renewal, but I am hoping for it.

I find that I told Albert about the German beer joint, and about the story of Pier's father on the prowl in Berlin. I know a lot of other stories, but I can't tell them now, and not only because of Mr. Farley.

How is Conrad? When you write give us the news about him. I wrote to them from Genoa, way back in August, to Conrad both a card and a letter since, and Cinina has written Jean [*sic*]. But not a word out of them. I wonder if they ever heard from us. And what about Duncan [Ferguson]? And the Kendalls?[5] And about "The Multiple Man, also called the Hunchback"? (W. B. Yeats: *A Vision*. New York: The Macmillan Company, 1939. pp. 176–179.)[6]

So long, and best love to you both. In which Cinina joins me.

As ever,

Red

P.S. Send the snapshots.

1. A simile taken from T. S. Eliot's "Rhapsody on a Windy Night."

2. The Brookses' dog, a Boston terrier.

3. The Mediterranean.

4. Givner notes that Porter's hopes for a financial boon from the magazine were disappointed (*Katherine Anne Porter: A Life*, 322).

5. Willmoore Kendall, the political theorist, was at the time a junior member of the government department at LSU.

6. Possibly a reference to Charles W. Pipkin. (Pier Pasinetti informs the editor that

Brooks and Warren surreptitiously nicknamed their titular superior Quasimodo, after Victor Hugo's legendary hunchback.)

TO CLEANTH BROOKS

TLS/YU   Rome
                                                          January 26, 1940

Dear Cleanth:

The immediate provocation for this letter is provided by a letter, received just this afternoon from John Palmer. He had just written Dr. Read, he said, asking for some sort of job for next year. He did not ask me to do anything about it—knowing, I suppose, that I couldn't do anything—but my first impulse was to sit down and write to Dr. Read. Then, on a little more reflection, I decided that a letter might not be the thing, that it might be better, if you happened to get a good opportunity and felt so disposed, for you to sound out the Doctor. Or, and this was decisive in my decision not to write to Dr. Read, it might be better to approach the matter through Bryan. In the light of the unsettled condition in the department, I thought it best to write to you about the matter and leave it up to your judgement. For all I know, John may have written to you or Albert [Erskine] already about the business, but just in case he hasn't I'm doing so on my own hook. Here is the way his situation stands. He has, for all intents and purposes, finished the thesis with Nichol Smith's blessing.[1] The blessing must be a very satisfied blessing, for Nichol Smith has agreed to back John strongly for a Carnegie grant for another year in England to pursue the study of the same topic, the history of literary patronage to the end of the 17th century. This was Secretary Allen's[2] idea—John seems to have made a hit with him—and Allen, it seems, is prepared to go to the bat with the Carnegie people to get John the Carnegie grant. In that case, John would pass up the B. Litt, get his status changed, and present the whole job for D. Phil, even though Nichol Smith tells him, on what grounds I don't know—thought [sic] this is of mild interest—that the B. Litt is the better degree. But John doesn't want to spend four years in England, especially under the present circumstances; that, it would seem, is easily comprehensible. If he can get a job he is coming on back to America. He is stalling, he says, but trying to burn no bridges behind him, until he knows something about LSU, which, he told me in August, was the place where he would like best to be situated. With the grant suggested to him by Allen, and strongly supported by Nichol Smith, however, it seems that his case for a job, if there is any kind of an opening, is extremely strong; and he told me last summer that he would come to LSU on a minimum salary. That's the dope, which I throw into your lap, and which you may be able to do something with. Perhaps John didn't put the full facts about his situation before Read—I mean about the idea of the Carnegie grant being Allen's, and about Nichol Smith's acting against his usual practice in backing up the idea.

John also wrote me that *Night Rider* is out in England, and he enclosed a lot of quotations from the *Times Lit. Sup.* Review.[3] He said that it was reviewed as the fiction choice of the week—which, the TLS being what it is, and there being fifty-two weeks in a year, and novels having been written for several hundred years, isn't exactly a thing to inflate the ego excessively. But it is mildly satisfactory. Here, in case you are interested, are some of the remarks from the review: "Once again it may come as a surprise to the reader unversed in the more serious fashion of the American novel at the present time that a subject of this sort, tobacco, etc., can be put to high and indeed subtle imaginative purpose." "It is this same awakened or heightened sense of the nation's experience that is at work in the more seriously analytical novel of social economic conditions, whether it deals with the present—like Mr. Steinbeck's *Grapes of Wrath*, for instance—or—like Mr. Warren's novel—with the past. In both instances, the novel takes on an added imaginative strength and urgency as a result." "—his are the story-teller's preoccupations, and the story he tells is full, adventurous, curiously tense and somber, genuine in tragedy." Then there is a reservation about the presentation of Munn's character, which, it says, is not worked out with full clarity: "one observes Munn, as it were, under all sorts of tests of character without feeling one really knows him. Yet the driving sincerity of Mr. Warren's interpretation of events triumphs over such weakness. The story is as distinctively American in spirit as in subject. If an English novelist chose to tackle a comparable theme of English economic history—the dock strike, say, or the rubber boom of almost the same period—what are the chances that he would produce a deeply felt and dramatic story and not an argumentative thesis?" I hope that the sales are satisfactory, though God knows, I get little enough of the royalty after the British Government and Houghton Mifflin have pawed over the sum. My share finally works out to a royalty of about three percent. In other words, a pretty good sale in England wouldn't do more than buy cigarettes for a year.

Speaking of money, I wrote to Holt some time back, asking for word about the Und[erstanding] Poetry. Yesterday I heard that they expected us to clear our indebtedness on the permissions this winter and probably have about $50 each on the black side of the ledger. But we don't get a statement until April. That of course, is an estimate and not a definite fact. By the way, Wilson has left them and gone to Reynal and Hitchcock.

No news with us, except that Tinkum's letter gave us great pleasure, in itself, and in the news that she is pretty well off with her insides.

I'm about half through with another longish poem—I've done some fifty lines on it—which I hope will be better than the one I sent the other day. That, certainly, is not a masterpiece.

Sunshine today, at last. And our colds are gone.

Love to you all and to Albert and KA.

As ever,
Red

1. David Nichol Smith had also directed Brooks's thesis at Oxford, and the two later collaborated on an edition of the Thomas Percy letters.
2. C. K. Allen, warden of Rhodes House at Oxford. (My thanks to John Palmer.)
3. "Drama in Tobacco," Times Literary Supplement (January 20, 1940).

TO ALLEN TATE

TLS/PU
American Express
Rome
January 29, 1940

Dear Allen:

I have been hoping to hear from you again. I know that you've scarcely had time to reply after receiving the last of the play, but I'm terribly anxious to know what you think of it. I haven't had anybody's reaction to it (except the first two scenes, last year), and naturally I'm in a sort of a twit. I've done scene revision since I sent the copy which you have, but nothing basic. I'd like to have any suggestions, however drastic they may be. I am rather of the opinion that HM will not want to publish it, since they turned down my poems, but I haven't heard from them about the matter. I think I told you that I had offered the thing to John [Ransom] for the Kenyon Review, not because I thought he'd take it but just on the off-chance that since he is planning to enlarge the magazine, he might have space for it; if he liked it. But I haven't heard from him, either.

Since finishing the play, I've been at the novel some, and have done a couple of long poems. I am enclosing one, on which I'd like to have your comment. I'll send the other when I get around to a few little revisions and get a copy made.

I just had a letter from John Palmer, the LSU boy who is at Oxford. He sent me some very full extracts from the Times Lit. Sup. review of Night Rider, which was treated, he says, as the fiction choice of the week; whatever that means. Except for a reservation about Munn's character, they went pretty well all out. It ended this way: "the story he tells is full, adventurous, curiously tense and sombre, genuine in tragedy. . . . One observes Munn, as it were, under all sorts of tests of character without feeling that one really knows him. Yet the driving sincerity of Mr. W's interpretation of events triumphs over such weaknesses. The story is as distinctively American in spirit as in subject. If an English novelist chose to tackle a comparable theme of English economic history . . . what are the chances that he would produce a deeply felt and dramatic story and not an argumentative thesis?" A good deal better than I expected. But since English royalties, after Chamberlain and Winston Churchill[1] and HM have had their cut[,] amount to about three percent on seven-and-six the copy; which won't make anybody rich on a probable sale of a few thousand copies; if that [sic].

I've given all my news, I guess. I'd like to have some of yours. I had a letter from Andrew recently, telling me about the farm.[2] I know that section; it's pretty fine through there. New[s] from LSU is satisfactory, but there are still some university matters in the air which I'd like to see settled and see settled my way.

Write when you can. Best to you all.

As ever,
Red

1. Neville Chamberlain, despite his "appeasement" of Hitler at Munich, was still prime minister. Churchill, first lord of the admiralty, would replace him in May 1940.
2. The Lytles had purchased a tract of land in Robertson County, Tennessee.

TO JOHN BERRYMAN

TLS/Minn

American Express
Rome
February 10, 1940

Mr. John Berryman
The Nation
New York City

Dear Mr. Berryman:

Some months ago you were kind enough to ask me to submit some poetry to you for publication in the *Nation.* Well, here, at last, is a poem. I hope that you will like it well enough to use it.[1]

I have done no short poems until a few weeks ago, for I was busy all last summer, and up until Christmas, with a verse-and-prose play. But that is now finished, and I hope to do some short poems this spring, when I can steal time from a new novel.

In case you do not like this poem well enough to publish it, will you do me the great favor of sending it to Mr. Albert Erskine, University, Louisiana, so that he may try to place it elsewhere for me? Since I intend to be here until next summer, that arrangement would save a good deal of time for me. And, of course, if you can manage to drop me a line about your decision, I shall appreciate it. This begins to sound like a Rube Goldberg cartoon,[2] and all over a few lines of verse. But thanks.

Sincerely yours,
Robert Penn Warren

P.S. I am enclosing an international reply coupon for postage.

1. "Crime" would be published in the May 25, 1940, issue.
2. Goldberg's comic strips typically depicted highly complicated devices intended to perform the simplest tasks.

TO ALLEN TATE

TLS/PU
American Express
Rome
February 10, 1940

Dear Allen:

Here is another poem. And by the way, have you received the one called "Terror"[1] which I mailed about two weeks ago? I'm anxious to know how you feel about them. And I'm anxious to have some news from you.

There isn't much to add to the last letter I sent you. The weather is still pretty bad, though breaking today. And we've had colds again. We stay in most of the time, except for the daily journey to the American Express for the mail which usually isn't there, and which, when it does come, has been opened by the British. But the work seems to be moving, for better or worse.

I have had several reports about the fate of Night Rider in England, by means of letters from friends there. Out of friendship they may be exaggerating a little in my favor, but the press seems to be quite good, and one writes me that the thing has been on the list of "Books which are being asked for at the shops." English papers, but not the literary supplements are to be had here; which means that I haven't seen any of the reviews myself. Palmer, my friend who is now at Oxford, writes me that the theater in London which goes in for experimental drama has re-opened, or is about to re-open, and suggests that I send him a copy of Proud Flesh so that he can try for a production there. Though I don't anticipate any luck on that score, Cinina has just made me another manuscript, which I am sending to Palmer on the off-chance.

How are things going with you all? Are you into your new novel yet? And how is Caroline's[?] What news of the Radfords?

Write when you get a chance.

As ever,
Red

[Handwritten] P.S. I have just reread Schwartz's piece on Tate in the SR.[2] I just can't see what he is talking about in the remarks on the metrics of the last stanza of Last Days of Alice. I feel, and wrote him to that effect last spring, that the end is dead right. But maybe he's right. There simply is a point where such matters are demonstrable.

1. Published in *Poetry* (February 1941).
2. Delmore Schwartz, "The Poetry of Allen Tate" (Winter 1940).

TO KATHERINE ANNE PORTER

TLS/Maryland   Rome
February 20, 1940

Dear Katherine Anne:

Your letter has reached me only a few days ago, having been held up, it seems, by the British examiners. I suppose that that accounts for the fact that a letter written on December 27 and mailed the next day comes tottering in here past the middle of February.

Things look more right for us now than when I wrote the letter in December which you answered. Except for the frightful weather during January and the first half of this month, with the accompanying colds in our little household, things would, in fact, have been very nice. But even as it as—and perhaps I say this because the sun is out today, and spring seems to be beginning—work has been moving. How good it is, I don't know, but by this time you may have some idea yourself, for I've sent off three poems to Albert (with the rather presumptuous request that he send them to another place if they are rejected at the places where I've sent them), and I sent the play, too, some time back. I'm well into the novel, and at moments feel that I see my way through the tangle; then at moments I feel like throwing the whole damned thing into the Tiber, which is high, swift, and muddy like turtle soup. We are, as you say, "pleasantly placed" for the year, that is, from the purely personal point of view; from a more general point of view, no, and the *no* probably ought to be written this way: NO.

As for the matter I wrote you about in December, and which you discuss in your letter, my own proper reply will, as you may guess, have to be postponed until the return which we look forward to. But for the moment, there is a little which maybe I can say.[1] Our friend Amos is one matter; the organ is another. I'll take up the first matter first. When I saw him last summer he was desperate and as far as his work went, or plans, completely paralyzed. He had just experienced, like Cinina, a very great personal grief,[2] and that matter, probably, had something to do with his situation, especially since the views of the dead man were what they were, views with which you and I would have the heartiest sympathy. I may be flattering myself and C., but I think that we did do a little something to get him to consider the future, that is, his own personal future. He knew what he wanted, but he was hopeless about it; as for his own work, the work of the past two years, it would be under the existing circumstances, buried, and had *better* be buried for sufficient reasons. We made some investigations, and found out what could be done from one end, and tried to put that program in effect—you know about it, Joe Brewer and such things, which are not *financial* in their immediate importance.[3] As for the other end of the situation, he has been, and upon our urging, pursuing what seems to be the only course that is not purely suicidal. At one time he did hold a view, when Albert and Cleanth knew him, for instance, which [w]as what you say, but then Amos was twenty-one, and the difference between a boy of twenty-one, under the special circumstances, and a man of the present years is very great. The change has been complete, violent, and I am convinced, irrevocable. I have some concrete evidence of this fact, which to my mind puts it beyond shadow of a doubt. But there is also the evidence that Amos wants to leave where he is now, where he enjoys certain things which he could never reasonably hope to enjoy elsewhere, and that he is willing, even anxious to make, and make permanently, certain very considerable material sacrifices for the issues which he sees. The question now is not one of saving the soul, which, it seems to me, is saved hands-down, but is a question of the disposition of the body. As for the violence of the change which [I] mention above, I have, at times, found myself in the position of trying to restrain public manifestations.

The other point of the organ itself is a different and more complicated kettle of fish. I cannot give an absolutely first-hand opinion, for no example of it has yet appeared. But I certainly would *not* undertake, *under any circumstances,* to give a clean bill of health to it. Nor would Amos, whose connection is, you might say, somewhat peripheral. I do not mean to imply that the nature of the thing would necessarily be overt, for I cannot know at the present; but there is bound to be a tacit definition of its limits.

There is another little thing, which I have almost forgotten to mention. Both Amos and I knew, of course, that Harcourt controlled your item. But after first considering writing to Harcourt, it was decided to write directly to you, because it was felt that your personal views ought to be consulted before the strictly business issue was raised with HB [Harcourt Brace]. And such matters must be on that strictly business basis to judge from the items which one can see with certain names.

You asked me to investigate the matter and give you an opinion. Well, my opinion is negative, for the question is already answered in my discussion above of the second point. I did not elaborate the first point in view of qualifying this opinion; I simply wanted you to know, as fully as I could tell you at the present, the position of Amos himself. (And he, God knows! is not alone. He is only different from others in that he has, at present at least, some hope for a personal release.) This reply to you is bound to be incomplete, but before too long we all can, I hope, talk about it together.

By the way, I just had a letter from my friend Corry, just back a few months ago from South America. I had mentioned, in an earlier letter, some of our little problems at LSU and had referred to the behavior of CWP.[4] Somewhat sardonically, Corry replied in the following terms: "I cannot see how you ever felt such a supple lad could ever have become self-hardened into a Meat-axe for the Lord." Well, that's it in a nut-shell, I reckon.

The description of the house with the new developments sounds pretty nice. The business about a ten-day notice and only the gas and water bills has its cheerful side, I might say, but I must also say that it strikes a little chill. Don't you all be going off and leaving a place like the place where the wisdom-tooth was. But the phrase about "the most solid foundation for permanence anywhere" is some comfort.[5] I hope that before too long we, too, can find exactly that solid foundation for permanence.

I must bring this to a close, for I have to get it off this afternoon if it is to catch the Conte di Savoia, which is the last boat out until early March. God knows when you'll receive this. The mails lately have been getting worse instead of better. I have not yet had answers to letters written to New York in late December.

Cinina joins me in all love to you both.

As ever,
Red

P.S. By the way, when you all write again, don't forget to tell us what has happened in the Departmental warfare. How is old Geryone[6] making out?

And by the way, the photographs which your Christmas letters promised haven't turned up yet.

1. Warren begins a long, encoded account of Pasinetti's situation and the status of his projected literary journal, which was to have carried translations of Porter's work. (See the December 12, 1939, letter to Porter, above.)

2. Pasinetti's father had recently died.

3. If Warren could persuade Joseph Brewer of Olivet College to hire Pasinetti, the latter's immigration to the United States would be greatly facilitated.

4. Pipkin, regarded as a toady of the Old Guard.

5. Ironically, Porter's marriage to Erskine was rapidly coming apart.

6. Geryoneo is a giant in Edmund Spenser's *Faerie Queene*, said to represent Phillip II of Spain. The allusion may refer to John Earle Uhler, Brooks and Warren's departmental nemesis. (Spenser had been much on Warren's mind as he worked at the first drafts of *Proud Flesh.*)

TO PAUL M. HEBERT

TLS/LSU
American Express
Rome, Italy
March 7, 1940

Dear President Hebert:[1]

You may recall the conversation which I had with you in your office last July, a few days before I sailed. At that time you suggested to me that I write you in the spring referring to our conversation and reviewing the matter of promotion, which was then discussed.

The situation is this. Mr. Cleanth Brooks and I, with the permission of Dr. Read, had an informal talk last winter with Dr. Smith on the subject of our promotion. At that time Dr. Smith said that he would look into the matter and would give us some word on it during the spring. Later, in the spring, I saw Dr. Smith in connection with another matter, but the subject of the promotion was again raised. At that time

I told Dr. Smith that, since I was to be away for a year or more, I had certain arrangements to make which were contingent upon the matter of the promotion, and asked what the situation then was. He replied, "The promotions are on the books for next year"—that is, for 1940. I then asked him if I could, with confidence, proceed on that assumption. He said, "Yes, definitely."

That sums up, I believe, all of the basic points in the conversation with Dr. Smith. But it may be pertinent for me to add that my promotion to the rank of Associate Professor, like that of Mr. Brooks, was made in the spring of 1936. Since that time we have done, in addition to our work in editing the Southern Review and in teaching, a considerable amount of publishing, in collaboration and independently.[2]

The winter here has been very pleasant except for the vile weather and influenza and the newspapers. I have managed to go on pretty consistently with the work I have on hand. This is not exactly the year I would have chosen to be here, but in some respects the special circumstances are proving a good deal more instructive than those of more normal and happy times.

With sincere regards,
Robert Penn Warren

P.S. I have just had a word from my English publishers that my book there has had "a good, in fact, an extraordinary good, press," and word from a friend that the advertisements, recently, were announcing the "second large printing."

[Enclosure]

Items since June, 1936, date of promotion.

Publications:

Books:	Night Rider, March, 1939, Houghton Mifflin.
	Night Rider (English Edition), January, 1940, Eyre & Spottiswoode.
	Understanding Poetry (with Cleanth Brooks), May, 1938, Henry Holt.

An Approach to Literature (with Cleanth Brooks and John Purser), Revised Edition, August, 1939, F. S. Crofts.

A Southern Harvest, October, 1937, Houghton Mifflin.

Articles, Stories and Verse:

Numerous magazines including the *Virginia Quarterly, Scribners,* the *Southern Review,* the *Kenyon Review,* the *American Review,* the *Nation, Poetry: A Magazine of Verse;* and three stories reprinted in O'Brien's *Best Stories* of each year and in the *O. Henry Memorial Prize Stories.*

Papers, Lectures, and Activities: (not complete)*

Modern Poetry (with Cleanth Brooks), The Modern Language Association, December, 1936.

Tradition, The Modern Language Association, December, 1938.

Phi Beta Kappa Address, University of Oklahoma, May, 1938.

Address, Phi Beta Kappa Alumni Association of Oklahoma City, May, 1938.

Writer's Conference, University of Colorado, July–August, 1936.

Chairman, Group XI, Modern Language Association, 1939 (resigned).

Awards:

Houghton Mifflin Fiction Award, June, 1936.

Caroline Sinkler Prize, June, 1936, June, 1937, June, 1938.

Levinson Prize (*Poetry: A Magazine of Verse*), October, 1936.

Guggenheim Fellowship, March, 1939.

*[Warren's note] During this period invitations for lectures and sets of lectures have been received, but were declined, from the University of Syracuse, Writer's Conference of the University of Colorado, and the University of Iowa.

1. Hebert, who succeeded the disgraced James Monroe Smith, was acting president of LSU. He was replaced in 1941 by General Campbell B. Hodges.

2. Nonetheless, Brooks and Warren would have to wait for their promotions to full professor.

TO CLEANTH BROOKS

TLS/YU   Rome
                                                  March 7, 1940

Dear Cleanth:

You remember that, last summer, I told you about my little call on Hebert in regard to the promotion business. I told him the little story of
our conversation and of my later conversation with James Monroe
[Smith]; and Hebert then suggested that I write him a summary of the
situation this spring and refer him to my conversation of last July. Well,
I've finally written him the letter which he suggested, and I am enclosing
a carbon for you to glance at. I hope that it looks OK to you in the light
of current events, whatever those current events are. And God knows, I
hope it doesn't backfire to queer anything. Anyway, let me know what
you think, and let me know how matters stand there. What line has Read
taken in the matter?

Speaking of department matters, a letter from Mrs. Daggett came
yesterday with a postscript to the effect that a faculty committee was
appointed to handle the matter of the headship of the English Department, and that Dolph was recommended, but has not yet been appointed officially.[1] For God's sake let me know when the glad news—if
it comes off—comes off. She also had some rather nice odds and ends
about politics—things which make our life here seem pretty sheltered.

How is the university politicking proceeding? Mrs. Daggett also said
that the president of the AAUP had resigned because of "ill health" but
that nobody believed that story. What happened? And what happened
to Ken?[2] And what is Ken going to do? God, that little item makes me
boil every time I think about it.

I had [a] note from John Palmer, a whoop of glee not a note, to the
effect that Read had written him that a recommendation for an instruc-
torship had been made. You all must have done some pretty nice work.
I do hope that the thing gets approved by the dean. The appointment of
John has a double value. First, and more important, it brings a damn
good man into the department, and second, it keeps somebody else out.
But this second advantage is not negligible.

The only pleasant thing I can think about to tell you is a beer party in Vatican City with two priests and two Associated Press men—one AP man who covered Spain and Bohemia and is now waiting here to bolt for the Balkans when the trouble starts there and the other AP man who is tagging about with Sumner and Myron[3]—or rather, I should say, was tagging about with them. But from their rich experience of men and events the two newshawks had little to offer except amiability.

Write to me when you have a chance. Cinina joins me in love to you all. And give our best to our friends, but don't be too liberal in the interpretation of the last word.

As ever,
Red

[P.S. at top of page] I am sending this in duplicate, since I want to have some confidence that you will get the enclosure.

1. Adolphus Bryan was passed over in favor of Thomas A. Kirby, a medievalist whose tenure as department head lasted three decades.
2. Willmoore Kendall.
3. Undersecretary of State Sumner Welles was in Europe on a fact-finding mission; Myron Charles Taylor, prominent industrialist and an authority on the refugee problem, had just been named President Roosevelt's personal representative to Pius XII.

TO ALLEN TATE

TLS/PU   Rome
                                                                   April 2, 1940

Dear Allen:

A letter from Don, one from Frank, and your own arrived simultaneously. I must say that you were particularly reticent about your own misfortunes and fortunes; for from Don's letter I learned that you had had an operation and are now well and feeling better than in years, and from Frank's letter I learned that you have had an offer to go back to Princeton at a greatly increased salary. I am delighted that you are so fully recovered from the operation, and delighted about the other, too. Will you be staying on, then?[1]

I would have answered your letter a great deal sooner but for the fact that the day after its arrival I took to my bed with a violent seizure, which four doctors finally decided was intestinal flu plus malaria.[2] Anyway, I vomited blood, had the highest kind of fever for five or six days, had the bone-ache, and in general felt like hell. But the fever is gone now, and yesterday, after some two weeks or so in bed, I got up for a few hours. I confess, however, that I don't feel like much yet. And I lost some fifteen or eighteen pounds in the process.

I have gone back over the poem Terror in the light of your comments. You are dead right about the conclusion; it is inflated. The last two lines would probably stand well enough if they were properly prepared for, but they aren't; and you are probably right that the poem ought to end with the stanzas before. The first two stanzas I'm still not convinced about. I do feel that I have to move into the poem in some such fashion (if not with those particular stanzas) and can't plunge in with stanza three, as you suggest. But I am convinced, upon reflection, about the other stanza which you suggest cutting. I am enclosing another poem, done after Terror, which I don't believe I ever sent you. What about this one?

As for the general question you raise, or the questions, for there are two, I wish I could think that haste were the cause of my troubles. I happened to have copies of the last two poems here and got them out to look at them in the light of your letter. [Handwritten in margin] I mean poems done a year and a half ago, or so [Typing resumes] And I must say that, whatever the cause, there's some justice in what you said. But I was on a cold trail with the three longish poems I did a year or two ago, and I shall do no more poems in that general style. The poetry in the play, I have felt, is much the best poetry I've done—that is, the best of it is, I believe, and the best of it seems to me to be in the second half, for I learned a little as I went along. (By the way, when you get a chance to write again, I'd like to know how you reacted to the play, as a whole, and then as far as the poetry, in isolation, is concerned. You say at the end of your present letter that you think I ought to come back to it in a few months. Certainly, I'm going to do some revising, but not before summer, anyway—I want to get a little more distance on it.) The other matter, that of a feeling on my part that I was accomplishing something if I got something down on paper—scarcely that, but I have had of late a sense of increasing pressure which may work out the same way. That is, there are a lot of things I want to do and the feeling that time is a little shorter than you had expected tends to make you put the pressure on. Anyway, I took my time on the play and willy-nilly I'm taking my time on the new novel, with the amount of illness we have had this winter. By the way, the novel is a bastard to write; I certainly don't feel that I've solved all of my problems about it, despite all the fine ideas which came to me when I had the fever but which have lost some of their lustre now.[3]

Write when you can. Meanwhile I hope that the various projects which you all have on hand are prospering. Best all around.

> As ever,
> Red

P.S. What has happened to John Ransom? I haven't had a word out of him for months, despite several letters. Nor from Manson? [*sic*]

1. The Tates would remain at Princeton until 1942.

2. The illness would later be diagnosed as typhus.

3. In interviews and conversations later in life, Warren credited his fevered delusions with freeing him up to finish *At Heaven's Gate*.

TO ANDREW LYTLE

TLS/VU
American Express
Rome
April 30, 1940

Dear Andrew:

Your letter reached me longer ago than I like to remember, but it looked like every time I sat down to answer it something happened. But here I am at the typewriter, impelled this time by my pleasure in the news, just received, that you and Mr. Moe got together.[1] Father sent me a clipping from one of the Nashville papers about the business. Well, I ought to be writing to Mr. Moe a letter of congratulations on the appointment, for that is where the honor is being done, I'm pretty sure. Further reflections on the event: It does seem, however, a little unsporting of the Foundation to give a grant for De Soto—a little bit like shooting a sitting bird with both barrels; a sure thing; for De Soto must be in the bag by this time. You are pretty well finished with it, aren't you? And the Fellowship carries with it a grave responsibility. You ought to come over and stop the war. The Warrens got a Guggenheim and came over to start it. There's a challenge for you.

The news of the farm you've bought sounds fine. That is a nice section through there, all right. Lon Cheney, too, wrote me about your new place, and about an expedition he took in that general direction with you. We are looking forward to seeing the place, and by that time, I imagine, you all will be settled. In a way, I must say, I envy you the business of putting the place in shape. We aren't entirely happy where we are, and have not yet built the house which we would regard as permanent. We are still hoping to find a place in the country; but Louisiana isn't like Tennessee and Kentucky in that respect. There simply aren't many houses; there are shacks and there are big pretentious places, now usually in ruins. Nothing much in between. But if we can't find a place in the country, the place where we now are represents a very satisfactory compromise. You may remember it—the wooded tract of some six or seven acres into which you saw me disappear with a brush-hook one afternoon three years ago?

News with us isn't very exciting. After Cinina got up from her flu I came down with a mysterious complaint which the fourth doctor decided was intestinal influenza crossed with malaria. My first experience with either ailment, and the mixture is, I tell you, a bastard. I'm not so attached to Louisiana that I want to be carrying that little sentimental record about the world with me. But we are both up and about our business, such as it is. My novel is moving along, toward what far-off divine event I don't pretend to know, and some days I don't give a damn. But I suppose such days are bound to be in the cards. I hope that you have already seen, or will see, the play. A copy is wandering about Baton Rouge and Nashville. But there's no haste. I do want, however, your advice on revision before I get back at it; but the advice would probably be best given face to face. The meeting, I hope, won't be too long off.

Plans with us are still uncertain. We did have our minds almost made up to coming home in early June or late May—I may say that we did have our minds made up and had begun to make arrangements; but now things have taken a turn here and it looks that our permit to remain may be given. Which means that we'll stay on a while longer.

Give our very best to Edna. Cinina joins me in all good wishes to you for farm, book, and self.

As ever,
Red

[P.S. at top of page] I suppose you are still a good isolationist. So am I, but I have moments lately when I waver.

1. Lytle had been awarded a Guggenheim.

TO FRANK LAWRENCE OWSLEY

ALS/VU   Rome
                                                              May 11, 1940

Dear Frank:

Here is a long overdue note of thanks to you all for the very handsome offer of the farm.[1] It sounds too damned good to be true, but I'm afraid that it's out for us. If things don't take a sudden change for the worse we shall go to north Italy as we had planned, to Sirmione again, where we shall be until late June.[2] Then in July I go west to Colorado, where I shall be doing two weeks work at the Writers' Conference again. After that everything looks vague to us, but we hope to get by Kentucky and Tennessee for a day or two anyway. I want to see my father and we want to see the Owsleys very much indeed, even if it has to be only a glimpse. But since we shan't have a car our movements may be determined by the routing I can get on our tickets without putting out a lot extra. And I can't find out anything about that until we get to New York.

I suppose that Cleanth has told you something about the trouble over the headship of our department. I have recently learned that our local s.o.b. didn't get in, and that a very good fellow is acting head.[3] But they are going out for a head, and I shudder to think what may be brought in. And this delay in the appointment probably means that all

the slimy politicking of our adversary will start all over again. And so on. I believe that a rotating chairmanship is probably a better system, and God knows anything which would avoid situations like the present would be desirable. It's all a Goddamned mess. This is under the hat: Iowa has started a flirtation with me—you know, asking me if I am happy at LSU, etc. and asked me to come next year to teach two hours a week as a visitor. But it's all in the air, and nothing decided yet.

We are well now and relatively happy and quite busy. My novel is moving, but I don't know how good it is, or how bad. I'm simply sort of [numb?] about it. I do hope that we can get by Nashville. Besides the constant [?] pleasure of seeing the Owsleys we'd like to see the improvements on the place.

Well, a good summer to you all and our best love all around.

As ever,
Red

1. The Owsleys had apparently invited the Warrens to stay at their farm outside Nashville upon their return from Europe.
2. A deterioration in the situation in Italy shortened the Warrens' stay; Mussolini officially entered the war in June 1940.
3. Kirby (the "local s.o.b." may have been Uhler).

When the Warrens finally left Italy, they did so under circumstances that resembled an escape more than a conventional departure. The possibility of finishing his play, Proud Flesh, *and seeing it staged had become a virtual obsession with Warren, and immediately after returning to America he took up residence at Bennington College, where he could gain practical advice toward that end. The summer of 1940 would include travels west as far as Colorado for writers' conferences, and there would be a pleasant extended visit with Warren's onetime mentor John Crowe Ransom in Ohio, before a swing back to Vermont for additional consultations on the play. With summer at an end, the Warrens would return to Baton Rouge via Nashville. Meanwhile an attractive possibility had presented itself, a visiting appointment teaching creative writing at the University of Iowa the following spring, evidence of Warren's burgeoning reputation.*

TO CLEANTH BROOKS

TLS/YU   General Delivery
North Bennington, Vermont
June 8, 1940

Dear Cleanth:

I wrote you a card a few days ago just to announce our arrival. We got out by the barest, I suppose, and on no notice at all. The manifestoes were put up on a Saturday; Sunday some of the beating-up occurred; Monday the demonstrations started. Monday morning I called Genoa to try to get our passage moved up to fifteenth of May. But no soap. We decided to go to Genoa and be on the spot if anything broke. So we went to Genoa on Tuesday night. By Thursday noon we had wangled passage, cots, not beds, but we could have scalped those for a mighty big profit if we had had a mind to do so. But I must confess that we didn't stay on the cots very long; on the second night out we both got beds, God knows how. Maybe some of the refugees jumped overboard. But Cinina was in with a gang of women and I was in with a gang of men. We spent the entire voyage listening to horror stories from Norwegians, Belgians, Germans, and French.

Poor Pier Pasinetti had finally managed to wangle his permit to come to America, after working all winter on the proposition. He is the saddest and the bitterest man you ever saw, and if he doesn't learn a little self-control he will shortly end in a concentration camp or with a busted head. He says anything and says it anywhere, in a voice like a fog-horn. The only chance he has for survival is that a lot of other people do the same thing, and I don't suppose they can arrest everybody. (All winter the anti-Fascist sentiment has been increasing, or has at least become more articulate; and the anti-German feeling is absolutely everywhere. We heard a German newsreel roundly hissed in a Roman theater, for instance.) But back to Pier: just a few days before he was supposed to sail, they revoked his permit. He was planning to come here and take out American citizenship.

I suppose we will be in the war in one way or another before long. I'm confused for the moment, I'm frank to say. I just don't know what we ought to do to save our own skins. But whatever we do, I'm pretty

sure of one thing; the things you and I are interested in will come damned near going by the board for some time to come.[1] Even in this little town, which is quite off the main line of activity, you can see the war attitudes pretty well formed. What do you think we ought to do?

Louisiana, I see from the evening paper, still commands some attention in the news. Alexandria this time. And I observe with pleasure that Leche got the rap. What about Maestri?[2] And how are the internal affairs of the University shaping up? Not too well, I imagine. I saw Crofts for a few minutes when I came through NY, and he said that there would, apparently, be a shut-down on money for LSU. What's the dope on that? (By the way, he also said that they had sold right at 800 copies of the *Approach* this spring, which means about seventy-five dollars each for us, in July. And, by the way, did Holt come across this spring?[3] And, if so, for how much? And Crofts also told me of his talk with you in the spring about our situation there, about promotions, etc. Has anything happened in that line? And if not, was any excuse offered? Crofts also told me of the flirtation which Cornell had begun with you. I have a little flirtation begun, too, but I don't know how far it will go. I'll write you details later. But I hope it will go far enough to give some sort of a stick to bat at the local dog with. I'm pretty damned sore if, after the various promises which have been made us, we don't get some satisfaction pretty soon.

As for news with us, the letter from Cinina to Tinkum, which I mailed a few days before we left Rome, and which was probably on the same boat with us, gave about all the news of the last period in Rome. For the present I'm here working with Francis Fergusson[4] on a revision of my play. (If you have any suggestions I wish you would spring them now, while I can bring them to bear on the present process of revision.) He is going to put on a couple of scenes experimentally this summer, and talks about doing the whole thing next year, if some of the revisions pan out. I despair of ever getting a commercial production. I hope to get a chunk of the revision done before I go to Colorado to teach two weeks in late July and early August. After that things look pretty vague, though we hope to be able to stop over on the way back for a short visit with John and Robb,[5] and then with my father. He had a touch of the flu this winter, not much, but is getting on in years now, and since he is simply never ill this seems to have depressed him considerably.

I hope that things are going beautifully with you all, and that Tin-

kum has finished her walk-building. Have you been keeping the raw material moving up to the point of production? Write and give us the news. Love to you all and to the Erskines, Albrizios, and Duncan. Cinina joins me in this.

As ever,

Red

[P.S.] Have you heard from John Palmer? I hope he is on the President Roosevelt.

1. A point reiterated by Brooks and Warren in their valedictory "Announcement" in the last issue of the *Southern Review* (Spring 1941).

2. Robert Sidney Maestri, mayor of New Orleans and ally of the indicted Governor Leche.

3. Publisher of *Understanding Poetry*.

4. Noted authority on drama and member of the faculty at Bennington. His "Notes on the Theater" had appeared in the Winter 1940 *Southern Review*.

5. The Ransoms.

TO ALLEN TATE

TLS/PU   North Bennington
                                              July 8, 1940

Dear Allen:

I have postponed from day to day giving an answer to your note, with the hope that I could set a date for coming down at least as far as New York for a day or so—thinking that we might at least get a meeting in there. I have the ticket, as a matter of fact, but now it seems that I probably shan't be able to use it before pulling out for Olivet, where I shall be for a week before going on to Colorado. But I shall probably get back here after Colorado, to put in another couple of weeks working with Fergusson on my play. That is what has kept me so consistently here—I've been out of town once during the whole period, and that only for less than a day. He has been helping me with revision from the point of view of staging, etc., and is putting on a scene so that we can get a notion of how the prose-verse mixtures, etc., will work out. He talks

about doing the whole thing later as his production here, but that isn't positive yet, and probably won't be until the revision is completed. In August we should get the job basically finished except for some rather drastic re-working of some of the verse. The main lines of the revision are something like this. The Chorus, according to his suggestion, becomes simply the surgeon, which, of course, focuses more definitely the notion of humanitarianism and science as related to the power idea in the play. But with the Chorus remains, in the introduction to each act, one other figure, patrolman in Act I, football player in Act II, etc. The Chorus also takes a more definite part in the dialogue, according to the traditional handling. This enables me, it seems, to clarify some of the actual characters. Then, the character of Anne has been more developed, and she takes a more hand [sic] in the plot. Next the whole thing has been compressed a lot and pointed up; the prose element has been reduced considerably. I have on my own hook been tinkering with the verse itself, trying to develop some adequate differentiation among the styles of the various characters. If it suits you, I'll send the MS to you in August when we get this preliminary revision done; then you, I hope, will give me a criticism of that before I get about the business of trying to put the thing in final shape. What do you think of the general lines of revision which I have indicated above? Do you think it is the right track? And if not, can you tell me what you think ou[gh]t to be the general objectives of the revision?

The weather has been cold here and rainy until recently, and that has kept us pretty steadily indoors. The fact that we have no car, too, has been somewhat hampering. But we hope to get some kind of car before we leave. I have been trying to get my credit transferred from the Louisiana dealer to a dealer in Albany, but that seems to have blown up. Now it's a question of getting something that will fill in for the summer and fall.

Andrew and Edna are there now, aren't they? I wrote Andrew a letter in April, but don't know that he ever got it. Ask him, will you? And did you get a long letter written in April, enclosing a poem? Everyday or so, I learn that I haven't received some letter or that some letter I wrote never got here.

I am anxious to know what you all think about the present political situation, and what you think about the chances we've got for the war.

John Ransom and his family came through here a little while back, stopping just for the night. We had a very nice evening—all too short. They asked us to come up to spend some time with them at Breadloaf [*sic*]. But we couldn't make it. We hope, however, to drop by Kenyon for a day on our way back to Louisiana, if we manage to get back here in August.

How are the novels in the house coming on? They both ought to [be] getting on to the end now, I suppose. I'm pretty anxious to see both. And what are you working on?

We leave this week for Olivet, and leave there the twentieth. If you don't write to me at Olivet, let me hear from you when I get to Colorado; care of Edward Davison, University of Colorado, Boulder. I'll be there until August 9. And tell Andrew to write.

Meanwhile best to all.

As ever,
Red

TO THOMAS A. KIRBY

TLS/LSU

Olivet College
Olivet, Michigan
[Summer 1940]

Dear Kirby:

I have just received an invitation from the University of Iowa to come there for the second term of 1940–41 to give a course. I am rather pleased with the arrangement they offer, since I shall have only one class meeting a week. I have written to Mr. Hebert about the matter of a leave for the second term, but I want to take up the matter with you. I imagine that a satisfactory arrangement can be made for my courses for the second term; and I imagine that the details of that can wait until my return when we can talk about it face to face. But I wanted to raise the general question with you now before I take the final plunge with Iowa.[1] I shall be leaving Olivet this week for Colorado. My address in Colorado will be: Care of Mr. Edward Davison, University of Colorado, Boulder.

I hope that your summer is a pleasant one. My wife joins me in regards to you both.[2]

Sincerely yours,
Red Warren

1. The request for leave was ultimately granted.
2. Kirby's wife, Josie, was popular with faculty, staff, and students alike.

TO THOMAS A. KIRBY

TLS/LSU

Kenyon College
Gambier, Ohio
August 16, 1940

Dear Kirby:

Thanks for the note, and for your undertaking to make the arrangement which I requested. However, after receiving the letter from President Hebert, I telephoned the people at Iowa and got an extension of time for a final decision. It now seems that I shall be able to wait until [the] term begins. That means that the matter can be settled after my return to Louisiana.

Colorado was pretty strenuous, and we staggered away from the place in not exactly the pink of condition; and the drag across Kansas didn't do much to improve matters. But a few days of quiet life here ought to put us back in shape before I have to leave for Vermont.

Goodbye, and best regards. Cinina asks to be remembered to you both.

Sincerely,
Red

TO FERRIS GREENSLET

TLS/Harv

Care of John Crowe Ransom
Gambier, Ohio
August 17, 1940

Dear Mr. Greenslet:[1]

Your note reached me just before I left Vermont for jobs at a couple of Writers Conferences—Olivet and Colorado. And, as you probably know, one fights for bare life at such a place; there simply wasn't that extra ounce of energy left over even for letters which I should have written and which I wanted to write. But I did get a little time in Colorado to put some of the novel manuscript in shape for a typist. I shall send that to you tomorrow or next day.

There are some things which I ought to tell you about the manuscript to help in the reading of it. Chapters I and IV, the chapters in dialect, need a little explanation—an explanation which would be given by a heading in the final version. These chapters are sections of a statement, or confession, written in the county jail in the city in which the story is laid. The man who writes them, Ashby Wyndham, is a mountaineer religious fanatic, who has founded a little sect and has come down the river on a shanty boat, trying to make converts. His departure from the mountains is an indirect result of the policy of one of the companies controlled by Bogan Murdock, the financier who appears in Chapter II. Throughout the period of the action of the novel, some two or three years, Wyndham and his little band are gradually approaching the city. In the end, Wyndham is the unwitting occasion of the collapse of Murdock's financial structure. This works out along the following lines: You will notice a reference to Private Porsum, a World War hero from the mountains, who is a cousin of Wyndham. Porsum has gone into politics and then has been used as a tool by Murdock and his outfit (he has other, personal connections with the general story), and at the end is the front used by Murdock for a last project undertaken in desperation as his affairs become more and more involved. Meanwhile, Wyndham and his band have arrived in the city and by accident are involved in a gun fight with the police who try to break up their water-front preaching. Wyndham, in jail, prepares the statement—which appears in the small sections in the novel—and the reporters, upon discovering that Wyndham is a cousin of Private Porsum, give a copy to Porsum and ask for a statement from him. Porsum goes to see his cousin in jail, and as a result of the visit goes back on Murdock's scheme. This is not the basic plot of the novel, but this part is probably necessary for you to grasp the general place of the inserted sections from Wyndham's confession. I have decided to introduce Porsum in Chapter II, at the Murdock's [sic] house, instead of the later Chapter, where he now appears, Chapter VI. But this is a mechanical detail which can be fixed up in a few minutes.

I haven't been able to get much done on the novel this summer. The jobs at the Conferences—which I had to take because of the cash in them—and the work which I have been doing on my play have just about cut the novel out for the present. Which, I feel now, was all to the good, for the rest from the novel has given me a fresh look at the whole thing. But I expect to be back at it this fall. With luck I should finish in the late spring. The University of Iowa has offered me a place there for the second term, a place which involves only two hours of teaching a week. That should permit me to work on the novel for four uninterrupted days a week, at the least. If I can get a leave from Louisiana, I shall take the place. But the situation at Louisiana is so confused now that I am not certain that satisfactory arrangements can be made there.

By the way, at Colorado I met Maurine Whipple,[2] whom I liked very much. But the life there was so strenuous that I didn't see nearly as much of her as I wanted. And something else about the Conference there. I found one novelist who looks quite good to me, a Mrs. Esther Chase.[3] She has two novels in pretty good shape—not final shape but far enough along so that one can have some sort of opinion. She is very intelligent and will be able, I believe, to fix up both books. She has promised to send me the manuscripts when she has completed the revisions, and I shall send them to you. In any case, she has also promised to get in touch with Houghton Mifflin before taking any steps about publication. I was also greatly impressed by the work of a Mrs. Surguine, who, I understand, offered something last year for the Fellowship. She isn't as far along as Mrs. Chase, but I have great confidence in her.

I shall be here, with Ransom, for a week or so. Then I shall be in Vermont for a couple of days before going back South. If you get a reading on the novel in the near future, I shall hope to hear from you here, for I am, naturally, anxious to know how you all feel about the thing.

Please give my regards to Mr. Linscott and Mr. Brooks.[4]

Sincerely yours,
Robert Penn Warren

1. Editor at Houghton Mifflin and author of biographies of James Russell Lowell, Thomas Bailey Aldrich, and Walter Pater.
2. Utah-born author best remembered for her novel of Mormon life *The Giant Joshua* (1941).

3. Esther Chase (under the pseudonym Anekke de Lange) brought out the novel *Anna Luhanna* in 1946.

4. Greenslet's Houghton Mifflin colleagues Robert Linscott and Paul Brooks.

TO PIER M. PASINETTI

TLS

Gambier, Ohio

August 23, 1940

Dear Pier:

We are now in Ohio, staying with John R[ansom] for a week or so before we go back to Vermont and New York. It is a delightful place here. The college, a[n] old-fashioned place with lots of fine trees, grass, and pleasant nondescript buildings, some of which go back to the Greek revival stuff of the early nineteenth century, is situated on top of a little plateau, from which you can look out for miles over the very beautiful, well-watered country. The R. house is a ramshackle, farmhousish [*sic*] sort of place, with an indefinite number of rooms, a big porch which looks out from the edge of the plateau, over the little river, and an active, handsome, and enterprising five-year old boy underfoot.[1] We have had a fine time here. We work in the mornings—they have given me an office in one of the college buildings—then we play bowls on the lawn for a few minutes before and after lunch, then back to work for a couple of hours, then volley ball played rather briskly for an hour and a half, then one of the R meals, for which they are justly celebrated, then conversation, reading or bridge. It's all too idyllic to last, and it won't last, for I have to go this week, that is within a few days. But it has been a kind of little oasis. By a kind of unspoken consent we haven't done much talking about the unpleasant things which are in the backs of our minds. We've just shelved them, apparently, for the moment, knowing that they will get a hearing soon enough, anyway. Colorado was fun, in its way, with which you are acquainted from your visit there. The staff was rather dull, the only person on it who interested me being a young playwright, Albert Maltz, some of whose stories you may have seen in the *SR* or in *Story*.[2] As for the other people, with the exception of Ralph Hodgson,[3] the English poet, I was frankly bored. There was Margaret Widdemer,[4] who writes a vile poetry and silly femalish novels which smell faintly of an old maid's upper bureau drawers, and who gave a lecture on Freud and modern fiction, which was enough to turn one's stomach. She sees nothing except collapse of the fine old moral values all around her— pornography to the right of her and pornography to the left—and she blames it all on Freud, just as she blames social ills on the novelists. As if the novelists and poets were ever, or rarely, responsible for ideas in her sense of the word. They use them—or rather, I should say, they *realize* them in the novel or poem, but in the way she is referring to, society does a lot more to make the novelist or poet, and to give him his ideas, than the novelist or poet does to make society what it is. Society is usually *acting,* perhaps unconsciously, on the ideas before the ideas find their way into literature;[5] then the novelist puts those ideas into fiction and society reads the novel and says: "My God, so I've been speaking prose all my life." When I was at Olivet, to give a lecture on my way out to Colorado, Margaret Widdemer was there to give the same thing on Freud and the novelists. Sherwood Anderson was present—he was one of the staff there—and after the lecture he and John Peale Bishop and Katherine Anne and I held a little indignation meeting over a fifth of scotch, ably encouraged by Cinina. Anderson, as you might guess, was one of Miss Widdemer's horrible examples, but she omitted him from the discussion, since he was present in the audience. (At Olivet, Brewer talked a lot about you and is greatly interested. A letter to me had miscarried.) The Widdemer lecture, some long talks with Katherine Anne and Bishop, and a julep party provided the high points at Olivet—by the way, the mint in Michigan is wonderful, they raise it there for chewing gum, but it goes a lot better with bourbon than it goes with chicle, or whatever it is they make gum out of. Well, let us push on to Colorado in the beautiful Packard, second-hand, which we bought in Vermont, at a great bargain, but with a frozen radiator. At Colorado we stayed with the Davisons, who were wonderfully nice to us. Ted, of course, is very preoccupied and sad, despite encouraging letters from his family. But he is holding up well, under the circumstances. After the Conference was over, we took an afternoon and evening off in Denver, eating and drinking. Then the next day, we went on a picnic up into the mountains, where Ted did two-inch thick steaks over a wood fire; we washed the steaks down with scotch and plain water and watched the sunset, and then lay back on the ground and waited for the mysteries of digestion to begin. On the way back we spent a day in Kansas City, where we discovered a wonderful restaurant and bar, 1890 murals, deep booths with dingy walls and very sparkling linen on the tables, and quart steins of beer and good salads and superb steaks. It is the kind of restaurant which can be found only in America, and is the only competition which we can put up against foreign parts. By the way, the beer here has improved enormously; really good now. Then on to Ohio, across a drouth-stricken Illinois and Indiana. (A crop failure there, but the wheat is a bumper crop in the West.) We heard Wilkie's [sic] speech accepting the Presidential nomination for the Republican Party[6]—by radio, that is. It struck me as a fairly weak performance, and the answer two days later, by Ickes,[7] was a clean job of massacre. The money looks about even for the election, though I think that the present incumbent will remain. As for my personal affairs, the Iowa job was reopened when I was in Michigan with a financial boost which made it very attractive. I asked for a one-term leave from LSU, and got it, but with some strings attached which I don't like. Therefore, I have asked Iowa for a postponement of decision and will not make up my mind definitely until I get back to LSU and can talk with the acting president. Cleanth is going to Columbia University in September to give a paper on criticism at a big pow-wow they are having there, but will be back at LSU for the regular term. Momentous events are apparently brooding at LSU, but the situation is too hot to be committed to paper, some of my friends tell me, and so I get only dark hints. I'm mystified, but not too apprehensive. I'll write the general outline as soon as I get back and can be sure of it. The Hardy issue of the SR was a great success, and got a fine press—including another long story in *Time*,[8] which I mention only because of the practical value which that organ's publicity has. They went all the way, again, in what they said about the SR. As for my personal projects, I am still rewriting my play, trying to reduce it enough to make production possible. I think that I have improved it, but the chance of getting commercial production for a verse play of this type is very remote. However, a little hope has been held out to me; and in any case, I shall do the best I can with the play, and not worry too much about its practical situation. Publication should be another matter, but the publishing business is in a bad way here, with the war. Many books slated for fall publication have been postponed. The *Atlantic Monthly* is tottering. It has recently been taken over by new people, and nobody knows how far the reorganization will go. This has affected me to some extent, because just two weeks before the reorganization, they asked me to handle the play in book form—they had read it in the unrevised version—about everything short of the signed contract. But now it seems that the man who wanted it, and perhaps the people who were with him on the idea, are out. What is the news about your book of stories?[9] Has it been held up? And if it has not been held up, would there be any chance of your getting a copy to us?—All of this chatter is probably pretty dull to you, but it is the only sort of thing which has been happening to us. Naturally, we have been rather sad this summer, and the old "alacrity of spirit" isn't exactly what it was a little while back. We talk of you often, and think of you more often, and look forward to a reunion. Which, we trust, may be not too far off. Everything that was said in the past, holds, and more. By the way, one of our cows died, but there are three left, but from other reports things go normally on our place. Mayme writes to us, at least, to that effect. There is a chance however, that we have found a farm farther out, which we shall look at when we get back. Goodbye, and our best love and all best wishes to you. Let us have news of Cini and Francesco.[10]

As ever,

Red

P.S. This summer I met Austin Warren,[11] whose book on Crashaw the LSU press published. He is, it seems, a friend of Praz,[12] and asked me that greetings be sent to him through you.

1. The Ransoms' son Jack (John James).

2. Maltz's story "Sunday Morning on Twentieth Street" appeared in the Winter 1940 *Southern Review*. After working in the theater in New York, he moved on to Hollywood, where his communist activities led to indictment and imprisonment during the Red Scare of the 1950s.

3. Ralph Edward Hodgson (1871–1962), prominent Georgian poet and associate of Walter de la Mare, T. S. Eliot, and Siegfried Sassoon.

4. In addition to publishing verse and fiction, Widdemer had edited *Best American Love Stories of the Year* in 1932.

5. Warren seems to anticipate an idea central to the "new historicism" of the 1980s and '90s, but he would clearly have rejected the cultural materialism at the heart of that critical school.

6. Wendell Willkie of Indiana was a dark horse candidate recruited to challenge Franklin Roosevelt in the 1940 election.

7. Harold Ickes, Roosevelt's secretary of the interior.

8. "Wessex and Louisiana," *Time* (June 10, 1940).

9. Pasinetti's collection *L'ira di Dio* would not appear until 1942.

10. Luigi Cini was a mutual friend; Francesco was Pasinetti's brother, a brilliant figure in Italian cinema before his premature death. (My thanks to Pier Pasinetti.)

11. Austin Warren was teaching at the University of Iowa and would soon be Warren's colleague during his visiting appointment there. With René Wellek, he published the classic *Theory of Literature* in 1948.

12. Mario Praz, the celebrated Italian critic.

TO FRANK LAWRENCE OWSLEY

TLS/VU   Gambier, Ohio
                                                   August 27, 1940

Dear Frank:

We survived two Writers Conferences this summer—one at Olivet and one at Colorado—and that, I am prepared to believe, is no mean achievement for anyone. Not that we didn't have some fun—that, too, must be admitted—but the combination of fun and the routine of the Conference, e[s]pecially that at Colorado, was almost more than the human frame could bear. For the work day didn't end until 10 PM, and the play-day didn't begin until 10:15 PM. The staff at both places was pleasant. Olivet had John Bishop, Sherwood Anderson, Katherine Anne Porter, Margaret Widdemer, and Glenway Westcott [*sic*]—or however he spells his name, I can never remember.¹ Colorado had Widdemer again, Albert Maltz, Frederick Lewis Allen,² Ralph Hodgson, and one or two others. But in the Colorado outfit the only person who really interested me was Maltz. Widdemer is a pleasant and rather amusing dunderhead, with a lecture on the influence of Freud on modern fiction, which was so uninformed and so stupid that it was painful. When she gave it at Olivet, Bishop, Anderson, Katherine Anne, Cinina, and I just went off and locked ourselves up with a bottle of scotch. Anderson observed, quite rightly, that he was one of her prize exhibits for her chamber of horrors, but she had simply said, "Since Mr. Anderson is in the audience, I shall omit him from my discussion." Anyway, we went on to Colorado, where we had a good time, winding up the more strenuous activities with a little mountain picnic with the Davisons. We hung round there a few days to recuperate before we started back East. We are now in Gambier, where we have been with the Ransoms for about a week, waiting for my summons to come on to Vermont. I am leaving immediately for Bennington. I shall be there a few days, then one day in New York, where I have a little modest business to transact, and then on to Tennessee. We hope to arrive in Nashville late in the afternoon of the fourth of September. We are hoping for a reunion with the Owsleys, needless to say. Cinina has a session pending with the dentist, but, except for a run up to see my father, I shall be free as air and honing for conversation. And I don't imagine Dr. Celia will entirely break Cinina's spirit, either.

I hope that things are going well with you all. We half way expect to see Margaret wearing long braids and riding on a bicycle, it's been so long since we left, or seems so long. But sober second thought tells us that that is scarcely possible.

Cinina joins me in all love to all of you.

As ever,
Red

P.S. I shall be in Gambier for a little while on September 3, and shall leave that afternoon, or early the next morning by automobile.

1. Glenway Wescott, an independently wealthy short-story writer and novelist born in Wisconsin, was a close friend of Katherine Anne Porter. His "Praise" ran in the Summer 1939 *Southern Review*.

2. Best remembered for his popular history of the 1920s *Only Yesterday* (1931).

TO JOHN BERRYMAN

TLS/Minn

The Southern Review
Louisiana State University
University
Louisiana
[Fall 1940]¹

Dear Mr. Berryman:

Thanks very much for the check for the poem.[2] The delay didn't matter a bit from my side—except that I am very sorry that it was occasioned by your illness. When I came through New York in late May or early June, I tried to get in touch with you for the conversation which you had suggested to me in your letter, but the people at the *Nation* told me that you were out of town. I am very sorry to have missed you.

As for the permission to reprint your poems from the *Southern Review,* there's no trouble about that.[3] Only we'd like an acknowledgment, if that can be managed.

Have you any new poems on hand? If so, we'd like a c[r]ack at them.[4]

Very sincerely yours,
Robert Penn Warren

1. The *Southern Review* letterhead and editorial tone of this letter suggest it was written after Warren's return to Baton Rouge, though the notation "27 Aug 40," not in Warren's hand, appears at the top of the page.
2. "Crime."
3. James Laughlin wanted to include Berryman's work in his seminal anthology *Five Young American Poets.*
4. No further Berryman poems appeared in the *Review.*

TO JOHN MALCOLM BRINNIN

TLS/UDel

The Southern Review
Louisiana State University
University
Louisiana
September 18, 1940

Mr. John Malcolm Brinnin
438 South State Street
Ann Arbor, Michigan

Dear Mr. Brinnin:[1]

We are departing from our usual policy this fall to publish a miscellany of poems, and we are anxious to include "At the Airport."[2] I am enclosing a copy of that poem in this letter, since we are suggesting the omission of one stanza, the third from the end, and want to have your opinion at the earliest possible moment. That stanza seems to us to have a different tone from the rest of the poem, and does not seem to advance the idea. Furthermore, it is our belief that that stanza actually breaks the d[r]amatic effect which would be gained by juxtaposing the stanzas which precede and follow it. Can you let us have a reply by air mail?

I hope that your summer at Bennington went well.

Sincerely yours,
Robert Penn Warren

1. The poet and future anthologist was concluding his undergraduate studies at the University of Michigan.
2. *Southern Review* (Autumn 1940).

TO JAMES T. FARRELL

TLS/Penn

The Southern Review
Louisiana State University
University
Louisiana
October 23, 1940

Dear Mr. Farrell:

I'm very sorry to report that, after a whole lot of discussion and pulling and hauling, we have decided not to use "Counting the Waves." But in the next breath, we want to ask a favor of you. Can we persuade you to do an essay on Mumford's *Faith for Living*,[1] with some reference to others who have taken the same general line? Say, about 3000 words. Will you do it? If you will, we'd like to have the piece before November 25 so that we can, if circumstances permit, use it in our winter issue. But please don't make your acceptance of the chore hinge on the matter of that date.

Warmest regards,
Robert Penn Warren

1. Farrell reviewed Lewis Mumford's book in the Winter 1941 issue.

TO JOSEPHINE MILES

TLS/UCal

The Southern Review
Louisiana State University
University
Louisiana
November 13, 1940

Miss Josephine Miles
2605 Haste St.
Berkeley, California

Dear Miss Miles:

Two of the poems, "Vacation" and "The Thoroughgoing" hit us pretty hard. Especially the first. If you have others to send, why not enclose these two? And we do hope that there will be others soon.[1]

Very sincerely yours,
Robert Penn Warren

1. Miles would have three poems in the Summer 1941 *Southern Review*.

TO LIONEL TRILLING

TLS/Col

The Southern Review
Louisiana State University
University
Louisiana
November 14, 1940

Dear Mr. Trilling:

I'm sorry to say that we have decided not to use the story. It's a little on the long side for us—and it may, it seems to us, be a little too long anyway. But excuse the impertinence of the comment. In any case, won't you let us have a look at other stories?[1]

I had hoped to be able to see you in Boston this Christmas,[2] but I've recently decided not to go up.

Sincerely yours,
Robert Penn Warren

1. None of Trilling's fiction appeared in the *Review*.
2. The Modern Language Association was meeting in Boston.

TO JAMES T. FARRELL

TLS/Penn

The Southern Review
Louisiana State University
University
Louisiana
November 14, 1940

Dear Farrell:

Fine. The outline you give for the article would certainly mean more space. So take it. How about something in the neighborhood of 5000 words, *more* or less, instead of the 3000 we first mentioned[?] We have to practice some economy in space, but we don't want you, certainly, to limit yourself arbitrarily. We are glad that you see a chance of getting the article to us this month, and we'd hope to be able to use it even i[f] it got here a few days after November 25—say before December 1. But the sooner the better, especially if you are to have a proof.

Thanks for your kind words about *Night Rider*. I appreciate them enormously. I'll look out for the piece in The Chicago Daily News.

Sincerely yours,
Robert Penn Warren

TO PAUL BROOKS

TLS/Harv

The Southern Review
Louisiana State University
University
Louisiana
December 14, 1940

Dear Brooks:

I am enclosing a sort of description and synopsis of my new novel, thinking that it may be of some interest to you all, at least in explanation of the chapters which you have. The finished job will be more closely organized than the synopsis, because a certain type of cross-reference and preparation can scarcely be handled in synopsis. But it may be that you can get a fairly good idea of the drift. Anyway, I'd certainly like to know how you all respond to it.

You may recall that I mentioned Mrs. Conrad Albrizio to you as a writer who might have a novel on hand for you pretty soon. (Your wife and she had lunch together.) She is working on a novel now. I am sending you a copy of the Winter issue of the *Southern Review,* in which you will find a novelette by Mrs. Albrizio.[1] If this strikes you as a good piece of work, it might be worthwhile for you to drop her a line—in care of Conrad Albrizio, Department of Fine Arts, University, Louisiana.

You may also recall that I mentioned the fact that I had never received the second half of the English advance on *Night Rider.* Half was to be paid in May, 1939, and the other half on publication. The second half never materialized. In this happy season, it would not come unhandy, either. Also, have you all ever had a statement from Eyre and Spottiswoode?

Those are all the loose ends which come to mind.

I hope that you all will come this way again before very long. It was good to see you. I'm sorry that the time was so short and that the conversations had to be so choppy and inconclusive.

> With our best regards to
> you both,
> Robert Penn Warren

1. "The Bereft" (Winter 1941).

TO ARTHUR MIZENER

TLS/VU
The Southern Review
Louisiana State University
University
Louisiana
December 19, 1940

Dear Mizener:[1]

Your piece has just come, and I've just read it.[2] It seems to do the job up pretty brown. Certainly, I don't see how you could have done more within the space available. And certainly, you have hit the very central fact for understanding the play. I hope that ours is as successful. I say "ours" because Cleanth and I talked the thing out together and collaborated on the actual writing. We had to do the thing under great pressure, and I'm sure it's not a masterpiece of prose. In fact, we shan't finish it until this afternoon. But, for better or worse, our piece does, I feel, tie in nicely with yours, at least in its intention. We have tried to define the "point" of the Killers, then show how the point is involved in the structure of the story, then how the "point" is related to Hemingway's basic attitude in all his work, and then how this basic "point" ties in with the literary history of the past century.[3] All pretty obvious stuff to you and a lot of others, and probably dreary because so obvious, but it may be worthwhile to put the stuff together in one piece. Or maybe I am flattering myself and Cleanth in being so sure of your agreement. Anyway, I'm anxious to know how you feel about the thing. I am getting a copy off to you tomorrow by air, so that you can have a glance at it before the CEA meeting. Cleanth, by the way, will read the thing. The Warrens are having a quiet home Christmas with the Ransoms, who arrive the night of the 26th. I want to say, however, that the Warrens greatly appreciate your invitation. I'm terribly sorry that our meeting will have to be postponed. Perhaps we can lure you down here again before another Louisiana meeting of the MLA.

A very Merry Christmas!

Sincerely yours,
Robert Penn Warren

1. Mizener, whose biography of Fitzgerald, *The Far Side of Paradise,* would become a classic, was at this time assistant professor of English at Wells College. He ultimately taught at Cornell.

2. Presumably a paper Mizener was to present at the 1940 meeting of the College English Association, held in conjunction with the Modern Language Association meeting in Boston.

3. Brooks and Warren's analysis of Hemingway's "The Killers" would be incorporated into *Understanding Fiction.*

1941

*The Writers' Workshop at the University
of Iowa, destined to become a model for creative writing programs throughout the nation, was in its infancy when Warren joined the faculty as a
visitor for the 1941 spring term. Always stimulated by new surroundings, he
would find the university, his colleagues, and the Midwest generally to his
liking, and after the demanding teaching loads he faced at LSU (even with
an "editorial" reduction) the time he could now devote to his own work
proved invaluable. At last, he would make steady progress on the novel he
had neglected in favor of his play. Its working title was "And Pastures
New," but it became* At Heaven's Gate.

TO ALLEN TATE

TLS/PU

Department of English
University of Iowa
Iowa City, Iowa
[Early 1941][1]

Dear Allen:

This will simply be a hasty note to say that we are in Iowa, with snow
on the ground and the temperature six below last night. But aside from
the weather, and a touch of flu which I had last week—very inconve-
niently, for it delayed a review I was doing for John—things have been
going very pleasantly. The trip up was nice, with a stop-over in Nashville,

where I had some good talks with Don and Frank, and a couple of days with my father, who is well. Things have been very agreeable here, so far anyway. Austin Warren, whom we met last summer in Bennington, is a hell of a nice fellow, and has put himself out to make things pleasant for us since our arrival. And there are some other very nice people about. For instance, a man named Wellek, from Prague, who is very interesting.[2] Schramm, too, turns out to be very likable.[3] My work seems to be pretty light. I have a class of twelve or fourteen, which means two hours a week. In addition to that, of course, I have conference[s], but since those are to be confined to two days a week, I ought to have an opportunity to get back at my own work seriously. I am now back at the play, which I hope to get revised this spring. I'll send it to you as soon as this draft is finished. I don't imagine that this draft will be final, but in any case, it will be vastly different from the one which I sent you last spring.

The war is about the only topic of conversation here, and suddenly it has begun to prey on my mind. The jitters are catching, I reckon, and the jitters are certainly going on around me here. How do you think we ought to act? I am inclined to feel that it's simply a military problem, and if our staff says to go ahead we ought to go ahead, but if they say we can't be effective, we certainly shouldn't allow any sentimental view to involve us. But I wonder whether FDR has taken military advice? Anyway, in another week or so we'll probably be so deep into the mess that we won't be able to turn back.

I recently had a nice offer for the Breadloaf [sic] School of English, but turned it down—although the summer looks pretty bleak financially. But I've got to be able to write next summer, and I suppose that we'll manage some way. But how, I'm not very sure. Maybe Houghton Mifflin will kick in with some dough. But I doubt it. They played so damned close about publishing the poems that I haven't got much confidence in their generosity.

Well, I've got to run to the University. Let me hear how things are going with you all. Best all around.

Red

1. Tate's notation is "[Early Winter 1941]."

2. René Wellek would leave Iowa in 1946 for Yale, where he would eventually be joined by both Brooks and Warren.

3. Wilbur L. Schramm, founder of the Writers' Workshop at Iowa.

TO JOHN PALMER

TLS
[Iowa City]
[Postmarked February 27, 1941]

Dear John:

A few lines, the first of which will be about business. Mr. Sidney Cox[1] (address: 26 East Wheelock Street, Hanover, New Hampshire) is planning on running a sort of one man writer's conference in New Hampshire this summer, and contemplates publishing a notice in the SR. He has written to me to ask about terms, but I referred him to you and have told him that you would write him immediately on the subject.[2]

I'm sorry that Harry has been hooked.[3] But tell him that he is probably grateful to me now for making him take those brisk walks last fall. And I'm sorry about Jean's illness.[4] Cinina and I do hope that it is a very unserious matter.

No great news with us. The things you'd expect, on the whole, except for the recent visit of James Laughlin.[5] He brings word that Albert is freezing to death and is [in] a terrible state of depression, but is a great social success in Boston and Cambridge, a seven-night-a-week diner-out.[6] Laughlin seemed like a very nice fellow.

Tell Cleanth I've made a little wax image with his name on it and that I'm going to begin sticking pins in it soon if he doesn't write. Meanwhile, send me some more MSS for the SR.

It's snowing again, worse luck, and I've got to get off to a class in a few minutes.

Our best love.

As ever,
Red

[P.S.] IMPORTANT: Tell Cleanth that I've just heard from Swallow, who is howling because he's had no word about the thesis.[7] Has the thing been read by Cleanth and passed on to Kirby, who in turn was to get another reader or two on it and then send it back to me[?] Swallow wants to finish up this June, you see.

1. Faculty member at Dartmouth and close friend of Robert Frost.
2. Palmer had taken Erskine's place on the *Southern Review* staff.

3. Harry Brague Jr. was a mutual friend. (My thanks to John Palmer.)

4. The future novelist Jean Stafford had taken the position of secretary at the *Southern Review*. Recently married to the poet Robert Lowell, who was determined to study with Brooks and Warren, she had followed him to Baton Rouge.

5. Founder of the New Directions press.

6. Erskine had gone to work for New Directions after leaving the *Southern Review*.

7. Warren means dissertation; Alan Swallow, founder of the Swallow Press, had taken the M.A. at LSU in 1939 and was now completing the Ph.D.

TO CLEANTH BROOKS AND JOHN PALMER

TLS/YU   [Iowa City]
                                                  March 3, 1941

Dear Cleanth and John:

I've spent a good bit of time reading Mr. Muller, who has taken an awful lot of space to say very little.¹ I seem to recall that we gave him a space limit—I'm not sure—but if we did, he certainly didn't pay any attention to it. I hate to see us pay out so much dough for this stuff. It is certainly wrong-headed. The notes on it which you, Cleanth, attached seem to me to be to the point, as polemics and more, but I'd like to suggest another (page 16) on the business of simple eloquence. For example, he cites the line from Dante—"In sua voluntade e nostra pace" [*sic*]²—which is indeed simple and eloquent—but not eloquent as a motto stuck up on a wall in isolation. Its effect grows out of a very complicated and ironical (in your sense) context. It might be said that the whole Comedy is filled with preparation for such a view, and the preparation frequently is accomplished by tensions—the giving of the full human value to a situation or person (Paolo and Francesca, Brunetto, Latino, Capaneo, Ulysses, etc.) in contrast to divine judgment. And the other two examples of simple eloquence have very complicated contexts, too—[the] dramatic context of Prospero, for example, which gives a very difficult job to Mr. Muller. He has completely misunderstood, or misrepresented, what you mean by ironic contemplation, it seems to me, and that is central. But off the point of Brooks, and on to other items in the piece—he has given Daiches³ a very superficial reading, sliding over the basi[c] self-contradiction in Daiches, and when he takes Mann⁴ as a stick to beat the bad poets with, he is doing a very dangerous thing, for Mann is full of the kind of irony which Muller disapproves of, and in method is very much like a symbolist poet sometimes. But enough of this, I guess.

I'm sorry, John, you had the tiff with Borth over the check.[5] The question with me was primarily one of knowing *when* or *if* so as to adjust my situation rather than of trying to get it immediately—but I'll be glad enough to see it when it comes. Why was Borth so touchy, anyway? I certainly think that you all took the right line in the statement to Hebert—about the principle that an editor can contribute.[6] But I certainly don't want to do so any more.

I had a long talk last night with Stoddard, Dean of the Graduate School, who was, you remember, one of the people mentioned for the LSU presidency.[7] He's a very plausible guy. We had the subject of education up for a couple of hours, and he's sending me a lot of his speeches. It's barely possible that we might get some ammunition from them for liberalizing the departmental situation at LSU, because he takes [a] crack at the institutions like Duke which, because unsure of themselves, try to lean over backward to be ultra-conservative in their interpretation of scholarship.

I'll sign off. Best all around. I hope that Jean is better.

As ever,

Red

[Handwritten in margin] I'm anxious to see [illegible] piece,[8] but don't bother to send it to me. But may I have a proof when it is ready?

1. In "The New Criticism in Poetry" (Spring 1941), Herbert Muller was less than complimentary in his assessment of Brooks and other "new" critics.

2. "E'n la sua volontade è nostra pace" (In His will is our peace), a line spoken by Piccarda Donati in Dante's *Paradiso*, Canto III.

3. Muller had some pointed remarks about the British critic David Daiches' *Poetry and the Modern World* (1940).

4. Thomas Mann (1875–1955), the distinguished German novelist whose "Olympian irony" Muller praised at the expense of that irony prized by the New Critics.

5. Daniel Borth was chief fiscal officer at LSU. (My thanks to Philip Uzee.)

6. Reformers in the new LSU administration had questioned the appropriateness of the *Southern Review* editors taking payment for their contributions. Warren's story "Goodwood Comes Back" had appeared in the Winter 1941 issue.

7. George Dinsmore Stoddard, a noted psychologist.

8. Warren's handwriting is particularly troublesome here; Grimshaw (in his edition of the Brooks-Warren correspondence) tentatively renders the name as "Allisy['s]," but no such individual appears in the *Southern Review* index.

TO PETER TAYLOR

TLS/VU   State University of Iowa
                                                                      Iowa City, Iowa
                                                                       March 4, 1941

Dear Peter:[1]

Your last story in the Southern Review[2] has excited quite a lot of enthusiastic comment about here and the comment has had, it appears, some concrete result. I have been asked to sound you out, as it were, on your coming here next year. Next year, for the first time, a special fellowship will be available, from funds raised privately, for some young man or woman who will live here for the college year. "Live here for the college year" is about the only requirement I can discover, though I suppose the recipient would be expected to attend the weekly work-shop meeting, and would be allowed to take any work in the University, without fee, which happened to interest him. That is, you would not be required to do any work for the stipend, either of a secretarial or teaching sort, or be required to take work toward a degree. You could, if you wished, do work entirely in the art school for instance; or you might devote yourself entirely to your own work. When I was asked about you I explained very fully your attitude—that you had resigned a fellowship at LSU, that you did not want to take an advanced degree, and that you had no desire to be a teacher. They said that that didn't matter on the terms of this special fellowship. But they did want to know how hard you took your own work. I told them that you worked like the devil. They didn't need any fight talk about the quality of your stuff, but I threw that in anyway. I believe that the fellowship is yours if you will indicate to me that you want it—of course, I can't be sure about this, but I am pretty sure. Will you let me know very soon how you respond to the idea[?] I am in no way trying to persuade you to take it, I simply want you to have it if you happen to want it. It pays about $500.[3]

I shall add that we are finding life here very pleasant indeed, in so far as the human element goes, and I imagine that you would find a fair number of very congenial people. Plus, naturally, some of the other kind.

A recent letter from John Palmer brought us the bad news about Jean. We hope that she is about all right now. Please give her and Cal[4] our very warmest regards. And we send them, likewise, to you. I hope that everything goes well for you.

As ever,
Red

1. Taylor, soon to prove himself a consummate master of short fiction, had studied with both Tate and Ransom prior to entering the graduate program at LSU. During his brief stay in Baton Rouge, he roomed with Jean Stafford and Robert Lowell.
2. "Sky Line" (Winter 1941).
3. The matter of the fellowship became moot. Taylor was drafted in the summer of 1941.
4. Robert Lowell's nickname, short for "Caligula."

TO JOHN PEALE BISHOP

TLS/PU
Department of English
University of Iowa
Iowa City, Iowa
[March 1941]

Dear John,

Because of my absence from Louisiana (I'm doing some visiting teaching this term) things are moving more slowly than usual for the SOUTHERN REVIEW, for Cleanth and I have to write back and forth. We'd like very much to have the paper you did for Princeton: we'd rather have it in fact, than your review of the New Directions anthology. And we still want the fiction review, if you will do it.[1] Will you notify Cleanth (or John Palmer, who is now with us in place of Erskine) if you have decided to do the novels? That arrangement would save a little time.

I want to tell you how much I think of the Fitzgerald poem in the New Republic.[2] It is very moving.

Good bye, and all best regards to you all.

As ever,
Red Warren

P.S. I hear that your collected poems are out.³ Fine!

1. Bishop had made his last contribution to the *Southern Review*.
2. "The Hours," *New Republic* (March 3, 1941). Bishop and F. Scott Fitzgerald, who died the year before, had been classmates at Princeton.
3. *Selected Poems* (1941).

TO CLEANTH BROOKS

TLS/YU   [Iowa City]
                                                             [March 1941]

Dear Cleanth:

Many, many thanks for your effort to relieve my mind about the appointment.¹ I do feel a little better about it, but that isn't to say that I'm going the rounds of the local beer parlors and setting up drinks on the house to celebrate. Hodges still has to prove himself. But if the Board tips him off as to his line, he may incline his ear in the right direction. I haven't yet given the SR stuff a thorough going-over, but I'll get off a report to you tomorrow on it. It isn't the most promising layout in the world, is it[?] While we are on the SR, yes, we did accept the piece on NeoPlatonism,² according to my recollection. And I have just written to Bishop to say that we did want a crack at his paper on Painting and Poetry, which he read at Princeton, and that we did want him to do the fiction review. Baker has written me that he's going to Mexico for a long stay to write—giving up Harvard because he can't do two things at once.³ And he would like to do some more long fiction reviews for us.⁴ So that would seem to indicate him for the piece after Bishop's. I shall write him to that effect if you give me the word.

Your name is on every tongue here. Last night we had a radio round table debate on "Ethical Considerations in Criticism"—Austin Warren, Norman Foerster,⁵ myself, and three other members of the Department—Warrens against Humanists. You received high compliments over the air from Foerster, who cited you as one of the four or five stars of the "new criticism"—with which, I must add, he feels ill at ease. Foerster is a genial and cunning Humanist, hard to pin. Baker,⁶ one of the other men, is a first-rate bigot with lots of learning. He even wants to deny that literature is an art at all—you can predict the rest. We had another session after the radio, and the hair-pulling reached an acute stage—with Baker referring to Ransom as "that charlatan" etc. Baker also said that any competent professor of English could read a poem—the sort of thing in *Understanding Poetry*—that that approach wasn't criticism because it didn't give moral evaluation, etc. I finally asked him what he thought about a play like Anthony and Cleopatra, in which there are no "good" people. He said he thought that the play was a study in elicit [*sic*] passion—yes, that that was the idea of the play, "guilty love." I said that I thought that Cleopatra was a "good" woman, and he almost went wild—she is good, it seems to me, in the sense that she is trying hard toward the end to establish [Rest of letter is missing]

1. General Campbell Blackshear Hodges had been appointed the new president of LSU.

2. Accepted or not, no readily identifiable piece on Neoplatonism appeared in the *Southern Review.*

3. Howard Baker had been teaching at Harvard.

4. Baker would contribute an omnibus review of new fiction to the Autumn 1941 number.

5. Foerster had directed the School of Letters at Iowa since 1930. Now remembered primarily as a pioneering Americanist, he carried on the New Humanist tradition associated with Irving Babbitt and Paul Elmer More.

6. Joseph Ellis Baker, a Victorian specialist.

TO PETER TAYLOR

TLS/VU   [Iowa City]
                                                                 [March 1941]

Dear Peter:

I was pleased to have your note, and to have some inking that your novel is moving.[1] As for next year, I may have overstated the case a little on the financial side—but it was because I was slightly misinformed. I gather now that you could expect something like fifty dollars a month while you are here, which would be a little less that the five hundred I mentioned in my letter. But not a great deal less. It seems that the best thing for you to do if you want to pursue the matter is: Write to the

Dean of the Graduate School (his name is Stoddard, and you can get his full name from a catalogue there—I advise you to do it) and ask for information about fellowships and assistantships, and tell him that you intend to apply for a post in the creative writing department of the School of Letters. Then write to Wilbur Schramm *and* Paul Engle,[2] both, saying that you are interested in coming here and asking what provisions could be made. (Schramm is director of the writing program and so rates a letter; Engle had a good deal to do with raising the money for the appointment, and so he should rate a letter out of courtesy and tact.) It seems to be in the bag, if you want it. The thing will have to go though the usual channels, that is, through the Graduate School office, because the money, which has been raised privately, will be paid into the University Treasury; but the appointment will be decide[d] by Schramm and Engle. You will, I understand, be technically a graduate assistant, but you will not be required to take any courses or work for a degree. You will be, however, expected to attend the weekly workshop in fiction and do some advising of other students in conferences. But, I am assured that the duties will be very light. If you wanted to take work in the School of Painting [*sic*], that would be all right, too. By the way, I think you would like Grant Wood[3] personally; and I have met another very nice fellow in the Art School.

I am delighted to learn, or to deduce, from a note Jean stuck in a bundle of MSS that she is well again. I hope that she has not rushed things by getting up. How is Cal? I'd like news of him and his doings. And we'd like mighty well to have news of you.

Things are going about as usual with us. I've been seeing a good deal of some of the men in the Department, who fall to, hammer-and-tongs, on the thing which they term the "new criticism." So I've got plenty of sparring partners—and some very shrewd ones. Austin Warren, I am glad to report, draws even more of their fire than I do; and he's a mean man to tackle. But it has been fun, with a radio debate and another debate coming up, and lots of private debates. And even Humanists drink whiskey—in moderation, of course.

Goodbye, and our best regards to you.

As ever,
Red

1. Taylor was never comfortable in the longer forms. His short "novel" *A Woman of Means* was not published until 1950.

2. A noted poet, Engle succeeded Schramm as director of the Writers' Workshop, which became under his leadership the nation's preeminent creative writing program.

3. A native Iowan celebrated for his paintings of midwestern rural life. His *American Gothic* has achieved iconic status.

TO PAUL BROOKS

TLS/Harv

Department of English
University of Iowa
Iowa City, Iowa
April 2, 1941

Dear Brooks:

I have been hoping to have some comment on the synopsis which I sent in just before Christmas, and, in addition, I'd like very much to have your remarks on the chapters which are in your office. I'm now back into the thing and hope, with luck, to finish up by fall, even though the book looks pretty long. I have declined some summer teaching offers, although one of them, the Breadloaf [*sic*] School of English, was rather attractive, so that I can put all my time on the novel. I'd appreciate it if you would send me all the manuscript which you have on hand, for the condition of my own is terrible—all scribbled over with revision, etc.— and I'd like, if possible, to have yours to splice in with the new stuff I'm on.

The situation here has been very pleasant, for I don't have much teaching, and my students are pretty good; and naturally I haven't had quite as much Southern Review work as usual. I've done another revision of my play and some new poems as well as the work on the novel— but the last now claims me full-time.

Goodbye, and my best. Thanks for sending me the stuff. And, as I said, I'd be grateful for any comments or suggestions.

Sincerely yours,
Red Warren

[P.S.] I was delighted to learn that Cheney got his Guggenheim.

TO BRAINARD CHENEY

TLS/VU
Department of English
University of Iowa
Iowa City
[Spring 1941]

Dear Lon:

I was delighted to have the news a few days ago that your Guggenheim came through properly. That's fine, and I'm sure that the novel will do them credit. I hope that it is moving fast.

Things have been going very pleasantly here. My work is light—two class hours a week, with fourteen students, and a weekly visit to the so-called "workshop," in which folks sit around and read each other their efforts. I do have, of course, some conferences, but I've got all my work concentrated on Tuesdays and Thursdays, and so I have a lot of time which should, but doesn't always, prove of benefit to me. I have done some of the things I had on the ticket, however. Pleasure, rather than work, is the hindrance here, for there are some very nice folks about, and they are rather sociably inclined. But a recent trip to Chicago, which had the slight excuse of a radio affair, has been our big debauch—and not very big at that. But it was fun. Except for the fact that we reached home late at night and found that our maid had locked us out and had locked the keys inside. So we had the necessity of a second-story job.

I suppose we'll be here until early June. Then we may get a day or so in Nashville—we hope so—and if we do we look forward to seeing you all. Meanwhile, all our best to you. Cinina joins me in all best wishes to Fanny.

As ever,
Red

TO PIER M. PASINETTI

TLS
714 East College Street
Iowa City, Iowa
April 16, 1941

Dear Pier:

Your letter, which came today, brought us the greatest pleasure. We had a letter from you in the fall, and I answered it. This time I am answering

in duplicate, a copy to you at Göttingen[1] and a carbon to your Rome address. Perhaps one will manage to reach you.

Yes. Mr. O'Brien (who, incidentally, died a few weeks ago) used a piece of yours, the last one in the magazine, and a copy of his collection, addressed to you, is now being held in Louisiana.[2] I didn't know what else to do with it under the circumstances. And, I may add, that the piece has attracted a lot of fine comment. And I like it better and better. I wish we had some more. We have been wondering—among so many other things—about your collection of novelettes. So they haven't appeared yet?

Yes, we came to Iowa. After our return, they raised the ante quite a bit and made it too attractive to turn down. I teach two class-meetings a week, two hours altogether, and visit the so-called workshop once a week. I have conferences on Tuesday and Thursday afternoons, but I get all my work done on those two days, and have five—think of it!—five full days a week for myself. I haven't any world-beaters in my little group, but do have some pretty intelligent people. There may be one world-beater—a lad named Brantley,[3] who was with me at Louisiana, and who has suddenly done some fine fiction. And, of course, [Shirley] Forgotson and Unger[4] are here, too, though they are not officially in my outfit; but they visit sometimes with the group and liven things up. I should get a lot done, but the social life here has been pretty active for us. I have, however, completely rewritten my play, and am on the novel, which I hope to finish by fall. If the summer goes well. I had an invitation, very attractive from both a practical and geographical point of view, to go to Vermont for six weeks this summer, but turned it down with the hope of squeezing through with the whole summer for the novel. We hope to go to Mexico, which is the *best* we can do under the circumstances. And we may not get to do that, of course.

Back to our life here. We arrived with suitcases only, and found that no furnished apartment was to be had. So we had to take an unfurnished one, and try to put it into shape for a five month stay. But friends rallied round and helped us. Grant Wood—you recall, the painter, "American Gothic" etc.—let us rifle his attic (by the way, his house here, an old place which he rebuilt, is a beauty) for furniture and rugs; and Austin Warren (a friend of Mario Praz, [and] author of a recent and very fine book on Crashaw) has decorated our walls with two Currier and Ives, and a very fine Japanese print. So we are pleasantly settled. There are a

lot of nice folks about. This you may recall, is the haunt of Neo-Humanism, with Norman Foerster brooding over the abyss; and I've been participating in debates, formal and informal, with Humanists since my arrival. It's just about Austin Warren and R. P. Warren against the field here, with one or two exceptions. A few weeks ago, we had a radio debate on criticism, and I have a transcript which I hope to show you before too long. I went to Chicago last week to give a radio program, and we had a very pleasant time, seeing old friends, Morton Zabel among them, and eating some very good food.

Cinina is taking work at the Art School here, and seems to be enjoying it. Aside from that she runs the house (we can get only a half-time maid here) and reads detective stories and Russian novels. The spring has just arrived in this latitude, and we shall soon be swimming in the lake here. The country is rather nice here, not prairie country, but rolling and somewhat wooded. Cinina is planning a picnic for this weekend, if [t]he streak of good weather holds.

News from Cleanth seems very good on the personal side. His book had a considerable success, followed by lectures at Columbia and Princeton. He goes to Texas this summer. Albert has left us to take a marvelous job as editor of the New Directions Press, double his previous salary, or near that. We had a fine blow-up with authorities when he left. He didn't even bid Quasimodo[5] farewell when he left. But the upshot of the affair was that we got a decent salary for his successor, who is John Palmer. The set-up is now changed: Palmer as managing editor and the rest of us as editors. But Albert and Katherine Anne are now separated, apparently for good. She is living up East, and has bought a farm in Northern New York State.[6] All very philosophic and friendly—but very sad. We miss them at Baton Rouge.

I suppose that you can gather from my foregoing remarks that life rocks along for us in pretty predictable channels. We do the same things, superficially at least. We talk of you constantly, and would give a great deal to see you. I shan't undertake to tell you how much we look forward to our next meeting.

As ever,

Red

P.S. We heard from Henri[7] recently. And Ray[8] in California—you remember him? A few nights ago I was talking to a friend and the tele-

phone rang. California was calling. Well, it was Ray. Why? Just said he felt like a conversation. So we had one. You may gather from the amiable freedom with which he indulges his impulses of friendship that he is still a big movie man.

Cinina is writing you under separate cover. Meanwhile, she joins me in love.

1. Pasinetti had left Italy to assume a lectureship at the University of Göttingen.

2. Edward J. O'Brien had reprinted Pasinetti's "Family History" in his *Best Short Stories of 1940*.

3. Frederick Brantley went on to edit *American Prefaces*.

4. Leonard Unger, later a distinguished critic and faculty member at the University of Minnesota.

5. Pipkin; see n. 6, letter to Porter (January 15, 1940), above.

6. Actually a farmhouse, near Saratoga Springs.

7. Henri Albert Arnaud, a graduate student from France during Pasinetti's stay in Baton Rouge.

8. Raymond Dannenbaum, a friend from Warren's Berkeley days working as a screenwriter in Hollywood. (My thanks to Pier Pasinetti.)

TO KATHERINE ANNE PORTER

TLS/Maryland

Department of English
University of Iowa
Iowa City, Iowa
April 25, 1941

Dear Katherine Anne:

A long overdue letter. We've talked about you and thought about you a lot, but somehow we just haven't brought ourselves down to business. I suppose that my immediate provocation grows out of the fact that I'm trying to do a piece on your fiction.[1] The University here sponsors radio talks now and then on literary subjects. I gave one on Hemingway recently, or rather gave a short talk, which was followed by a debate (Humanists are, as you may suppose, anti-Hemingway, and the Humanist Society had its meeting in the radio room), and next month I'm supposed to do another. So I have thought I'd do it on KAP. I've been using some of the stories in my work here, and begin to feel that I've got a few

ideas on the subject. I wish I could talk them over with you. But that's impossible, and I shan't bore you with the stuff in the form of a letter. If the paper seems to turn out well, I'll send you a copy and shall use it for a lecture which I'm giving here in June before we tear out.

We have had many small things happen to us this winter, but nothing very big or unpredictable. We left Baton Rouge in late January, somewhat embittered and worn-out by all the confusion about university reorganization and the presidency. Now, recently, they've appointed a doddering Major general in the U.S. Army, as president, and things on the whole look black. He may turn out to be an intelligent man, and I'm willing to assume that he's an honest man; but honesty and intelligence won't fill the bill there. If he hasn't had enough special training to make him aware of the issues at LSU, it will take him years to do anything; and we can't wait years. Suppose he does want to do something. The people on whom he will naturally depend for information and advice will be the same old gang of deans and department heads who have put things in the present shape. And you can bet your bottom dollar that they won't cut their own throats in the cause of higher education. And you can also bet that the new appointments (there are almost a dozen headships to be filled) will be made on the advice of the deans, etc. And, one of those headships is our own. So I'm pretty gloomy and though Cleanth writes that there is a little ray of hope from the Board, he too is gloomy. I'm in a state of mind to begin looking around hard for a job, if things aren't on the mend when we get back next fall.

We stopped in Nashville for a few days on our way up here, and in Kentucky to see my father. (Since our arrival here he has had a light case of pneumonia, his first illness of any kind in thirty years, but he seems to be well now. But he's getting on, over seventy now.) We fought our way north through snow and sleet, and arrived to find that there are no furnished apartments in this fair little city. So we had to take an unfurnished one. Cinina made the rounds of the second hand furniture stores and bought herself a lot of paint and brushes and started in. She did wonders, and then Grant Wood and Austin Warren helped—Wood rifling his attic and Austin going down into his supply of Currier and Ives and Japanese prints. So things are rather pleasant, after all. There are a lot of nice folks here. Austin Warren is a swell fellow, and has been wonderful to us. Schramm is very nice. René Wellek, from the University of Prague, is a monument of learning in the European style. And there are several very keen fellows among the younger men in the department. Grant Wood is kind and amusing. And three of my students from LSU are here in the graduate school. Debates with Humanists rage here— Austin Warren, Wellek and yours truly against the field. But it has been fun. My work has been light, one class with two meetings a week, and, of course, conferences. But I get it all in on two days, and so have a reasonable amount of time for myself. Since I get paid about the same for this as I get at LSU for working like a navvy, it has been a pleasant change. But I do have SR stuff to read. (Speaking of the SR, haven't you something for us[?] We need fiction desperately these days. Haven't you a nice story all ready for the summer issue? Please, please.)[2] As for my own work, I've completely redone the play, and, I trust, have improved it. And I've done a few poems, which I am enclosing for your inspection. I'm on the novel now and hope to push it through by fall—or, at least, I tell myself that. I have turned down my chances for summer teaching—a very nice job at Breadloaf [sic] School of English—and we are set to scrape through somehow, but the somehow looks a little thin. We haven't decided definitely what we shall do or can do. We hope to go to Mexico if the exchange stays right, and if we can get a line on a quiet place where there's swimming. I have been studying Spanish all winter, and would like to go on with that this summer.

The spring has finally arrived here, and is doing a very decent job of itself, too. The country in this little section is very nice, rolling hills, several little rivers and woods. So we are ready for a few picnics and some trips to the lake. Cinina spends a good deal of time with her work at the University, but she can get off in the afternoons. So tomorrow afternoon we take our first jaunt out to get an impulse from a vernal wood for the season.

We'd like to have a lot of news from you. The grape-vine tells us that you have bought a farm and will be at Yaddo for a little while longer. But that is all we know, and we'd like to hear a lot more. About yourself and about your novel and about whatever else pops into your head.

Goodbye.

As ever,

Red

[Postscript in Cinina Warren's hand]

Dear Katherine Anne:

This has been too long a silence on our part, and we are in debt to you for a letter. Red's remarks about L.S.U. unpleasantness are really understatements. We missed you terribly and then Albert went. On top of that Conrad and Duncan were tied up in a "movement"[3] which entitled them to even give up old friends (in Spartan cold blood). It was a messy return, but of course it drew *us survivors* closer. It's been nice here, but I'll be delighted to get South again. Is there *any* chance that you might come to see us[?] You have no idea how we'd love it, and how much we would love seeing you.

> Affectionately,
> Cinina

[Handwritten in margin] Do come—Red.

1. Ultimately published as "Katherine Anne Porter: Irony with a Center," *Kenyon Review* (Winter 1942).
2. Porter's novelette "The Leaning Tower" would run in the Autumn 1941 issue.
3. A flirtation with Trotskyite politics. (My thanks to Robert B. Heilman.)

TO PAUL BROOKS

TLS/Harv

> Department of English
> University of Iowa
> Iowa City, Iowa
> May 14, 1941

Dear Brooks:

Many thanks for sending me the manuscripts. I agree that the Ashby Wyndham story should not open the novel, and I also agree that the section devoted to him should be very short—that is, until the time when his story is fused with the general situation. I've done some re-working of that material since you saw it, but I'm spending most of my time on the new part of the book. Things are going pretty fast now, for I'm getting some six hours a day at the typewriter, and by early June I'll have another considerable wad of stuff to send you all. I shan't send you what I now have on hand, for I don't want to take the time out right now to make the copy, and my only version is in such a shape that no typist could figure it out. But when I finish the section I'm now working on I'll make a copy and send it. That is, if you want the thing bit by bit. In any case, if I can hold my present pace, I shall finish in September.

I shall be here until about June 12.

> Goodbye, and warm
> regards,
> Red Warren

TO PAUL BROOKS

TLS/Harv

> University of Iowa
> Iowa City, Iowa
> [May 1941]

Dear Brooks:

This is an SOS. I am in dire need of an advance to tide me over the summer. I have been on a twelve month basis at LSU, the year running from July to July. Not long back, I learned that they are reorganizing their system, and will not begin payments until October 10, which makes the period from June 13, when I leave here, to the fall look long and lean. Before I learned of the new system of payments, I had turned down a very pretty little summer job at the Breadloaf [*sic*] School of English, and another little job. And now, of course, it's far too late to do anything about summer teaching. Anyway, I wanted, if possible, to push the novel through by fall. That seems to be entirely possible, at the present rate of composition, if I don't have to try to do a lot of incidental writing during the summer to get a little extra money. Five or six hundred dollars would just about make the difference for me, which, with the five hundred already advanced against the book, would require a sale of four thousand copies or so, wouldn't it?

I'd much prefer not to have to have an advance, God knows. But now it seems to be my only recourse, for, as I said above, the situation looks very black.

> Goodbye, and best regards,
> Robert Penn Warren

TO KATHERINE ANNE PORTER

TLS/Maryland   [Iowa City]

June 9, 1941

Dear Katherine Anne:

Forgive the long delay in answering your letter, which we enjoyed very much. But the last few weeks have been pretty damned hectic from every point of view, exams, last-minute parties since we are leaving now, last-minute conferences with students who insisted on leaving their work until the end of term, and the thousand and one predictable confusions contingent upon pulling up stakes from a place. But, as I said, we greatly enjoyed the full letter. The description of the farm sounds too damned fine to be convincing, and we, who don't know where we shall really be able to settle, really settle, are pretty green with envy.

I am hoping to find the novelette you spoke of waiting in Baton Rouge, when we arrive there next week. I can't wait to read it. And how is the novel coming? But—not to rush ahead of myself—naturally we want to publish the novelette. I rather imagine that we can—and that we should. It will simply be a matter of some space calculations, and even that, I don't imagine, would matter if you don't mind waiting an issue or two for publication. You see, the fact of a special Yeats issue in December throws our general program a little out of gear. But you will hear definitely from us as soon as I get to Louisiana and we can add and subtract. As for the MS, I hope it is there, since you and Cleanth had communicated on the subject. But if it isn't there will you send it PDQ and win the gratitude of yours truly?

I gave the radio piece on your stories, and since that time have been working up a larger lecture which I shall give here next Thursday night as the opening general lecture of the summer school. Then I hope to put it into shape for an essay, which I shall send you a copy of. The problem I have been chiefly concerned with is this—in addition to certain obvious things which need to be said by way of a general introduction to the work: I have tried to define the basic attitude (not specifically *literary*) which underlines the stories and have tried to see how this finds its special technical manifestations in structure and style. I am using Old Mortality, Flowering Judas (the story), Noon Wine, and Theft as the central pieces. Magic, Hacienda, and Pale Horse seem to me to be more peripheral—by which I do not mean any pejorative judgment, though I do think that Hacienda and Magic lie below the best, and well populated best, level of the stories. I shan't go more into detail now, for I would find myself summarizing the essay. And I shan't ask you for a judgment now, for I think that is cheating some, to make the author help write the essay on his own work or, in this case, *her* own work. But this term we spen[t] three weeks in the class on the stories and now I feel that I know them better than before, though I thought that I knew them very well indeed.

We are leaving Iowa in a few days, heading for Louisiana, where we shall be for a short time. Then Mexico, if things go well. Some time back we almost decided to go to Vermont, where I had a very nice job for six weeks, but I knew that if I taught I wouldn't get much work done on the novel. I was wavering, however, when Cinina put her foot down and said "no teaching" even if we had to do something pretty drastic to get through. And now, no teaching, and I'm happy to report that the novel is moving briskly. The financial worries for the summer have been somewhat alleviated too, by the fact that HM has kicked in a second advance on the novel, just today. So after we put the fall issue to bed, or almost to bed, in Baton Rouge, we shall shove off again. We shall stay with Tinkum a day or so, and then shall go by way of Austin, Texas, where Cleanth is teaching. The University of Texas, I have heard, though not from Brer Brooks, is carrying on a flirtation with him. I hope that they will make him a handsome offer, and then he will use it as a club on the heads at LSU. But Cleanth has recently written me that things in general (not personally) are looking up. Apparently the radicals got across the line of communications of the deans with the Board, and have captured the ear and confidence of the Board, temporarily, at least. But until I see the death warrants for several I don't believe in the new day. But I hear that two deans will bite the dust. It has gone to the point, I hear, that some deans are snitching on other deans, and turning state's evidence. Pretty, huh[?] When you hear of a Saint Valentine's day massacre of deans you know that the DA will be after the other deans for bumping off their late confederates. (By confederates, I mean no aspersions on the late political organization, of the Mississippi, the bank sinister, of the Ohio, the bank sinister, to adopt the phrase from a poem by JCR.)[1]

Goodbye, and all best luck. Looking forward to the novelette in Baton Rouge.

As ever,
Red

[In Cinina Warren's hand]

Dear Katherine Anne:

I'm in the middle of that abomination called packing. Tomorrow I go to have a wisdom tooth removed, in the midst of this mess. Life has been spinning desperately around here, but I have managed to get through an art course, and Red has gotten a very great deal done. Morton Zabel came by and stayed with us much to our delight. He was here about three days.

We will be very happy indeed to get home. It seems there is a rift now between D.F. and C.A.[2] (dog eat dog stuff). That part of Baton Rouge depresses me, but still it will seem like home. It's Syria now— Damascus of all places![3] What will happen there? Well, we just live from thin hope to thin hope. Your farm sounds lovely, and we hope you will be very happy there.

Our love,
Cinina

1. See John Crowe Ransom's poem "Antique Harvesters."
2. Duncan Ferguson and Conrad Albrizio.
3. Free French and other Allied forces had invaded Syria and Lebanon to preempt an Axis takeover.

TO PAUL BROOKS

TLS/Harv

Iowa City
June 13, 1941

Dear Paul:

The contract came this morning, and I am getting it back by what ought to be return mail. I'm very much relieved that you all settled the advance question, for the summer now looks much brighter. Thanks very much for writing me about it.

I gather that you all aren't particularly interested in seeing the stuff I've done this spring. When I stop in Louisiana I may be able to get some copies made, and if you want I'll send them. But I imagine that you'd rather have the thing in one chunk and not in sections. Will you please let me have the material now in your hands? Perhaps the best thing is to send it to me at the Southern Review, marked personal, so it will be there for me next week.

We are leaving tomorrow morning after a very pleasant time here. Again thanks. And best regards.

Sincerely,
Red Warren

P.S. I forgot the very important item of the check. Can you send that to me at the Southern Review, too? Thanks. I'd be mighty grateful to you if [it] is waiting for me upon my arrival a few days hence.

In late June 1941, the Warrens—with a quixotic haste that seems character-istic—set out for a summer vacation in Mexico, planning to visit Brooks (guest-teaching at the University of Texas) on their way. The summer was to prove eventful in several respects.

TO JOHN PALMER

ALS

Charleston Hotel
Lake Charles, LA
[Postmarked June 29, 1941]

Dear John:

As you know by this time, I left the car. If you want it, it is yours on whatever basis is agreeable to you. If you don't need it, will you dispose of it for me? The people who offered me three fifty on a trade said that it should bring between two fifty and three hundred to a dealer. I am in no immediate press for cash, and so if you take it there is no rush; but if you decide not to take it I'd appreciate early steps in disposing of it. The car papers, as Jean will tell you, are in the office, and Cal has the keys. By the way, the license plates if returned to the Bureau of motor vehicles [*sic*], Court House, Iowa City, Iowa, will mean a refund of eleven dollars for me. So if you are keeping the car, will you register it in your name immediately so that my rebate will be good, and will you send the plates back? I'm sorry to burden you with this but I didn't know how else to manage.

But I did forget one important thing in the rush of buying the farm yesterday[1] and packing. I forgot to get my draft papers which will permit me to cross the border. Mr. Upton,[2] of Board #2, at the Old State Capitol, has them prepared, and I'd be enormously grateful if you'd pick them up as soon as you conveniently can and send them, special delivery, in care of Cleanth. It was a damned fool thing to do, forgetting them, but I did it.

Good bye and all best to you from us both. You *must* join us in Mexico, even if for a few days.

As ever,
Red

[P.S.] Best to *Lowells.*

1. Always attracted to country living, the Warrens had arranged to purchase a house and acreage in the Prairieville area, a clear sign of their intention to remain in Louisiana.
2. Probably Malcolm R. Upton (Baton Rouge City Directory). In preparation for America's eventual entry into the war, President Roosevelt had activated the Selective Service, and Warren's status would come to preoccupy him in the next few years.

TO JOHN PALMER

TLS   Austin, Texas
                                                                   June 30, 1941

Dear John:

Among other things I forgot was the batch of MSS which I am to read. Can they be sent to me in care of Wells Fargo, Mexico City[?] And, also,

Heilman's essay is lying in the office.[1] After you have read that will you send it on to me, too, please?

I forgot to tell you in the note from Saint [sic] Charles, that the car caught on fire the night before we left. The lead wire from the battery slipped off and rubbed against the metal plate above the battery. Some stuff lying on top of the plate ignited. Not [sic] damage, however, was done, and I had the thing fixed up the next day and a piece of insulation put under the plate to prevent a recurrence of the trouble.

We are, I hope, pulling out tomorrow. That, of course, contingent upon the arrival of the draft paper. I'm sorry to have forgotten that.

Again, all thanks. And again, please try to join us for your vacation.

We have had a pleasant time here with the Brookses. Cleanth has wowed them here, it seems.

Love to Lowells.

As ever,
Red

P.S. [Typed at top of page] I am enclosing a couple of hat checks, one for a panama, which I forgot, and the other for a hat which was taken out from the shop—but I don't know which is for which. If you ever pass by the joint I'd appreciate your picking up the panama; if you don't, it's mighty little loss.

I expect a couple of checks in before long, one from Crofts and one from Holt. Will you open anything addressed to me from these firms, and if the checks come deposit them at your convenience[?] Naturally, I have some curiosity about the amount involved. Toodle-oo.

[Handwritten at bottom of page] Your note and the draft papers have just come. (I delayed mailing this.) Many thanks!

Best,
Red

[In left margin in Cinina Warren's hand]

Dear John: A mattress (inner spring) will come by freight for me. Please have the Globe Storage Co. charge the delivery to me, and have it put on your bed (as we had agreed). Lots of love to all. I've been in bed with a cold, but am now well alkalinized, and I hope, healthier. Thank you.

Cinina

[In right margin in Warren's hand] Do come to Mexico—return trip won't cost you a penny. We ought to sit in some [illegible]

1. Robert Becthold Heilman's "Notes on the Renaissance," *Southern Review* (Spring 1942). Heilman was among Brooks and Warren's most valued colleagues.

TO JOHN PALMER

TLS   Hotel Nido
                                                   Chapala,
                                                    Jalisco,
                                                     Mexico
                                                July 17, 1941

Dear John:

This isn't exactly Sirmione, but it's a pretty good Mexican version. It's a tiny town, picture-postcard in appearance and smelly on close acquaintance, situated on an eighty-mile lake surrounded by mountains, with a wonderful climate. We have a tiny house, new and never before occupied—which means that we haven't inherited any animal life. For the house we pay six dollars a month, but a screening job raised the rent several dollars a month—and God knows screens are necessary at this season. Our cook costs a dollar a week and food costs damned little, except meat, of which we don't eat much. There is fine boating and swimming. And some rather funny and agreeable people, including a fly-weight Olympic wrestling champion (1920), Witter Bynner,[1] a Hollywood lady and her novelist husband, an alcoholic and hefty and humorous widow of some forty-five summers from Florida (dead husband an army man, I gather), an old lady from Virginia who has lived here forty-odd years and is full of lore, mostly erroneous, I surmise, and some other folks. But we live out of the center of town and down there the hordes gather and drink; we go down for our swim and take a walk in the evening, and stick pretty close to home otherwise. We are still hoping that you will come down. You can get a room and breakfast for from fifty cents to a dollar and quarter, according to your tastes, and can take dinner and lunch with us. It would cost you practically nothing, once you got here, and rail fare is quite cheap here, as you know. And, there are the busses [sic]. If you come you get a ticket to Guadalajara, where we'll meet you by car. Only thirty miles away. And do come if you possibly can. It would be fine to have you here.

My mail which Jean sent on Bastille day arrived this afternoon. The mail which was returned from Wells Fargo—the bastards, who simply declined, it appears, to forward the stuff to me here despite two cards of instructions. Thank her for me. But I'll write in a day or so, anyway. Meanwhile, I hope she is improving and that the plans for leaving Louisiana are thriving, like a peach tree the rabbits have been gnawing.

I had a garbled note today from the Iowa license people, who, it seems, are trying to welch on the money they owe me. If you happen to have kept somewhere the little yellow registration card from Iowa, which was attached to the steering post in a little celluloid folder, it might help matters along. But I have no hope of being able to get anything from them. They claim that the fact the car is to be sold lets them out—or something of the sort. Their letter was so garbled and illiterate that I could scarcely make any sense out [of] it. But if you do happen to have the little yellow ticket, stick it in an air mail envelope to me, and receive my thanks.

Also, I'd love to have the MSS for the SR, and Heilman's essay, which is lying in the office. And we'd love to have news from the home front. Speaking of fronts, the Russians don't seem to be doing so well, if my halting spelling out of the local newspapers means anything.[2]

Goodbye, and our love to all. I'm writing to Cleanth in Texas, not being sure when he leaves. We had a fine visit at Austin.

As ever,
Red

1. Born in 1881 and educated at Harvard, the modernist poet Bynner had settled in Santa Fe, New Mexico. He had contributed to the *Fugitive* in the 1920s.
2. Hitler had invaded the Soviet Union in June.

TO JOHN PALMER

TLS   Hotel Nido
                                                    Chapala, Jalisco,
                                                            Mexico
                                          [Postmarked July 22, 1941]

Dear John:

Thanks very much for your letter, which came this evening, and for the various chores you have done for us, such as depositing the check.

We're distressed to hear about the accident to your eye. For God's sake take all precautions. I do hope that it will be all right. But don't take one doctor's opinion, unless it simply amounts to nothing—as I trust will be the case.[1] And let us hear very soon the state of affairs. We'll be anxious to know.

As for the thirty-five dollars for the battery, etc. for the car—sure. And a tip. You don't need a full-size battery. The size now in the car is perfectly all right, and don't let them sell you the regular size Packard battery, which costs a lot of money. I used the battery in the car for a year and many a mile, and it was old when I got the car; so I know that this size is all right. As for the general condition of the car, I do hope that it was all we anticipated. That was why I was anxious for you to get the opinion of a mechanic before you bought it.

As for Chapala, we like it better and better. It definitely grows on you, day by day. And we are extremely anxious for you to come. I have just been down town, after receiving your somewhat encouraging letter, to price accommodations for you. The Nido Hotel, where we get our mail, is scrupulously clean and quite newly painted, etc. You can get a room without bath there for four pesos a day, which means about eighty cents. Breakfast would cost you from fifteen to thirty cents. [W]e live on about sixty cents a day for all food; so you can see that eating would be a negligible expense. If the Nido sounds high—and it was for us, for we were cutting things as close as possible—there is the Chapala Hotel, across the street from the Nido. I went there to get a price tonight, but the proprietor was out. But I do know that an English family stay there for nine pesos a day for three people, including all food. The accommodations there would be clean enough, but [bring] a few yards of mosquito netting with you to tack on your window or put over your bed, for the hotel is not screened. The Nido is well screened—at least for Mexico. Bus fare is very little in Mexico, but there is a train to Guadalajara, which is only thirty miles from Chapala. If you come by train we'll meet you there—or if you come by bus, for that matter. As for the return trip, you will have no expense, except, perhaps, the cost of shipping a little displaced baggage to make room for you. It ought to be a very cheap trip, and I think you would really like it here. And certainly you would add a great deal to our pleasure in the place. By the way, if you have to wait over between trains or buses in Mexico City, they say that the Monte Carlo or the Regis is a good quiet, clean, cheap place. We got badly stung in a luxury spot on our night in the City, and in addition had a bed bug.

So much for the present. We'll expect you here. And let us know about your eye. And let us know about the trip, so that we can be sure accommodations are available.[2]

Goodbye, and our best to Brookses and Lowells.

As ever,
Red

P.S. I'm assuming that, since the car deal is a deal, that I can send a few checks out against the amount of two sixty-five, [Handwritten] not for more than $125 now. [Typing resumes] This will come to you by air, and the checks will go ordinary mail, and so there will be a several day lag. So long.

[Typed at top of page] If—when—you come, please bring a quart of Pompeian olive oil (Capitol Stores) and a two-pound can of Union Leader smoking tobacco and your own cigarettes. Thanks.

[Typed in margin] We have been to the Chapala Hotel to get a rate. It is two and a half pesos a day, fifty cents American, for [a] good room and breakfast. Our lunch today, 12 1/2 cents each: vegetable soup, broiled white fish with lime juice and olive oil sauce, avocados and French vinegar, fried potatoes, rolls, mangos and bananas.

[Cinina Warren's postscript]

Dear John, We both hope you'll see your way to getting here. We like it better and better all the time. Witter Bynner and his friend Bob Hunt have a house here: Bynner will be away, but we can get Bob to show us the house which is really a beauty! There is boating of all kinds—rowing, motor boat, etc. . . . Chapala is on Lake Chapala which is 85 miles long (the lake). It is 35 miles directly south of Guadalajara which is the second largest city in Mexico. That will help place it on the map. Our house costs 6 dollars a month, plus about 4 that we spent on screening. The maid, or helper, who at least shops and washes dishes and scrubs, is paid 4 a month, and food is really cheap. Laundry is not too cheap, although less than at home, and so seersuckers, and things that don't have to be washed too often would be better. There are some pleasant people here, and the natives seem extremely kind. It is getting more and more like a Mexican Sirmione, only of course, not quite as lovely to me. I've simply slaved getting the place in order; my Spanish comes back more every day, and altogether, barring trouble, we should have a profitable and completely pleasant time. Our house is very tiny—next to the Mexicans and out of the swank section, but it is completely new and has never been lived in. There are natural warm water springs here, and one can bathe in them—in individual tubs, for less than five cents a bath. The hotel Chapala is very very cheap, although a little primitive [Handwritten in margins] but English and Americans stay there. Your food (lunch and dinner) should cost no more than 25 to 30¢ a day. I haven't been here long enough to average properly. [Typing resumes] Red has started working his head off, and he is doing beautifully with the Spanish, and he is already exchanging lessons. We do live a *sober,* tranquil life, with only and [*sic*] occasional tequila or rum collins. Give our love to all and get here if you can. I hope the eye situation progresses satisfactorily. We will be very anxious to know.

Our love,
Cinina

1. Given the loss of his own left eye due to an accident in his youth, Warren's concern with Palmer's injury takes on special poignance.
2. In the end, Palmer was unable to join the Warrens in Mexico.

TO JOHN PALMER AND CLEANTH BROOKS

TLS

Hotel Nido
Chapala,
Jalisco,
Mexico
[Postmarked August 2, 1941]

Dear John: Dear Cleanth:

Your exciting letter has just arrived. You did a marvelous job of depicting the little scene in the dusky parlor.[1] I can get the whole sense of it. And I must say, I wish I had been there. I imagine that after the first three minutes it ceased to be painful and a kind of exhilaration set in—a sort of compliment to the inevitable. Certainly, things are now in an impossible condition and we must put our heads together. I have a few scattered ideas, but you all probably have a more coherent plan of action than I. And every thing that occurs to me is tentative. This for what it may be worth: Cleanth, you probably have received an official slip from Hebert saying you were reappointed with one quarter of your salary on the SR budget. That is worth investigating, it seems to me, in the light of the current situation. If the policy has been generally applied in the University—say to Stevenson [sic],[2] and all the other folks who edit journals—then it ought to be applied to Pipkin. Anyway, if it is applied to us it ought to be applied to him. If it is said that he really shouldn't have his salary distributed so, that it doesn't fit the facts, then there is an admission that he doesn't do anything. And if he doesn't do anything why is he on the masthead at all? This might require some careful handling, and there are probably better ways of going about things—for instance, the plan suggested by you in Austin. Do let me hear how things seem to be shaping up on those lines.

Well, as I wrote to Jean Lowell, we had a little trouble, the details of which I'm sure she passed on to you all.[3] I wasn't up to writing but one letter that day and had to write Jean on business for Cinina, who was laid up. Then, for two days we had to be in Guadalajara arranging for the repairs on the car. In Mexico a thing like that—finding a man to do a simple job—takes forever. And since we didn't know the city, we had to shop around for advice. But the car will be all right by August 27—so the garage says, and we don't believe them. It needs a lot of body work, and that is slow. We were not covered by insurance—for everything else under the sun—fire, theft, public liability, etc. But not for what is quaintly termed in the profession "upset." And we were upset twice, and maybe three times.

John, I want to ask a great favor of you. I am enclosing a check for fifty bucks made out to you. Will you please buy me a New York draft, made out to me, and send it to me here, *Air mail, registered,* as soon as you decently can[?] Our Guadalajara expenses sadly cut into our modest country budget, and we are verging toward starvation. I had the bank send me a draft earlier, and they simply took forever, and then didn't send the thing by air, even though I enclosed money for postage. By the way, I am making the check for enough above fifty to cover registration and air postage.

We hope that New York goes well, Cleanth, and we hope that we shall see you here, John. Do let us have a bit of news, when there is any. And give our love to Tinkum and the Lowells.

As ever,

Red

1. Palmer recalls a confrontation between Brooks and the titular editor of the *Southern Review,* Pipkin—whose physical and psychological health was rapidly failing.

2. Wendell Holmes Stephenson edited the *Journal of Southern History* at LSU.

3. The Warrens had been involved in a serious automobile accident, but escaped with relatively minor injuries.

TO CLEANTH BROOKS AND JOHN PALMER

TLS/YU

Chapala

August 5, 1941

Dear Cleanth and John:

You can well imagine my shock this afternoon when I went to the hotel for my mail and found a telegram telling of Pipkin's death.[1] It came from his secretary, and gave no information beyond the statement that he was to be cremated in Memphis this morning. I assume that he died there. The whole thing has been a sad, bitter, nasty business, and I suppose this is the predictable end—at least, it is the one which has been predicted for some time. Heart attack or stroke or suicide or the case of pneumonia. My one-time feelings for him have long since been converted into the feelings which we have shared; and now I only have the thought that he is probably a lot better off than he was.

I may add that the same mail brought the package from the office with the letterheads. But the whole business is too pat.

As for SR business I shall get a batch of MSS off within a day or two with my reports. But several other items of a rather pressing nature have found their way to me. As they come to mind they are:

(1) Sam Monk writes that he fears his piece wasn't satisfactory and was therefore excluded from the summer issue;[2] and also mentions that he had hoped to have the money this summer. I imagine that the expenses occasioned by his wife's death, etc. have something to do with the situation. I can only write him that he ought to know that we are subject to delays and last-minute shifts of publication, and that if anything can be done about the check it will be done. Could you, John, drop him a note or a card, Southwestern College, Memphis? I am writing, but there ought to be a definite word from the office.

(2) Leonard Unger writes that he understands that a new poem by Eliot is to appear in the fall,[3] and asks to do a piece on it & Dry Salvages incorporating his other stuff on *Burnt Norton,* etc., along the line of his work on *Ash Wednesday* and *East Coker.*[4] He has some corrections to make, you may recall, on the *East Coker* piece we published.[5] [Handwritten in left margin] Can you, John, let Leonard have a card at 60 University Street, Nashville, Tenn.? [Typing resumes]

(3) Shirley Forgotson writes to ask if we can't let him have some reviewing for the fall issue. I had told him that I would take the matter up with you all for some reviewing in the winter (you all may have seen his reviews for *Poetry, American Prefaces,* and the *Nation,* and he is to do some for the *New Republic*), telling him that I was sure we could at least give him a trial piece. Can anything be thrown his way now, as trial anyway? I know he'll need the money badly. I am writing him that he will have a word from the office, that I have written in, etc.[6]

I want to thank you all for the several letters and notes of recent date, and Cinina wishes to thank you all and Tinkum and Jean. She is writing Tinkum and Jean right away, but she is still ailing a little with her shoulder—in bed again today. Tinkum's description, by the way, of the General's call was pretty damned funny.

It's a blow that Jean is leaving us—and a blow that Cal and Peter won't be about. But the Jean business raises an immediate question. You ask for the Bennington girl's address. She is Barbara Deming, 2096 Abington Road, Cleveland, Ohio, but the envelope should be marked with a request for forwarding. I don't know that she types, but she does everything else—has been publisher's assistant, stage manager for Orson Welles, graduate assistant at Western Reserve, a novelist's secretary, and God knows what. And she has a fine record at Bennington. If she types and will take the job she sounds like our best bet. But it should be made clear to her that it will be something like a full-time job, and that she can take little or no graduate work. I say this, because she is applying for a SR scholarship, and might get the things confused. If she doesn't take the job, or perhaps even as a first try, it might be worth getting into contact with Mary Jane Forgotson,[7] who is smart as hell and is an expert at short-hand and typing and is very systematic. But she has a secretarial job in Alexandria and might not want to come back to LSU. I don't know. I am simply trying to think of possibilities, for if we don't get a good secretary we'll be in bad shape next year, with the student help lopped off. Another possibility occurs to me. At Iowa there was a very nice girl named Frances Stewart,[8] daughter of a Methodist preacher in Missouri, very intelligent—A's in graduate work with Austin Warren and Wellek—and very, *very* quiet. I am pretty sure that she types, for I seem to remember that she was typing theses last spring. About the short-hand, I don't know, but that, of course, isn't of paramount importance. If she seems desirable, just address her in care of the English department at Iowa, with a request to forward. Sad to relate, the Deming and Forgotson girls probably have better jobs than the SR job. I wouldn't mind trying the Stewart girl at all, if the others—or some other you all have in mind—don't pan out. And it's possible—I really don't know how you all feel about it—that the Forgotson girl might annoy you. She doesn't annoy me, and I've definitely grown to like her and she's smart as hell. But no virtue amounts to a damn if the girl gets in the hair.

Well, that's about all that occurs to me now. Except thoughts about the future. I don't suppose that there will be any movement to give us a new editor in Pipkin's place. Or will there be? Unless it's Frey.[9]

Goodbye, and my best and most affectionate greetings to both you gents and all that.

As ever,

Red

P.S. The word sent to Shirley would reach him through the English Department of Iowa, I'm pretty sure. I can't lay hand to his New York address. I am writing him a note to say that he will get a card or a line from the office on the review situation. [Handwritten at bottom] Have found Shirley's address: 7614 20th Ave., Brooklyn.

1. Pipkin died suddenly on August 4.

2. Samuel Holt Monk's "From Jacobean to Augustan" would run in the Autumn 1941 number.

3. "Little Gidding," the last of Eliot's *Four Quartets*.

4. Unger's "T. S. Eliot's Rose Garden: A Persistent Theme," was included in the final issue of the *Southern Review* (Spring 1942).

5. James Johnson Sweeney, "East Coker: A Reading," *Southern Review* (Spring 1941).

6. Forgotson would have an omnibus review of poetry in the Spring 1942 number.

7. Presumably Shirley Forgotson's sister.

8. Stewart took the job.

9. Fred C. Frey, a sociologist and dean of the College of Arts and Sciences, was no ally of Brooks and Warren.

TO ALLEN TATE

TLS/PU

Hotel Nido
Chapala,
Jalisco,
Mexico
September 1, 1941

Dear Allen:

I got your card quite a while back, but my ordinary tendency to procrastination is encouraged in the present spot, where I should have plenty of time for correspondence. It is a nice place and on the whole, we have had a nice time here. It's a tiny town, some thirty miles from Guadalajara, on a very large lake—some eighty miles long, in fact—with a perfect climate. We got a native house, but one absolutely new and therefore clean, screened it, furnished it—all for the price of about ten dollars a month. There have been some pleasant people staying here, too, and that, to paraphrase Dr. Johnson, improves any landscape. And it has been a good place to work. I'm on the down grade with the novel I've been working at, on and off, for a long time, and hope to finish it by Christmas. HM has contracted for it, and, I suppose, will publish it in the spring. I have the usual jitters about it, of course, as I approach the end. And I've managed to get some poetry done; one poem[1] I enclose for your inspection. The other two need a lot of reworking; I'll send them when I get back home and can get at them again.

We leave in a day or two to get back in time for registration. If we don't have any car trouble. This trip we got smashed by an army convoy in Texas, but Uncle Sam pays the bill; and a month or so ago, returning at night from Guadalajara, we saw a cow on the road, got into a skid because of wet brakes—it was raining and we had had to ford a stream swollen across the road—and turned over two or three times, coming to rest, on the side of a car, in a rather deep ditch. Cinina, who was driving, took a beating on the wheel, and had a rather badly wrenched back and had to stay strapped up for a few days, but I and a friend who was with us escaped with nothing worse than a shaking-up. But having the body of the car fixed cost quite a lot of money, though probably not as much as it would cost in the U.S. Fortunately the motor and running gear were not harmed, and the repair work done here on the body was excellent. But our insurance covered everything except what happened, our Mexican insurance, that is; and the U.S. insurance does not apply here.

I suppose we'll reach Baton Rouge about September 8. Let me hear from you. What has been going on this summer? What about next year? Princeton, again, I presume? And what are you working on, both of you?

Best all around.

As ever,
Red

1. "End of Season."

Back from Mexico, Warren settled into what must have seemed a routine semester of teaching, writing, and editing the Southern Review. *He was pressing forward with work on his new novel, and he and Brooks had ambitious plans for the quarterly. The Warrens busied themselves with improvements on their newly acquired property near Prairieville, but all the while ominous events on the international level were taking shape that would forever change the course of history and have a direct and unexpected impact on Warren's career.*

TO OLIVER ST. JOHN GOGARTY

TLS/Harv

The Southern Review
University Station
Baton Rouge, Louisiana
Sept. 22, 1941

Dr. Oliver St. John Gogarty
c/o Mrs. Roden Ryan
1807 North Highland
Hollywood, California

Dear Dr. Gogarty:[1]

In December the Southern Review is bringing out a special Yeats issue, which will contain some fifteen essays on various aspects of the poet's work. The contributors who have already committed themselves are I. A. Richards, L.C. Knights, Allen Tate, R. P. Blackmur, Randall Jarrell, Arthur Mizener, and several other poets and critics.[2] We are hoping to persuade you to do an essay for us, perhaps of a personal nature. However, if you have any special topic which seems more attractive to you, please do not feel that we are attempting to dictate the kind of essay. We would like to have an essay of some 5000 words. The deadline is November 20. Our rate of payment is six dollars and a half a page.

Again I wish to say that we are extremely anxious to have you among our contributors for this issue, or, for that matter, for other issues.

Very sincerely yours,
Robert Penn Warren

P.S. We cabled you in Dublin, and were informed that you were in this country. Your publishers in Toronto supplied us with two addresses, to both of which we are sending copies of this letter.

1. Playwright, poet, novelist, and practicing physician, Gogarty had been a leading figure in the Irish Renaissance and a close friend and associate of William Butler Yeats.

2. The Yeats special issue featured pieces by Knights, Tate, Blackmur, Jarrell, Mizener, Howard Baker, Kenneth Burke, F. O. Matthiessen, Donald Davidson, T. S. Eliot, Horace Gregory, John Crowe Ransom, Austin Warren, Delmore Schwartz, and Morton Dauwen Zabel. (The British critic I. A. Richards, whose early work had done much to initiate the New Criticism, did not come through.)

TO PAUL BROOKS

TLS/Harv

The Southern Review
University Station
Baton Rouge, Louisiana
October 21, 1941

Dear Brooks:

Your news sheet came today, and with mixed feelings I observe that the new novel is announced. The statement goes that the novel will "deal with the downfall of a Nashville, Tennessee, banker." I'd go to the stake denying that, for reasons too numerous to mention, and I devoutly hope that in future publicity—of which I candidly admit I hope there will be a lot—the scene is the Aleutian Islands or Buenos Aires.[1]

The thing is moving, all right, but not at breath-taking speed. With luck I'll finish in December. I don't know how much cleaning-up it will have to have. You all will be able to tell me when you get the manuscript. I know that the first part has to be revised, but I have the revisions pretty clearly in mind already. I could make better time if I didn't keep getting ideas for poems (I've done quite a few in the last several months and they'll be coming out in several magazines this fall)[2] and hadn't very foolishly committed myself, months ago, to a paper at the Southern Historical Association.[3] But the cursed thing will soon be behind me for better or worse.

Did you ever get in touch with Peter Taylor? And what was the word on Moreau's manuscript?[4]

Dixon Wecter wrote me yesterday that he has seen you this summer.

Goodbye and best regards,
Red Warren

1. Mindful of the possible legal consequences, Warren resists any attempt to present *At Heaven's Gate* as a roman à clef based on actual persons.

2. "Pursuit," "Revelation," "End of Season," and "Original Sin: A Short Story" would appear in early 1942.

3. The Southern Historical Association was meeting in Atlanta in November. Warren's paper was "Literature of the New South."

4. Taylor and Louis Moreau (who had stories in the Autumn 1936 and Summer 1937 issues of the *Southern Review*) were nominees for the Houghton Mifflin fiction fellowship.

TO ANDREW LYTLE

TLS/VU

The Southern Review
University Station
Baton Rouge, Louisiana
November 3, 1941

Dear Andrew:

Your "Alchemy" reached us on [*sic*] the early mail today, and Cleanth and I have read it, Cleanth this morning, and I this afternoon. And well worth reading it is, as a brilliant piece of narrative. But—hastily, since you asked for an early word—we have reached a decision. The real reason for our not using it is a purely practical one. We have already run one long novelette this year, and the Yeats special issue in December will further reduce the space we have available for fiction. We try to keep up a certain number of fiction titles—for we have found that to be a useful policy—and with the set-back from the KAP novelette and from the Yeats issue, we are running close to the last margin. That was a heavy factor in our decision. Another, and less significant, factor is this. The resolution of the piece, especially the last paragraph, would, we can see, serve beautifully in a novel, where the total context would point up and give meaning to the narrative. We grasp the implications because we know something of the theme of your book. But it is probable, it seems to us, that the reader who lacked our special information would be left a little uncertain as to the final reference. But as I said, this consideration was not very important, and, in fact, we aren't too sure we are right on this point. But we are hurrying the manuscript back to you so that you can, as you say is your intention, put it elsewhere.[1]

I have been intending to write you for a long time, to get the news about Edna's progress.[2] But, in the rush of things, I had assumed that no news was good news, and had trusted to know all in due course. I do hope the cold disappears and all goes well. You must let us know as soon as there is anything very definite.

The news about Bill is very sad.[3] Where is he now? Let me know, for I want to write to him.

The Sewanee thing sounds pretty good.[4] Certainly, it might develop into a very nice thing. And Sewanee would be close enough to your farm, for some traveling back and forth.

There's not much news with us. We have bought a place some eighteen miles from town and are now in the midst of remodeling. We hope you all will come down to inspect it before too long a time. I'm working on my novel, which nears the end. I hope to finish it in December, for they are announcing it for spring. But a paper for the Southern Historical Association meeting in Atlanta has delayed me. And the SR and teaching still claim their part of daylight and energy.

Goodbye, and our best and best wishes to you both.

As ever,

Red

1. "Alchemy" would eventually be published in the *Kenyon Review* (Autumn 1942).

2. She was pregnant with the Lytles' first child, Pamela.

3. Saville T. (Bill) Clark was among Warren's closest friends from his Vanderbilt days and had achieved uncommon distinction as a marine officer. He suffered a serious illness in 1941 that almost brought his career to an end. (My thanks to Saville T. Clark Jr.)

4. Lytle had entered into an informal relationship with the University of the South that eventually led to a teaching appointment and editorship of the *Sewanee Review*.

TO KATHERINE ANNE PORTER

TLS/Maryland

The Southern Review
University Station
Baton Rouge, Louisiana
November 3, 1941

Dear Katherine Anne:

We were very distressed to learn of your trouble,[1] and devoutly hope that all is now well with you. Let us know, won't you[?] And let us know how the house develops.

House. The word has been a sort of nightmare, though not an altogether unpleasant nightmare, since our return here. Where the old night club on the Jefferson Highway burned—you may recall the spot, some eighteen miles from Baton Rouge—that's where our new house is. When we passed through in June on the way to Mexico, we bought it, almost on the moment, but maybe our impulse was right. Anyway, the place, though ugly as sin externally, has very good rooms, enormous ones, in fact, and is well arranged and proportioned. The living room, for instance, is thirty-nine feet long, with an ell to it twenty-five feet long. The study and two bedrooms aren't that big, but are big. The ceilings are high. The walls are all of cypress which has gone to a nice rich gold brown—we shall keep the natural wood throughout the house. Every room except the dining room has a fire place, and, thank God, wood is cheap in this neighborhood, $2.25 a cord, delivered. We have installed a gas heating system, have pretty good plumbing in the two baths, and have a working windmill for water. (I say "working," but it hasn't worked for two weeks. Some bastard broke a hydrant in the yard and drained our tank, and as soon as we got it fixed, the wind died. We haven't had any wind for two weeks.) The grounds are very, very nice, with several first-rate big live oaks, numerous magnolias, and a lot of odd stuff about. It seems that there will be an artificial lake, some thirty acres in extent, which will border our lawn on two sides. We aren't doing anything as ambitious as that, but Dutton—the famous Tom Dutton[2]— from whom we are buying the place, is putting in the lake on some of his land and it will come over on us for several acres. But there is still some hitch about getting a state permit for the lake. We have been living in the midst of carpenters, plumbers, electricians, and nigger boys for a month. And Cinina has been cookless. So life hasn't been too simple.

By the way, the *Kenyon* is bringing out my essay on your stories in the winter issue. I hope it's a good essay. I want to send proofs to you to get you to check the little bibliographical information in it, but if the proofs don't come soon enough, will would [*sic*] give me a list of your published work, with dates, by which I can correct the essay? It isn't, of course, imperative, but I had the thought that some of the more serious readers might want to explore items which hadn't reached them in the ordinary course of events. I know about all books, of course, but I'm also listing some of the more important pieces which have never been in book form. I just want to be sure that the list is accurate. I know that this is an imposition, but maybe you'll consider it one in a good cause.

Another matter! Cleanth and I are busy on our book on fiction, a companion book to *Understanding Poetry* done with the same method. We want, of course, to use one of your stories for analysis. In fact, we already have an analysis of *Old Mortality,* which we shall include if our budget which Crofts allows us is big enough. If the budget doesn't permit, we shall have to use a shorter, and therefore cheaper, story.³ One feature of the book may be a few short essays by authors represented on the backgrounds of the particular pieces included—a sort of natural history of the story, how it was suggested, how it grew, what the problems were which the material presented, etc. If we find that we can use this feature, could we persuade you to do about 2500 words on some story, to be selected in consultation with you? We intend to run the essays in the SR and so there would be some moderately substantial payment for the trouble in addition to the pittance which we hope to be able to salvage from our Crofts budget. I say "hope," for we haven't yet had final word from him. But what do you think of the general idea, anyway, of the essays by the authors? Our feeling is that they might answer some of the questions which students are always asking about how much did the author actually mean. But we aren't too sure.

Except for the nightmare of the house, already mentioned, things go fairly well with us. I'm on the down grade with my novel, which I hope to finish by January. This week I go to Atlanta to do a paper for the Southern Historical Association, which means an interruption. And a more pleasant interruption will be a visit by my father in late November. But it's moving, and I'm in that final dither.

Brookses are well, Palmer well, University politics go on as usual. Duncan recently came down to judge an art exhibit in N.O., and moved about in a holy trance the whole time, still wrapped up in his God-damned nonsense. Conrad seems about recovered from the attack. We read Dante every Monday night with him and Jean [*sic*]—a very pleasant arrangement.

Cinina asks me to say that as soon as she can lay down the broom and get her hands out of dishwater she will write. Meanwhile she says to give you her love. And she joins me in the hope of a letter before too long.

As ever,

Red

1. A cryptic reference, though Givner notes that this period was a particularly stressful one for Porter, who had overextended herself in acquiring the farmhouse near Saratoga Springs.

2. A prominent figure in the Baton Rouge community and a member of the board overseeing LSU. (My thanks to Charles East.)

3. Brooks and Warren *were* able to include *Old Mortality* in *Understanding Fiction* (1943), along with a series of study questions.

TO DAVID M. CLAY

TLS/YU

Atlanta Biltmore

Atlanta, Georgia

November 8, 1941

Dear David:[1]

In accordance with our conversation at lunch today, I am setting down a few facts about my literary work. Here are the things I have published so far.

John Brown: The Making of a Martyr (Brewer and Warren)—1929
essay in I'll Take ·my Stand (Harpers)—1930—two editions
" Who Owns America—(Houghton Mifflin)—4000 copies (?)
Night Rider (Houghton Mifflin)—4500 copies (?)—1939
(Eyre and Spottiswood[e])—5000 copies (?) 1940
XXXVI Poems (Alcestis Press)—1936

Approach to Literature (with Brooks and Purser)—(LSU Press, F. S. Crofts)—1936—9000 copies (?)

Understanding Poetry (with Brooks)—(Holt)—1938—14000 copies

Contributions to various anthologies and magazines, such as Literary Opinion in America, ed. Zabel, American Poetry, ed. Untermeyer, the Nation, New Republic, Virginia Quarterly, Scribners, etc.

Here is a list of the things I have in preparation:

And Pastures New (novel) to be published by Houghton Mifflin in March, 1942.[2]

Bearded Oaks and Other Poems[3] (poems) to be published by New Directions [in] February, 1942.

Proud Flesh (in collaboration with Francis Fergusson) (play)— entering fourth draft, probably final—conversations with [Paul] Brooks of Houghton Mifflin but no contract—HM could exercise Literary Fellowship option if contract reads "book" and not "novel." Otherwise I am committed to the[m] for one more novel, *I think*. (I'll check contract when I get home.) (New Directions and Atlantic Monthly Press have expressed much interest. AM Press has read it unofficially.)[4]

Selected Poems, including those in XXXVI Poems and Bearded Oaks, and new pieces—verbal agreement with Brooks of Houghton Mifflin, though they'd probably be willing to release it.[5] Word came from Breadloaf [*sic*] this summer that H. was talking about bringing out both Proud Flesh and poems in one volume, but I do not have this information direct from them.

Manuscripts planned, with some work done:

Two novels. Novel one, based on Huey Long situation,[6] but not an exposé—on theme of power versus values, means versus ends—some academic setting, but not central to the novel. I plan to begin work on this next summer. Novel two, very short—an allegorical fantasy, about 50000 words—What Says Don Martin—locale in Mexico.[7] No commitments on either book, unless HM can exercise option on one of them. Will look up contract.

With Brooks I am working on a book on Shakespeare as a poet—the "poetry" of the plays as well as the sonnets.[8] There is no book on this subject. It will attempt to correlate the poetry with dramatic situation, with historical context, with development of Shakespeare, etc. No commitment of any kind.

In addition, I have two novels in manuscript, one which I would not want published, God's Own Time, under *any* circumstances. The second, But not the Lark, is complete in manuscript but needs drastic revision. If I ever get the right idea for revision it would take about three months to put it in shape. Time is 1910, locale, small town in Kentucky.[9]

You have explained to [me] Harcourt Brace's wish to publish all my subsequent books which, after full consideration, I might feel really warrant publication, in trade or text field. I understand that books of a series type are to be exempt from the foregoing provisions and that all textbook ideas are to be discussed with your firm before execution.

The idea of having one publisher permanently appeals to me,[10] and I should be very pleased to be with Harcourt Brace under such an arrangement. I want to give more and more time to writing and that means that I shall want to avoid teaching summer school and shall want to reduce my regular teaching hours and thus my potential earning power, in order to get the writing done. If I do this this will necessitate my having as advance of $750 each summer, with the expectation of my completing every two years a novel or a comparably valuable trade or text book. At my present rate of composition I expect to have a book of poems ready about every three years. I find myself doing fewer short stories.[11] My royalty arrangement with HM on And Pastures New is 10% list price up to 2500 copies, 12 1/2% up to 5000 copies—I don't remember further scaling, but I can check on contract. I would expect a parallel arrangement on my novels and a comparable arrangement on other books, and you have explained to me your sliding scale arrangement in your text book department—12% of net wholesale in any year up to a fixed number, 15% net wholesale on increase, and 18% in any one year at a still greater number to be fixed—this on books written rather than collections edited. I agree with you that a permanent association with Harcourt Brace would advantageously be conducted without the use of an agent for film, second serial, and foreign rights, but only if HB conducts a department for systematically handling such business, and exhausts the possibilities before publication of any given item.

I'll send you any other information as soon as I can get it together and in so far as satisfactory details can be worked out at both ends, this letter can be said to constitute a tentative arrangement depending on satisfactory releases and satisfactory agreement on trade royalty.

Very sincerely,
RPW

P.S. I forgot to mention that in conjunction with Allen Tate and Cleanth Brooks I am under contract with Scribners to do a critical and analytical anthology of modern poetry. But this contract has been in force some six years, and I am inclined to believe that the facts of separation of the collaborators from each other (Tate is at Princeton now) and of more pressing interests will probably prevent the fulfillment of the contract. Tate received an advance on the book, but I waived an advance, and so have no financial obligation. Brooks, too, has had no advance for the book. Tate, being a Scribner's author, has his own arrangement with them. I don't imagine I would have any difficulty in getting a release from the contract, if it seems desirable.[12]

And another matter, which involves my personal situation. I have a note falling due October 1, 1942, for extra payment on a house I am buying, the sum of $600. I have an opportunity of going to Iowa for the summer term, it seems, with a light schedule (several days a week free for writing) at a very good salary, good enough to see me through the summer. But I would like, for next summer, to be able to take the Iowa job, *if* it can be arranged so as to give me at least three uninterrupted days a week for writing, and take a reduced advance from HB—$600 to take care of the note. This would enable me to avoid burdening myself with a loan in the fall to handle the note. Then, after that time, I would avoid regular summer teaching, though I would like to feel free to take a short lecture appointment, say up to two weeks, if such an opportunity should present itself.

[Handwritten at bottom of page] A good clear account of our conversation of 11/8/41 DMC [David M. Clay]

1. Clay and Warren had been friends since their student days at Vanderbilt. Meeting at the annual convention of the Southern Historical Association in Atlanta, the two explored the possibility of Warren leaving Houghton Mifflin for Clay's firm, Harcourt Brace and Company. Warren followed through on their plan.

2. "And Pastures New" became *At Heaven's Gate* and was published under the Harcourt Brace imprint in 1943.

3. Published as *Eleven Poems on the Same Theme.*

4. "Proud Flesh" went unpublished.

5. Retitled *Selected Poems, 1923–1943* and published by Harcourt Brace in 1944.

6. A first reference to *All the King's Men* (1946).

7. Never completed.

8. Another abandoned project.

9. Like "God's Own Time" (or "The Apple Tree"), this apprentice work was ultimately deemed unfit for publication.

10. Warren had moved on to Random House by 1950 and would remain there for the rest of his career.

11. In later interviews, Warren suggested that the writing of short fiction interfered with his verse. He abandoned the form altogether after the late 1940s.

12. The project was dropped.

With the Japanese attack on Pearl Harbor on December 7, 1941, the United States entered World War II, and the LSU administration responded with a series of institutional economies that included cutting off funding for the Southern Review. *Warren's initial reaction was mixed, but other considerations soon conspired to bring about his departure from the university—and from the South.*

TO ALLEN TATE

TLS/PU
The Southern Review
University Station
Baton Rouge, Louisiana
December 24, 1941

Dear Allen:

Cleanth and I have greeted with great enthusiasm your idea for the symposium,[1] and shall try to execute it. The only catch is that the University has just cut us off without a cent—you can imagine the excuses—war, economy, etc. But the question of institutional economy is always a matter of choices among various items. We are budgeting for the spring issue, but we have, naturally, a pile of stuff on hand, and several outstanding commitments. We shall have to try to get some extra money if we are to float the symposium. And we shall try, desperately, for the symposium is the appropriate swan song for the Review. So we are going to write the people right away—I've already written to John—to ask for the essays. Naturally, we want you to do one.

The Yeats issue came of[f] the press today. At the moment it looks

better than the Hardy issue. I hope that it will have some success. My hope is not without a touch of vindictiveness.

I wish that I could be in Indianapolis to see you.[2] But work here swamps me—I'm trying to push the novel through within a month—and besides it is probably best that the editors of the SR are *not* in Indianapolis at this fateful moment. They should be anywhere but Indianapolis.

I am hoping to get a few hours of quiet reading done this week. I have, for instance, been able to give only the most superficial reading to the novels by Caroline and Andrew.[3] And I would like to get a few days on a poem I've been working at. If you happen to have seen the revised version of the poem I sent you last spring—in the current Virginia—I'd like to know what you think of it.[4] And of the one I sent you this fall.

And, how about some news from your end of the line? How are things going?

Goodbye, and a good Christmas to all.

Red

1. The *Southern Review* had recently featured two symposia on topical issues: "Literature and the Professors" (Autumn 1940) and "American Culture" (Spring 1941). Tate was apparently proposing a symposium on war and literature.
2. The Modern Language Association was meeting there.
3. *Green Centuries* and *At the Moon's Inn* respectively.
4. "Pursuit," *Virginia Quarterly Review* (January 1942).

TO PAUL BROOKS

TLS/Harv

The Southern Review
University Station
Baton Rouge, Louisiana
December 24, 1941

Mr. Paul Brooks
Houghton Mifflin Company
Boston, Mass.

Dear Brooks:

This is to report my progress on the novel. I have about a month of work left, or perhaps five weeks. But I am definitely on the down grade and feel the pull of gravity. The fall has been full of disturbances, among them a fight to get the University to continue with the Southern Review. We lost the fight. Last Saturday we received the death warrant. Personally, I can't grieve, for I shall now have a lot more time for my own work. Brooks feels the same way. But the situation has aspects which prevent me from feeling merely like a kid let out of school. After you've put seven years on something, you are bound to develop certain attachments.

But to get back to *And Pastures New* (by the way, how does that strike you as a title?), I want to ask if early February delivery precludes spring publication. That is, assuming that you all do not find too many drastic revisions necessary.

I hope that all goes well with you all. And Merry Christmas to you in the midst of your air raids.[1]

Sincerely yours,
Red Warren

1. A grim joke, worthy of Jack Burden in *All the King's Men*. Hysteria was sweeping many American cities in the wake of the Japanese attack on Pearl Harbor.

TO J. KERKER QUINN

TLS/Ill

The Southern Review
University Station
Baton Rouge, Louisiana
January 8, 194[2]

Dear Mr. Quinn:[1]

Thank you very much indeed for your letter. As for the SR, we are not very optimistic that the "arrangements not now foreseen" will materialize. I imagine that it would take a good deal to make the University Budget Committee change its mind, unless higher authorities got busy. In matters of economy, it is always a matter of what economies, and the Committee has its own standard of values.[2]

We are very glad to hear that *Accent* is determined to keep going. It even seems to me that you all might be in a stronger position now than before. I hope so.

I am very pleased that you all would like to consider some of my work. I have no poems on hand—except parts of a verse-prose play, on which I am still working, and which, I think, I shall keep by me for the present. I have some poems in process of construction, but they need more work. I do have, however, a couple of stories, written a year or so ago and turned down by *Harper's, Atlantic,* etc. If you want to see them, I shall be happy to submit them. If I can find them. Let me know, and if you want to look at them, I'll hunt them up.[3]

With best wishes for the New Year which is beginning so inauspiciously,

Robert Penn Warren

[Handwritten P.S.] Please give my warm regards to Moses.[4]

1. Quinn was an editor of *Accent,* a literary magazine headquartered at the University of Illinois, and had apparently written to voice solidarity with the *Southern Review.*

2. In later years, Warren would often wryly observe that monies which might have saved the *Southern Review* went to feed the university mascot, Mike the tiger.

3. Though none of Warren's short fiction appeared in *Accent,* he did review e. e. cummings' *1 x 1* in the Summer 1944 issue.

4. The poet W. R. Moses was on the editorial board.

BROOKS AND WARREN TO ALLEN TATE

TLS/PU

The Southern Review
University Station
Baton Rouge, Louisiana
Jan 13 [1942][1]

Dear Allen,

Your two letters have got in—the last one, of the 11th, only a few minutes ago. I hasten to answer. The efforts made by our friends fill us with admiration and gratitude. And we are honestly surprised to see how much protest is coming from the students and the faculty.[2] How much of this is bearing fruit, I don't know. But the local protests are increasing, if anything; and there is at least one bit of tangible evidence that they (local and outside protests) are having some kind of effect. The Board of Supervisors met yesterday, and it was announced this morning that it was deferring action on the S.R. until March. I'm not sure that I know what this means. I understand that they adopted the budget submitted to them. If this is true, it would seem to settle us; for I imagine that the chances of taking away funds from something else in order to give them to us would be very difficult to do. Indeed, as far as we are concerned, we are finished. That was our understanding of the matter; and I believe the General's.[3] The unforeseen circumstances would be the raising of funds from outside the U., or the rather remote chance that the administration would change its mind. I believe that you could tell [Henry Allen] Moe that the chances of our getting funds from the U. rest still where they rested when this whole matter came up: on the chance that the General will decide to buck the advice of his committee and make provision for us. On the other hand, one ought to be accurate, and I imagine that our affair is not formally closed until the Board acts in March.

To sum up: the only conclusion that I can draw from the Board's action is that they (or the president) are beginning to feel more pressure, but we know no more than we knew before. The postponement of final decision by the board may be no more than the business of putting the tail to the wind until the gust subsides. It is feared that Zabel may have had a rosier impression than is warranted by the facts. [Handwritten at bottom of page] I may have inadvertently given him this impression from a hint that came out of the President's office. But it turned out [not] worth building on. C[leanth].

[Typing resumes] As for your essay in the spring issue—why not take your own line? The general question is clear enough and you can make your own approach to it.[4] We have written to Wilson, Zabel, Katherine Anne, Ransom, and Matthiessen. Zabel, Ransom, and K.A. have already replied that they will be in the symposium.[5] Zabel is developing some ideas which occurred toward the end of his MacLeish piece, and John is, apparently, discussing the case of secondary and primary literature.

Our best,
Cleanth [and] Red

1. Tate's bracketed notation.

2. The student newspaper, the *Reveille,* carried an editorial by the undergraduate John Edward Hardy (in time a noted critic), and a faculty resolution in favor of continuing the *Southern Review* had been passed. See Thomas W. Cutrer's indispensable *Parnassus on the Mississippi* for similar details.

3. LSU President Campbell Blackshear Hodges.

4. The final issue was given up primarily to previously accepted pieces. Nothing by Tate was included.

5. The symposium on war and literature that Tate had proposed earlier (see Warren's letter to Tate of December 24, 1941, above) came to naught.

TO PAUL ENGLE

TLS/Iowa   [Baton Rouge]
                                                           January 21, 1942

Dear Paul:

Forgive me for the long delay, but your letter reached me just when we were most occupied with the effort to keep the Southern Review from being killed by the University Budget Committee. But now that the Committee has had its way, I can turn to the pleasure of personal correspondence and reading books and playing a little bridge and doing a little carpentering.[1] At least, I hope now to get to those things. It almost seems like a holiday to me, and I am looking forward to doing some work of my own which I have been postponing because of the damned confusion of the fall. I confess to a certain irritation at the Committee, not because of their handling of the Review but because of their handling of other matters. The live tiger, for example, still gets his beefsteaks. But I imagine that one can scarcely expect a university to do more than reflect the society of which it is a part; and our society generally prefers live tigers to reading matter.

Our life goes rather uneventfully. Cinina has been very busy all fall trying to supervise the remodeling on a house we have taken over, and the war situation didn't make things easier. Labor was hard to get and certain materials scarce, even common things, and original estimates, made in October, weren't very trustworthy by the middle of December. I have recently finished my novel, and am now doing some last-minute tinkering with it. I suppose I'll get another shot at it in proofs. It is slated for May or June.

The academic life here is pretty turgid lately. The war, of course, has unsettled everything, but the unsettling caused by the war is minor in comparison with the unsettling which seems to be chronic around here. It seems that I've spent half my time in committee and department meetings, and I can't be too sure that a great deal has been accomplished. But some reorganization has taken place.

Fred Brantley and his wife came through here for an evening and spent the night with us.[2] They brought pleasant but not very detailed news of Iowa, and I've recently had a note from Fred. But it was not exactly crammed with news.

I was distressed to have your news about Shirley [Forgotson]'s showing on the examination. But I hear since that the matter was finally settled. I have, as you know, very great confidence in his ability, and only hope that he doesn't get himself into another jam.

How is your work going? I hope that a letter from you will bring more cheerful information about you and Mary[3] than the last one did. I gathered from a letter from Mr. Foerster that you all will be around next summer. I hope so. We are looking forward with great pleasure to being in Iowa City again for a few weeks.

Cinina joins me in very [w]arm regards to you, Mary, and The Mouse.[4]

Sincerely,

Red

1. Warren enjoyed working with his hands throughout his life. The vacation home he and his second wife built in Vermont still bears evidence of his handiwork.

2. Brantley had married another of Warren's students, Sheila Corley, who became Warren's assistant while he was Consultant in Poetry at the Library of Congress, 1944–1945.

3. Engle's wife.

4. Presumably one of the Engles' two daughters.

TO KATHERINE ANNE PORTER

TLS/Maryland

The Southern Review
University Station
Baton Rouge, Louisiana
February 13, 1942

Dear Katherine Anne:

This is simply the briefest of notes to tell you how our project for the little symposium on war and literature is going—or rather, how it may not be going. We are in a jam financially, for reasons that are probably all too easily surmised. We have on hand a large mass of stuff which was accepted or contracted for before we knew that we were in for really rough weather. This means that to honor our commitments, we shall have to publish an over-size issue, and that means that what remains in our budget will have to [be] divided a good many ways. We have some hope of getting a little sweetening from the University, a penny for the boatman on the black river,[1] as it were, but our hope is not too high. We have been trying to get appointments with the Big Boss, but have not yet succeeded; and our last meeting with him, some two or three weeks ago, was not conclusive. All of this probably would mean that we shall be forced to tell you and other contributors to the symposium that if you write the pieces it will have to be for love and not even the little cash we used to pay. But we don't want anyone to do this unless the desire to get something off the chest is a burning desire. Certainly, we don't want to get a friend to do it for friendship's sake. We don't want to close our books with the exploitation of the good will of our contributors. So please don't feel that you have any shred of commitment to us in the matter. If you have been working on the piece, we must apologize for having led you on—even though we know that anything from your pen will almost certainly find honorable harbor. We are trying to get an appointment with the President for a wind-up session next Wednesday. Then we shall know the full nature of the situation and shall inform you immediately. So this is the preliminary note.

I have to rush out and do some little chores and go to the train to meet Lambert Davis,[2] who will be here a day or two. So I shan't burden you with news. But we are well, or, as well as could be expected in the face of the horrible news and the generally bad situation on the LSU front. I have finally finished my novel. I wish you were on hand to give it a little work with the currycomb. But, alas.

Cinina joins me in love to you.

As ever,
Red

1. In classical mythology, the dead had to bribe Charon to row them over the Styx into the underworld.
2. Formerly editor of the *Virginia Quarterly Review,* Davis was now with Harcourt Brace, Warren's new publishers.

TO CAROLINE GORDON

TLS/PU   Baton Rouge, Louisiana
                                           February 17, 1942

Dear Caroline:

I got a hasty and choppy reading of *Green Centuries* when it first came,
but it came at a time when hell was breaking loose pretty generally here
with the Review troubles, etc., and when I was just trying to push my
novel through to the end. But recently things have slacked off a bit, and
I have been able to go back to *Green Centuries* with an easier mind. I
want to thank you for the book and thank you for the very real pleasure
it gave me. I can't think of many novels which have so successfully recre-
ated their worlds. There is a very fine solidity in this respect—a pervasive
familiarity, the proper casualness, no "set jobs." You don't get the feeling
that it came out of a library and that you can punch your finger through
the surface. As far as the people are concerned, Archy is the big thing for
me.[1] His whole business is a beauty. In fact, the Indian sections, all the
way through, excited me greatly. You got a great deal of variety into
them, too, and a great deal of variety into the Indian characters. Cassie
[*sic*] comes next for me, as character, especially toward the end of the
book.[2] I think that my only real criticism of the book would be that
Rion,[3] who occupies a great deal of foreground of the novel, is less developed as a person than Archy, Cassie, or even Canoe.[4] I suppose that the
reason for this comes from the fact that Archy, Cassie, and Canoe have
positive questions at their center—there is a dramatic frame for everything they do and say that derives from their central questions. While
with Rion no question develops except in relation to Cassie—and that
comes pretty late. Rion's story is more of an outside job. I don't mean
to say that this impairs the novel, really, because it isn't Rion's novel—it
isn't any one person's novel, of course. And the basic line of the book is
strong enough and rich enough. I'll say again that I enjoyed it, and admire it very much, indeed. It is, to my mind, by far your best book since
Alec[k] Maury, which is saying enough.

    As I said above, things have slacked off a little with me lately. The
death of the Review has given both Cleanth and me a little more time
than we had, and now I am taking a breather between finishing my novel

and getting at revision. But that will have to start in a day or so. As far as the Review is concerned, the issue seems to be definitely settled. The protests in the magazines, which God knows were strong enough, didn't dent the situation. Some squirming was done, and that was all. So we shall wind up with the spring issue. That is, unless money drops from the blue. I rather imagine that the administration would put up some money if substantial help came, for I have it direct from one member of the Budget Committee that there would be rejoicing if a way to save face turned up. He didn't put it in that language, but he wanted to get Cleanth and me to go to the President and try to start a begging campaign. That isn't our job, as things are set up here. We wo[u]ld do what we could to help, if the Administration called us in, but we've shot our wad now.

What are you up to next? And what is Allen doing? I just heard a rumor from Nashville that he is going into the Navy.[5] Is that true[?] And tell him for Christ's sake to write a letter.

> Best to all,
> Red

1. Archy Outlaw, a character in Gordon's novel who lived among the Indians.
2. Cassy Dawson is the novel's female lead.
3. Rion Outlaw, the novel's protagonist.
4. Dragging Canoe, an Indian chief and counterpart of Rion.
5. Though he considered seeking a commission early on, Tate managed to avoid military service during the war.

TO PETER TAYLOR

TLS/VU   [Baton Rouge]
                                   February 28, 1942

Dear Peter:

It is fine to know that we may have the pleasure of seeing you soon. Cinina and I urge you to come up and stay with us. We are now living in Prairieville, some eighteen miles from Baton Rouge, on the N.O. road. Since we are hoarding our precious tires,[1] we shan't offer to come to get you, but you can descend from the bus at our very door, or almost.

When you come, get off at the Prairieville stop, which is merely a little filling station and bar, and ask the man there, a Mr. McCory, or Mc-Crory, where we live. He is a very nice fellow, and will direct you or, perhaps, bring you. But we only live a quarter of a mile from his place. I give you the directions now, so that you will be able to notify us and come on without waiting for a reply, if events move that fast when you finally know your dates. We are rarely in town on Tuesday or Thursday, and almost never on Saturday. So if you come on those days, the best thing is to come directly to our house. The only catch is this: I hope to God, you don't arrive before March 11, for I am leaving in a few days for a jaunt up to Minnesota,[2] and shan't be back until the morning of the eleventh. So tell the army they'll have to adjust their convoying to that date.

As for the SR, there's not much chance of the Board's reversing the Budget Committee's decision. But we'll know in a few days, I imagine. Personally, we don't mind, for we feel freer for our own work than ever before, and we are behind on all our commitments. But certain aspects of the process irk us a bit. Sure, i[f] any money should come in from the blue, say from your friend in Michigan, the Administration would probably leap at the chance of continuing the SR and putting up part of the dough necessary. It seems that some of the boys have become very sensitive on the subject. We'll talk over all these things when you come.

Goodbye. Cinina sends her best. And we are both anxious to see you.

Sincerely yours,
Red

1. As the nation began to operate on a wartime footing, rubber tires, gasoline, and other strategic essentials were being rationed.
2. As part of the University of Minnesota's successful attempt to lure Warren away from LSU.

TO ALLEN TATE

TLS/PU

The Southern Review
University Station
Baton Rouge, Louisiana
March 23, 1942

Dear Allen:

Just a note in answer to your request for a title.[1] Actually, I am floundering around a good deal about the subject. I have been thinking of taking some Elizabethan poems and trying to work out some sort of pattern, but I don't know how far I can go with this, exactly, or how well it will suit the occasion. In that connection I have been thinking over some of Wyatt's translations and trying to define the principle he followed in adapting from his Italian sources. Is this too far off base? I have also been thinking some about the matter you proposed—the dramatic context business. But I don't seem to get very far with it. So could you be satisfied for the moment with something pretty vague? Some title which would give me leeway? The questions I've mentioned above would hinge on imagery for the most part. How about this: "Imagery and Structure." Almost anything could happen to that.

One reason I'm so slow and confused is that I'm trying to reach some major decisions about my future plans. It looks probable that I'll leave LSU. Primarily because I don't think they want me—or Cleanth either, for that matter. It seems that we are frozen here as long as the present Administration is in. So I'm considering an offer at Minnesota. There are strong personal reasons for staying here, the work with Cleanth being one of the biggest. But I am certain that he won't be here very long. Well, I shan't bother you with more of this.

Goodbye, and my best,
Red

P.S. Cleanth and I are very much concerned about the Georgia business.[2] For one thing, we cannot take any steps about setting up our last issue until we know how things are going. What is the latest dope? Will you wire us the instant you have final word one way or the other? We would want to pass on some MS to you if the thing goes through in order to give our contributors a better break about payment for the last issue. Would that be OK?

1. Through Tate's good offices, Warren had been invited to deliver a Mesures Lecture at Princeton. His talk developed into one of his most significant essays, "Pure and Impure Poetry," *Kenyon Review* (Spring 1943).

2. In a letter to Lytle of February 17, 1942 (included in the Young-Sarcone edition of *The Lytle-Tate Letters*), Tate reports that Agnes Scott College, the University of Georgia, and Emory University were interested in founding a new quarterly to take the place of the *Southern Review* and had offered him the editorship.

TO KATHERINE ANNE PORTER

TLS/Maryland

The Southern Review
University Station
Baton Rouge, Louisiana
March 24, 1942

Dear Katherine Anne:

I have been trying to answer your letter for days, but the days have been full of alarums and excursions and labors. I shan't, at the moment, describe them all, but take my word for them. I haven't written Albert yet to tell him what a nice job of book-making he did for me.[1]

About the SR business: We were aware that our announcement looked pretty weak.[2] But on the matter, we had, at the time it was prepared, to consider certain aspects of the situation which did not, and could not, appear to the general view. When we prepared the statement (which, by the way, was revised downward by the General), we still had some hope of keeping the magazine. The question was not, at that time, settled. If we had taken a high line at that moment, we would have killed all chance of keeping the SR as a going concern. It seemed to us that if we [were] interested in keeping the magazine we had to prepare such a statement. We have been severely criticized for the tone of the statement, but we felt at the time that our first obligation was to save the magazine if possible. As far as the fear of [our] job[s] was concerned—that was entirely out of the question. We have academic tenure, and it would take a pretty big effort to dislodge us as long as we stay out of jail. To touch us on the magazine question would have brought down investigations and God knows what on this place—and that is one thing they fear. They tried to fire Allen Stanley[3] this spring, and as soon as he showed fight, they reinstated him and tore up the charges. So the fact that we didn't worry about [our] job[s] wasn't nobility; it was simply that we felt we had the drop completely on Frey. But to continue, as soon as it seemed to be a certainty that the magazine was done for, we gave a full statement of our personal views to TIME. But the TIME editors didn't run them in the story on the SR.[4] Why, we can't say. But we have been planning all along for a closing editorial, signed by us, which will clarify our own personal attitude toward the state of mind which is typified by the boys who killed the SR. We are writing something on war and literature, etc. We simply did not feel that we could indulge ourselves until we knew what bearing our statement would have on the fate of the magazine.

We may have played our hand wrong all along, but I did want you to know the exact situation and know the nature of our motives.

Among the disturbing factors in my life at the moment is the necessity of making a decision about staying at LSU. Minnesota has offered me a full professorship and raise, etc., and I am as yet undecided. On the purely practical side I ought to go. But I hate to leave here because of some pretty strong personal ties—though the personal ties become fewer every year. You and Albert gone, John Palmer going in June,[5] etc. Valente[6] leaving—fired (no academic tenure). Then the work with Cleanth has been valuable to me, and enormously pleasant. We have on hand a project about Shakespeare, and I don't know what would become of that. But I'm pretty sure—very sure—that the time is growing short for him here. The University might meet an offer made him, and he might stay. But they haven't, to date, shown any inclination to meet the offer made me.[7] Also, we are trying, or have been trying, to get settled here in some permanent way. That isn't crucial, but it does bear on the decision. So.

Other news isn't very exciting. I'm trying to do an essay for the Mesure thing at Princeton, and have a job of revision on the novel staring me in the face. The only bright spot we see ahead is a visit from Zabel, who is to make a speech here. I like him enormously, and look forward to a couple of days of conversation.

The *Parrot* has just come in, and I snatched it first. I've just read the introduction with pleasure, a typical KAP job.[8] Next week I hope to finish the book.

Goodbye. Cinina joins me in love.

As ever,
Red

1. Now an editor at New Directions, Erskine had overseen the publication of *Eleven Poems on the Same Theme.*

2. The editorial announcing the quarterly's demise (*Southern Review* [Winter 1942]) had taken a stoic and conciliatory stance that disappointed many of the journal's supporters.

3. Stanley taught biology at LSU.

4. "Obit in Baton Rouge," *Time* (February 2, 1942).

5. Palmer entered the navy.

6. Richard Valente was on the music faculty.

7. Though LSU eventually promised Warren a promotion to full professor, their counteroffer of a raise in pay fell a few hundred dollars short of Minnesota's. Warren regarded this as "an invitation to leave."

8. Porter had translated and furnished an introduction for José Joaquin Fernandez de Lizardi's *The Itching Parrot.*

TO R. P. BLACKMUR

TLS/PU

The Southern Review
University Station
Baton Rouge, Louisiana
[Spring 1942]
Monday

Dear Blackmur:[1]

Your letter came this afternoon, and I am dashing off a sort of preliminary reply. Palmer, who has the records, is not here, and so the secretary is trying to patch together some provisional figures, which may help you. These are fairly accurate, and may serve your purpose. In any case, I shall leave your letter here for Palmer, who will answer it within a day or two if my figures seem too far off base.

Loss: This may be best arrived at by setting up our costs.

Editorial costs:	$3000
Secretary:	1200
Manufacture:	3200
Contributors:	4800
Incidental:	500
	$12500 [*sic*]
Income 1941:	3000
Loss:	9500

The actual loss to the University was somewhat less than this, because the part of my salary and that of Brooks which is charged to the Review would have been paid out anyway; the University would simply have saved the cost of a couple of teaching fellows, and not the amount of our salaries allocated to the Review.

I haven't the figures for minimum and maximum losses, but I can say that our income has steadily gone up, and we had expected about $3500 this year.

The maximum circulation was about 2000 copies (Hardy issue), the minimum just under 1000.

A few hundred dollars would cover our take from advertising. Palmer would have to write you [about] this.

For the subscriber-stand circulation, I'll give you fall, 1941:

Subscriber —	600 +
Single —	70
Stand —	250
	920

The Hardy and Yeats issues presumably will double the circulation. It is a little early to give figures on Yeats, but the Hardy is still moving well.

This is about all I can give you. All the figures are approximate, but they are very close, I think. So I'll send these on and leave your letter for Palmer to work up in the next day or so.

I hope that you all can swing your project.

Warmest regards,
Warren

1. Blackmur wanted to found a literary magazine along the lines of the defunct *North American Review* and had written to explore the question of costs.

Deeply hurt and offended, Warren decided to leave Louisiana State University when the administration declined to match the salary he had been offered by Minnesota. En route to take up his new appointment, he stopped for a time in Iowa City, where he did some hurried summer teaching at the university and visited friends he and Cinina had made the year before. As the nation adjusted to a wartime footing, the inevitable social disruptions and personal uncertainties multiplied. Given the effects of rapid mobilization, the Warrens had to scramble to find suitable housing in Minneapolis for the fall, but with that mission accomplished they managed to retreat to the Minnesota countryside for what Warren liked to call the "shank" of the summer.

TO JOHN PALMER

TLS   care of A. A. Secord
                                                    Brown's Point
                                              Alexandria, Minnesota
                                                  August 10, 1942

Dear John:

I've been meaning to write for a heck of a long time; and you, no doubt, have been meaning to do the same. I shan't plead the pressure of day-to-day affairs, for that would sound a little silly to you, who are certainly a lot more under such pressure than I am. We made Iowa without any serious mishap, though the effort of getting off from Baton Rouge was terrible. I stopped by to see my father [in Guthrie, Kentucky] for one day and made the University of Iowa just under the wire. So our hope for a few quiet days between LSU and SUI[1] was an idle dream. But the period at Iowa, though well filled (I had six Ph.D. and M.A. theses to read and committees to sit on—the little joker in the deck), was pleasant enough. It was especially nice to see Austin Warren and John McGalliard.[2] And the new Mrs. Warren is a damned fine woman.[3] We really enjoyed her society a lot. Austin and John Mc. have been trying for months to get into the Navy, in the Deck Volunteer Specialists thing. Just two days before we left Iowa City, however, Austin got his orders to report to the army for induction as a buck private. He had received a lot of encouragement from the Navy people, and so began to wire frantically around to see how his application was progressing for the DVS. Des Moines and Chicago blandly denied any knowledge of the whereabouts of his papers. Des Moines stoutly claimed that they had sent the papers to Chicago, and Chicago stoutly claimed that they had never heard of any such papers. All in all, it was a very nice mess. We haven't yet heard the sequel. Speaking of the Navy, Edward Donahoe came to Iowa City for a week to visit us, took his physical there for the Army, and then went on to Chicago to try to get into some branch of the Navy. (He'd tried something earlier in New York without luck.) He called on Jimmy Caffrey,[4] and one night we received a long-distance from Chicago from Jimmy and Edward and had a conversation with them to the off-stage noises of music, clinking glasses, and laughter. They must have been telephoning from a night club. Jimmy, who had written us earlier that he would try to get up to Iowa City for a week-end, then said that he would try to come up to Minnesota for a few days with us in August. We're hoping to see him soon. As for Edward, it appears that he got his orders to report to the Army before he made any progress with the Navy. So I reckon he's now wearing army shoes and working off his incipient pot. When we saw him, he was facing the prospect with great cheerfulness. Well, after Iowa, where besides the damned theses and dissertations and a lot of lousy short stories—for the most part lousy, for the war was taking all the bright boys and nothing was left but the schoolteachers from Sioux City and Grand Rapids—we went to Minneapolis, where we put in a week or so hunting an apartment for next year. It's a defense area, so called, and the city i[s] crawling with apartment hunters. The real estate people simply don't have any listings. But we finally lucked a place which promises to be moderately satisfactory. It's tiny, but it overlooks a nice lake and has a lot of greenery about. It's to hell and gone from the University, however, and I see myself standing in the twenty-below, at seven-thirty in the morning, waiting for the bus which doesn't come. After that rather dreary period in Minneapolis—which, by the way, is a very nice place, as far as we could make out in our brief stay—we came on here. Alexandria is a small town west of Minneapolis, in the middle of one of the lake sections, but a modest lake section. We have found a quiet place and are, I trust, settled here until early September. We'd like to stay until term opens, but we had to take our apartment for September 1, and can't very well let it stand empty. Andrew Corry, who is now in Washington preparing some sort of report for the State

Department, may come by for a week or so, he says. We saw him for a couple of days in Baton Rouge when he was on his way up from South America. If things turn out right here, I'll finish up most of the novel revision. I didn't get anything done on it worth mentioning in Iowa City, because the follow-up stuff on the fiction text book killed that time, when there was any time. But day by day, my occupations seem more and more trivial to me as I read the newspapers. Maybe I shan't have this mild complaint to make very much longer—I'm not romantic enough to call it more than mild—for the draft board in Baton Rouge, and the district boss to whom I wrote, come mighty near promising to classify me out of 3A this fall into 1B.[5] So maybe I'll do my bit as a $600 a year man in Camp Livingston, shoveling gravel before too long. I'm sure going to try to beat that rap, however, and get some other job if they begin to blow hot on the back of my neck. I have been in pretty close touch with Cleanth about the text book business, but he hasn't had much to say about Michigan, except that he likes his place there.[6] The Minnesota place looks rather nice at the moment, for I've got a pleasant set-up of courses for the next year—Literary Criticism and Sixteenth Century as the other two courses, and a Modern Literature for the first term while Lewis is taking on the writers.[7] All scheduled on three days a week. But I've got to bone on the Criticism course. I taught it once, exactly ten years ago and I've gone pretty vague on Lord Kames and Leigh Hunt[8] and a million other folks. Not to mention the great masters, with whom I've never been very much better than vague. But, as I suggested above, a lot of this seems pretty trivial to me right now, and it must sound damned trivial to you lively little lads in Navy Blue.

Thank you for your telegram about the little ailment you had on your mind. It was a relief to know that things were working out all right for you. And thanks for the kind reference to the money.[9] Until the present there hasn't been any pressure with me on that score, but a little pressure is making itself felt now, for I'm without visible means for the coming two months. The moving was heinous and the damned house in Baton Rouge takes out great chunks. We finally rented it for $15 a month and there seems to be no prospect of a sale until the Peace of Berlin is written. (I'd like to dictate that, for I've got a little personal grudge now entirely separate from my more impersonal and high-minded considerations.) But to return to the pressure: if you can scrape up a penny for the Old Guy,[10] it would not come unhandy right now.

But if you can't, don't let it prey on your mind, and spoil your efficiency in Omaha, where, of course, you will spend the duration.

When you get time, let us know how things go with you. I don't expect you to tell me Admiral King's innermost thoughts,[11] but I'd like to know how you are getting along. My address is the above for the next three weeks. And if you've seen Albert, tell us how he is. I wrote him a little while back, but haven't had a reply. I can't say that I blame him, for I hadn't written since seeing him in New York.

Goodbye, and all luck. Cinina joins me in the last.

As ever,

Red

[P.S.] Upon reflection, I've decided to register this, for it'll probably be kicking around a dozen addresses if I don't. Frances[12] wrote me your New York address, but I've lost it, and the English Department at LSU seems like the safest bet now. The P.O. in Baton Rouge must have information for the first stage of the journey. I imagine that you're in Washington now from what Frances said.

[Handwritten] P.S. Cinina said tell you that she went by Rosenf[i]elds[13] before leaving, and that they said you had been by. But they had balled things up somehow and were very vague about the business, and ended by saying they would wait for further instructions from you. By the way, I recently heard from Conrad that his brother has been appointed to the sculpture post at Iowa.[14]

1. State University of Iowa (Iowa City), not to be confused with the present Iowa State University at Ames.

2. John Calvin McGalliard was a medievalist.

3. Austin Warren had married Eleanor Blake in 1941.

4. A member of the Warren's social set in Baton Rouge, nephew of the diplomat Jefferson Caffrey. (My thanks to Philip Uzee.)

5. The 1B classification would have meant limited service, but Warren's status, despite the obvious handicap of a missing eye, remained problematic for some time.

6. Brooks was teaching in the summer term at the University of Michigan.

7. Sinclair Lewis, whose novels *Main Street* (1920) and *Babbitt* (1922) were already American classics, taught creative writing at Minnesota.

8. Henry House, Lord Kames (1696–1782) was the author of *Elements of Criticism;*

Hunt (1784–1859) was a major figure in the romantic movement and an associate of Shelley and Keats.

9. Palmer recalls offering to repay money he owed the Warrens.

10. See the epigraph to Eliot's "The Hollow Men."

11. Ernest Joseph King was chief of naval operations and thus the ranking officer in the navy during World War II.

12. Stewart, formerly the secretary at the *Southern Review.*

13. A Baton Rouge department store.

14. Humbert Albrizio, who had studied sculpture at the Institute for Design at the New School in New York. (Special thanks to Judith L. Macy.)

TO BRAINARD CHENEY

TLS/VU   care of A. A. Secord
                                                          Brown's Point
                                                  Alexandria, Minnesota
                                                        [18 Aug. 1942]¹

Dear Lon:

The review which I have recently read of River Rogue in Time prompts me to write this note and say that I'm happy to see such a favorable reception.² I trust that it has been duplicated, and bettered, elsewhere. I've been rather cut off from magazines and newspapers, except the local sheet, for some time, and so the Time review is the only thing I've seen.

We left Iowa City toward the end of July, after a rather pleasant but hectic time. I suppose the fact that so many of our friends there were waiting to be called to the war or had applied for commissions and were twiddling their thumbs in suspense, had a good deal to do with the surcharged atmosphere. But it wasn't a bad period. Especially the week when Edward D[onahoe] turned up to introduce a more carefree note than is usual. But he left in a hurry to go to Chicago to try to join the Navy. Then, apparently, his draft board called him back to New York. He passed his physical while in Iowa City, and is a 1A.

After Iowa we went to Minneapolis, where we put in a week house-hunting. A rather dreary occupation in a city which is a defense center with people pouring in from all over. But we finally got that matter arranged, and came to the country. We're just outside a small town on some lakes, somewhat northwest of Minneapolis. It's a very nice country here, very different from anything I've ever seen. And I've become a strong pro-Scandinavian, if I can judge from the rather numerous samples I've encountered in these parts.

We go into Minneapolis in early September, since we've signed a lease for September, and can't well afford not to use shelter that's paid for. But before then, or shortly after, we'd love to hear from you all. Cinina joins me in best to you and Fanny—and Beatty's, Starr's and Owsley's outfits.

As ever,

Red

P.S. If you go to Monteagle please pass on my remembrance to Lytles and Tates. And when you write, let me know what has become of the Zibart boys.[3]

1. Bracketed notation in an unidentified hand.

2. The August 10, 1942, issue of *Time* carried an unsigned review of Cheney's novel and Robert Richards' *I Can Lick Seven.*

3. The Zibart family operated Nashville's leading bookstore. (My thanks to Martha and Arthur Goldsmith.)

TO FRANK LAWRENCE OWSLEY

TLS/VU
care of A. A. Secord
Brown's Point
Alexandria, Minnesota
[August 1942]

Dear Frank:

Well, we're finally in Minnesota, hard as that is for us to believe. After summer term in Iowa, which wasn't bad—as a matter of fact, I like the place—we went up to Minneapolis and had a rather hellish week trying to find an apartment in a city which is swamped with defense workers, all of whom make more money than college professors, if one is to judge from the rent scale. But we finally got settled in a rather pleasant apartment, very small but overlooking one of the dozen or so lakes in the city and with a got [*sic*] bit of greenery. I suppose that before long the greenery will be whitery, for they say that winter starts early. And with tires threadbare and our apartment some six or seven miles from the University, yours truly will be standing in the twenty below three mornings a week at seven-thirty, waiting for his bus with the morning paper wrapped around his torso under his overcoat. And I don't forget, either, that seven-thirty, war time, is six-thirty by God's time,[1] which is damned early under the pole.

After our Minneapolis period we came to the country, and are now settled in a rather pleasant cottage on the shore of a lake, just outside of a small town northwest of Minneapolis. The weather hasn't been any too good, though we've managed to get into the water most days. But the evenings are chilly enough to make us relish a fire on the hearth. I suppose we'll go back into town shortly after the first of September. I'm trying to give another curry-combing to the novel, which is slated for February. But I may have more to do than I realize, or it may take me longer to do than I anticipate. So the February date is tentative.

Aside from the rather unexciting narrative above, we haven't any real news. I spend far too much time reading the papers about the war, but here, thank God, we haven't a radio at least, and that gives me a little time for myself. In Iowa City I was on the radio five or six times a day listening to the details of the Russian retreat.[2] Which promises to go on, it seems, forever. I comfort myself with the reflection that it could be a hell of a lot worse, and remember that the Germans aren't at the Suez, as I damned well thought they would be at the fall of Tobruk.[3] But it's all very slim comfort. I believe that we will win, all right, but I sure God hope we'll take the easy way and not the hard way to do it. I'm afraid that our side simply hasn't got much imagination, and will be a jump behind all the way to the last round. As for me and the war, it seems that I shall probably be classified out of 3A this fall, according to my draft board and the director of the area in which Louisiana lies. That might mean 1B—limited military service. But they have been very cagey about answering my questions, and I can't feel that I have any real indication of my status. I'd sure hate to be building latrines at some camp, which is what a 1B has a good chance of doing for the duration.

Write to me when you get a chance. I hope that the summer has been a nice one for you all. We still think how pleasant it would have been to be in your house in the country in June, but as it was I made Iowa just in time to meet my first class.

SELECTED LETTERS OF ROBERT PENN WARREN

Cinina joins me in love to all. And don't forget to include Isabel in the all, too, when you see her.

As ever,

Red

1. Since February, the United States had operated on "war time," with all clocks set forward one hour.
2. The Germans were closing in on the key city of Stalingrad.
3. General Rommel had overwhelmed the British garrison at Tobruk, but the Allies would retake the North African city later in the year.

Settled in for the fall term, Warren found the University of Minnesota and his new colleagues much to his liking. Still, he maintained a keen interest in events and individuals back in Baton Rouge. The war provided a grim backdrop as he finished work on At Heaven's Gate *and* Understanding Fiction *(the third of his textbooks with Brooks), and though he had claimed in earlier letters that editing had become a somewhat onerous task and even expressed mixed feelings about the demise of the* Southern Review, *he soon found himself putting together a special issue of John Crowe Ransom's* Ken-yon Review.

TO JOHN PALMER

TLS

3124 West Calhoun Boulevard
Apartment 405
Minneapolis, Minnesota
September 16, 1942

Dear John:

A letter of mine (from Alexandria, Minnesota) and yours of early August must have crossed in the mails. It was, and is, fine to know that you could make your living wearing a leopard skin and bulging your biceps in a side show, or by playing Mr. Weissmuller's roles[1] when the grim reaper overtakes him, if the teaching profession gave down. As for the teaching profession, I don't see why you would ever want to get out of a nice quiet life like the navy. Right now, I am inclined to envy you, for this afternoon my stuff begins. No classes, however, for ten days or so. And I'll need that time. We've barely started to get things straight here in our apartment. Junk is piled to the ceiling, bookcases have to be built, papers have to be sorted, etc. And in addition, there are a few little details like winding up the novel revision and putting the last few hellish days on Understanding Fiction. (For instance, the problem of finding out the date of composition of a few stories by Chekov and Pirandello[2]—nasty little chores of that sort.)

The stay in Alexandria was very successful. It is a fine place and we found no flies, scarcely gnats, in the ointment. The weather wasn't always ideal, but it was good enough. You must come and spend some time with us there in the days we look forward to after the mess is over. (After—maybe a rather long *after,* for Stalingrad was tottering last night and I haven't seen a morning paper.[3] But we'll count on your coming, if we can't make Sirmione again right away. I suppose you could be persuaded to try that again.) Since our return here, we've seen a few people in the department. The Huntington Browns are very fine folks. (He's doing the Elizabethan courses, exclusive of my 16th century affair; a marvelous linguist, good sense of humor, has six children and a nice little Bostonian wife who reminds me of Mrs. Ransom, likes the bottle in a pleasant way.)[4] We've seen the Beaches once, and like them.[5] We're going out to their camp this coming week-end, it appears. If we pull out of our colds—we're both pretty low right now with coughs and sniffles.

There's not much news from LSU except word of the disintegration of the place. Caffee[6] is in an officer's training camp; Turner[7] in the Navy; Wildman and Woolf[8] in the army; Daspitt[9] in Washington. Stanley has gone to St. John's,[10] and according to reports likes it. Dana Russell[11] has gone with the Government in some geological capacity, but before his departure wrote a six page indictment to the Board naming all names and itemizing the crimes of the LSU bosses. Bourgeois' trial comes up in October in Judge [James D.] Womack's court, with K. K. Kennedy as his lawyer.[12] Broussard will leave a bed of pain in a New Orleans hospital for the doubtful relief of the witness chair.[13] It seems that Daddyboy Bradsher [*sic*][14] has tried a new strategy: He forbade his classes to read a Farewell to Arms on grounds of immorality and went to Hodges with the complaint that Kirby and his sect were corrupting the students. Kirby got hold of him and gave him hell, I hear. I am not sure that he suggested Cane Juice as nice clean reading for the boys and girls, but he should have to make the picture complete.[15] Heilman writes me a dolorous letter and asks for arsenic by return mail. Conrad writes that his brother got the Iowa job and will be teaching there this fall in the Art department. I recently had a long letter from Albert, who doesn't give much news except the news of the marriage.[16] We are hoping to see Jimmy Caffrey this fall, if he hasn't changed his mind about coming up here. That is about all the news I have. Except that the Kenyon has reorganized with Brooks and Warren as members of the staff. A James issue (1943 is the hundredth anniversary) will appear next year.[17] That's all the news I can think of.

Thank you for the kind words about the money, in your letter. It would come in handy, all right, for I don't get paid here for some time to come.

Write when you get a chance and let us know how things go. I'll say again how good it was to hear from you. Cinina joins me in love.

As ever,
Red

1. Johnny Weissmuller was a former Olympic swimming champion who starred in a popular series of Tarzan movies.

2. Chekhov's "The Lament" and Pirandello's "War" were among the stories included in *Understanding Fiction.*

3. Stalingrad held out, and the failure of the German army to take the city is regarded as a turning point in the war on the eastern front.

4. During Warren's Minnesota years, Brown became one of his closest friends, and a particularly deep affection developed between Warren and "Biddie" Brown. (My gratitude to Leonard and Sherley Unger.)

5. Joseph Warren Beach, the department chair, and his wife, Dagmar.

6. Nathaniel Caffee had joined the LSU English department in 1935.

7. Arlin Turner, ultimately a distinguished Americanist.

8. The poet John Wildman and lexicographer Bosley Woolf were members of the English faculty.

9. Alex Daspitt, a political scientist, went on to work for the State Department.

10. Allen Stanley; he moved on to the University of Oklahoma.

11. Russell taught physics at LSU.

12. Eugene O. Bourgeois, of the Romance languages department, had been dismissed over an alleged indiscretion with a student and was suing for reinstatement. Kemble K. Kennedy was a flamboyant and controversial attorney. (Special thanks to the redoubtable Charles East.)

13. James F. Broussard, a member of the Old Guard on the faculty, died without testifying. (My thanks to Charles East.)

14. Earl Lockridge Bradshear, a departmental enemy of Brooks and Warren.

15. Warren relishes an irony; his nemesis John Earle Uhler, now an opponent of reform, had once almost lost his job when his novel *Cane Juice* (1931) was denounced as obscene.

16. Erskine married Peggy Griffin Anthony in 1942.

17. The Henry James issue of the *Kenyon Review*, assembled by Warren, came out in autumn 1943.

TO JOHN PALMER

TLS

3124 West Calhoun Boulevard
Apartment 405
Minneapolis
September 23, 1942

Dear John:

It is too bad about the trench mouth, even if you are getting a chance to read and listen to your radio. I hope that your next letter will bring better news. As for the headquarters job, that would certainly be better than Omaha; but I believe that if I were in, I too would like a taste of the briny. Anyway I hope things work out according to your desires.

Many thanks for the check, which was, by the way, too big by four bits.[1] So I am sticking in stamps for the four bits in the hope that you will use the better part of them on the Warrens, who would like to have news from you whenever you find time to write. By way of Edward Donahoe (who, by the way, was finally turned down by the army because of his cracked arm) we hear that Jimmy Caffrey will be going to sea in a month or so. But we are hoping that he will get up here before that. I hear also that Austin Warren seems to be in line for a Navy place similar to yours after all the comedy of his lost application and his notice to report to the army.

Things go pretty well here except for our colds and the apparently impossible job of getting our apartment into order. I began my official duties last Monday with a grim three-hour Ph.D. examination. And this morning I sat in a department conference for a while. I have a nice schedule, nine hours, Monday, Wednesday, and Friday, and have a pleasant office-mate, Professor Hessler,[2] a jolly fellow who has easy chairs in the office and a lot of enormous and beautiful and properly framed Brueghels. So I am in the lap of luxury in comparison to the amiable disorder of the SR office—for which I hone already. I shan't dare drop a pin or a postage stamp in my present quarters, and I could use some of the Brooks-Palmer conversation. So far, however, things go smoothly and I like my colleagues. We have seen the Huntington Browns for drinks and a dinner, and Sunday went out to the Beach lodge on the St. Croix river for the day. A very pleasant expedition. The only other piece of news is that I'm trying to sell the car, and plan to use street cars for the duration. But the gas rationing has knocked the bottom out of the market; so I may not have much luck.

Again, thanks for the check. And again, thanks for the letter. Another soon, I hope.

Cinina joins me in love.

Red

1. See n. 9, in the August 10, 1942, letter to Palmer, above.
2. Lewis Burtron Hessler, a philologist of the old school.

TO HENRY HOLT AND COMPANY

TLS/PU

3124 West Calhoun Boulevard
Apartment 405
Minneapolis, Minnesota
September 28, 1942

Henry Holt and Company
Text Book Department
New York City

Dear Sirs:

I wish to call attention to a permanent change of address. My new address is as given above.

I also wish to ask a favor. If you can now give me my share of the payment due in late October, on *Understanding Poetry,* I shall be grateful, since I have some unusual expenses for the first of the month. In any case, will you please let me know what the amount of royalty will be for this period?

Thank you very much.

Sincerely yours,
Robert Penn Warren

TO ALLEN TATE

TLS/PU
3124 West Calhoun Boulevard
Apartment 405
Minneapolis, Minnesota
October 19, 1942

Dear Allen:

First, about the James issue of the Kenyon Review. Will you do a piece for it? There is no use for me to say how anxious I am for you to contribute.[1] But, for the grimmer side of the question—the deadline, I am told, is July 1. And the maximum length is about 4500 to 5000 words. If you will do the essay, can you let me have, at your earliest convenience, a statement about the subjects which would interest you[?] John is anxious to avoid duplication, and we want to get the subjects lined up before people start actual work on their contributions.

After Iowa, we came to Minneapolis for a few days to hunt a place to live, and finally located an apartment which is proving to be very pleasant. But we're pretty far from the University, and it will be colder than hell on the street corners waiting for the bus. We had a little snow in September, but the weather since that time has been beautiful. After we found the apartment, we went to the country for three weeks—three very nice weeks on one of the ten thousand lakes which the Chambers of Commerce boast about. Then we turned up here in early September and began the hell of unpacking. I've been teaching now for about fo[u]r weeks and begin to have some notion of the place. On the whole, I am very well pleased. I have the courses I want, but of course the new draft age will probably draw off all students except those in the lower division. In my graduate course in criticism I now have only five, and God know[s] what will be the situation next term. I find the department quite agreeable—or rather, I should say that I find those agreeable whom I have come to know. The place is enormous, and I'll probably never know gangs of my colleagues. Beach is as fine and frosty an old gent as you ever saw.[2] You couldn't ask for a more considerate department head. He has made every effort to smooth the way. For instance, my work was arranged so that I only have to go [to] the place three days a week, and in my big class in modern literature I have a very capable assistant.[3] Minneapolis itself is a very handsome city, and I've become a great admirer of the Scandinavians. So for the present things look fine. I'll know more a little later, but I hope that what I then know won't contradict my first impressions.

I'm on the verge of finishing the revision of my novel, and haven't the slightest notion of what it is like. For the moment I feel that I have done all to it that I can do, and that it will have to stand or fall as it is. But after it cools off a little I'll probably want to tinker some more.

Zabel writes me that he has recently heard from you all, and that you will remain at Monteagle for the winter. Is that right? Have you begun the novel? I'd like to have the news. And when you write tell me about the Sewanee Review. Andrew, in a recent note, told me a little but not much. What has become of Knickerbocker? That news seems to be sweeping the country, with every version contradicting every other version.[4]

I haven't heard from Baton Rouge in some weeks. The last letters from Cleanth have been devoted to the last-minute problems of our text book, which is due out this winter, and so I don't know much about developments there. But what I do hear is gloomy. Apparently the General has gone from bad to worse—has killed faculty participation in administration, etc. But I am missing the General, for he filled a big part of my life last year.

Goodbye, and best to you all. Tell Andrew I am getting a note off to him right away.

As ever,
Red

1. Tate was not among the final contributors.
2. Beach and Warren grew especially fond of one another over the next several years.

3. Probably Mary Lund Wyvell, who stayed on after completing her graduate work at Minnesota.

4. William S. Knickerbocker had edited the *Sewanee Review* since 1926 and was leaving under duress.

TO MORTON DAUWEN ZABEL

TLS/Newb

3124 West Calhoun Boulevard
Apartment 405
Minneapolis
October 19, 1942

Dear Morton:

Thanks a lot for the note, which came today to fill me with shame for my delay in answering your California letter. But once we left Iowa City time seemed to disappear from calculations, until we settled in Minneapolis and there ceased to be any time for anything. From Iowa we came here for a few days to hunt a place to live. After some bad days (the city is overcrowded) we found a place which seems to be very satisfactory, despite its great distance from the University. Anyway, we want you to come and pay us a visit in it very soon. (But I'll return to this point a little later in my letter.) Then we went up to Alexandria and took a cottage on a lake for a little over three weeks. It was a good period, filled with swimming and reading and work on my novel (which I have been revising for winter or spring publication) and croquet. In early September we came back to town, and began the hellish process of unpacking and trying to get settled. But every other aspect of our life since the return has been pleasant. I like my classes and I find the department very agreeable. Of course, I have not yet really talked with a large number of the members, but I have seen quite a bit of Huntington Brown, the Beaches, Moore,[1] McDowell,[2] and one or two others.

To return to the matter of your visit here: Why don't you plan to get up for a week-end this fall? We'd love to have you, and you have other friends here who would share our view of the matter. Consult your program and let us know about when you would be able to come. Thank you a lot for the suggestion that we come to Chicago, but that doesn't seem to be in the cards for the immediate future. Perhaps Christmas, but not earlier, I should say. So try to come up soon—for if you do have to go to the Army we'd like to have that glimpse of you before you begin your soldiering. It's too damned bad (and stupid) that you haven't been able to get into the Intelligence or another special service. I suppose you knew that Austin Warren had been in an awful mix-up too. His Navy papers were lost in some office, he was ordered to appear for induction in the Army, had to go to Washington to work on the Navy business, and the last I heard was waiting around Iowa City in great uncertainty. His father, too, died this fall. As for my own status—I am still 3A, but expect reclassification. I don't know what would be the result of that.

About the James issue: I have been very slow about getting out letters on the subject, and have only written three or four. Your name is on the original list which Ransom, Rice,[3] and I drew up, and it is my fault that you have not heard. Certainly, we are hoping to have you, and the subject which you propose sounds fine.[4] Do you mean that you have the essay already written? If so, we shan't discuss the question of your subject. But if you haven't written it already, could you let us have a choice of a couple of subjects? I ask this because we want to try to avoid duplications as much a possible. I am trying to get the subjects together to iron out duplications. But if any contributor has his heart set on a special subject, we don't want to steer him off it. There is another point which I should mention, the matter of length. Since the Kenyon is somewhat smaller than the SR was, we shall have to be pretty definite about length. We want to hold all essays absolutely down to 5000 words. I know that this will create difficulties, but it seems to be necessary. Can you manage in that space? We hope to get some down to 4000 or 4500 words. But in any case, 5000 will be the maximum.

Do let us hear from you. And give us the assurance that you will come to see us. Cinina joins me in warmest regards.

As ever,

Red

1. Cecil A. Moore, a senior member of the English department.
2. Tremaine McDowell, who started the American studies program at Minnesota.
3. Philip Blair Rice was managing editor of the *Kenyon Review*.
4. Zabel was not represented in the James issue.

TO MORTON DAUWEN ZABEL

TLS/Newb
3124 West Calhoun Blvd.
Apartment 405 Minneapolis
October 29, 1942

Dear Morton:

It is good to know that we shall probably see you here next month. We have no commitments, and all weeks look alike to us. So you pick the time and let us know. I'd like to know as far ahead as is convenient for you, for I want to be sure to get Beach, Moore, and a couple of other people for an evening.

It is also good to know that you will do the James piece. Since you have the essay ready on James's idea of the literary vocation, let's say that that is your title. And thank you for the suggestion about Marianne Moore. That sounds very good. I'll have to check back on my list, and see how space looks. But I'm sorry that I didn't think of her earlier.[1]

It is definitely not good to know that your various efforts to get into the services have failed. I can't believe that your going in by [w]ay of the draft will mean more than a delay in getting a commission. I have heard some encouraging things about the handling of such cases as yours once the man is in. My own situation is unchanged. I have no word yet about reclassification. But I have heard from Austin Warren that he has been ordered up for induction. He has a little delay, and is still hoping for his Navy commission. John McGalliard has definitely received a commission, I believe. The blackest part of Austin's picture is the illness of his wife. This fall she had another bad bout with her spine, and was in the hospital two weeks. Since that time she has been laid up at home.

I shan't try to give a proper answer to your letter. I'll save up for your visit. Don't forget that we are counting on that. Meanwhile, Cinina joins me in all good wishes.

As ever,
Red

---

1. Warren lost Moore's address (letter to Zabel, December 15, 1942, below), and it is unclear if he ever wrote her.

TO ALLEN TATE

TLS/PU   Department of English
                                          University of Minnesota
                                          Minneapolis, Minnesota
                                          November 2, 1942

Dear Allen:

Your topic for the James issue sounds fine. As for the matter of length, I simply don't know what to say at this moment. You know that the Kenyon is limited in space, and it is hard this early to tell exactly how things will pan out. I have written to John to ask him exactly how much space will be available, and as soon as I hear from him I'll know better what to say. My guess is that 6000 words would work out all right, but I don't want to be positive until I hear from him.

I was glad to have the dope about the Sewanee Review. Yes, it would be too bad to let that fall into certain hands. And certainly, I want to do anything I can. As for the Mesures piece, it has been in John's hands for some time, and he has said that he wants to use it.[1] He also has a story,[2] which he asked me for, but I haven't had word from him about it. I'll send that along if he doesn't like it. I don't imagine that he will, but then, I don't imagine that Andrew would like it either.[3] In fact, I am not optimistic enough to believe that anybody would like it very much. I only sent it to John because he asked. It's an old one—in fact, I think that you have seen it. I am working on some poems, and I shall certainly send them to Andrew before they go elsewhere. Andrew asks if some part of the novel might not stand alone. I'm not sure, but as soon as a decent copy is available (probably not soon) I'll send the thing along. Then he can decide.

Is there any chance that Guerry will see the light and try to get some money for contributors?[4] It wouldn't have to be much, but it is almost essential to pay something.

News is scarce with me. I'm doing a lot of reading and working on one of my courses—a new one for me which requires a lot of attention. I've just sent a version of the novel off, and I am recuperating from that. I don't know whether it is ready yet, but at the moment I don't see anything else I can do on it.

I am glad to hear that life in the mountains goes pleasantly. The Lowells are an asset to any community, aren't they? Has Jean finished her novel yet?[5] What is Cal doing? Give them best regards. Is Nancy going to school up there?

Goodbye, and best.

As ever,
Red

1. Ransom did indeed publish the piece (see n. 1, letter to Tate, March 23, 1942, above).

2. Possibly "The Life and Work of Professor Roy Millen."

3. Though the masthead listed Tudor S. Long as editor of the *Sewanee Review* after Knickerbocker's departure, Lytle, as managing editor, seems to have been in charge. Tate would himself assume the editorship a year later.

4. Alexander Guerry was vice chancellor of the University of the South and, as such, its highest ranking administrator. (My thanks to George Core.)

5. Stafford's first novel was *Boston Adventure* (1944).

TO CLEANTH BROOKS

TLS/YU
[Minneapolis]
November 11, 1942

Dear Cleanth:

I have finished the proofs of Understanding Fiction, and am sending them under separate cover. Here, in addition to the things I have marked on the proof itself, are several items of greater importance than punctuation and spelling.

1. Should not the Glossary follow, rather that precede, the Appendixes? Especially since it serves as a sort of index for the book?

2. Should not the Appendixes have titles of some sort? How about this for Appendix I: "Some Technical Problems and Principles in the Composition of Fiction"? It is a little cumbersome, but it is, I guess, fairly accurate. And for Appendix II: "Chronologies of Stories in this Volume." You will probably be able to better this attempt, if you accept the idea of the titles.

3. Exercise on "A Simple Heart."[1] I have made out one and

have attached it to the proof. Will you revise it, amplify it, or rewrite it according to your views[?]

4. In the Glossary the word *convention* is not treated, although in our text we give one or two references to the Glossary for this word. Furthermore, although we have the word *conventional* in the Glossary, we simply refer to the head FORM. But under FORM we make not the slightest reference to the idea, much less the word itself. This is a very bad lag, and we ought to do something about it. I propose that we cut out the reference to FORM, and treat the two words *convention* and *conventional* under a separate head from FORM.

5. On galley 107 I have changed "point of view" to "focus of narration" to make the interpretation consistent with the principle laid down in Appendix I. Will you give this a careful look and see what you think?

6. On galley 121 I have questioned a point of style.

7. On galley 178 there may be a piece of bad paragraphing. It should be checked with the original of "Old Mortality." I haven't got a copy (my books are not unpacked yet).

That is about the works as far as I can judge.

By the way, Crofts was just here. He doesn't seem too optimistic about the immediate prospects of the book—the war, etc. But he is talking about revising the Approach before too long.[2] I told him that you and I had signed up with Harcourt for the freshman text.[3] He said that he wished that he had it, but he didn't give the impression that he thought we had betrayed him.

General news with us is thin. We had to stand in a line for three hours at the President's reception for new Faculty members and take the beating of our lives. We are filling out gas ration blanks. We are hanging on the radio, as you no doubt are, for news of North Africa and the French fleet.[4] I have just done the last work on my novel, and tried to follow the suggestions you and Bob [Heilman] gave me—changing the lynching scene, for example. Harcourt now has the MS. I've recently done a couple of pieces for the Chicago Tribune's new literary supplement—one short and one long thing. The long one is on *The Valley of Decision* which affords a perfect example of corrupt patriotism, the debasing effect of war on literature. I got pretty rough (especially for the

Chicago Tribune) and rather expect they'll refuse to use the piece.⁵ If they do that I'm going to try to have some fun with them. So you see what I said is true—our news is thin. But I've heard from Morton Zabel that he is definitely out of the war. He tried to get into the Navy and was turned down, and now the Army has turned him down, too, for good and all. The last I heard from Austin, he was ready to report to the Army, but was not [sic] hoping for his Naval commission to come through in time to save him. My status is still unchanged, but I expect a reclassification, as you know.

But what about news with the Brookses? I learned from the Rhodes Scholar magazine that you had been promoted to a professorship. I suppose I should write Hodges and congratulate him on a gleam of intelligence in the administration. And I know, from a letter from Allen, that you were expected in Sewanee on Sewanee Review business.⁶ I'd like to know what happened. And I'd like to know the rest about things and your activities.

Speaking of activities, I am inclined to think that we might do well to begin work on two of our projects. First, we've got to give Harcourt some sort of idea about that damned freshman book before too long. They want some statement of plan in December. Second, isn't it possible for us to divide up the reading in terms of periods, and begin to put together an anthology of criticisms of Shakespeare as poet? I think that we could get that stuff together pretty fast, and would have no difficulty in getting a publisher for it. Then, we could do a long introduction, an essay outlining our findings about (1) the state of criticism on the subject, (2) the problems that need investigation, and (3) our views on certain of those problems. I am afraid that if we don't stake out our line by some such preliminary thing we shall wake up and find we have been beaten to the draw. For instance, here is an aspect of the project which might be pretty interesting to you: the critical assumptions underlying eighteenth-century textual emendations. It strikes me that there is a lot of concealed criticism in that field. What do you think? If you are inclined to get on with this, I'll start reading right away and making copies of the excerpts which I think we would use in the book. It won't be much fun doing this in isolation, but I hate to see the thing evaporate. And if we don't get started, it will evaporate.

Well, so long, and all best to you both. Cinina joins me.

As ever,
Red

1. A story by Gustave Flaubert.

2. The next edition of *An Approach to Literature* was not issued until 1952, a full decade away (James A. Grimshaw Jr., *Robert Penn Warren: A Descriptive Bibliography*).

3. *Modern Rhetoric* (1949).

4. To keep it out of Axis hands, what remained of the French fleet was scuttled at Toulon.

5. Grimshaw indicates that the Chicago *Sunday Tribune* books section ran four reviews by Warren in March and April of 1943, but the critique of Marcia Davenport's novel was not among them.

6. Brooks had been offered the editorship. Though he declined, he did agree to serve on the editorial board.

TO DR. KATE ZERFOSS

TLS/VU
Department of English
University of Minnesota
Minneapolis, Minnesota
November 19, 1942

Dear Dr. Kate:[1]

I want to ask a great favor of you, and knowing how busy you are, I am almost ashamed to do so. But the favor is this: Could you let me have a copy of the operation record of the operation on my eye, and a statement concerning the cause of the operation[?] The record is for the use of a doctor here who is thinking about the possibility of changing the type of artificial eye, and the statement is for an insurance company with which I am planning to take out some accident and health insurance. Perhaps I should be more definite on the matter of the insurance. I am told that if the loss of the eye was occasioned by accident and that if there was no disease or infection which might directly endanger the other eye, the policy will give coverage for the remaining eye; if, however, that is not the case, trouble with the remaining eye will not be covered by the insurance. It is my understanding that I will be able to get coverage, but, of course, the company wants a statement from the doctor whose patient I was. As for my present condition, Dr. Stanford,[2] whom I have just seen, tells me that my vision is excellent and that the left socket is perfectly healthy. (Dr. Stanford is a professor at the Medical School here.)

We are liking Minneapolis, and I like my job very much. The department is a very pleasant one, and I have a very light schedule, three days a week. I hated to leave Louisiana for personal reasons, and I hate to think that my visits to Nashville will be fewer from now on, but my situation in the University here is more pleasant than the one I had at LSU.

Please give my warmest regards to Dr. Tom.[3] And Cinina wants to be remembered to both of you. We often talk of you all, and we shall always be grateful to you for your many kindnesses.

Very sincerely yours,
Robert Penn Warren

1. Zerfoss was the highly respected Nashville eye specialist who had removed Warren's damaged left eye in 1934.
2. Charles E. Stanford, an ophthalmologist and adjunct professor.
3. Thomas Zerfoss, M.D., husband of Kate, directed medical services at Vanderbilt.

TO ROBERT B. HEILMAN

TLS/UWash   University of Minnesota
                                             November 27, 1942

Dear Bob:

Many thanks for the letter, which I truly appreciate. I don't want us to lose touch, even though I can't worry you on Monday, Wednesdays, and Fridays at 9:00 A.M., as I used to do. And I appreciated the reprint of your education piece, which I applaud. Not only for the basic views and applications—you would know that anyway from our conversation—but for the skill and force of the presentation. I have not seen your review in the AAUP Bulletin,[1] but I shall certainly hunt it up. As for the letter from the big boy at Chicago, it sounds very mysterious. Is he a vigilante committee of one, or something? But my curiosity is well aroused. And I don't want to close this paragraph without saying that I was glad to have the Broussard-Middleton remark.[2]

Well, lately the Department here has been having a reorganization—new council set-up, new system of election of members, and such. It was just like old times. Any moment I expected to see Cleanth pop in with his derby and cigar. But such things lack color here. People just sat around for hours and corrected the grammar in the document. And there was nobody to take John Earl[e]'s place in debate. The meeting was just like the performance of *Hamlet* without the prince.

By this time next week I may be in the Army. The Navy has told me that they can't use me, not even to sharpen pencils for crippled vice-admirals. The Army won't have me as a volunteer, but they will have me—at least the Colonel who has charge of Selective Service for this area told me—as a draftee. I'll know my fate definitely next week, it appears.[3] I wonder how you stand with Uncle Sam? Any new developments? To return to my case, if I am taken it will be for limited service. That means, I presume, that I'll be stuck somewhere at a pine desk adding up columns of figures. It doesn't sound very romantic. They probably won't even let me play with a Garand[4] on my afternoon off. And speaking of the war, has anybody heard from John Palmer? I wrote him about a month or more ago at the hospital in New Orleans,[5] but I haven't had any answer. Do you have his present address?

I like my work here. I have some very good students in the Criticism course and some good ones in a big mob course in Twentieth Century (juniors mostly). My freshman section (which I drop next term for the Graduate Writing) is a nondescript lot, but agreeable enough. It's rather sad in that class to see a dozen big lads wearing the Navy Blue or the Army or Air Force uniforms sitting with their brows wrinkled over restrictive and non-restrictive clauses. I drop the Twentieth Century next term—January—for the Sixteenth Century, if there are enough Graduate students to make up the class. The Graduate School is hard hit, and will probably be harder hit after Christmas. The only two men I had in the Criticism didn't last out the first three weeks. In a way, it would be better just to go on with the Twentieth Century. That course is pleasant and requires little preparation; and I have a very good assistant. All of this, of course, if I last out.

By the way, Hunt Brown, whom you said you knew, or knew about, at Harvard is almost a neighbor of ours. He is a hell of a nice fellow and full of stuff. I've recently met Stoll.[6] Brown took me around to Stoll's for tea, and then yesterday the Stoll[s] had Thanksgiving dinner at the Brown's [*sic*] with us. Stoll is very un-dragonlike on such occasions, but I suppose he keeps his fires banked for high days and holy days.

I'll end this jabber. Write to me again when you have time. Let me know the news and the news about yourselves. How is the drama book coming?[7] For the present give my best regards, and Cinina's, to your family.

As ever,

Red

1. Heilman had reviewed Newton Edwards' *Education in a Democracy* for the *AAUP Bulletin* (October 1942).

2. Heilman was unable to recall the substance of this anecdote involving James F. Broussard and Troy H. Middleton, the former commandant of cadets at LSU, vice president under Hebert, and eventually president of the university in his own right.

3. Warren was overly optimistic.

4. The M1 rifle.

5. See letter to Palmer, September 23, 1942, above.

6. E. E. Stoll, prolific Shakespearean scholar.

7. Probably an early reference to Heilman's textbook anthology *Understanding Drama* (1945), done in collaboration with Brooks.

TO F. O. MATTHIESSEN

TLS/YU   3124 West Calhoun Boulevard
                                                            Apartment 405
                                                            Minneapolis
                                                       December 5, 1942

Dear Matthiessen:

I am very sorry to hear that the odds are against your being able to do a piece for the James issue of the Kenyon. But I do not want to take no for an answer as long as there is the slightest chance that you will be able to do the job. May I hold the place open for you a time longer? Then as soon as you have some absolutely definite information you can let me know, one way or the other.[1]

It now seems that I too am bound for the Army. I have been reclassified out of 1A and have had my first examination. The Navy turned me down some time back because of eyes, but from all I can find out the Army is yearning for my services. So maybe I'll see you in Cairo or Omaha before long.

As for my poems, I wouldn't have sent them to you in the first place if I hadn't wanted, and expected, you to speak your mind. Naturally, I would have been happier if you had liked them better. But that simply follows from my respect for your critical judgment. In the future I shall send you others, and shall hope that they are better. In any case, I shall expect the same candor.

I do hope that you can fit the James essay into your program. But I suppose that will be possible only if you get a def[e]rment until June. Anyway, the place is open until I hear definitely from you.

Sincerely yours,
Robert Penn Warren

1. Matthiessen's "James and the Plastic Arts" was included in the James issue.

TO ALAN SWALLOW

TLS/Syracuse

Department of English
University of Minnesota
Minneapolis
December 7, 1942

Dear Alan:

Some weeks ago your letter came, was laid on my desk, and promptly disappeared—before I had even had a chance to break the envelope. I have searched high and low for it, and from day to day have expected to find it; but now all I can do is to write and say that the letter is lost and that I don't know what was in it and that I most positively do want to know and that I hope you will forgive my combination of bad luck, negligence, and procrastination. Plus a very stiff period of work—new courses, etc.

But this fall I was thinking more and more about your dissertation and have reread more than once (which usually means twice, and does mean twice in this case) the section on Wyatt and Surrey, and the general introductory material. I have also looked again at Wyatt and through my own notes. I feel that especially on the theoretical material on the inductive-deductive stuff, etc., some further work is needed—more qualification. What you say about the actual difference in style between pre-Wyatt English poetry is undoubtedly true (with a few minor exceptions, odd lines etc., which I have picked up here and there—exceptions which do not effect [*sic*] the principle). But the thing does not fit as patly in Italian poetry—there is much more blurring of the distinction, and in the greatest scholastic poem—"deductive poem"—the *Commedia*, the "inductive method" i[s] worked for all it is worth in the detailed use of imagery and rhythms. In other words, some recognition must be made of this fact, and of the fact that in some of the religious writing the same situation prevails. I still think that the pre-Wyatt prose of a religious type, sermons, etc., would have to be investigated in English to see how the imagery worked. (I am sure it was more complicated than in the poetry, from the relatively small amount of it which I have read.) Those are the general comments which occur to me. Here and there, I have noted some [que]stions, and occasionally, objections, to particular pieces of scansion. But that can be discussed later.

You may recall that when the subject of the thesis was first discussed we decided that we would treat some of the matter in collaboration, the Wyatt material. I hope to get a piece done on that right away, if you are willing. What I propose is this: I shall take your section on Wyatt's imagery and recast [it] into an article and send it to you for revision and criticism in the light of your later thinking. Then we can offer the article for publication over our names as a joint piece. This would seem to divide the effort pretty well, for I had done the original Italian work and you had done the French work and had located the Chaucerian reference. If the piece has any modest success, then we might try the piece on Wyatt's metrics (though in the present piece we might make some reference to the metrical situation and give some key examples as related to the inductive style). How does this strike you? If you'll let me hear right away—and if, of course, you accept the proposal—I'll put the Christmas vacation on the matter and shall try to give you a manuscript in middle or late January. But if you feel that the matter is unsatisfactory, simply say so.[1] As for the relation of such a project to your general book,[2] you could, of course, incorporate the article into the book with whatever later revisions or alterations you saw fit. I have the feeling that the thing, the book I mean, needs some more working over along the lines I have suggested. And the publication of some articles on the subject (say one or two in collaboration with me and then, perhaps, one or two, say on

Sidney by you alone) would help toward the book publication. Naturally, there is no certainty that we could get the piece published, but we have to take that gamble.

Coming to Minnesota was somewhat of a wrench, for I had some strong personal attachments in Baton Rouge. But the University situation was, as the military language has it, "deteriorating," and I didn't see much chance of immediate improvement. Then LSU met the promotion offered here but met it after a long time and much haggling, but did not meet the salary and did not meet the schedule. I am finding the situation here very pleasant. I like a lot of the people in the department and have courses which interest me. The History of Criticism, which I am now giving, interests me a lot, and I have an agreeable undergraduate class in Twentieth Century. I shall continue with the Sixteenth Century (which I am not giving this term) if the registration in the Graduate School permits. But, of course, that bracket is hard hit here as elsewhere. My schedule is very pleasant—three days a week, nine hours, with an able assistant. And the weather doesn't seem as severe as I had anticipated. It has been ten below several times in the last few weeks, but I haven't even taken out my heavy overcoat yet—I've been using a reversible raincoat and find it adequate. I'll save the overcoat for thirty below. As for my private activities, I've finished the revision of my novel, have done a little poetry, and several articles, or rather, reviews, this fall. But the Criticism Course has kept me humping, for I had grown mighty remote from some of the stuff—Lord Kames and Blair[3] and such worthies.

I'll look forward to a letter from you. I hope that your doings are happy ones and that the printing and poetry writing and such things go apace. I'd like to see any poems which you have on hand. How is the war affecting the University there?[4] Not too badly, I hope. Please give my best regards to your wife.[5]

Sincerely yours,
Red Warren

P.S. I forgot to say that my proposal would hold only if I stay out of the army. It looks like there's a good chance for me not to stay. The Navy turned me down, but I believe that I may pass the Army physical.

1. There is no indication the project went forward, but Warren's keen interest is telling.

1. Army Air Force; Cheney had been trying to get a commission.

2. Cheney was going to Washington as an adviser to U.S. Senator Tom Stewart of Tennessee.

3. The *Saturday Review* (September 19, 1942) had carried Warren's review of Cheney's second novel.

4. Most likely a swipe at Edwin Mims, longtime head of the English department at Vanderbilt, who had refused to renew Warren's annual contract in 1934, thus precipitating the move to Baton Rouge.

5. The actor Joseph Cotten had just played major roles in Orson Welles's *Citizen Kane* (1941) and *The Magnificent Ambersons* (1942).

6. Randolph Churchill, already regarded as something of a difficult case.

TO JAMES T. FARRELL

TLS/Penn   Department of English
                                                           University of Minnesota
                                                           Minneapolis, Minnesota
                                                           December 16, 1942

Dear Mr. Farrell:

I have just received the copy of the editorial from the New Republic.[1] I had not seen it, and am glad to have a copy. The whole situation seems to be disgraceful. If there is any organized protest to the ALA,[2] I should like to participate. I feel that something ought to [be] done about a protest, but I don't imagine that individual letters would do any good. Except to let off the writer's steam.

You see, I have a new address. Since the death of the SR, I've come up here. If you get into this part of the country, please let me know.

Merry Christmas, and best wishes,
Robert Penn Warren

1. "Censorship by Timidity," *New Republic,* November 30, 1942.

2. The American Library Association had omitted Farrell's Studs Lonigan trilogy from a list of approved books reflecting American life in a positive way, thus affecting its distribution abroad.

TO JOHN PALMER

TLS
3124 West Calhoun Boulevard
Apartment 405
Minneapolis
December 24, 1942

Dear John:

It's fine to have the note. When I got no reply to my letter acknowledging the lifeline you threw me, I began to have dire surmises. I have written to several people in Baton Rouge in the last month, asking in the course of my letters for news of you and for news of your address. Nary an answer to that question. I could have written to you in N.O. if I hadn't promptly lost your address, and I suppose I could have taken a chance on Mr. John Palmer, USNR, Admiral-to-be-hereafter, N.O. But I kept waiting for the address to turn up.

I must say that your note doesn't exactly provide a glut of information, but if you are able to keep the midnight watch, you must be strong enough to stand, and if you are strong enough to stand, you must be able to take nourishment; so we suppose you're all right. Do you know anything about your immediate future? Will you continue in New Orleans? Do you ever get up to Baton Rouge? Or have you been in Memphis? The day before yesterday we got a letter from Mary Elizabeth Harsh,[1] who said that she had seen John. But what John, we wondered? We know a John in Memphis, too, who also is known to M.E.H. In the same letter she remarked that she was getting married, but not to the "John" referred to in the letter. We met the lad last summer—a dark-browed, handsome Christer from Southwestern—a very nice fellow, as a matter of fact, as far as one can tell with a half hour conversation in the Memphis gloaming, sitting in deck chairs on the lawn, slapping mosquitoes and wishing for the highball to come. (I believe that his presence forbade the highball. But I can't be too sure of this.)

Well, there's no world-shaking news with us, except that I may be in the Service in time to win the war, and that Cinina is fighting off the flu or something without sensational success. I have been classified 1A. Sometime back I tried the Navy, and was turned down cold. Eyes. Then I tried the Army, but was told that they didn't want me until the draft got round to me. I didn't have any talents which interested them. Then I got reclassified. I have seen an oculist and am told that I am a cinch to pass the Army on that count, and last sp[r]ing when I had all those physical examinations, the doctor told me that I was a cinch for the Army physical. The Office of Director of Selective Service in the area has recently told me that the new age ruling does not apply in my case. The University, without any prompting from me, appealed my case; I would have been willing to prompt them, for I don't like the idea of that pine desk in Omaha, which I thought was to be yours for the duration. I wouldn't mind the Army, as a matter of fact, if they would give me something more than fifty bucks a month. That would be a little bit rough on Cinina, especially when we've got so many millstones around our necks right now.

Minneapolis has turned out to be a very pleasant place. I really do like the town, and find a good deal of pleasant and stimulating companionship. It's better than I had anticipated in that respect, and if the wit and rage here is not quite at the temperature to which I had grown accustomed in the SR office, I still survive agreeably enough. Brown is always good for a Shakespeare argument, and knows a hell of a lot, and Beach is a fine fellow. I have had a sort of burst of poetry, too. I can't say that I've pushed anything quite over the line yet, but I've got drafts of seven or eight poems, which only need the last tinkering. And I've got starts on others.[2] The novel is in the hands of Harcourt, and I've just heard that it is in their spring catalogue, or will be—for they have written me for material, etc. They claim they like it, but they always claim that. But I know that [Lambert] Davis was damned nervous about sales possibilities. And God knows I am. By the way, I discovered in the most pleasant way possible—by opening the envelope and finding a check for an advance fall out—that Night Rider has been bought by an English Book Club, for a very nice figure. Unfortunately, by the time the British Government had taxed the figure and Houghton had taken their fifty-percent, there wasn't enough left for me to retire on. But it was enough to fill the gap moving caused, or close to it. Such small blessings are making life possible, as a matter of fact, these days. Mademoiselle—God save the mark!—has just taken a story,[3] which will shortly appear among the bra ads and the pantie illustrations. It's a poor story about a poor old professor. I don't imagine you ever saw it. I wrote it a couple of years ago, and reworked it this fall. And I learned a few days ago that I split the Shelley Memorial Award this year for 11 Poems. The Old Colony Trust Company in Boston is my informant—they handle the trust fund, and have to do their adding and subtracting for the year before they send me a check. They say they don't know what it will be. Well, I hope they've been grinding widows and orphans or have some airplane stock this year. I had to borrow money this fall to pay for the Prairieville place—the extra payment fell due in October—and so Shelley ought to come in handy. I'm going to read "Alastor" and the "Sensitive Plant" immediately, and then work through the complete works of all the Romantic poets.

Except for the fact that we've had plenty of cold weat[h]er—ten and twelve below—that about exhausts our news. Oh, yes, I haven't yet taken out my heavy overcoat. I still wear a light reversible raincoat. So you see, I've grown damned hardy. Oh, yes, there's one small item. One of our friends from Rome, an AP man, has turned up here as editorial writer for the local paper. It has been very pleasant to see him. Oh, yes, again. Albert writes that he has just become an editor of [sic] Doubleday Doran. Pretty nice, huh? He ought to make a great success of that. But I suppose that you had heard that bit of news.

Cinina joins me in lots of love and in all best wishes. Write when you can, and I'll file your address this time.

As ever,

Red

1. A graduate student at LSU from Memphis. (My thanks to Charles East.)

2. The sequence "Mexico Is a Foreign Country" and the poems "Variation: Ode to Fear" and *The Ballad of Billie Potts* date from this period, but by his own admission Warren found it increasingly difficult to complete short poems for nearly a decade afterward. The book-length "tale in verse and voices" *Brother to Dragons* was published in 1953, but the shorter poems that made up *Promises* (1957) did not begin to appear until 1955.

3. "The Life and Work of Professor Roy Millen," *Mademoiselle* (February 1943).

TO MORTON DAUWEN ZABEL

TLS/Newb

> 3124 West Calhoun Boulevard
> Apartment 405
> Minneapolis
> Christmas, 1942

Dear Morton:

The occasion for this note isn't a very pleasant one. Cinina has been ailing for several days—fever and aches in the bones—and yesterday the doctor told her that she had to stay in bed for some days at the best. She has been in bed for four days already, but the flu, or whatever it is, doesn't seem to be losing out in the struggle. This, I fear, will make it necessary for me to ask you to postpone the visit a little while. And we had counted on it so much, too. It was going to give us the high point of our Christmas. I'm terribly sorry to have to write you in this strain. But you must come soon, anyway—if I'm not in the Army next month. I still don't have any definite word on that business.

I'll close with a word of business. I have had a check up on length with Ransom for the James issue. He says that something in the neighborhood of 50,000 words will be available for the James essays. Since there are twelve contributors listed, this means that the essays will have to be a little under 5,000 words each. I'm writing around to the various people now to let them know the state of things.

I hope that your Christmas has been a good one. And Cinina and I wish you every good thing for the New Year.

> As ever,
> Red

TO FRANK LAWRENCE OWSLEY

TLS/VU

> 3124 West Calhoun Boulevard
> Apartment 405
> Minneapolis, Minnesota
> Christmas Day, 1942

Dear Frank:

I must not read the right newspaper or something. Last night I went to the telephone to send you all a wire to let you know that we are thinking of you, and was told, after giving my message, that no messages of a non-business nature are to be accepted. So our greeting will have to come to you somewhat tardily in this fashion. But it is warm. We wish you all a very happy Christmas and all sorts of good things for the New Year.

We've missed hearing from you all. In fact, we've had no news from Nashville all fall. Except a letter from Lon, which came in a few days ago in answer to a note of mine in August. (Since I'm such a poor letter writer myself, I always seize any opportunity to take a high position in these matters.) He told me about his tribulations with the Air Force and about his new job in Washington, but there wasn't much other news. I'll ho[p]e to have some of that and a lot of Owsley news in particular when you write. May that be soon.

As for news with us, it's not very great. We like Minneapolis, and I find the University quite pleasant. People in the department have gone out of their way to be nice. (For instance: Cinina has been flu-y for the last several days, and so today Huntington Brown, one of my colleagues, and his wife brought a Christmas dinner, complete, over here and set it up in our apartment.) And, in addition to the Browns, and some other people whom we have come to know, there are the Beaches—Joseph Warren and wife. He is a fine gentlemen, keen and broadly read and charming. He's the head here—somewhat different from one of two heads whom I have known.[1] He has done everything in the world to make things pleasant for me in my work, and we see a good deal of him and his wife outside of work days. My classes are the ones I want—and the schedule is arranged so that I have to go to the University only three days a week. This past term I've had Literary Criticism, Twentieth Century Literature, and one Freshman course. Next term I have Criticism, Twentieth Century, and Graduate Writing. I wa[s] slated for Sixteenth Century instead of the second term of Twentieth Century, but the decline in graduate enrollment has knocked that course out, it seems. I'm just as happy about that, for it means I have more time of my own. A graduate course is bound to take up more time than an undergraduate one (and I have a very able and experienced assistant in the Twentieth Century, anyway). And I already have the Literary Criticism, which is a graduate course, with one precocious undergraduate in it. Sinclair Lewis had the Graduate Writing this term, but he only teaches the one term.

The good schedule has meant that I've had some time of my own. I finished the revision of the new novel—At Heaven's Gate—and it is now in the hands of Harcourt. It is slated for spring publication, they tell me. As I asked you before informally, I now ask you more formally, for permission to dedicate the book to you.[2] I hope that it won't disgrace you.

Aside from the novel, I've been working on a new batch of poems. I have five or six in complete draft, but they need some more tinkering. Speaking of poetry, I learned the other day that I split the Shelley Memorial Award this year for 11 Poems—which is convenient, unless the Old Colony Trust of Boston, which handles the fund, has failed to invest in the airplane stock this year. And if you'll look, about February, among the brassiere advertisements and the illustrations of young ladies in pink panties in the pages of Mademoiselle (no, I didn't know anything about that fashion magazine, either, until they asked me for a story) you'll see a very bad story about a poor old professor. But don't look, for the story isn't any good. I wrote it two years ago, and retouched it this fall, but the retouching didn't improve matters much.

The news with us is that I seem to be army-bound. I was reclassified 1A some time back, after being rejected by the navy on account of eyes. But an oculist has recently told me that I'll get [b]y the Army on that count. And when I had a very complete physical last spring, the doctor told me that I looked like a cinch for the Army. The office of the Director of Selective Service in this area informs me, too, that the new age ruling will not affect my case. The University has appealed, but they don't seem to be optimistic. I don't imagine that they have much weight with a Louisiana board—and I'm still attached down there. So I'm waiting.

It has been pretty cold for the last month—down around ten and twelve quite a few times. But we haven't felt it, somehow. The old notion that the "dry cold" doesn't bother you seems to have some sense to it. As I think I wrote Lon the other day—proudly—I haven't even worn my heavy overcoat yet—I've been using a light reversible raincoat, saving up my overcoat until it hits twenty-five below.

This about drains me of the Warren news. But the news of the great world is enough to make me more cheerful than I've been in some time.[3] It begins to appear that we may have something on the ball to worry Adolph. And the Russians sure-God have plenty on the ball to give him his worries. I read that Lloyds of London is now giving even money that Hitler will be knocked out in the early summer. I'm not that optimistic, but I'd take a guess on fall of 1943. I don't see how they can take what the air is going to bring them this winter and next spring. The heavy bomber has really never been used, it would seem. Cologne and London will probably look [like] fun compared to what will probably happen to West Germany in June. Speaking of the Air Force, Ransom writes me that his son is now an aviation cadet in college.[4] But I guess that you all don't mind the fact that Larry[5] is a little on the young side for the show. And I don't blame you.

Cinina joins me in love to all Owsleys, and in the hope that we shall soon hear from them. Best to Don and Theresa[6] and to the Cheneys and Isabel.

As ever,
Red

1. See n. 4, letter to Cheney of December 16, 1942, above.
2. *At Heaven's Gate* does carry a dedication to the Owsleys.
3. A series of Allied successes came late in 1942.
4. David Reavill Ransom.
5. The Owsleys' son, Frank Lawrence Jr.
6. Donald Davidson's wife.

Though Warren entered upon his new life in the North with characteristic energy and enthusiasm, he did so out of a sense of compulsion. Over three decades later, in a 1977 conversation with Louis D. Rubin Jr. and William Styron, he put it this way: "I left Louisiana only because I felt I wasn't wanted. I felt pressure to leave. It wasn't a choice. I had settled myself down and bought a house in the country—settled down for life, I assumed. . . . I wasn't fired. I left out of pride." Though Warren did not recognize it at the time, his departure from Baton Rouge was in effect an act of final expatriation. He lived outside the South for the rest of his life; whenever he returned to the region that had shaped him (whether the Border South of his boyhood and youth or the Deep South of his Southern Review years) it would be as a visitor, an estranged observer. As Lewis P. Simpson suggests, Warren left Baton Rouge to pursue "a vocation to exile," and it is the voice of the exile that registers most compellingly in his mature work. To recast the matter in terms loosely appropriated from the "new theory," Warren's "absence" from the South came to be an abiding "presence" in his finest fiction, poetry, and social commentary. In that respect, one might argue that Warren never quite severed his ties with Louisiana, for he carried the rich legacy of his time there with him throughout his life. This would account for his implacable decision to travel to Baton Rouge—against the expressed recommendations of his physicians—for the fiftieth anniversary of the founding of the Southern Review *in 1985. Desperately ill, unable to finish his scheduled reading on his own, Warren was nevertheless determined to be part of this homecoming and belated vindication. His gaunt presence was itself a symbolic act of reconciliation, eloquent testimony to the role LSU had played in the making of Robert Penn Warren.*

Selected Bibliography

Aaron, Daniel. *Writers on the Left: Episodes in American Literary Communism.* New York: Harcourt Brace and World, 1961.

Altman, Janet Gurkin. *Epistolarity: Approaches to a Form.* Columbus: Ohio State University Press, 1982.

Atlas, James. *Delmore Schwartz: The Life of an American Poet.* New York: Farrar, Straus, and Giroux, 1977.

Bayley, Isabel, ed. *Letters of Katherine Anne Porter.* New York: Atlantic Monthly Press, 1990.

Bedsole, V. L., and Oscar Richard, eds. *Louisiana State University: A Pictorial History of the First Hundred Years.* Baton Rouge: Louisiana State University Press, 1959.

Blotner, Joseph. *Robert Penn Warren: A Biography.* New York: Random House, 1997.

Carpenter, Lucas. *John Gould Fletcher and Southern Modernism.* Fayetteville: University of Arkansas Press, 1990.

Conkin, Paul. *The Southern Agrarians.* Knoxville: University of Tennessee Press, 1988.

Cowan, Louise. *The Fugitive Group: A Literary History.* Baton Rouge: Louisiana State University Press, 1959.

Cutrer, Thomas W. *Parnassus on the Mississippi: The "Southern Review" and the Baton Rouge Literary Community, 1935–1942.* Baton Rouge: Louisiana State University Press, 1984.

Donald, David Herbert. *Look Homeward: A Life of Thomas Wolfe.* Boston: Little, Brown, and Co., 1987.

Fain, John Tyree, and Thomas Daniel Young, eds. *The Literary Correspondence of Donald Davidson and Allen Tate.* Athens: University of Georgia Press, 1974.

Fallwell, Marshall. *Allen Tate: A Bibliography*. New York: David Lewis, 1969.

Fraser, Russell. *A Mingled Yarn: The Life of R. P. Blackmur*. New York: Harcourt Brace Jovanovich, 1981.

Gerber, John. *The Teaching of English at the University of Iowa*. Vol. 1, *1861–1961*. Iowa City: Maecenas Press, 1995.

Givner, Joan. *Katherine Anne Porter: A Life*. New York: Simon and Schuster, 1982.

Griffith, Albert J. *Peter Taylor*. Rev. ed. Boston: Twayne, 1990.

Grimshaw, James A., Jr. *Robert Penn Warren: A Descriptive Bibliography*. Charlottesville: University Press of Virginia, 1981.

Grimshaw, James A., Jr., ed. *Cleanth Brooks and Robert Penn Warren: A Literary Correspondence*. Columbia: University of Missouri Press, 1998.

Heilman, Robert B. *The Southern Connection*. Baton Rouge: Louisiana State University Press, 1991.

Hobson, Fred C. *Mencken: A Life*. Baltimore: Johns Hopkins University Press, 1994.

———. *Serpent in Eden: H. L. Mencken and the South*. Chapel Hill: University of North Carolina Press, 1974.

Hoffman, Frederick J., Charles Allen, and Carolyn F. Ulrich. *The Little Magazine: A History and a Bibliography*. Princeton: Princeton University Press, 1946.

Jarrell, Mary, ed. *Randall Jarrell's Letters: An Autobiographical and Literary Selection*. Boston: Houghton Mifflin, 1985.

Kane, Harnett T. *Louisiana Hayride: The American Rehearsal for Dictatorship*. New York: Morrow, 1941.

Kenny, Vincent F. *Paul Green*. New York: Twayne, 1971.

Linebarger, J. M. *John Berryman*. New York: Twayne, 1974.

Makowsky, Veronica A. *Caroline Gordon: A Biography*. New York: Oxford University Press, 1985.

Mariani, Paul. *Dream Song: The Life of John Berryman*. New York: Morrow, 1990.

Owsley, Harriet. *Frank Lawrence Owsley: Historian of the Old South*. Nashville: Vanderbilt University Press, 1990.

Pannick, Gerald J. *Richard Palmer Blackmur*. Boston: Twayne, 1981.

Paul, Jay. *The Selected Correspondence of Kenneth Burke and Malcolm Cowley, 1915–1981*. New York: Viking, 1988.

Pilkington, John. *Stark Young, a Life in the Arts: Letters, 1900–1962*. 2 vols. Baton Rouge: Louisiana State University Press, 1975.

Prenshaw, Peggy Whitman. *More Conversations with Eudora Welty*. Jackson: University Press of Mississippi, 1996.

Pritchard, William H. *Randall Jarrell: A Literary Life*. New York: Farrar, Straus, and Giroux, 1990.

Richardson, H. Edward. *Jesse: The Biography of an American Writer, Jesse Hilton Stuart*. New York: McGraw-Hill, 1984.

Simpson, Lewis P. *The Fable of the Southern Writer.* Baton Rouge: Louisiana State University Press, 1994.

Simpson, Lewis P., James Olney, and Jo Gulledge, eds. *The "Southern Review" and Modern Literature, 1935–1985.* Baton Rouge: Louisiana State University Press, 1988.

van de Kieft, Ruth M. *Eudora Welty.* Rev. ed. Boston: Twayne, 1987.

Vinh, Alphonse, ed. *Cleanth Brooks and Allen Tate: Collected Letters, 1933–1976.* Columbia: University of Missouri Press, 1998.

Waldron, Ann. *Close Connections: Caroline Gordon and the Southern Renaissance.* Knoxville: University of Tennessee Press, 1987.

Watkins, Floyd C., John T. Hiers, and Mary Louise Weaks, eds. *Talking with Robert Penn Warren.* Athens: University of Georgia Press, 1990.

Watson, James G. *William Faulkner: Letters and Fictions.* Austin: University of Texas Press, 1987.

Williams, T. Harry. *Huey Long.* New York: Knopf, 1969.

Wilson, Edmund. *Letters on Literature and Politics.* New York: Farrar, Straus, and Giroux, 1977.

Winchell, Mark Royden. *Cleanth Brooks and the Rise of Modern Criticism.* Charlottesville: University Press of Virginia, 1996.

Wood, Sally, ed. *The Southern Mandarins: Letters of Caroline Gordon to Sally Wood, 1924–1937.* Baton Rouge: Louisiana State University Press, 1984.

Young, Thomas Daniel, and Elizabeth Sarcone, eds. *The Lytle-Tate Letters.* Jackson: University Press of Mississippi, 1987.

Young, Thomas Daniel, and John J. Hindle, eds. *The Republic of Letters in America: The Correspondence of John Peale Bishop and Allen Tate.* Lexington: University Press of Kentucky, 1981.

Young, Thomas Daniel, and George Core, eds. *Selected Letters of John Crowe Ransom.* Baton Rouge: Louisiana State University Press, 1985.

Index

Page numbers in italics refer to photographs.

205–6, 236, 236*n*1, 241, 266, 300, 323*n*1; Columbia and Princeton lectures by, 288, 311; and Cornell University, 279; and correspondence with Warren generally, 229, 300; and critique of Warren's writing, 253–54; and dean of LSU English Department, 271, 276–77, 313; and demise of *Southern Review*, 348–49, 353; as editor of *Southern Review*, 2, 7, 24, 29, 35, 39, 45, 47, 54, 57, 69, 74, 75*n*1, 76*n*1, 86*n*1, 120, 137–38, 148, 151, 189–90, 205*n*2, 250, 252–53, 280*n*1, 301–2, 304, 317, 328, 329*n*1, 330–32, 336, 344, 356, 360; as editor of *Southwest Review*, 7, 9, 10*n*2; eye problems of, 202, 202*n*4, 205; and father's stroke, 10, 13*n*3; future of, at LSU, 356, 358; and *Kenyon Review*, 370; letters cosigned with Warren, 65–66, 86–87, 104–5, 189–90, 348–49; letters to, 252–55, 259–61, 271–72, 278–80, 301–2, 305–6, 328–32, 379–81; literary criticism and other writings by, 19, 21, 58, 59*n*6, 63–64, 64*n*1, 67, 67*n*2, 69, 82*nn*8–9, 91, 96*n*2, 98, 145–46, 147*n*7, 156, 157*n*5, 158–59, 253, 255*n*7, 255*n*9, 302*n*1, 305, 311; and LSU scandals, 218, 232, 234*n*1, 237, 245, 249; *Modern Rhetoric* by Warren and, 380, 382*n*3; Oxford thesis of, 261*n*1; pet of, 256, 258*n*2; and Phi Beta Kappa, 248; photograph of, *following p. 167*; promotion for, at LSU, 254, 268–69, 270*n*2, 318, 381, 392; salary of, 328, 360; and Scribner's contract for anthology of modern poetry, 92–93, 94*n*4, 156, 157*n*5, 343, 344*n*12; and *Sewanee Review*, 381, 382*n*6, 392; and Shakespeare project with War-

ren, 358; textbooks with Warren generally, 3, 49, 363, 374; *Understanding Drama* by Heilman and, 385, 385*n*7; *Understanding Fiction* by Warren and, 297, 297*n*3, 339, 340*n*3, 368, 379–80, 392; *Understanding Poetry* by Warren and, 81, 82*n*6, 86–87, 87*n*1, 89–90, 92, 100, 104–5, 105*n*1, 108–9, 118–19, 120, 126–27, 127*n*2, 135, 136*n*1, 145, 185, 188, 200, 216, 253, 255*nn*11, 261, 269, 280*n*3, 306, 339, 341, 372–73, 392; at University of Michigan, 363, 364*n*6; at University of Texas, 311, 318, 320, 322, 324; Warren on value of work and friendship with, 356, 358, 383–84. *See also* specific works
Brooks, Cleanth, Sr., 10, 13*n*3
Brooks, Edith Blanchard (Tinkum), 202, 202*n*5, 255, 261, 279–80, 329, 331
Brooks, Paul, 140, 214, 285, 286*n*4, 341; letters to, 295–96, 308, 315–16, 319–20, 335–36, 345–46
Brooks, Van Wyck, 67
Brother to Dragons (Warren), 396*n*2
Broussard, James F., 30*n*3, 198, 199*n*2, 369, 371*n*13, 383, 385*n*2
Brown, "Biddie," 369, 370*n*4, 372, 398
Brown, Harry, 129, 129*n*1
Brown, Heidel, 200, 200*n*2
Brown, Huntington, 369, 370*n*4, 372, 375, 384, 395, 398
Brown, John, 2, 6
Browning, Robert, 257
Bryan, Adolphus Jerome (Dolph), 254, 256*n*13, 259, 271, 272*n*1
"Bryan, Bryan, and Bryan" (Lindsay), 126
Burke, Kenneth, 3, 33*n*1, 36, 36*n*6, 39, 45, 139, 179, 180*n*5, 213, 240–41, 241*n*2, 335*n*2; letter to, 234–36